Radical Passion

Radical Passion
Sacred Love and Wisdom in Action

ANDREW HARVEY

North Atlantic Books

Berkeley, California

Published by
North Atlantic Books   Cover photo by David Sutton of Sutton Studios
P.O. Box 12327   Cover and book design by Suzanne Albertson
Berkeley, California 94712

Printed in the United States of America

Permissions begin on page 563.

Many of the pieces in this collection were previously published. For several of them, the original capitalization of nouns and pronouns has been retained.

Radical Passion: Sacred Love and Wisdom in Action is sponsored by the Society for the Study of Native Arts and Sciences, a nonprofit educational corporation whose goals are to develop an educational and cross-cultural perspective linking various scientific, social, and artistic fields; to nurture a holistic view of arts, sciences, humanities, and healing; and to publish and distribute literature on the relationship of mind, body, and nature.

North Atlantic Books' publications are available through most bookstores. For further information, visit our website at www.northatlanticbooks.com or call 800-733-3000.

Library of Congress Cataloging-in-Publication Data

Harvey, Andrew, 1952–
    Radical passion : sacred love and wisdom in action / Andrew Harvey.
       p. cm.
    Summary: "Radical Passion, the culmination of award-winning author Andrew Harvey's life's work, explores the catastrophes of our current times and celebrates the ecstatic hope and divinity that is possible—right now and in the future"—Provided by publisher.
    ISBN 978-1-58394-503-2
1. Spiritual life. 2. Religions. 3. Harvey, Andrew, 1952- -Authorship. I. Title.
    BL624.H3443 2012
    204—dc23   2012012223
          1 2 3 4 5 6 7 8 9 Malloy 17 16 15 14 13 12

To Matthew Fox
prophet, mentor, heart-friend

Acknowledgments

Immense gratitude to Janet Thomas for her wonderful vision and for seeing it through; to Emily Reed for her editing sensibilities and the tenacity and faith she brought to this book; to my good friend Nancy Steinbeck for her brilliance and support; to Emily Boyd and the team at North Atlantic Books for their meticulous attention to the complexities of putting this book together; to editor Jennifer Eastman for creating consistency, insisting upon accuracy, and being patient with my writing eccentricities as all these pieces were compiled; to Jill Angelo whose loyalty knows no bounds; to Charlene and Tony Marshall for their dignity and example of true love; to my Arkansas family, Frances and Mike Cohoon; and to all the friends and colleagues who contributed to *Radical Passion* and whose works inspire and enlighten our lives.

Contents

Contents

Chapter Three

The Body of Love–The Embodiment of Love in the Mystics from All Spiritual Traditions   179

Contents

Chapter Four

The Light of Love—Honoring the Divine Within 293

Chapter Five

The Shadow of Love—The Dark Side of Guru Worship and the Essential Nature of Spiritual Discernment 371

Contents

Chapter Six

The Suffering of Love—The Spiritual Path of the Broken Open Heart 411

Chapter Seven

The Power of Love—Becoming a Sacred Activist in Service of Self, Other, the Planet, and the Divine 481

Introduction

Wherever I travel in the world, people who respond to the message of love in action that I am giving ask me, "When will it happen and how?"

The "it," of course, is the great catastrophe (or series of catastrophes) that more and more of us are feeling is now inevitable. I point out, as gently as I can, that we are already in an apocalyptic situation—one that is worsening spectacularly, month by month. A global financial elite, drunk on greed and desire for total control, manipulates the banks, markets, media, and all political parties. The gap between the tiny handful of the rich and the billions of destitute or deeply struggling human beings widens daily. Nothing real is being done to address the now lethal menace of global warming. Our food and water are increasingly poisoned. Ninety percent of the sea is polluted. Many of our crucial individual liberties have been so drastically curtailed that the foundations of a global fascist state are now visible to all those with the eyes to see. Hundreds of animal and plant species are vanishing every month, in the largest continuing extinction event since the last ice age. What more evidence should any awake human being need to show that we are in extreme danger and must respond comprehensively and urgently before spreading disaster becomes irreversible extinction?

Perhaps the most alarming, even devastating, aspect of this unprecedented crisis is the denial, apathy, and paralysis of the great majority of the human race. In the time of our greatest danger, we are at our most hapless, distracted, and narcissistic. The promise of the Arab Spring is leaking away into the brutal, toxic swamp of religious and power politics. The Occupy Movement, for all its global courage, is being deeply hobbled by the self-interest of the corporate media. To occupy the future in time, the movement needs knowledge,

Introduction

patience, resilience, and an interminable spiritual persistence if it is to help birth the global, grassroots revolution of love and wisdom in action that is our last and best hope.

As for the various religions, mystical systems, or New Age philosophies, they are mired either in fundamentalism; meaningless brutal repetition of outworn dogma; addiction to transcendence; or the kind of obscene, magical thinking that prompts Ahmadinejad to believe that plunging the world into war will bring the Twelfth Imam and legions of New Agers to expect, on the turning of the Mayan calendar, to be whisked away from our mad, burning world on ships of rainbow light.

The reason I still have hope, as I approach my sixtieth birthday, is not because I believe the human race is going to find a technological, political, or economic solution to this devastation. I do not believe in the potential transformation of the existing corporate nightmare; I do not believe in the magic of technology; I do not believe in the ability of a corrupt and greedy political class to deconstruct its own power. I do not believe in the spiritual depth and sincerity of the great majority of religious and New Age leaders, or in their capacity either to tell the truth about what is happening or to galvanize human beings to react urgently and wisely to it. Our inherited notions of salvation, redemption, and enlightenment are as dissociated and ineffectual in this immense evolutionary storm as our continuing tragic obsession with perpetual growth and technological wizardry. Nothing undertaken from our current level of consciousness will now work. This crisis is the destined graveyard of all human "isms": all religious, political, and economic agendas, fantasies, and projects. The grandiose mask we have constructed for ourselves out of our demented narcissism is being stripped from our faces to reveal us as we are—terrified, lost, and helpless before a global agony of our own making.

The hope I live for and explore in all my work and teachings has nothing to do, then, with the current smorgasbord of fantasies for sale in the corporate bazaar. My hope is grounded in three interlinked truths, derived from a lifetime of mystical and personal search. These truths are: first, that the human race is now in an unprecedented and destined evolutionary crisis—a global dark night. Second, that this global dark night is potentially the birth canal for a new, embodied divine humanity chastened by tragedy and illumined by grace. Third, that the birthing force of the divine human is the force of the Motherhood of God, expressed not only in a new and radically evolutionary mysticism, but also in sacredly inspired, radical action on every level and in every arena.

It is this vision that I have been working on for three decades. It is this vision that works itself out, fugally, throughout this collection of my introductions and interviews called *Radical Passion*.

The passion I'm referring to has nothing whatever to do with emotionalism, theatricality, or even conventional and understandable forms of anger and outrage at injustice. It is a divine and sacred passion—a vast, focused love energy—grounded in peace and knowledge of divine identity, increasingly purified of shadow and demonizing judgment and directed like a laser to the radical and urgent transformation of both our inner version of awakening and our outer practice of political and economic reality. As always, Rumi expresses the divine truth of this passion when he writes:

> *Passion burns down every branch of exhaustion*
> *Passion is the supreme elixir and renews all hope*
> *Run far away, my friends, from all false solutions*
> *Let Divine passion triumph and rebirth you in yourself.*

It is this steady, peaceful, compassionate passion that fuels the work of all those who now, seeing where we are, are prepared to gamble away their lives and resources for the possible creation of a new world.

In its ultimate divine origin, this passion, as you will see in the pages that follow, is nothing less than the power, or Shakti, of the Mother side of God and of Her evolutionary will. Aligned with and inspired by this passion, there is nothing we cannot—even at this late desperate hour—accomplish. Without its radiant, clear, illumining energy, the energy of evolutionary wisdom itself, we will not be able to rise to the challenge of our times, and we will die out, taking a great deal of the already debilitated natural world with us. The word *radical* derives from the Latin *radix*, "root." The passion I am describing and trying to live springs from the root of the Divine itself and focuses its wild, pure energy on the roots of our evolutionary nightmare—our abandonment of the authentically sacred and mystical, our fatal dissociation from the glory and healing of the creation, our addiction to technology and science, our separation—so convenient to the elites who dominate our world—of divine reality and justice from active socioeconomic and political reality. It is "radical" in the deepest and highest sense, because in order to be born in sufficient power, it requires—even demands—the death of the collective false human self, a total inner revolution that expresses itself directly in a rehaul of all current ways of being and doing everything. Millions of years ago, a group of brave, prescient, and desperate fish left the toxic sea that was killing them. They endured whatever they had to in order to be slowly and gruelingly transformed, in a wholly new dimension, into birds. The radical passion that drove them is the one that will have to drive us if we are to transform in time from our current dark and poisoned narcissism into joyful and humble servants of the birth of a new divine humanity.

Such a revolutionary transformation, although ferocious and extremely difficult, is, I believe, still possible, because it is willed by the Divine and supported by torrential divine grace. Whether the human race will choose its rigors and demands remains to be seen and is not by any means certain. We are as likely to choose the destructive shadow of global fascism and die out in a series of manmade and natural disasters as we are to be galvanized by revelation and heartbreak into sacred action. The very worst and the very best, the rivers of blood and the rivers of milk, as Rumi put it, now run side by side. Everything now depends on us, on our willingness to let all the myths of the past die, on our courage in accepting almost unbearable ordeal as the gateway into new life and growth, on our radical passion to put the will of the Divine for a transformed humanity into inner and outer urgent action, on our creativity renewed in and inspired by divine peace, wisdom, and passionate compassion.

Radical Passion is organized in seven chapters: "The Heart of Love," "The Language of Love," "The Body of Love," "The Light of Love," "The Shadow of Love," "The Suffering of Love," and "The Power of Love." This organization is the heart-child of my brilliant, indefatigable editor, Janet Thomas, without whom I could never have undertaken this project, and whose profound understanding of the themes of my work have greatly inspired and heartened me. I conceive *Radical Passion* as an immense fugue in which central themes—of the Divine Feminine, mystical empowerment, the dark night, and the birth of divine humanity in and through an inner revolution expressed in sacred action—return again and again in different configurations and intensities to be concentrated in the call to transformative service of the last chapter, "The Power of Love."

When my great teacher and beloved, Father Bede Griffiths was dying, I asked him, "Do you really believe, with all you now see and know so clearly, that humanity will survive and transform?" He withdrew deeply into himself for one long moment and then said, "Yes, I do. What is to come will be harder than any of us can imagine, but a birth will take place." Then he smiled. "It will be a great adventure, the greatest adventure of all."

In this great adventure, whose terrors, rigors, ordeals, and amazing possibilities are now becoming clear to those who dare to understand, radical, divine passion in action will be our fundamental fuel and source of creative wisdom and purpose. Anything we have to go through will be worth it in order to realize its power. Nothing we do, inspired by its fire, will be wasted. Whether you or I survive the coming storm of chaos does not matter as much as the peaceful, clear, and impassioned spirit with which we set about, right now, building in ourselves the divine strength and compassion necessary to go on going on and building in the world the humble and tenacious structures of action that can weather whatever unfolds. On the rock of these truths we can build a house for a new humanity if we are illumined, fearless, and brave enough to risk everything.

Two years ago, when I was visiting the white lions in Timbavati, South Africa, my gall bladder exploded, and I came within an hour or two of dying. My life was saved by a wry, brilliant, half-drunk Afrikaner doctor. When I returned to recover in the camp near the white lions, I was told that Mandla, the king of the white lions, considered by the African shamanic tradition to be the animal avatar of all transforming divine light, had also been through a near fatal encounter with another lion. As soon as I could walk, I went to pay my respects to him in the small fenced enclosure in which he was recovering from his fierce wounds. I stood by the wire fence and waited in silence. Slowly, with a breathtaking poise and majesty, Mandla strode to within six feet of me and sat down, gazing into my eyes with his piercing, incandescent, sky-blue gaze, in which all the purity and grandeur of creation seemed focused with an almost blinding intensity of sacred passion. Then, the King of the Natural Creation blinked once and his entire body shook with a long, vast, infinitely powerful yet gentle roar that penetrated, beyond words or concepts, my mind, heart, soul, and every cell of my body. What this roar thundered to me was, "Abandon all fear and all self-pity. Do not worry about the wounds or sufferings of the past or about what is to come. Claim your inner divine royalty and live out to the end your sacred purpose, whatever happens. Be fierce, tender, humble, and majestic. Give everything, as I am giving everything, for the transformation of the world."

It is my deepest hope and prayer that this soft, wild roar echoes through this book and inspires you to rise fearlessly to your greatest truth, to enact it in humble splendor, giving up all the fruits of action to the grace of God, not counting the cost or labor or heartbreak, so that you may remain poised in, inflamed by, and drunk on the fiery wine of a divine love that no horror can dissolve and no ordeal can defeat.

Chapter One

The Heart of Love–
The Return of the Divine Feminine

Introduction

The greatest of humanity's evolutionary mystics, Sri Aurobindo, wrote at the end of his life, "If there is to be a future, it will wear the crown of feminine design." The Hopis have told us that if we do not turn to the Mother side of God, we will be "shaken off the face of the earth as a dog shakes off fleas."

At its deepest level, our crisis is one born from a long rejection and degradation of the Sacred Feminine, or the feminine as sacred. The return of the power and peace of the Mother, along with Her wisdom and passion, is now not only essential to the survival of the human race and a great deal of nature but is also essential to the birth of the divine human. It is the Mother side of God that is the energy behind the creation of the universe.

As an increasingly fear-driven and frenzied patriarchy degrades and destroys the world in an orgy of greed and violence, the celebration of the Mother becomes imperative. It is She who is the force of the all-embracing, passionate divine love that lives in, for, and as the divine creation. She offers a saving balance of reverence for the created world, an honoring of all diversity, and a new respect for feminine modes of intuition and cooperation. The celebration of God as Mother also offers a fresh, urgent vision of love in action—of what I call *Sacred Activism,* which I believe to be the destined birthing force of a new embodied humanity.

One of the central aspects of this return of the Mother, as you will see in this chapter, is an astonishing revival of interest in and passion for Mary. The Mary who is emerging in humanity's mystical experience of Her is not only the transcendent Queen of Heaven, but also a revolutionary of love and justice, passionate for the triumph of God's kingdom on behalf of the poor, humiliated, and dispossessed, and of an increasingly ravaged nature. She is the cosmic Mother of all creation. She is Maryam, the mother of Jesus, who, in the Magnificat, called for a triple revolution—spiritual, cultural, and political—that would overturn the forces of oppression. She is the Black Madonna, enraged beyond endurance at human folly, inequality, and cruelty, but also gifted with the vast divine power of creative destruction and divine ferocity.

This Mother-force, known in its full passion, majesty, outrage, and demand, released from the limitations of the sentimentality of patriarchal religious and mystical systems, unleashes a tremendous, radical power that menaces all elites and hierarchies, all ways of being and actions that do not revere or protect the harmony and dignity of life. The force of the Mother, returning now at this terminal crisis in our evolution, wills nothing less than a complete upheaval of the brutal "systems of cold evil" and all inner and outer structures that keep people and nature enslaved. From the Mother flows not only the vision of a new creation and transformed humanity, but also the revolutionary birthing powers and energy of sacred passion in action necessary to birth it into being.

Andrew Harvey

"Blaze of Light, Blood of Creation"
from *The Unknown She*, by Hilary Hart

What is a mystic? A mystic is a king or queen of paradox. A mystic knows that death is not death, life is not life, the body is not the body, and the spirit is not the spirit. The mystic knows that he or she is an eternal being in a dying body, and that this is the supreme experience—the experience of transcendence and the experience of immanence, both the experience of the divine emptiness that is creating and the experience of being the creation.

Do you understand the gift? The gift is death, the gift is time, the gift is pain, the gift is love, the gift is extremity. When you receive the gift full in the blood of the heart you dance as Shiva. You dance as the unborn one, you dance as the divine one, you dance as the child of the Mother, you dance as Christ did, you dance as the liberated one in the complete divine experience, the complete divine madness, which is to be in unity with everything that lives and dies, that has ever lived or died. That is the supreme experience and that is what is being offered to humankind.

Andrew Harvey, *The Way of Passion*

Hot Chocolate at the Edge of the Desert

I leave my room at the Hard Rock Hotel in Las Vegas, closing the door on the bright-colored modern furniture and the gigantic poster of Janis Joplin—her head pulled back in rock-and-roll ecstasy, her hair wild and sweaty—that hangs above the bed. I have come to Las Vegas to meet with Andrew Harvey, a highly respected spiritual scholar and teacher, author of thirty books, renowned as passionate, brilliant, unpredictable, and deeply committed to a spiritual vision that can help guide our collective consciousness into a new relationship with the Divine. I am eager to meet him and hear more of his views, which are grounded in an extensive understanding of the Divine Feminine, and I am intrigued to find out what kind of modern mystic lives and works in this city of celebration and degradation, extreme need and lavish abandon.

I drive up to Andrew and his husband Eryk's pale pink stucco house, one of what seems like a thousand others just like it in the flat and endless suburban landscape spreading away from the city. He welcomes me with a generous and enthusiastic smile and the proposal to talk in a desert park a few miles away. We climb into my car, which soon fills with the luscious smell of roses—Andrew's perfume choice—and sail beyond the sea of stucco into the explosion of color and emptiness that is the desert at dusk.

We sit and talk on a bench in a roadside pullout, the vast sky spreading out above us in endlessly forming and reforming patterns of blue and white, high cliffs jutting upward like a splendid warning against the dangers of too much space. The sun sinks slowly behind

5

us, and the dry winter air gets colder by the minute. The visitors who
have been pulling into this overlook during the last hour are beginning to thin out, and Andrew and I are left mostly alone, his passion
and despair mirroring the vivid intensity of the desert.

In Andrew's vision of the Divine Mother, the Mother is enraged.
She is enraged at spiritual systems that emphasize transcendence and
detachment over a passionate and loving relationship with what is
here, embodied in the earth and our own humanness. She is enraged
that the teachings of the Father have been twisted and misused by
patriarchal power systems more intent on maintaining control and
domination over the world's precious resources than in doing the real
spiritual work of transforming consciousness so it can relate to all of
life as the divine reality it is. She is enraged that we are not finding
joy and love in our lives, enjoying the gifts She has given us, honoring and embracing our life here with Her. And She is enraged that it
is taking so long for Her children to understand that life is precious,
that every atom of creation contains the love and light of God, that
by ignoring this fundamental truth we are spiraling Her world into
irreversible darkness and destruction.

But She is not only enraged. Through Andrew, She shows Herself
as sweet and loving, and generous in the true sense of the word—
creative and regenerative. She is deeply sorrowful as She watches us
struggle to realize what is truly available within this world, and also
outrageously passionate about sanctifying all the aspects of life that
are so easily dismissed as base or crude. For in Andrew Harvey, She
offers us a way to Her through passion and despair, kindness and
outrage. She allows a sometimes deranged entry into a world we are
not used to, a world where the distinctions between the sacred and
the profane are dissolved in divine love and divine hilarity, where
purity and earthiness infuse each other, where eating a peach in conscious gratitude and celebrating its juice running down your chin is as
holy as prostrating in silence before a crucified Jesus until your knees
bleed. In this world—in Her world as reflected through Andrew—life
is a chance to be shipwrecked again and again on an island of holy

longing and desire until every last cell of your body and every thought and action of your life is fused into a song of divine joy.

There are times with Andrew when I find myself questioning his passion and his excessiveness—is it really the rage of the Mother, or is it his own? Is he an authentic living representation of the Mother's energy, or is he sometimes just an ordinary man with his own personal agenda and personal desires? But the more time I spend with him, the more irrelevant these questions become. For in Andrew I experience passion and joy that seem to defy definition and limitation, a vision of real freedom that comes from unabashedly being oneself despite what others might think. And, ultimately, an inspiring and refreshing potential in a contemporary spiritual atmosphere that seems sometimes depressingly old and stale, fueled and defined by the conventions that it could be shattering.

And when I sit drinking hot chocolate with him late into the night, in the bar at the edge of the desert, on cowhide lounge chairs, under dollar bills that hang from every inch of the ceiling, I feel so much joy that I have to abandon any interest in distinguishing what I suppose is "spiritual" from what I experience as "ordinary." And maybe this is Andrew's greatest gift—he brings such laughter, he encourages a way to live in this world that is so joyful that one has to ask, who cares about the rest? The freedom in going beyond these opposites, these doubts, these distinctions, is intoxicating. Andrew's humor and inspired irreverence send me, relentlessly, into fits of laugher. His compassionate and desperate longing for humanity to take its next step into divine consciousness draw up a deep and ancient sadness. These swirling realities are the basis of my experience with Andrew, and I'd forego what the experts sell as "enlightenment" to drink his cocktails any day of the week.

The Masculine and the Feminine

As we sit in the desert pullout, looking at the beautiful sandstone cliffs and the vast space surrounding them, I ask Andrew to describe his understanding of masculine and feminine energy, and how they relate with each other both within an individual and in all creation.

"Ramakrishna said it so beautifully," he begins, his enthusiasm shining from his eyes behind his glasses. "He said Brahman (masculine energy) and Shakti (feminine energy) are two aspects of the same reality beyond name. The wonderful way of envisioning it is the masculine as the diamond and the Shakti as the radiance of light. Or milk and white. Or in an even more beautiful analogy, like the serpent and its wriggle. So the Mother and the Father are the same thing, but the Mother—and I think this is the most wonderful way of looking at it—She is the love power that arises out of the depths of the silence of transcendence and then expresses itself as the creation and lives in creation. Ramakrishna compared it, dazzlingly, to a spider who spins the entire creation out of herself and then goes and lives in every aspect of the web.

"Of course," he continues, "the love power and the silence are two aspects of the same reality beyond the Mother-Father."

Andrew and I sit watching the cliffs slowly become the canvas for the dance of vermilion and luminous gold orchestrated by the sun's submission to the encroaching dusk. In front of this glowing spectacle of heaven and earth, sky and rock, rays and shadows, Andrew speaks of the roles of the masculine and feminine, insisting that it is the role of the masculine to protect and illuminate the feminine. When he refers to masculine properties, he means the transcendent, detached, clear, and active aspects of the godhead. When he speaks of feminine qualities, he means the immanent, creative, life-sustaining, receptive, embodied aspects of the godhead.

"We can't possibly have a sane world," he says, "until we realize that the function of the masculine is to allow itself to be irradiated by the feminine, so that it can truly be a protector and guardian and warrior for those forces that actually ensure the continuance of life. If the masculine doesn't allow this deep and intense permeation by the feminine, it very easily becomes psychotic, addicted to transcendence, power, and control, and while pretending to be the guardian of life, actually becomes its secret destroyer.

"There is an image in *Judges* describing Samson, describing the masculine as the lion's mane with a river of honey running through it. To me this is a marvelous example of the fusion, the power, and force and lucidity and resolute courage that belong to the masculine, with the intense sweetness and tenderness and intimate love for all things that belong to the feminine. I believe the whole of reality is a sacred marriage, a marriage between heaven and earth, transcendence and immanence, feminine and masculine, life and death, the body and soul. It's a marriage that's reflected in all of these dimensions, and the task of every human being is to come into their own unique version of the sacred androgyny, to infuse it in the way it's meant to happen in their own personalities—the masculine and feminine within them.

"I see the Christ force as a result of the marriage of the Transcendent and Immanent, the force that is totally aware of the Transcendent but is also totally aware of how much the Transcendent loves the Immanent, and works to preserve and honor that love with everything it is."

Andrew's voice fills with intensity as he tells me that within most aspects of society, including our spiritual systems, we are out of balance, caught in a masculine dimension, focused on transcendence and devaluing the Immanent. His enthusiasm is contagious, and I become eager to hear how one can bring oneself back in balance, and how one can help the world become more balanced.

Descending Transcendence

"First you have to realize that everything you have ever been told about the Divine is prejudiced by patriarchal distortions that define the Divine almost obsessively in transcendent and not immanent terms," he says with urgency. "The addiction to transcendence keeps everybody in a coma, tells you your emotions are too much, your desires are absurd and obscene, your passions for justice are naïve. This addiction, in fact, is the ultimate heroin, because it keeps you high, self-absorbed, and falsely detached. It's a brilliant way of policing the human race, and the deepest reason why Karl Marx dismissed religion as the 'opiate of the people.'

"Supposing you told people the truth?" he continues, raising his voice. "Suppose you told people that the real use of detachment is only to help you fight for truth and love more purely? It is only so your love can become more intense and focused. What would you have then? You'd have an empowered human race that wouldn't accept anything it didn't know for itself as true!

"Let's get real around here!" Andrew almost yells, and I feel his intensity and eagerness sweep through me. I pull back a bit, and he continues. "Transcendence is the first real knowledge on the path. It's crucial, but then you have to learn about love. Don't you think that Jesus could have made all these transcendent junkies look like twerps? He could have materialized things, he could do anything, because he was in touch with transcendence, but he knew *Her!*

"He knew that the only truth lay in serving and loving every single living thing!" His voice now is shaking with frustration and sadness. "So you have to go down on your hands and knees and kiss every living thing. That's about service. About service and being a slave. It has nothing to do with authority, nothing to do with being enlightened. That's the patriarchal world! She's bringing in a wholly different world in which the last really are the first. And there are no masters who aren't slaves! The last thing Jesus tried to do was break people's projections on him by dressing as a female slave and washing their feet. Of course, no one got the meaning of that, because it's too deranging. The Mother's world is too deranging!

"Supposing we see that eternity really is in a grain of sand?" he asks, softly now. "Supposing we see that a cat is a totally holy creature, incredibly wise, and instead of thinking of it as stuck on the lower end of the evolutionary scale, we start talking to the cat and learning from the cat the secrets of serenity and secrets of divine mischief?

"Supposing we do reverse the whole human craziness and start listening to Her? All of this stuff goes! The whole authority structure goes, the elite goes, the churches go, the mystical systems with their prizes to the boys who play the game go. It all goes! And only *She* is here, radiating love between hearts, between all the hearts of all the creation, and that's what She's trying to bring here. Because from that will come the real harmony, the real community of all human beings.

"And all of the powers that don't want that to be born are trying to appropriate Her for their patriarchal games. That's why all the women gurus are Jehovahs in drag, or all the men gurus talking about the Mother can only talk about the sweet aspects of the Mother, never the tremendously tortured or torturing or justice aspects. That's why this realization is such a hard realization to get through, because it is a realization that menaces in the most absolute way everything that we think is holy to reveal a much holier world than anything the transcendent junkies could ever imagine. There is a marvelous story that Ramakrishna tells describing real holiness, holiness that makes no distinctions between above and below:

> A few days after the dedication of the temple at Dakshineswar, a madman came there who was really a sage endowed with the Knowledge of Brahman. He had a bamboo twig in one hand and a potted mango plant in the other, and was wearing torn shoes. He didn't follow any social conventions. After bathing in the Ganges he didn't perform any religious rites. He ate something that he carried in a corner of his wearing-cloth. Then he entered the Kali temple and chanted hymns to the Deity. The temple trembled.... The madman wasn't allowed to eat at the guest house, but he paid no attention to this slight. He searched for food in the rubbish heap, where the dogs were eating crumbs from the discarded leaf-plates. Now and then he pushed the dogs aside to get the crumbs. The dogs didn't mind either. Haladhari followed him and asked, "Who are you? Are you a *purnajnani* [a perfect knower of Brahman]?" The madman whispered, "Shh! Yes, I am a *purnajnani*." Haladhari followed him a great way when he left the garden. After passing the gate he said to Haladhari, "What

else shall I say to you? When you no longer make any distinction between the water of this pool and the water of the Ganges, then you will know that you have Perfect Knowledge." Saying this he walked rapidly away.

"You see, Ramakrishna got there! Ramakrishna was there! *Here* I mean!" Andrew says, shaking his head, his voice rising again, the Mother's deranged world shining through. "I think of him as a supreme sign of what I'm talking about. Our addiction to transcendence—to splitting the world in two and rejecting half our experience—is madness!

"I heard this wonderful story about Ramakrishna by a man who walked across India to meet him." Andrew now becomes like a child listening to a bedtime story, big-eyed and sweet and enraptured. "I heard this story from the man's family.

"This man arrived in Ramakrishna's village and went out to the fields. And what did he see? He saw Ramakrishna lying on the ground talking to some rabbits *in rabbit!* This man asked him what he was doing, and Ramakrishna said, 'Well, I'm telling them that there are some terrible snakes over there, and they've got to stop being so naïve, because if they go across the field, they're going to be bitten by those snakes.' They all nodded their heads and went off. So then Ramakrishna went to the other side of the field and lay down, and snakes came out of their holes, and he gave them *hell!* In the snake language, he told them, 'Look, you're clever, you know those rabbits are stupid over there, and you just wait for them to come over and you bite them! And that's got to stop, you've got to have more responsibility about yourself! There are other things to eat!'

"The point being that he wasn't standing up!" Andrew insists. "He was lying on the ground in his *dhoti* talking their language! Was he crazy or are we crazy? If the real mystics are right, then Blake was not lying when he said eternity is in a grain of sand. In the whole universe, everything is one of God's names and in God's name everything is reflected. Everything is not some bloody illusion that's going to evaporate, but this fantastic, surreal, *glorious* emanation of divine splendor!"

The Joy of Life

We sit quietly for a while, mesmerized by the desert sunset that is now alive and dancing all around us, watching the cliffs change color in the evening light. Engulfed in this brilliance, Andrew explains that the simplest way to descend transcendence is by celebrating all that we love here, by accepting everything in our lives as divine. Life and love are how the Divine comes to us. That which makes us feel alive, that which awakens our senses, engages and encourages us, is how God comes to us in this world.

"Do you think you are here to suffer and learn a few lessons so as not to be here?" he asks me, pointing out the absurdity of striving for a detached and transcendent relationship with the world. "Or do you think you are here so as to finally arrive here and be here in the fullness of your real being?

"And the fullness of your real being isn't realized by seeing this world as a place where you can have sex, drugs, and rock-and-roll," he says, before adding, with a mischievous smile, "though that's not so bad!" He goes on, serious again, "It's seeing this world as a place in which you can fully realize your divine nature and fully realize your human nature and fully realize the marriage between the two and fully realize the bliss that comes from the marriage between the two.

"Kabir has a line I love: 'More than all else do I cherish at heart that love that makes one to live a limitless life in this world.' To live this limitless life is why we are here. And this limitless life is the child of the marriage I've just described.

"If you believe all these patriarchal religions," he continues, taking up again the absurd reasoning, "they're saying to you that you're on this planet as a terrible school in which you have to go through all these dreary lessons so that you can finally get out of being on this planet and be one with the light. That is such a depressing, such a wearying vision of what we are here for!

"Be honest with yourself! Do you really believe that when you make passionate love with someone you truly love, that it's not glorious? Do you really believe that when your heart thrills to the music of, say, Tina Turner, you are not having an authentic experience? Do you really believe that when you're eating a peach and savoring every bit of juice in the peach, you're not actually doing something miraculous? Do you really believe that your body is given to you as a kind of prison?

"Or is this life, is this body," he continues sweetly, "the most overwhelming opportunity to have an overwhelming array of experiences that can help you really celebrate this existence as the dancing ground of joy, bliss, and illumination?

"And if you're honest with yourself, and if you suddenly just abstract yourself from all the garbage you've been told about being a sinful and imperfect creature, you will, if you look at your own experience, realize that it's actually already been filled with all kinds of illuminations of the joy that is the core of reality. I think that will be a wonderful place to start.

"You see, we're *in* the Mother. The universe is the Mother, life is the Mother, and everything that happens in life is designed to move us into this deeper dimension of love. And knowing this truth increasingly is the great reward of the mystic devotion to the Mother. And really embracing this truth is the courage of that distinct devotion. Then from that can come an overwhelming fearlessness, and you can become what the Mother really wants us all to be, which is radioactive nuisances! Unbelievable rebels of love!" He looks intently at me as I try to imagine what it means to be a radioactive nuisance. And then he yells, "YES!" as though I had just figured it out.

I am sent into fits of laughter. I see in Andrew what it might look like to be a radioactive nuisance and a rebel of love, and am giddy with possibility of being in a similar state. I ask him how he became so aware of the joy of being here on the earth, especially since his spiritual background included involvement in Buddhism, Hinduism, and Christianity, traditions that so often accentuate transcendent elements.

"Well, I was born in India," he says smiling. "I think being in India was a tremendous help. Temples are fun; priests are fun, with their gold robes and the sweets they give you. And Indians have hilarious sacred holidays like Holi, where they rush around and shriek and fling paint on everything. And the actual gods are fun. It's great to have an elephant god! Hinduism has at its core a hilarity, a joie de vivre, a phenomenal acceptance of the gaiety of the human world. That was a terrific antidote to any Judeo-Christian horror I might have been exposed to.

"I remember my mother telling me at an early age, 'Why would Jesus's first miracle be the turning of water into wine at a wedding if Christ wasn't about joy?' And that's something I got from all of my family. They were not hot on sin. They believed that joy was the source of strength, and so it is!

"The real answer," he continues, "is to start getting people out of their spiritual conditioning and into the real mystical dimension by hook or by crook, because as soon as they're in that dimension, what they're going to have is an overwhelming experience of bliss! They're going to have that eruption in the heart that nobody, not even Rumi, has been able to describe, in which it's clear beyond any shadow of a doubt that the essence of God is a joy and a peace and a bliss beyond any imagining. If you really open your heart to the possibility of a direct encounter with the Divine, what you'll discover very, very fast is that the Divine has nothing to do with all these rules and regulations and glooms and despairs. The Divine is *here,* in life, in the world as rapture and the fire of eternal joy."

Creation Spun Out of Transcendent Light

I only mind a bit that the air has become very cold, and that the coldness of the bench easily cuts through the thin skirt I chose to wear, not knowing we would be talking out in the desert. I can see that Andrew hasn't noticed the drop in temperature as he eagerly tells me that one of the most important myths to dispel is that the body holds one back from spiritual life.

"If the Divine has chosen to be embodied, it's not because the Divine is playing some mad game of being embodied so as to get out of being embodied," he laughs. "The Divine is embodying itself because it's experiencing another level of rapture through being embodied. Creation is a flaming out of this joy. Everything we are is an expression of this joy, including this body, because it's through the body that we can have the experience of this joy here in creation.

"The body, in fact, reveals itself as the grail," he continues. "The reason why they couldn't find the grail is because they were looking for the grail in the light. They were actually in the grail! The grail is the cup that holds the blood of the incarnation. What holds the blood of incarnation? The body.

"It's important to understand the body is not your enemy. The body is, in fact, the condition on which this experience is possible, the way in which you can partake in both aspects of the Divine. You see, the Divine is transcendent light and the Divine is also the creation that is spun out of transcendent light. If we were only transcendent light, we would only be able to experience one half of the Divine. If we were only matter, we would only be able to experience one half of the Divine. The fact that we are transcendent and immanent, soul and body, spirit and flesh, means in the most *astounding* way that we can in our lives experience the fullness of the godhead. That's what the human experience is really about! God loves us so much that God has given us the full experience of God. Not just the light, not just matter, but the amazing dance between the two.

"And you don't need to be apart from this world in an ashram or monastery to be or live this dance. Kabir says, 'Why put on the robe of the monk and live aloof from the world in lonely pride? Behold, my heart dances in the delight of a hundred arts, and the Creator is well pleased.'

"The real Mother is both transcendent and immanent," he tells me, first waving his hands toward vast space, then pounding the bench, "and is trying to help all people to be birthed simultaneously into the Absolute and the Immanent. She is helping us to be in the deathless presence that is beyond both, and to know that the bodies that seem to be taking us to death and limitation and heartbreak and sorrow and loss are in fact the grail from which we can drink this astounding wine—this mixture of the blaze of the eternal light and the blood of creation."

Andrew explains that this coming together of the Immanent and Transcendent is, in part, an aspect of what is possible now, in the evolution of consciousness. Historically, we have yet to collectively embrace this union.

"This is the teaching of the marriage," he says, "the teaching of the feast. And it's because the human race has chosen either the transcendental or the material that it has missed the fusion and the ecstasy and the real transformation. Because not only in this transformation do you have a total awakening to your transcendent origin—that's just the first step—then you descend from that awakening, with that awakening into the actual details of your life. You include the emotional and physical and you use the light to transform your body and your body's actions and thoughts and emotions consciously so that your body then becomes the living experience, a living instrument of the light."

I ask Andrew how a person comes to use her consciousness to transform her body into an instrument of light. His answer points to a harmony between one's body and the rest of creation, to the oneness of all life, the inclusion of love in the body.

"You use your body as an instrument of divine love," he answers, "which means you move to the rhythm of divine love, you open to loving all beings in reality. A very simple example would be someone who uses his body to really stroke his cat. When you are aware that you're a divine being in a relationship with another divine being, it transforms the way in which you touch that divine being, speak to that divine being. So by using your body as an instrument of divine tenderness and divine love you gradually infuse it with light and it starts to transform. This isn't poetry, this actually happens."

Crucifixion and Resurrection

The process of transformation includes a variety of stages, taking one beyond transcendence to the final illumination of matter by spirit. "In the real journey, not the fake journey of most modern New Age mystics," Andrew tells me, "several things happen. First, you have to separate the spirit from matter so you really taste and know your transcendent origin. This is perhaps best done through the practices of meditation, prayer, and even contemplation. But that's where most people's diagram ends. People believe they have achieved a very high state, but what they don't understand is that they are actually living in this unconscious dualism that they celebrate as transcendence." This dualism is based on the lived rejection of the Immanent, the unconscious disgust of all that one has left behind.

"The next step," he continues, "is the really difficult aspect of the path. Now you have to marry consciously the spirit to matter. In a civilization in which matter was celebrated as divine from the beginning, that marriage would be a great deal easier than it is for us today. What in fact and in practice happens for most of us is that after the recognition of our origins as transcendent spirit, most of us have to go through some immense crucifixion that forces us to embody again." This descent can seem so counterintuitive, and is, in fact, counter to so much of our spiritual conditioning that many people have to be forced back to earth through a process of intense suffering.

"In my case what happened was that after years and years of sailing off into the light, the woman I worshiped as the Divine Mother on earth told me to leave the man I was in love with and say that her forces had transformed me into a heterosexual. The blessing of that experience was that it compelled me to accept my sexuality as divine in a way that I hadn't been able to before. I had to decide—is my attraction to Eryk an inefficient expression of transcendence, or is it a further stage along the path?"

Circumstances that bring an individual back into life, into the simple aspects of being, often require a withdrawal of a projection of the Divine outside oneself, and the claiming of power, love, or the Divine within oneself and within ordinary aspects of life.

"What was happening through my love for Eryk," Andrew continues, "was a radical embodying of the light in my body. Once I really chose my love for him over my infatuation with this spiritual figure, everything became lit up by the flames of our love, and I knew that human love was divine! Slowly this came. I had to choose it again and again, and suffer through the loss of what I had thought was 'spiritual.'

"I had always understood in my mind that sexuality was a blessing. But I had to actually experience my sexuality as a tremendous initiation of passion and of love, and experience the healing of the shame and humiliations and the wounds and the body-hatred that had been so stored in me, in order to really accept the divine nature of my own sexuality."

Andrew tells me that at this time in his life he suffered a severe back problem that left him incapacitated physically. "It was as if the Mother just took an axe and felled me, and I think She did that because I had just been floating around, I hadn't really considered my body. And having a terrible backache brought me right back into the core of my body, made me really, really start to look at all the ways in which I had fled my body. And I began to attend to my body, bring myself back to it, and this process became a way to really bless my body. I think you can't heal your body until you've blessed your body, and that long process helped me reenter my life.

"Loving Eryk helped me reenter my life," he continues. "Healing my back helped me reenter my life. Seeing the guru system as a power-brokering of transcendence helped me to realize that the real path was into matter, into life, into social and political action inspired by divine passion. And this totally transfigured me and brought me really into the path of the authentic Mother. The path of the authentic Mother is a path of tantra, which means the marrying of light to matter, which means not only experiencing the Divine in the way you make a cup of tea, the way you stroke your cat, the way you make love to the person who is your sacred partner, but also expressing the Divine in creativity and expressing the Divine in political and social action.

"To really come back to life, back to the body, back to matter, you have to smash so many of the concepts that have been handed down to you, concepts that have even been enshrined as wisdom," Andrew insists. "And what the Mother sends to help you do this is known in traditional terms as the dark night of the soul. This corresponds mystically to what the Sufis know as *fana* and what Jesus experienced in the crucifixion. This crucifixion, both of the false self and of the false self's dualism and its fear and shame at matter, births the resurrection. And what is the resurrection? It's the transfiguration of matter; it's the birth in matter of the light of the Divine.

"That is exactly what happens at the higher levels of the Mother's path. It is a crucifixion, and it happens in terms of your own temperament, in terms of your own life, and actually usually in terms of your own body all at the same time.

"My life was annihilated by death threats," Andrew says, shaking his head at the memory, "by the craziness that reigned around all those people, by the guru's lying, by my back being out, by Eryk's nearly dying of cancer, by a whole holocaust. It was really a crucifixion. By being dismembered I was actually able to be remade in the light of the Mother and reenter my life…. That's what happens."

This process of crucifixion is an aspect of transformation, for rebirth can never occur without death, without the shedding of one's self at whatever stage one is. "All the different props of the self," Andrew goes on, "the emotional, religious, physical, conceptual props, are dissolved in the acid of atrocious suffering. Those props are actually walls against the Real. Walls against an overwhelming experience of divine love that, when all the walls are annihilated, can come in and flood and possess the center of the entire being.

"What Jesus did in the resurrection was give an eternal sign of this rebirth on the childbed of the cross," Andrew continues. "The crucifixion and the dark night are best understood as a kind of maternity bed in which one body, one spirit, and one mind all are broken apart to birth the resurrected consciousness, resurrected mind, and resurrected body. This is known in traditions of alchemy, Taoism, and I think by the Mahayana Buddhists in the Vajrayana path; it's known in the Christian esoteric tradition; and it is the fundamental Mother knowledge.

"We are here to have this double birth," he tells me, excited by the idea. "We are here to be born into this extraordinary dimension and then to be reborn, which does not mean going off into transcendence but bringing transcendence *down*. Because the aim of the Divine in the human race and the aim of the Mother-Father—and I think it's especially the work of the Mother, because I think She is the emanating embodying power—is to birth beings on this planet who then can use this Shakti, this power, to transform this whole planet and all its institutions, all of its arts, all of its sciences, into burning mirrors of love and justice. That's what we are here for!"

Extreme Emotions

Andrew and I are sitting now in the gentle and full evening dusk. Hunting birds are barely visible against the dimming sky as they make their last turn before dark, and the cliff's edges melt slowly into the desert landscape beyond. We begin to speak about daily life as the arena for practice, and how to include the intensity of one's desire for truth in the sometimes banal ordinariness of the day. Andrew assures me that it is not only possible but necessary to focus on life as completely as one focuses on more formal spiritual practices. One place to start is in the transformation of ordinary human desires and emotions. Simple human needs, according to Andrew, are not to be denied, repressed, or relegated to the shadowlands of the antispiritual. On the contrary, they are the energy of life and the ground for transformation. And in accordance with his way of turning things entirely upside down, Andrew is the living possibility that the wilder the emotions and the more desperate the needs, the more fuel there is for realization.

"I particularly revere Sufism and esoteric Christianity," he tells me, his excitement growing again, "because they never, ever, ran away from extreme emotions. They realized that in the extreme emotions, if purified by adoration and by profound clarity, is the living Shakti.

"If you look at the Hubble Telescope's pictures of the birth of supernovas, you see a great shout of light with billions and billions of miles of streaking fire coming out of it," he continues, extreme emotions beginning to manifest in his voice.

"Does this seem to express to you that there's an extremity, a gorgeous extremity at the heart of the universe? And that this gorgeous extremity might have something to do with a God who tosses off a few universes before breakfast, and creates fish at the bottom of the Philippine Trench that look like they were designed by Faberge on drugs?

"This extremity, this fabulous, gorgeous too-muchness is part of the essence of the essence of God, and if you're going to find your way to that power, you're going to *have* to bless the extreme emotions inside you. You're going to have to purify them without annihilating the source of them.

"I was helped very much by a crazy friend of mine in Paris," he says, like a child again with a good story to tell, "who is a wild old countess. She was shamelessly angry at everything, and she was so out there, nobody could control her. She would go up to the president and tell him off. She would talk to the so-called great artists of Paris and tell them what rubbish their work was—which it usually was—and she would criticize to their faces the famous film stars. And nobody could control Helene. And one day she was doing her thing at a dinner party, and I was there, and a man sitting next to her said, 'Helene, you are too much,' and she turned to him and said, 'Bertrand, you are not *nearly* enough!'"

I'm laughing at Andrew, his story, and his snobby French accent, and he goes on, smiling and big-eyed, "I always remember that! People come to me and say you care too much about the environment, or you care too much about the poor. But if you think I am too much, wait till you see Jesus! And wait until you experience the volcano of the Mother's outrage and the volcano of the Mother's love! Then you'll think that anything I'm showing you is a tiny firefly compared to the Krakatoa of what She really is. So let's get real around here!"

Consecrating Desires

"You really have to turn toward the values of the heart," Andrew continues as the darkness begins to settle in, wrapping us both in the timeless magic of the desert sky at night. "You have to understand that in emotion and love and passion are tremendous truths. You can find these truths, release them, by dedicating your emotions and your desires to divine love and divine adoration. This is the key of the tantra.

"If you have tremendous sexual desire—and most people do, let's face it—" He stops speaking, turns to me and says with a mischievous smile, "Thank God!" And then he looks into the dark sky, throws his arms upward, and yells loudly, "Thank God!" And we laugh, forgetting where we were in the conversation.

"Bede Griffiths said this so beautifully," he continues, still laughing. "I got the highest teaching from an eighty-six-year-old monk sitting under a tree in south India who told me, 'It's quite clear to me what the answer is.'" Andrew pinches his face now and speaks in a high-pitched, ambiguous foreign accent.

"'You certainly can't indulge it! Because look at all these unhappy people, they've done things I can't even spell! I didn't know one could do such things! And they're clearly not happy. And you clearly can't repress it, because the monks are all crazy! All the monasteries are filled with absolute lunatics in all religions.'" Andrew's accent reaches a particularly hilarious pitch, before it evens out back to his normal voice. "'The only way through is to consecrate it. Is to offer it.'"

It is Andrew again, speaking to me. "And there's only one way to do it. I mean, you read these tantric manuals, and they're so hilarious, because after you've read them, you think it's a form of gymnastics! If you can throw your leg over this shoulder, then you've managed tantra. This is such materialistic horseshit!

"The only way in which to experience tantra is to be profoundly, and wildly, and passionately, and holily in love with somebody. So that extreme love will take you into the dimension of adoration, and then in that dimension of that extreme love and adoration all the sexual desire that you *explode* in the relationship will *explode* in the divine dimension! Because love is divine! And holy love is holiness itself in action. And then desire becomes the Shakti creating the world. And then sexual meeting becomes the dancing ground of Shiva and Shakti, the site of consummation of the marriage. Then you realize what Kalidasa, the Hindu Sanskrit poet, meant when he said that the entire universe is wet with the love-juices of the gods and goddesses."

I ask Andrew to say more about divine adoration. "Adoration is the devotion to the Divine in all things," he tells me. "That's the clue to the experience of the Mother."

He reminds me that I asked him at the beginning of our conversation how we can really come down from transcendence. "To get back to that question you put at the beginning," he says, smiling at me. "It was asked to Ramakrishna. An old lady came to Ramakrishna and said, 'Look, I know you're supposed to be a great saint, and you've got to give me an answer to this, because I'm dying and I've got to know, because otherwise I'll die ignorant as a dog. I've never done any meditation, because I hate meditation. I can't pray, because it bores me to death, all those Sanskrit words. You've got to give me a way of connecting with the Divine Mother in the core of my life— otherwise I will hold you personally responsible!'

"And Ramakrishna laughed and laughed and laughed, and said to her the amazing phrase, 'Well, who do you love most?' And she said, 'I love my granddaughter the most.' And he said, 'Well then it's quite simple, you go home and you worship your granddaughter as the Divine Mother. You treat her as if she were the Divine Mother on earth, and you will have realization.'

"What he was trying to do," Andrew explains, "was to say— Look at your life! What do you really love in your life? Personally, I really loved my cat, and treated her like the Divine Mother. She *was* for me the Divine Mother!

"In the middle of writing my last book, *The Direct Path,* I asked for a sign that I wasn't crazy to believe that human beings could have a direct connection with God beyond religions, dogma, and all mediators. And I thought, of course, being me, that there would be lightning that would spell my name in the sky. Or something at least dramatic. And I was very disappointed for a whole evening, because nothing was happening. And I walked outside my study, and there was Purrball, my tabby, absolutely irradiated with divine light. *She* was the sign. It was my cat who was the sign, because I loved her! And it is love that gives us the eyes to see the divine world more directly.

"It is so much simpler than we think," Andrew says softly. "The divine Motherhood of God is pure love. And when we love purely, we are living in Her. Whatever we love like that, whether it's a rose or a cat or a piece of music or four lines of a poem, we're experiencing a part of that great love that is taking and binding together all of those experiences.

"And it doesn't matter what you love!" He raises his voice again. "You could love a peach! I mean, I love spaghetti Bolognese!" We both laugh at his example, and he continues. "It's wonderful! I love it. I really love it! And if I can take the essence of that love and link it to the essences of all the other forms of love, then I'm coming to intuit something of *my* capacity for love and something of the love that is trying to reach me through all these different aspects of life.

"Rumi says it so clearly, 'Everything that you love and enjoy is a ray from the sun of the Beloved.' As you really love and enjoy something, anything, just remember where it's coming from. And in the love and the enjoyment is threaded the intense memory of its source. So you know you are eating the Divine. And you feel through that the incredible mercy and blessing of this experience.

"I try to be always conscious that the enjoyment I feel in life is Her, and is Her enjoyment. When you know who you are and whose child you are, all of what we call private ordinary pleasures are seen as unbroken miracles. And I try to live, more and more, in Her dimension of ordinary miracle. The whole of life is threaded with Her miracle.

"And then the difficulty," he says softly, "is to see Her presence in pain and suffering and death and darkness. But that comes later, through an initiation into heartbreak, and the acceptance of the price of love."

Initiation into Heartbreak

When one takes a transcendent stance and limits life and the world as an illusion, it becomes difficult to engage in the problems of the world and to work to resolve these problems. Passionate engagement in life includes the willingness to experience, deeply, the needs of the world and the suffering within life.

"When I think of somebody who came into the complete consciousness I'm trying to describe, I think of St. Francis," Andrew tells me. "And I think of a particular detail. When he was dying, it was spring. And he spent a lot of his last energy in this world going out from his deathbed into the little paths around Tuscany, picking the little slugs up from the paths to save their lives. Each of these little slugs kindled in his heart infinite love.

"Don't tell me that he thinks of reality as an illusion! Because he experienced the full mystical initiation, he came to understand that the illusory nature of the world is actually an element of one's own senses, of the limitations of one's senses before they are transformed. He saw that one's senses create the illusion of separation, the illusion that the forms of the world are not real. And he saw that underneath and in all of these forms is light, this whole creation is, in fact, a creation of the dance of different-colored lights that emanates from the one white light.

"The Upanishads tell us there are three progressive levels of illumination. The first reveals the world as an illusion. The second reveals that only Brahman, the absolute transcendent presence, is real. In the third, the world itself is unveiled as a manifestation of Brahman. So the world, finally, is not an illusion. The world, as the divinized senses experience it, is saturated with divinity—it is absolutely, absolutely divine, super-real, not unreal." Andrew is now yelling again. "If we go on saying this world is an illusion, we'll kill the whole planet!"

We sit in the dark stillness. After a moment, he says calmly, "It is essential to know and see and experience that the world is the living manifestation of the glory, the power, the radiance, of the Father-Mother's unbelievable passion and unbelievable love. And when you have experienced the dissolution of the ignorance of the senses, when you have experienced the whole world vanishing into light, and when you have experienced the world reappearing from that light, when you see each single object saturated with light and vibrating with light in every single moment, then what you come into, interwoven into the bliss and wonder, is heartbreak. Because at that moment what you share is the heartbreak of the Mother at what is being done to *Her* body, *Her* world, *Her* children, *Her* reality, *Her!* As a result of ignorance and craziness!

"So, you see the world as totally holy. And when you see the world as totally holy, you see yourself as totally responsible for the protection of every living thing in the world, and of beauty and of joy in the world, so the Mother's truth can play out everywhere.

"A Sufi text I love says, 'When you attain union, you are drawn near, and when you are drawn near, you never fall asleep, and the rays of sublime heartbreak engulf you.' You see, on the path of the Mother, you're being led to the moment when you can be strong and surrendered enough to see the world in its total divine glory and also to feel the infinite pain of the infinite love that has created this glory and is trying to awaken the entire creation to its presence so that creation can become transfigured with its power and divine justice.

"That is a completely different model, and we have to get there. And it doesn't deny the nothingness or emptiness. It just includes the very real initiation into heartbreak, and into the tremendous passion and compassion that arise from that heartbreak, and into the living commitment to direct action in the world that is born from that tremendous compassion. That's Jesus's path, that's the Sufi path, that's the Buddha's path, that's St. Francis's path.

"St. Francis was able to talk to the plants because he was able to realize they *weren't* an illusion! They weren't unreal! They were *super*-real! So that his being with them in that state of intense divine humility allowed them to speak to him! It's because we think we're superior and because we've used transcendence as a way of reinforcing this ridiculous arrogance that we don't talk to the plants, that we don't speak to the animals, that we are burning the world and killing the environment.

"We are being led by human history to the moment when either we awaken to this, or we don't. And if we don't awaken, we will be talking about transcendence, going on about the sixteen types of emptiness, when the last tree in the last forest is burned down, and then we will suddenly discover that there's no more bloody oxygen. And at the moment, where *will* our transcendence be?" Tears are forming in Andrew's eyes, and he is now shaking with anger and frustration.

"What set of disasters will it take for us to see that this is why She appears in tears? What more could She do? She's appearing everywhere, She's constantly trying to give us messages, She's erupting in human hearts, She's organizing this huge catastrophe. You would have thought we would have done something about it, but we've done nothing! Nobody's talking about it! The churches aren't talking about it, all those supposed masters are going on about transcendence and how to worship *them,* when we're in the middle of a holocaust that threatens the life of every single living creature! Does that suggest that we are crazy?"

The Price of Love

Andrew's desperation moves me deeply, and I ask him why people won't pay attention, why we don't recognize the impending disaster around us. He tells me that the price is simply too high.

"To face it requires facing that we do not have all the answers, that science, reason, and human wisdom are simply going to prove inadequate to the situation. We're going to have to take an evolutionary leap if we're going to solve it. That's the first reason.

"The second reason is that facing it is like facing, finally, that you may die from the cancer that is ravaging you. It is a terrifying experience full of extreme grief.

"And the third reason is that the only possible response to facing it is dedicating your entire life to transforming the conditions that are creating it.

"This heartbreak is so painful," he continues. "You realize you have to accept the derision, you have to accept the cruelty, you have to accept the upset you're going to feel with the price of real action in the real world. All of it has to be accepted; you have to shoulder it and get on with it.

"People want illumination, they say they do!" he says, shaking his head. "People want divine love, they say they do! But do people really want to see the glory and the agony together? Because if they do, they'll plunge into the fire of transformation and give themselves wholly up to the work that's required now.

"I think everybody who has even the beginnings of this realization understands that if they do this work, they are going to have to go against all the churches, they're going to have to go against the transcendence-selling mystical systems, they're going to have to go against the material jamborees of our culture, and they're going to have to go against everything that the human race has been addicted to! And this is terribly scary for most people."

And Andrew explains that we can't do it alone, or within the systems already established. "It's only by connecting directly with the force, the power, and the majesty and the extreme compassion of the Mother that we are going to be given the strength to accept it, to accept the stern terms of the transformation, and to actually start infusing ourselves with the Divine, so that we can become servants of this transformation. It can happen only through Her because She is the power of the embodiment of the light."

The Darkness of the Mother

Andrew and I are now sitting in the desert night. The stars are beginning to show themselves—vivid and alive—as they only do in the uninterrupted vastness of wilderness. The black space and the light of the stars seem equally brilliant and engaging. Andrew's face comes in and out of distinction as the occasional headlights of departing park visitors sweep by us. I am growing colder and colder, but still absorbed by Andrew's passionate description of the path of the Mother.

"People fear this vision because it's so fiery and demands so much responsibility and also calls for a frank acceptance of ordeal. But there are so many people thrilled at last to hear people say, 'Look at the facts, look at what's going on, look at how the solutions can't possibly be solutions. Accept that there is a way through, and it's the way of love in action, and that way is a way that depends on honoring the feminine as sacred.' Many people are thrilled when that is voiced.

"Passion is the key," he continues. "Rumi says it so beautifully:

> Passion burns down every branch of exhaustion;
> Passion is the Supreme Elixir and renews all things ...
> Run my friends, run far away from all false solutions
> Let divine passion triumph and rebirth you in yourself.

"It is essential on this path to be naked to the passion and emotion that the death of the planet potentially causes you. It's very important to get at the agony of the Mother, the rage, the suffering of the Divine inside us, at what's going on, and to stop buying their version that being realized means being calm and peaceful. That's such a stupid idea! Was Jesus calm and peaceful all the time? No, he got furious at the people selling God at the temple! He raged at the priests at falsifying the relationship between the Divine and human beings.

"The Mother is a tigress," Andrew says, fiercely. "A tigress protecting Her children. And sometimes She roars, and She can roar with rage, and She can roar with agony, and She can roar with ferocity, and She can roar with terrifying lucidity.

"It's very important not to buy into the dreary, spiritually correct categories of what people describe as 'holy.' I mean, I live in Las Vegas, I'm gay, I have a marriage with a man I absolutely adore, and I talk about sexuality being one of the experiences of the radiant empowerment of the Mother. I enjoy Tina Turner, opera, and cabaret singers. I believe enjoyment is a divine gift. I don't believe that I have to stand on one leg at the top of a mountain, or wear standardized clothes, or change my name to 'something Ananda' or any of that garbage! The realization that the Mother's grace feeds me in the core of my ordinary life is enough for me!

"I just encourage everyone out there to be their wildest, deepest, passionate, compassionate selves!" he says so enthusiastically that it is hard to imagine any other solution to the problems of the world. "That itself would be a tremendous witness! Some people don't get it, other people are thrilled!

"If you buy this transcendence stuff, you have to be totally awake before you can have an opinion on anything, and totally awake means totally calm about the destruction of this illusion. The Mother isn't going to sit around saying, 'It's okay if everything is destroyed and the planet is destroyed and human beings suffer appallingly,' because She is all of those human beings suffering!

"This is another level of awareness! You know why they stress being calm and peaceful as the ultimate?" he asks me. "Because that's the easy part! Then you don't bother about social conditions, you don't bother about the caste system, you don't bother about women being burned or homosexuals being tortured and crucified. You don't bother about any of that, because it's all only an illusion, which means that the power of divine realization can never inspire society to transfigure it! Calm and peace is one half of the godhead, but the other half of the godhead is tremendous passion, tremendous burning outrage at cruelty, and enormous commitment to just action! And that's the Mother!

"And Jesus is such an extraordinary example of this. He is as much Her son as he is the Father's. He lived life! *Not* the life of transcendence. He was offered transcendence and all its powers. He could have dined like the gurus do with all the famous rich people and sold them transcendence over martinis any day of the week!

"But he didn't. He married the masculine and feminine within him, transcendent awareness with the passion for justice of divine love, entered into the world and fought against all forms of oppression and was killed because he was so bloody uncompromising about his vision of how society must be changed. And that to me is the violent, pure, sweet love of the Mother coming through and possessing him and making him. And his whole yoga is the yoga of the transfiguration of matter into spirit through the crucifixion through the Absolute, opening in the depths of his being to the blazing power of divine love."

Detachment and Passion

At the end of our visit we have finally moved out of the cold into Bonnie Springs, a desert saloon reminiscent of the old West, with an unlikely pond outside filled with swans, dollar bills hanging from the ceiling, and Western music playing from a hidden jukebox. I feel oddly at home with Andrew, sheltered from the desert by the unavoidably peculiar atmosphere of the bar. We drink our hot chocolate, sitting on cowhide lounge chairs in front of an open fire, amongst a vague combination of gamblers and cowboys. Here, we speak about the balance between detachment and passion, between transcendence and immanence, between hot and cool spiritual practices.

"We need these technologies of transcendence," Andrew tells me, "as developed so skillfully through Buddhist practices, to purify the mind so we can bring down the light more effectively. I truly honor Buddhism. Buddhism has given us great techniques, and I call them the "cool techniques." I use Buddhist forms of meditation, of visualization, walking meditation, sitting meditation, but I use them in conjunction with Sufi heart forms and the Christian sacred-heart forms to marry the masculine and the feminine. You need them to cool you down, and you need these other practices to heat you up, inspire you, and get you *thrilled* abut life and about compassionate engaged communication with it.

"No one can live a life of dedicated passion without rooting their passion in deep prayer, meditation, and profound contemplation. Because only prayer, meditation, and contemplation can clear away all of those neuroses and obscurations in the psyche that prevent it from being a pure and vibrant instrument of holy passion.

"Look," he says, "detachment is there to make passion more white hot, to purify passion and make it diamond-pure. Someone put it so well when he said, 'Passion is a long patience.' And this is so true. How can there be patience without true detachment? And how can you wait and wait and wait unless you are passionate about what you wait for? Passion not rooted in detachment is useless, will just burn itself out.

"Detachment without passion is death, and passion without detachment is chaos. And passion fed off the silence and peace of detachment will find endless energy. The Mother's boundless fire draws its strength from the boundless silence of the Father. The Mother's boundless ecstasy draws its passion from the endless peace of the Father.

"At every level we are talking about a marriage of opposites. The greatest realization comes from this marriage. Life and death, good and evil, detachment and passion, masculine and feminine, heaven and earth. In marriage, both qualities interpenetrate each other to create the mysterious third that is both and neither.

"From the marriage of passion and detachment," he tells me, looking into the fire, "is born a laser and a passion that is pure as wind. Birthed from passion and detachment is the third—the fire presence of the awakening ones who are at once surreally calm and wildly extravagantly passionate in ways that confuse all categories."

Sipping his hot chocolate, he adds, "Passion is so wonderful. But without discrimination to balance your passion, it's like climbing the Eiger in a tutu."

Andrew and I look at each other and burst out laughing at the absurd image, and as at other times during our meeting, I let the fun flood through the seriousness of the point. I am grateful to be overwhelmed by laughter again with this extremely joyful and passionate man, and by now I trust that the power and urgency of his vision are not lost within these moments of hilarity, but infused within them.

Andrew insists on paying for the hot chocolate, but I sneak the waitress a bill while he isn't looking. We leave the warmth of the bar and head into the night, driving down mysteriously wide streets, often in the wrong direction, drifting through a sea of pale pink suburban stucco, trailing the scent of wild roses, toward the lights of Las Vegas.

Conclusion to *The Return of the Mother* (1993)

There is very little time left. The next few years are going to reveal the full horror of what we have done to the planet and to ourselves. How much time do we have? Twenty years at the utmost, twenty years in which to undergo a vast transformation of all our ways of thinking and acting, twenty years in which we will have to make major decisions in every arena or abandon the fate of the world to chaos. And if we do not change? The human race could die out in unimaginable suffering and take most of life on the planet with it.

Any spiritual vision that does not ask us to calmly face the appalling facts is, I believe, whether consciously or unconsciously, conspiring in our infantilization and so in our destruction. I am often asked whether I am optimistic or pessimistic about the future. I reply that both optimism and pessimism are now luxuries we can ill afford. Optimism is crazy, given the facts—the facts of overpopulation, environmental destruction, the pollution of the air and water, the facts of escalating nationalism and tribal hatred, the facts of still-continuing nuclear proliferation, the facts of obscene frivolity and denial in all of the media of the nightmares we face. There is nothing whatever to be optimistic about. Yet pessimism is also crazy; it just conspires with catastrophe by imagining it to be inevitable. Catastrophe may be likely, but it is never inevitable.

The only response that I find honorable in this potentially terminal situation is that of dedicated love. Whatever happens, whatever horror or destruction unfurls upon the world, however terrible the suffering of human beings and nature becomes, such a response keeps the heart open and keeps alive courage and compassion. This response of dedicated love, committed love, of love in action, springs directly from the sacred heart of the Divine Mother, of the Mother of the cosmos and the Mother within us. "I am the Queen of Peace," Mary says again and again as She appears; peace can only be engendered by love and sustained in love in action.

The essential message of the Divine Mother to us can be summed up, I believe, in the following Ten Sacred Suggestions. I have called them "suggestions," and not "commands" or "commandments," because the Mother does not issue commands. At all moments in our relation to Her, we are left free—free to rise through Her grace into our own human divinity and take the journey into Her love, or free to deny Her and Her laws and destroy ourselves. Not even the Mother can help us if we do not wish to be saved; not even the Mother can help us if we turn from Her help. Everything now depends on us, on the authenticity of our sincerity, on the passion and wisdom with which we turn to the Divine.

I have tried to impart the flavor of these suggestions as richly and comprehensively as possible. On how deeply and fully we *imagine* the Mother depends how much strength, courage, and inspiration we can draw from Her. Incomplete imagination of Her will lead to incomplete contact and incomplete help. It is crucial now, with such worldwide disaster and agony, not to repeat any of the past mistakes, exaggerations, or limitations of our understanding of Her.

We need the largest possible vision of the Mother and of Her relationship with us and of how we can sustain, interpret, and enact that relationship. All the clearest insights and highest awakenings of all the traditions that celebrate Her, however partially, have now to be fused together. She is calling on us to unite in one all-embracing and all-encompassing knowledge all the separate ways of knowing Her. Neither a purely transcendental vision of Her nor a purely immanent apprehension of Her can help us now; we need *both*, fused in a sacred marriage of truth.

We need Ramakrishna's vision of the all-transcendent Kali and the Aboriginal celebration of the wallaby as the guide to motherhood; we need the Sufi understanding of the transformatory powers of suffering as well as the Mahayana Buddhist knowledge of the void-as-Mother and the sacred mystery of the Tao. We need a restored Mary and a restored Christ. We need, in fact, all the help we can get in order to make conscious and full radical range of the great and healing mystery of the Sacred Feminine, that mystery we have betrayed for so long, but must now reclaim in its completeness and complete challenge, or perish.

These, then, are the Mother's Ten Sacred Suggestions as I understand them now in my journey into Her:

1. I am the Mother. I am both transcendent and immanent, source and all that streams from it. I am one with all things in creation and one in boundless light within and beyond it. Adore me.

2. Adore every being and thing, from the whale to the ladybird, as life of my life. I am appearing in everything as everything.

3. Honor yourself humbly as my divine child, and see, know, and celebrate all other beings as my divine children. Whatever you do to or for anyone, you do to or for me.

4. See through constant practice of adoration that nature is the sacred body of my sacred light, and do everything at all

times to honor its laws, which are my laws, and to protect it from destruction. I and you and nature are one love, one glory; protecting nature is protecting yourselves.

5. Dissolve forever all schisms and separations between sects and religions. Whatever you adore is a face of me, and everyone is on his or her own unique path. Know that there are as many paths as there are people.

6. Dissolve forever through repeated holy inner experience of my unity all barriers between what has been called "sacred" and what has been called "profane." Know the whole of life as my feast. Realize ordinary life as an unbroken flow of normal miracle.

7. End all hatred of the body, all guilt and sexual shame, and discover and celebrate my sacred eros in all its ecstatic connections and revelations. Preserve its purity and power, in my name, with truth and fidelity and mutual honor.

8. Unlearn all the "religious" propaganda that tries to tell you that you need intermediaries in your relationship with me. I can be contacted by anyone, anywhere, at any time, and in any circumstance, simply by saying my name, however you imagine it. No intermediaries—no gurus, priests, "experts"—are ever needed. You and I are always, already, one.

9. Do not make of my worship another dogma, another mind-prison. Remember always there is no "Mother" without the "Father," no "Goddess" without "God." I do not want a new religion in my name; I want the whole of experience on the earth to become holy and integrated in love. I want the return of harmony and sacred peace and balance; the union of the sacred marriage at the greatest depth; and in everyone, of "masculine" and "feminine," "earth" and "heaven," body and soul, heart and intellect, prayer and action. Men are as much my children as women; the wound of the loss of the Mother is felt by women as well as

men. Any separatist or prejudiced or one-sided attempt to worship me worships only a distorted image of me. Dare to know me in my full majesty and all-encompassing humility, and know that there is never any end to the journey into me and that the conditions for that journey are ever-deepening faith, radical trust, and radical humility.

10. If you trust and love me, put your trust and love into action in every aspect of your life—emotional, sexual, spiritual, social, political—with my passion, my clarity, my unsentimental practicality. Know that my revelation is a *revolution,* a revolution that demands calmly a transformation of all the terms and conditions of life on earth. Establish justice for all in my world, in my name, and in my spirit of all-embracing, inexhaustible compassion. Let no one be poor or discriminated against; may all sentient beings everywhere be cherished and safe and protected from harm by law and by love. Turn to me now and I will fill you with all the grace, strength, courage, and passion you need to transform the world at every level into a living mirror of my truth, my love, and my justice. If you truly love me, change everything for me.

How can we most richly, wisely, and comprehensively respond to the Mother's Ten Sacred Suggestions? When I first wrote them down, I had a sudden inner vision of a burning gold heart with five flames leaping from it. I heard the words: *This is my Sacred Heart in you, and the five flames are Five Sacred Passions.*

These Five Sacred Passions are: The passion for the Divine beyond forms, the transcendent source; the passion for nature as the immanent manifestation of the source, instinct everywhere with its glory; the passion for all sentient beings and all human beings; the holy passion for one other human being, a tantric passion devoted to tantric transformation in the Mother; and finally, focusing and fulfilling all the others, a passion for *service* and *action.* All Five Sacred Passions draw from, enthuse, infuse, strengthen, sustain, and interilluminate each other. Lived together in every dimension for Her and *in* Her, they represent the full alchemical force in reality of divine human love. Living them together, alone and together, is what will help us transform not only ourselves but the world.

> *Let my Sacred Heart become yours.*
> *Live and act from my love.*
> *Risk everything while there is still time.*
> *Give everything while there is still time.*

The First Sacred Passion—the passion for the Source, the Transcendent, the transcendent Mother of Light—fuels all the others. While it is true that the patriarchal bias toward transcendence has resulted in a destructive rejection of women, nature, and the body, it is also true that contemporary overemphasis on the Immanent can cut us off from those sources of transforming power that are the gift of the invisible and Transcendent. It is from the one beyond all forms, names, dogmas, and concepts that the light of grace streams; if we do not love origin passionately, it cannot send us the strength and inspiration we need—and need all the more intensely now as catastrophe deepens. To be in continual, loving contact with the Transcendent is vital for the stamina and illumined wisdom we need to survive. As Ruysbroeck reminds us in his *Mirror of Eternal Blessedness:*

> At the beginning of the world when God resolved to create the first human beings, God said ... "Let us make the human being to our own image and to our likeness." God is a spirit and so God's word is God's knowledge and God's action is God's will. God has created each person's soul as a living mirror, on which God has impressed the image of God's nature.... Our created life is one, without intermediary, with this image and this life that we have eternally in God. That life that we have in God is one in God, without intermediary.... We thus live eternally in God and God in us, for our created being lives in our eternal image.... This eternal

image is one with God's wisdom and lives in our created being.

For this reason the eternal birth is always being renewed, and the flowing forth of the Holy Spirit into the emptiness of our soul is always occurring without interruption, for God has known, loved, called, and chosen us from all eternity. If we resolve to know, love, and choose him in return, then we are holy, blessed, and chosen from all eternity. God … will then reveal his divine resplendence in the topmost part of our soul, for we are his kingdom, in which God lives and reigns. Just as the sun in the heavens pervades and enlightens all the world with its rays and makes it fruitful, so too does God's resplendence as it reigns in the topmost part of our mind, for upon all our powers it sheds its bright, brilliant rays, namely, its divine gifts: knowledge, wisdom, clear understanding, and a rational discerning insight into all the virtues. It is in this way that the kingdom of God in our souls is adorned.

To connect profoundly with the transcendent source, the transcendent Mother-Father, is not to devalue immanence in any way, for when we come to see the Mother as Ruysbroeck's "resplendence as it reigns in the topmost part of our mind," then, as Ramakrishna also said, and in fact all the Mother-mystics make clear, we also see and know reality as entirely saturated and radiant with Her glory. We come to know that nature is entirely holy with Her, is in fact Her body. "God's grandeur," Gerard Manley Hopkins wrote, "will flame out, like shining from shook foil." Nature *is* that "shook foil" from which the grandeur of the Divine Mother is continually and incessantly flashing, if the eyes of love are open in us. From this immanent knowledge of Her splendor in every fern and dolphin and wave and rose and deer and hippopotamus and orchid and windswept sand dune arises, then, the Second Sacred Passion—the passion for nature. It is this that Ramakrishna was living and expressing when, after his vision of Kali as the light-consciousness pervading and manifesting all things, he "threw flowers in all directions." It was this sacred passion for the blazing of the source in all created things and for the humility of the source's presence in and as all things that possessed St. Francis of Assisi and made him talk with sparrows, wolves, snakes, turtledoves, and all the elements as his brothers and sisters and equals, that led him to that state in which, as one of his biographers tells us, "worms kindled in him infinite love." This sacred passion for nature is not something we can afford to leave to the saints; we must all know it, live it, and act from it now if we and nature are to survive. When we know nature as the Mother's body and everything in nature as utterly sacred, then, and then only, will we do everything in our power to preserve, honor, and protect nature.

Knowing the "resplendence" and its radiant dance in nature is not, however, all we must do; we must also know all sentient beings as Her, and see, know, and celebrate all human beings, whatever their caste or creed or color or gender or sexuality, as Her divine children, each unique, each holy, each loved unconditionally by the Mother. From this Third Sacred Passion—the sacred passion for all sentient and human beings—the passion of the bodhisattva, of the Sufi lover, of all those who give themselves to Christ to be "Christed"—arises that loving knowledge of our interbeing with all being, of our total and fundamental interconnectedness with everyone and everything in the entire cosmos.

Unless all of us now realize at greater and ever greater depths of truth and integration this Mother-law of interdependence, and unless we translate its truth into action at every level and in every arena, humankind will not survive. Christ said: "Feed my sheep"—his sheep are *our* sheep. The animals perishing in the burning forests are burning in us; the old woman dying alone and abandoned in Rio or Los Angeles or Calcutta is dying in us; the acid rain falls on us when it falls on the trees; it is into ourselves that we release clouds of deadly chemicals and it is in ourselves that we bury nuclear waste that no known technology can contain. We are implicated in every life and every death, in every injustice, in every crime, in every casual premeditated or unconscious brutality. Allowing this Third Sacred Passion for all beings to begin to awaken in us is a terrifying experience, one that many celebrate but few want to live, because this awakening shows us that there is no escape anywhere into any mystical state or other world from this tremendous responsibility of love. All our fantasies of "progress" or "spiritual transformation" will not save us—and cannot—if we do not see, know, explore, and enact more and more fully, comprehensively, and passionately our interconnection with absolutely everyone and everything. Such an opening to Her web of love, however terrifying, however demanding, however devastating to all our private agendas and notions of separateness, is now essential. There will not be any significant turning-around of our contemporary catastrophe without it.

In the Fourth Sacred Passion—for one other human being with whom we live in consecrated tantric communion, in sacred marriage—the Mother brings us the tender opportunity not merely to go on *talking* about healing the split between body and soul, but actually to do it. When consecrated to Her and protected by fidelity, the sexual, spiritual, and emotional passion for another being becomes the site of an encounter with Her in every dimension and at every level, the site of an always-unfolding empowering *direct* teaching by Her of us in the ground of our daily lives. A massive worldwide healing of sexual pain is now essential if human beings are to be freed to love themselves and honor the body and so love and honor nature. Through exercising this Fourth Sacred Passion in and with all the other passions, human beings will discover, without any need of any church or dogma or intermediary, the *unity* of the Mother, Her radical blessing of *all* of life, Her love-presence in all things, and so taste ever more deeply their own divine human power and freedom. Couples—heterosexual or homosexual—who allow themselves to experience this tantric teaching (and submit to its necessary rules of mutual honor, service, respect, and, above all and always, fidelity) will find that psychological and spiritual suffering are greatly diminished through it, that revelations dance naturally around and in them, and that humble self-reliance in and for Her becomes increasingly instinctual and increasingly joyful. I am living this great teaching with Eryk in Her and for Her and know that its promise is genuine.

All of these four Sacred Passions, lived separately or together, could become decadent, narcissistic, or escapist if they are not *always* linked—and felt and known to be linked—to the Fifth Sacred Passion, which focuses and fulfills them all—the Sacred Passion for service and for love in action.

"Those who are near to me are near the fire," Christ tells us in the Gospel of Thomas; those who are near to the Mother now are near to Her great fire of change. The return of the Mother, I have continually argued in this book, is not merely a revelation but also a *revolution*—a call to emotional, sexual, spiritual, social, economic, political revolution. Daring to allow the fire of the Mother into our lives is daring our lives to burn away in that fire, to be transformed continually to reflect ever more richly and intensely the Mother's laws of love and justice.

It must never again be forgotten, as it has been forgotten for millennia, that one of the Mother's holiest names is Justice. To awaken the Mother's Sacred Heart in us is to awaken a passion to serve, honor, and protect all of nature and all living beings. The human race will not really be honoring the Mother until every starving person is fed; until every homeless person is housed; until every sick and poor old person has free access to medicine; until every woman everywhere is free from all kinds of oppression; until every human being everywhere, whatever his or her sexuality, feels free to love openly; until, in fact, *all* the man-made distinctions between white and black, male and female, poor and rich, straight and gay, are radically transformed so as to express in both individual and social, spiritual and political ways, the equal love of the Mother.

Every sea must be cleaned for Her, every ravaged forest restored, every endangered species—including those parts of the human population facing a kind of selective genocide—protected, every commercial arrangement that threatens the creation in any way forbidden. The force of the Mother is a revolutionary force of love that works incessantly to break down *all* barriers and separations in the name of love and hungers to see *this* world become the stable paradise it already is in Her mind of truth. Unless we serve this force, and will and strive to put into living practice its unsparingly radical injunctions, we are not loving the Mother but a watered-down, personally tailored version of Her that can only keep us trapped in illusion, and the world on its headlong rush toward annihilation.

The revolution of the Mother demands of each of us unstinting service. And what does such service mean? It means dedicating our every gift and power, our every prayer, our every thought and emotion and perception, to the welfare of others in the world. It means having the courage and patience to learn all the dreadful facts about what is happening and how we—all of us—conspire in what is happening. It means taking *personal* political responsibility on local, national, and global levels, alone and together. It means scrutinizing who we vote for, who we give power to, and holding them to their promise of change. It means realizing, once and for all, with no false consolation of any kind, in just what terrible danger we are and how each of us will have to dedicate our entire being and intelligence to focused, thoughtful acts of loving service to all, if we are going to have a chance to survive.

It may mean in the near future taking to the streets all over the world in a massive peaceful but adamant protest against what the politicians, generals, and corporations are doing. It may even mean being prepared to die. The service the Mother is asking of us in this catastrophe is as humble, supple, many-faceted, loyal, indefatigable, and extreme as Hers. If we claim to love Her or to know Her love, that claim must be made good in tireless love in action using all of our gifts and resources; and it must be fed, illumined, balanced, and informed, as I have said, by all the other Sacred Passions.

And when these Five Sacred Passions live in us and we in them, then we will be living the full human divine life in the Mother, and we will be awake in Her Sacred Heart and living and acting from it and with its blessing and serving power.

Know that my revelation is a revolution.
Establish justice for all in my world.
If you truly love me, change everything for me.

There is very little time left.

The dark forces that want the human experiment to fail and the world to be destroyed are everywhere more and more powerful, subtle, deadly, and ingenious. But the Mother is always in us and with us, and Her strength will never fail us. "I am with you always," Mary has said again and again. "I am with you always."

And, as St. Bernard of Clairvaux reminds us, the Mother and Her power is always, *always,* there to be drawn on in love's name:

When you follow Her, you do not take a wrong turn.
When you pray to Her, you do not lose hope.
When She occupies your mind, you are sheltered from error.
When She holds you up, you cannot fall.
When She protects you, you do not fear.
When She leads you forward, you do not get exhausted.
When Her star shines on you, you arrive at the harbor of Liberation.

Foreword to *Spiritual Writings on Mary,* by Mary Ford-Grabowsky

Perhaps the single most significant mystical event of our time is the return to human consciousness, on a massive scale, of the awareness of the Motherhood of God. As an increasingly fear-driven and frenzied patriarchy degrades and destroys the world in an orgy of greed and violence, the return of the celebration of God as Mother-of-God—as the force of all-embracing divine love that lives in, for, and as the creation—offers a saving balance of reverence for the created world, an honoring of all diversity, and a new respect for feminine modes of intuition and cooperation. This revival in spiritual thinking also offers a fresh, urgent, and radical vision of love in action and a "mystical activism" that gives birth to what may well be humanity's last—and best—hope.

At the center of this return of the Mother is an astonishing revival of interest in and passion for Mary, both within Christianity and outside it. Increasingly—and for seekers of many kinds and paths—the figure of Mary is embodying all the grandeurs and powers of the complete Divine Mother, of a Mother who not only governs the transcendent realms but also wills the transformation of *this* earth into the "kingdom-queendom" of which Jesus spoke continually and to which his entire mission was dedicated. The traditional limits that male theologians of the past have placed on Mary's power and significance and on Her role in the Christ revelation are being shattered, and a new revelation of Her role in the birth of divine humanity is being acknowledged at the very moment when the human race needs its inspiration most.

This vision of Mary as the complete and completely empowered Divine Mother does not, however, deny the different truths of Mary's presence as celebrated in the Christian mystical tradition. In fact, one way of experiencing the Christian mystical tradition—as Mary Ford-Grabowsky's exemplary and brilliant anthology makes clear—is as a continually self-transforming unfolding of the truth of Mary's role in the birth of Christ-consciousness, an unfolding that begins with Her relatively minor role in the Gospel, expands through Her growing glorification in the third and fourth century CE, explodes in the many-sided ecstatic celebration of Her mystical power and glory in the late Middle Ages—in the visions of Dante, Julian of Norwich, and Hildegard of Bingen—and comes to a triumphant consummation in the work of the prophetic Marian mystic of the eighteenth century, St. Louis-Marie Grignion de Montfort, who declared in his *Secret of Mary:*

> It is through the Very Holy Virgin that Jesus Christ came into the world to begin with, and it is also through her that he will reign

in the world.... Until now, the divine Mary had been unknown, and this is one of the reasons why Jesus Christ is hardly known as he should be. If then—as is certain—the knowledge and reign of Jesus Christ arrive in the world, it will be a necessary consequence of the knowledge and reign of the Very Holy Virgin, who birthed him into the world the first time and will make him burst out everywhere the second.... Mary is the dawn that precedes and reveals the Sun of Justice.

De Montfort's tremendous vision of Mary as a cosmic Mother-force that is indispensable and crucial to the birth of authentic Christ-consciousness in apocalyptic times has had the essential purpose of providing an expanded mystical context for the apparitions of Mary that began in the 1830s and are still continuing. Mary warns humanity of the dire consequences of continuing on its path of suicidal self-destruction and offers a way out through prayer, repentance, mutual respect, and sacred action. However hard the guard-dog theologians of the Roman Catholic Church try to contain the cosmic reach and implications of the Mary of the apparitions, it is clear to anyone who studies them that *this* Mary is speaking not only to Christians and the Church, but to all beings everywhere as a universal Mother with all transcendent powers at Her disposal and a burning compassion to use them for humanity's transformation and for the creation, out of the ashes of nightmarish destruction, of a new human race and a new world. The coming of the apocalypse has called out of the depths of human memory and divine awareness an ever-richer image of Mary as the focus and conduit of an all-powerful and all-redeeming divine feminine love and knowledge dedicated to helping us preserve and transform our world.

Perhaps the most important aspect of this new vision of Mary is its insistence that this all-powerful and all-redeeming divine feminine love is, in its essential nature, radical, even revolutionary. The Mary who is emerging in humanity's mystical experience of Her is not only the transcendent Queen of Heaven but also a revolutionary of love and justice, passionate for the triumph of God's kingdom on behalf of the poor, humiliated, and dispossessed, and of an increasingly ravaged nature. She is at once the cosmic Mother of all; Maryam, the Mother of Jesus, who called in the Magnificat for a triple revolution—spiritual, cultural, and political—a complete overturning of all the forces of oppression; and the Black Madonna, enraged beyond endurance at human folly, inequality, and cruelty, and gifted with vast divine powers of creative destruction and sacred wrath. This composite Mary-force, known in its full majesty, outrage, and demand, unleashes a tremendous radical power that menaces all elites and hierarchies and all ways of being and acting that do not revere the harmony and dignity of life. The force of the Mother, it is becoming clear, wills, in and through Mary, nothing less than a complete upheaval of the brutal facts of the world and of all those oppressive structures that keep people and nature enslaved.

The emergence of the "complete" Mary—at once transcendent and immanent, divine and human, all-loving and revolutionary— allows, as de Montfort in the eighteenth century prophesied it would, for the birth at last of the complete and authentic Christ-consciousness, as much the child of the Mother as of the Father, and which is profoundly revolutionary in its intent. In the Gospel of Thomas, Jesus proclaims, "He who is near to me is near to the fire." The revelation of the divine Mary, of the Mother as both compassion and prophetic hunger to see all institutions, arts, sciences, and ways of doing politics and business transformed to reflect God's love and God's justice, makes possible the birth of this "fire" on a massive scale in the world. The drama is set, at the heart of the apocalypse, for the potential creation of a new humanity, on fire with divine wisdom, peace, power, sacred outrage, and sacred energy; and inspired and empowered to act in every dimension to preserve and transform the world. The "fire" that Jesus proclaimed the creative agent in the kingdom-queendom is not only an inward experience but also an outward way of acting. What Mary as the birthing force of the "fire" can guide the whole human race to at the moment is a new vision both of what it is to be a mystic and what it is to be an activist. Just as the historical Maryam filled in her being and life all the opposites of peace and passion, transcendent knowledge and radical embodied action, stillness, and energy, so Mary the complete Mother can help birth in the human race the potentially all-transforming fire in action of mystical activism that fuses all the sacred powers of mystical strength, stamina, wisdom, and compassion with all the sacred passion of the Mother's vast hunger to see the world transfigured. From Mary as Divine Mother flow not only the vision of a new creation but also the birthing powers and passion necessary to bring it into being.

In 1986 Mary announced to the world at Medjugorje in Yugoslavia: "These are the times of the great return. Yes, after the time of the great suffering there will be the time of the great rebirth and all will blossom again. Humanity will again be a new garden of life and beauty." For those of us who are aware that humanity and the world are now entering the hurricane of the great suffering, this promise of a new garden by the Mother is not only a prophetic consolation but also a call to action, a call to all of us to summon up all the creative powers of our being and place them under Her guidance, inspiration, and protection so that the great rebirth can, in de Montfort's phrase, "burst out everywhere."

Introduction to *Mary's Vineyard*, by Andrew Harvey and Eryk Hanut

> Mary is the unrecognized Mother Goddess of Christianity.
>
> Anne Baring and Jules Cashford, *The Myth of the Goddess*

> I love you, my little ones, and I do not wish to see you destroy one another.
>
> Our Lady to Estela Ruiz, Phoenix, 1991

Many seekers and lovers of God of all kinds and faiths are agreed that the single most important aspect of the spiritual life of the world today is that everywhere we are witnessing a return to the Mother, to the long-forgotten, long-derided Mother aspect of God.

For too long the major religions and mystical traditions have been biased toward transcendence and attached to detachment. This bias and this subtle attachment to a vision of the Divine that separates it and us from our bodies, our ordinary lives, our sexuality, and nature have, it is becoming clear, abetted the destruction of the planet and not worked to prevent it. Those who love the Mother know that unless we turn to Her and allow Her profound and passionate knowledge of interdependence and love in action at every level and in every dimension to penetrate, transform, inspire, and guide us—we will not find in ourselves the vision or passion or wisdom necessary to preserve the planet.

To a world ravaged by disunity, the Mother offers the revelation of oneness; to an age inwardly destroyed by apathy and anxiety, the Mother offers the grace of a holy and peaceful passion that blesses, loves, and protects all things and knows all things and beings as sacred emanations of a common source; to beings panicked by the threat of a worldwide ecological catastrophe, the Mother offers strength, hope, and the inner power to effect a change of heart, and the radical political and economic action that must follow such a change; to those depressed by the harshness of working for justice and transformation in so deluded and secretly devastated an age, the Mother offers Her protection and Her humble stamina and that force of unconditional love that is Her essence and Her gift, and that no power can defeat.

In this worldwide return to the Mother and to the healing and invigorating wisdom of the Sacred Feminine, nothing is more signifi-cant or inspiring, especially for those brought up, however difficultly, in the Christian tradition, than the extraordinary attention being paid by seekers of all kinds to Mary. During the last 150 years, Mary has been appearing all over the world, delivering short, simple messages of infinite love, wisdom, and urgency, trying to wake Her children up to the enormity of the danger they are facing and to the remedies of prayer, mutual honor, and hard work in every dimension that alone can save the situation. Increasingly, and for people of all faiths, Mary is being liberated from the golden cage of patriarchal adoration that has kept Her prisoner for so long, and is being revealed for what She is: the Divine Mother in full force and splendor, as essential to the working out of the Christian mystery as Her Son—the most human of all the faces of the Mother, the one turned with the most urgent and passionate love toward humankind.

Kali and Saraswati, Isis and Astarte, and the great Goddesses of South America and Africa are all marvelous cosmic revelations of the Mother. Mary has the power and range of all of these, but being also once human, it is clear to anyone devoted to Her that She has a very personal interest in the world, a very anxious interest, one that emphasizes—as none of the other aspects of the Mother do with quite such intimacy or anguished passion—the glory of this world and the absolute necessity of doing everything in our power to preserve it.

Mary's message is a simple one: "Realize the essential unity in my Sacred Heart of everything that lives; ripen that knowledge and love through continual prayer; enact that knowledge in every aspect of life to irradiate life with my power, truth, tenderness, and passion for justice." All the old barriers between faiths, peoples, sexualities, castes must now be dissolved, for differences create division, and there is no more time left for the dubious luxury of divisiveness.

Mary knows—and makes clear again and again that She knows—that our situation is desperate, that evil is extremely powerful, and nature—the body of the light—is in appalling danger. She knows that we cannot preserve ourselves unless we undergo a massive change of heart that leads to a commitment at every level to make love real in action and to implement justice in every arena. She knows that there are immense forces ranged against us, ranged against the success of the human enterprise.

Mary also knows that if we can turn to the Mother, to Her mercy and Her power and Her love that live in us as our deepest identity and heart-truth, miracles of transformation are possible—miracles that are not simply personal and spiritual, but ones that effect the changes that will save the whales and the dolphins and Antarctica and Amazonia, as well as the future of the soul of every human being. Nothing is impossible to Her children, if they recognize, honor, and pray to their Mother. Together with the Mother, we can still, even at this late hour, do anything.

"My Immaculate Heart will triumph," Mary said to the children at Fatima, after being terrifyingly clear about the dangers ahead. Mary's heart—and the heart of Her Son—will triumph, but only if we all turn to them now, with humility and confidence and complete lack of illusion about the potentially terminal danger we are in.

Eryk and I have made this book as an aid in this turning of the whole being toward Her. Mary, our Mother, needs no elaborate address, no fancy meditations, no complex prayers. Saying Her rosary and talking to Her from a full heart are always enough, and She will answer every request directed to Her, as everyone who risks intimacy with Her knows beyond doubt. We have brought together here those prayers, meditations, and mystical insights culled from Her greatest lovers over two thousand years that have most intimately helped us in our longing to be close to Her and to realize Her love in the world.

Weave the meditation we have given into your prayers, thoughts, and actions each day, and you will find, as we have, that your whole being will be strengthened in the fire of the Mother's hope and truth. And with that hope and that truth increasingly established in our hearts, minds, bodies, and souls, nothing will be impossible to us, Her children.

The Virgin said to Sister Faustina in the 1930s, "Mankind will not have peace until it turns with trust to my mercy." To Father Stefano Gobbi, the Virgin said in 1987, "I am gathering my children from every part of the earth and enclosing them in the refuge of my

Immaculate Heart so that they may be defended and saved by me at the moment of the Great Trial that has now arrived for all. So in the very years when evil is triumphing by leading humanity along the road of its own destruction, my maternal heart is also triumphing, as I bring my children along the way of salvation and peace." She added, "My light will become stronger and stronger the more you enter into the decisive moments of the battle."

This battle for the future of humanity is now raging in every field of human life. Everything depends on the intensity and the seriousness and the comprehensiveness with which we summon the Mother's love and power, and enact it.

We pray that this book will furnish all who come to it those arms of love, mystical trust, and insight that we all need to endure, to struggle calmly, and to win, in Her name and for Her glory.

O Divine Mother, Save, Inspire, Elevate, Stabilize, Humble, and Embolden us all.

I dedicate this text to my mother, Kathleen Elizabeth Harvey.

"On the Black Madonna" Interview with Fred Gustafson from *The Moonlit Path*

This interview took place between Andrew Harvey and Fred Gustafson on January 24, 2001. Following the terrorist attack on the World Trade Center on September 11, 2001, they reconvened to reflect on the bearing that the Dark Feminine has upon that terrible event.

Fred Gustafson: Andrew, when you hear "Black Madonna" or "dark virgin," what thoughts, feelings, dreams, and personal experiences come to you?

Andrew Harvey: The Black Madonna is a very important part of my inmost life and has been now for almost ten years. I first met

Her in a book by Anne Baring titled *The Myth of the Goddess*. I realized when I read Anne's book that what was coming together in this symbol were the two sides of my own quest for the Divine Feminine. I was then a devotee of an Indian woman, Mother Meera, whom I believed, at that time, to be the Divine Mother. I was also very moved by the whole vision of Mary that was being opened up to me by the Christian mystics such as Louis Grignion de Montfort. However, I had not found the inner connection between an Eastern understanding of the Divine Mother as the force of destruction as well as creation and the Western vision of Her as this transcendent force that unifies and unites all things.

When I met the dark Black Madonna in a book, I suddenly realized that was the force that I had been looking for to bring together my Eastern passions and my Western inheritance. Although this realization was quite profound, it remained on a mental level, until I actually left my guru under very painful circumstances. Briefly, Mother Meera told me on December 27, 1993, to get rid of my lover, Eryk (who is now my husband), get married to a woman, and write a book about how I was transformed into a heterosexual. At that moment I realized that fifteen years of passionate devotion to Meera had been lunacy. This sent my whole life into a whirlwind of suffering. During the weeks that followed as I was battling with myself and with my past and with the craziness of this extraordinary situation, I made a pilgrimage to Chartres, where I worshiped for the first time, with the fullness of my being, the Black Madonna in the "Virgin of the Pillar." I came to begin to understand very deep things about Her because I had come to the moment when Her agony, power, and extreme vibrant, violent purity of compassion could be revealed to me.

That day I realized that I had been projecting onto Meera my soul's secret passion to come into direct connection with the Black Madonna beyond name and form. In meeting the Black Madonna in my state of misery and psychological and spiritual torment, I was being opened to Her presence in the cosmos and in present history.

On that day, I think what I understood most of all was that the Black Madonna is the force of divine destruction and creation, the nondual Mother whose absolute ferocious power is manifesting the entire cosmos. I also understood that what was astounding about this particular symbol was that in Her burned blackness, it was quite clear that the Black Madonna was sharing the pain of the whole creation; in fact, She was suffering and sobbing and howling and screaming and dying in and with all of Her creations so that there was an extreme sense not only of Her transcendent power but also of Her absolute and final, immanent compassion. I realized that the only force that could see me through the tremendous crisis that Eryk and I were in would be the Black Madonna.

The whole of the rest of the crisis that Eryk and I were to live through was lived through very consciously on my part in the atmosphere of the Black Madonna. What I came to realize was that She was helping me birth my inner nondual Christ-consciousness, which is only possible in and under Her because only She can take the adept into the depths of a nondual identification both with the Transcendent and with the suffering of the Immanent. Only She has the symbolic and actual power to birth the realization that can only be born through an experience of the dark night of the soul, the total shattering of all the agendas, concepts, visions, and spiritual understandings that have accompanied the adept up to then. So to me the Black Madonna was the force of the Divine Mother that I met at the very moment when I needed to plunge into unfathomable pain and suffering in order to dissolve the old structures of myself. It was only Her force that could sustain and see me through that suffering and, through divine grace, birth the new being that that suffering was preparing. So I saw Her as the womb, if you like, in which the crucifixion of the false self takes place. It is Her power that both enforces the death and engenders and protects the new life of the Christ-self that is born from the death.

At the end of a particular set of devastating experiences, in which I had to face the betrayals of my old friends as well as my own complicity in those betrayals, because I had been deliberately blind to what they had been doing for years, I decided that the only way to survive such knowledge would be to "die" in life. So I lay down on the ground and found myself sinking through layer after layer of divine knowledge and awareness until finally I reached an unfathomable darkness, which was calm and broad as the universe and wide as infinity and ultimately peaceful. At that moment I understood beyond knowledge that I was the child of the Black Madonna. I had been birthed into a dimension of transcendent and immanent divine identity.

When I surfaced from this experience, the whole of the room around me (I was actually in the bath)—the bath, the taps, the walls—all were brilliant with divine light. I understood that the unraveling of my own agendas, programs, and visions of myself had taken me to a point of total surrender, where She could reveal the dark divinity at the core of myself. This experience led to many other unfoldings that I also recognized to be Her gift. I had, first of all, projected onto a guru my own self secret need to meet the Black Madonna. Then, through the shattering of that illusion of the guru, I actually came in increasing intensity to meet the Black Madonna and, in increasing intensity, to be stripped, seared, and burned by Her in Her crucible of the dark night of the soul. It was also here, however, that I was reborn by Her. I feel I have been graced the initiation of the Black Madonna, and that this is a very crucial initiation for our planet at this moment.

When I was living through the initiation, I remembered that I had already been informed of its deepest secrets by somebody that I had met only a year before, Father Bede Griffiths. I was invited by an Australian film director to go to south India to the ashram where Father Griffiths lived to be involved in the making of a film about him. He was eighty-six at the time. When we met, we fell spiritually in love, and he opened the treasure chest of his emotional and mystical journey to me. The account of what he said in the tapes we made is published in a book titled *The Human Search*, which has a marvelous description of his meeting with the Black Madonna. What happened to Bede was that in his eighties, he had a series of strokes that he interpreted as the dark Mother coming to shatter his patriarchal addiction to the left-brain understanding that he had adhered to all his life. Through Her shattering of this, he had come into a deeper and much broader, wider, wilder vision of the cosmos, of his own relationship with it and into a far deeper understanding of what the sacred marriage between body and spirit really is. So as I was going through my own initiation I was being fed, if you like, the wisdom of what Bede himself had told me. Now I was living it for myself in the terms of my own temperament and the terms of my own dark night.

FG: And what did you actually discover as you lived this initiation?

AH: What I discovered was two things, which many people discover when they come into the crucible of the Black Madonna. The first thing is, of course, that all your plans, agendas, projects, and visions are systematically and with a terrifying precision unraveled by Her. They are annihilated because they belong to a world of division and separation. They belong to the pride of the false self and to a way of acting that has to become immeasurably deepened by radiant awareness. The second thing that you discover is that She is not only transcendent, She is also the most passionately profound natural process, and that the birth into Her and through Her is very much a physical birth. This is what Bede, in his eighties, discovered. He discovered that being annihilated by Her actually birthed him into the dimension of the body for the first time and into the dimension of a consecrated and sublime sexuality and into the marriage of the body and spirit at a level and intensity that he never before imagined.

What happened during the annihilation process that I went through with the Black Madonna is that just as my external life and concepts were being destroyed, so in my love for Eryk and in our lovemaking, in our deepest and most passionate meeting, She revealed to me some of the most transfiguring truths of the tantra. The birth in Her was simultaneously the destruction of all fantasies and an initiation into the divinity of the body, and the divine secrets that consecrated, tantric love reveals about the body and physical life when transfigured by spiritual passion. So it was clear to me and became clearer still that this birth into the Black Madonna is a birth simultaneously into this "dark transcendent," the source and womb and spring of all manifestation, and a birth into the splendor of tantric fullness and the glory of tantric being. The two *together,* as they deepen, create what only can be described as the resurrection consciousness, the consciousness of divine humanity. Though this process is very far from complete, I have experienced how She is the birthing force of authentic divine humanity. What She does to birth it is to destroy all of the fantasies that block the Transcendent as well as destroy all of the fears, loathing, self-hatreds, and all of the terrors of the body that block the glory of the flaming out of the body's own most sacred truth. This is essential information for all seekers at this moment, because unless we come to this birth of divine humanity here on the earth with fully consecrated sacred powers and sacred creativity of every kind, we are simply not going to be able to survive.

FG: How would you describe what the Black Madonna is now doing on a world-scale? With the whole planet?

AH: First of all, I believe She is allowing the crucifixion of the planet by our arrogance, pride, greed, and horrible lust of power to take place, because it is the only way in which we will now, at this late moment, wake up to the terror and horror of our pride, greed, and arrogance and lust for destruction.

Second, and as part of this, She is shattering all human agendas. All of our fantasies about ourselves are being exposed horribly by this crucifixion that is clearly the result of our own madness. Every single belief that humanity ever had about itself, about its worth, its holiness, its sweetness, its reason, its technological power, its divine truth—all of them are being rubbled by this destruction, which is increasingly revealing to anybody with half a mind and half a heart that everything that we have ever known or believed about ourselves is illusion. This is a terrible process and involves not only a crucifixion of nature but also a crucifixion of our inmost spirit and agendas as well as everything we believed in that is now an outmoded version of our own nature. The Black Madonna is doing this because it is only through this that we will become abandoned and surrendered and humbled enough to Her to call upon Her to take us through the dark birthing process of the "annihilation adventure" into the new consciousness that She alone can bring us. Everything in human history now depends on whether or not this fierce and frightening knowledge, with its glorious conclusions and possibilities, can be revealed to human beings clearly and accurately enough so that as many people as possible can give themselves over to the birthing powers of the Black Madonna, and go through whatever is necessary to birth the divine human creatively.

FG: I can't help but see a parallel between your personal journey—specifically, your being with Mother Meera with the pain that brought, and how you dealt with that—and what is happening on the planet and the planet's need, the peoples of the earth's need, to withdraw their projection and to take a look with how they are living on the earth and crucifying it. It seems to me the Black Madonna was behind the events around Mother Meera for you.

AH: Three weeks before I broke with Mother Meera, I received a postcard from a friend's exhibition in Zurich. It was of Kali. The week before that, I had a dream that I now realize was my first experience of the chthonic power of the Black Madonna. I had just finished writing *The Way of Passion*, about Rumi. I had a dream in which I went to a window, opened it, and saw this great, blue wave, which reared like a vast cobra and turned black. From the center of this swarming, boiling darkness flashed out a lightning flash that actually caused me to faint away. After that, the Kali picture came and the dark night I have described started to unfold.

It became very clear to me that the entire process was ruled by the Black Madonna. The crucifixion initiation I underwent burned me free from my own projections of my own divinity onto someone else and forced me to take back those projections, and to honor them, and to consecrate my whole life to honoring them not only in myself but also in other people, without illusion. It compelled me to stop being a secret junkie of transcendence and realize my own body, sexuality, love, and desire were all potentially, wholly, and completely sacred.

Also, because I suffered in my inmost core the horror of the abuse of power, it made me a permanent mystical revolutionary. If you suffer the abuse of power in one area, it initiates you into all the nuances of abusive power in all the different institutions of the world. One of the major gifts of the Black Madonna to anybody who worships Her is that She wakes them up starkly to all the games of manipulation that mask abuse and to the presence of the corruption of power in every institution, media, and way of being and doing that is not directly illumined by democratic egalitarian compassion. This is a terrifying initiation, because once you see, or begin to see, with Her eyes, what you see is a world gone mad, a world in which the essential truths of divine humanity are rubbled, betrayed, and degraded on every side, not merely by the materialists or by those who deny God, but with horrible ingenuity by those who claim to represent God both in the established religions and in the guru systems—all of which are addicted to power and not to the true transmission of sacred empowerment.

FG: I do not see the Black Madonna in any way being benign. But I do see Her being patient except when we ignore what She represents. Then She becomes like Kali. Then She will tear you apart, lovingly.

AH: Yes, She will tear you apart within yourself to rebirth you in your true, divine self. I have found that the most important way of seeing the Black Madonna is actually to bring together three seemingly contradictory aspects. It is my experience that you experience them all together like music. The first aspect is that She is the transcendent Queen of Darkness—the "dazzling darkness" of Dionysius the Areopagite. This is the darkness beyond name and form. It is the darkness of the Tao. It is the transcendence from which even the light, even the godhead is born.

The phrase of Ruysbroeck that Bede used when he was talking of Her is very moving. He says, "She is the darkness in which lovers lose themselves." The Dark One is the Queen of final Mystery, the One who through all transformations is leading us on, ever onward, while "hiding" in a kind of cloud of darkness, forever distant from any formulation or concept we may have of Her.

In the second aspect, the Black Madonna is the Queen of Nature, the Queen of Tantra, and the Queen of all the dark, rich, gorgeous, fertile processes of Nature and of Tantra. The sum of these processes is often destructive, because for the true divine nature to emerge and for true tantra to be born, all kinds of fears and self-presentations have to be rubbled. That can be searingly painful, but the purpose of the pain is to open you up to the gorgeous textures of Her transformations. That is what streams through the destruction: one of Her hands is tearing you apart while the other is pouring into the torn-apart self the perfumes and unguents and revelations of a new kind of being. This is important to remember. The more you experience the holiness and the exquisite and acute precision of Her destruction, the more you will be helped by Her and understand why She is stripping you, because almost immediately afterward, into the dark empty hole that She has dug in your psyche, She will pour a wholly new vision and new awareness.

The third aspect is also revelatory. I think that one of the reasons why the Black Madonna haunts us all so much is that She very clearly represents the cost, the price, the anguish, and the sacred agony of the Divine Feminine in each of us. She is that part of us that is burned, wounded, seared, and broken by the world, by what we suffer in the world. There She is, standing in front of us as the Queen of the great and final Mystery, and as Queen of Nature and Tantra, but also as what Jacopone da Todi calls Mary in one of his great poems to the Virgin, "La Donna Bruciata," the burned woman, the woman who has been burned by love, burned by the price of love, by the constant, unavoidable opening of the heart to the misery of life, and to the injustice of human beings, and to the cruelty of the false self. I think what She is doing in standing in front of us in Her burned, black dignity is giving us a way of enduring without closing down, of standing in the fire and being burned and charred by the fire without ever turning away from the necessity of loving in a complete and total way and of giving everything.

There is a great Sufi text of the ninth century that I think goes right to the heart of this third aspect of the Black Madonna. It says, "Those who are taken into union are drawn near. And those who are drawn near never fall asleep, and the sublime rays of heartbreak engulf them." When you connect with Her in the third aspect, La Donna Bruciata, what you connect with in the depths of yourself are those "rays of sublime heartbreak." What She gives to you is the ability to participate in Her own life of final fiery compassion beyond hope, beyond agenda, beyond all plans, beyond any kind of transcendental justification. This aspect of the Black Madonna is an initiation into the burning furnace of charity, that is, the broken and burned heart of the Mother. You are taken into the depths of the mystery of the Mother because the Mother is not simply the great, dark cloud of final mystery that is uplifting everything from revelation to revelation. She is not simply the Queen of Nature and the Queen of Tantra, the Queen of all the fertile processes that transform life itself into a mirror of the Divine. She is also Herself living as every dying animal, as every dying plant, as every raped child, as every broken-hearted gay man and woman, as every abused person, as every killer, as every being of every kind on the planet suffering all the different forms of torment, ignorance, and grief.

Knowing Her in these three aspects together is a mind-, heart-, and soul-shattering experience, because if you only know Her in the transcendent aspect, then you can leave this world and reality behind. However, your realization is going to be incomplete. And if you only know Her as the Queen of Nature and Tantra, you have no knowledge of Her as the transcendent Mystery or as absolute and final compassion. Again, your realization will be incomplete. However, if you only know Her as final suffering and final compassion, you will not be able to bear such knowledge, because you will not know Her also as the Queen of the Processes and as the Queen of the Mysteries. You really have to come to a knowledge of Her in all three aspects and link them all in the inmost part of yourself beyond thought and paradox so that you can come into Her true dimension. When you do this, what you find happening within yourself is that you start to birth a being and a way of being and doing that reflects all of the three aspects, together, of Her great identity. It is only through facing, inviting, and saturating your whole practice with all of those three aspects that you can do that. You have, in fact, to "invite in" consciously the whole glory of the Sacred Feminine, since in the Black Madonna you have the whole radical glory of the Sacred Feminine in one symbol.

The universe and all mystical traditions tell us about a sacred marriage between matter and spirit, the "feminine" and the "masculine." For millennia, the bride in the marriage, the Black Madonna, has been kept in a dark, filthy, stinking cellar with Her hands tied behind Her back and Her feet tied to a chair, with black tape over Her mouth. No sacred marriage has been able to take place within human beings, no marriage of spirit and matter, of transcendence and immanence, body and soul. Releasing the bride from the cellar, taking the black tape from over Her mouth so She can speak Her own sacred wisdom in us is the present task before all of us. If She does not turn up at our inner wedding in Her full splendor, there will be no sacred marriage. The only way in which the world can be saved is through a personal initiation into that sacred marriage by millions of people and a flooding of all the world's arenas and institutions with the powers awakened by that sacred marriage. These powers are celebratory, earth-rooted, earth-grounded, justice-making, and create in the name of love and justice a new world of equality for all beings. That is the future, if there is a future. So bringing the Black Madonna back is not a luxury for a few intellectuals or a private passion of a few mystics.

FG: Yes, and isn't honesty the chief thing that the Black Madonna asks of us?

AH: In my experience, She demands something even more frightening than honesty. She demands the most extreme abandon, because She demands the most total acceptance of the terms on which She manifests the whole universe. And those terms are extremely shocking not only to the rational mind but also to the religious mind. Remember how Ramakrishna describes the Mother. He had a dream about Her. He dreamed he saw this beautiful pregnant woman arising out of the waves of the Ganges, looking glorious. Pregnant, she goes to the shore, births her child, and with a smile of ecstasy on her face, tears her child limb from limb, eats the child with the blood running down the sides of her mouth and, still ecstatic, goes back into the Ganges and drowns. Then the whole process begins again. What Ramakrishna is trying to make us aware of is the shocking, terrifying coexistence of crucifixion and resurrection at every single level of the universe.

This simultaneously creative/destructive force is something our rational minds have been constructed to try and block us from. Our religious minds also have been "constructed" to try and save us from the full shock of recognition of Her real nature. The deep reason for the addiction to transcendence in all the patriarchal mystical systems is that they simply cannot face the extremity of what She is up to. They choose to devalue the creation, life, relationships, the body, and the earth because they cannot embrace the cost of crucifixion and resurrection that the immanent aspects of the Mother demand and exact. In refusing to embrace the immanent aspects of the Mother, what they have done is effectively to castrate themselves. They have made themselves impotent. If you are addicted to transcendence, you may have a certain kind of realization of divine Being, but you can never have the realization of divine Becoming that belongs to the Mother and is the Mother's supreme gift. In choosing to privilege the realization of divine Being exclusively, what you ensure is that those realizations never flood Becoming, never transfigure or transform it, never form a radical, revolutionary core of insight and transfiguring wisdom that can actually turn the institutional axis of the world around.

It is only by facing what Ramakrishna faced in the story and plunging beyond the mind and the frightened heart, beyond the lust for transcendence, and into the full, outrageous gorgeous lunacy of Her nondual bliss that you can ever be taken into the divine truth of your own divine humanity and initiated into the creative powers that come from an acceptance of the terms in which this whole experience happens.

So, it is not just honesty the Black Madonna requires. She requires the most searing imaginable abandon and the most extreme imaginable plunging into the total embrace of Her conditions. When that is mature in you, in the depths of yourself, you become a part of the Cosmic Resurrected Christ, simultaneously awake to your divinity and also initiated into your total connection in suffering with every being everywhere. Think of those vivid Mexican representations of the Cosmic Christ. You are at once divine and yet carrying the stigmata, whether outwardly or inwardly. Marrying transcendent identity with a broken and crucified immanent identity, you finally become useful. On the one hand, there is a transcendent being, or light body, that you feel at one with and part of; that light body, and held up and nourished by it, is the crucified Christ. The Black Madonna ensouls and sustains both as necessary for Her initiation. It is not just honesty She wants. She wants, in the end, our commitment to be crucified so as to be resurrected.

The Heart of Love

FG: When you lived in India and prior to Mother Meera, did you have any personal or spiritual connection with Kali or Amba?

AH: India is itself a living Kali, because India is the total coincidence of opposites. As a child, I experienced, with the child's vulnerability, nakedness, and sacred imagination, the coincidence of opposites that is India. On one hand, there are the glorious tombs and the Taj Mahal, jasmine in the air, the aromas, maharanis wrapped in silk that looks like spun moonlight. On the other hand, mad people masturbating in the street, crazy yogis eating shit, rabid dogs howling in the night, and the poor starving and dying under crumbling bridges.

FG: That is the full spectrum of life right there.

AH: The genius of India is to expose you to both the glory and horror of life at the same time. So I feel it is not that I just experienced the Black Madonna in some meeting with Kali or Amba. By being born in India, I was born into Her directly.

FG: And through your crisis with Mother Meera, you completed, in a certain way, a process that had begun at birth.

AH: Yes, when I look back, it makes sense that I would try and project onto an Indian woman what I experienced of India as a child. I came to understand the difficulties and horror of my own imperial inheritance. As a child, I woke up to the fact that I belonged to a culture that had used, exploited, and betrayed India in all kinds of ways. The equivalence as an American would be waking up to the fact you were the son or daughter of a Southern plantation family and had the blood of black Americans on your hands.

FG: Yes, or red Americans.

AH: Yes, or red Americans. Basically what I did, in retrospect, was

66

to project the choice to love Meera because what I wanted to do was to honor the Black Madonna as India. Meera was a wonderfully convenient way of psychologically killing my own mother and of revenging myself psychologically on my "imperial" family. Nothing you could imagine would make them crazier and angrier than their distinguished, intellectual son choosing to worship an illiterate Indian woman with a mustache and call her the Divine Mother on earth! Looking back at it, I realize psychologically I needed to project India onto Meera and to try and destroy my own mother by projecting true motherhood onto someone else. I needed to have this bizarre revenge on my own imperial past. Thank God I unmasked these games and was able to take back these projections and heal my relationship with my mother—my real mother—by finding the real Black Madonna. I also was able to heal my relationship with my family and my past. I came to understand all this in a much subtler way. As a young person, however, I could not see any other way out of my own psyche except by doing what I did.

What I see now is that I was born to the Black Madonna. I could not face that early on because I did not know enough about Her. I probably, psychologically, was too fragile and complicated to face Her full on, so She gave me a false master and Mother on which I could project Her. Out of Her even more paradoxical mercy, She shattered that projection in a terrible way. She also gave me as a companion to that shattering, my husband, who has been an amazing warrior for Her and in Her. She birthed me into a wholly new awareness that I pray and hope is now helping a lot of people.

FG: That is an excellent analysis of your story. I think, in America, it is similar for our own imperial past in terms of the need to reconnect with our own indigenous roots. This has a direct connection with the Black Madonna that is our own earth, here in America.

AH: It is the only way, because, on the one hand, what She will do is to make you face the full horror of it and, on the other hand, Her compassion will give you the strength to go through it. Her strength will hold you up as you are crucified. That is what America has to go through both in its relationship with black people and Native Americans. She is the only force that can bring about the debt of recognition, the debt to sorrow, and the debt of crucifixion.

FG: I am now reading *The Woman with the Alabaster Jar* by Margaret Starbird. She relies heavily on the work in *Holy Blood, Holy Grail.* What do you think of that? That is a movement that suggests Jesus was married, has a bloodline, in southern France....

AH: Well, I think the bloodline stuff cannot be proved or disproved. However, the understanding that Jesus may have been married to Mary Magdalene is what I think would be crucial. It is entirely possible and opens up what I have been talking about. It opens up the real truth of the resurrection: namely, that resurrection is about the transfiguration of the body. One of Jesus's tremendous powers, as well as the Mother's, is tantric. I believe actually that Jesus was bisexual and that he had a sacred relationship with John as well as with Mary Magdalene. There is a heterosexual and homosexual tantra that comes out of the Black Madonna, and Jesus realized them both. One of the tremendous benefits of opening up to the Christ as the Cosmic Androgyne would be the healing of all human sexual shame and all human sexual division and the initiation of the human race into the great secret of the tantra that springs directly from the force of the Cosmic Christ and is birthed by the force of the Black Madonna. Awakening to this tantric force might give us as a race the power and sacred energy to change all things in Her and for Her before it's too late.

In every arena of life, there is a massive shift to be made, and very fast. Only the Black Madonna, I feel, can give us the passion, vision, strength, and complete realization necessary to make this shift in time. These days there is a prayer I keep saying in Her honor, a prayer I first prayed in Chartres to the Black "Virgin of the Pillar":

O Black Madonna, my Dark Mother, who births all those who love and surrender enough into divine humanity, keep me close to your wild and burning heart, and grace me the courage to go through all I need to become your instrument.

I have found that if you pray this prayer sincerely or "dangerously" enough, it will be answered.

After September 11, 2001

This interview addresses the attack on the World Trade Towers, September 11, 2001, in New York City. It is meant as an addendum to the previous interview with Andrew Harvey and describes, through this specific historical event, the relevance of the eruption of the Dark Feminine archetype. The interview was held on November 18, 2001.

FG: The tragic event of September 11 changed not only the American psyche but also the world's psyche.

AH: Yes, for me it seems like the eruption of the Black Madonna into the center of life. Fundamentally, I think of the planes going to the towers in two ways: the first image that comes to me is that of the spear opening the heart of Christ on the cross. It is the spear that lances the boil of a very long coma of denial. The other way in which I think of those planes going into the side of the towers is like the breaking of the waters. When the towers dissolved, it seemed as if the waters of a vast, pregnant woman had broken. A birth was going to take place. For me, both ways of looking at this disaster are as a huge immersion in the acid of the shadow. I see the crisis as a vast shattering-open of all the fantasies, so as to confront the world with the seriousness, gravity, and horror of real evil, and people on all sides with the necessity for a real transformation of the heart and mind, if we are going to survive. This event has brought together in a death or birth dance the two different sides of the world: Jihad and McWorld. Jihad is the fanatical, extremist wing of Islam, and

McWorld, the fundamentalism of the dollar, of the corporate mind, of the oil multimillionaire, and the world of the domination over nature by economic greed. Both sides are fundamentalists disconnected from the feminine—mass-murderers, in fact, of the feminine in women, in relationships, in nature. They are being brought together now to fight each other to the death so that the dark in both will be destroyed.

This is terrifying. Both sides are not only responsible already for enormous suffering but also have to face enormous suffering. Both sides will have to claim the truth of their shadows if they are going to change and be creative, if there is going to be a birth of a new humanity and not a death.

I believe strongly this tremendous clash has come for a prophetic purpose. It comes at the very time in which all the terms for a Great Birth of a divine humanity are ready, despite everything, and waiting to be implemented. All the technological and philosophical possibilities and skills are there. All of the mystical systems have flooded the world with the treasures of their knowledge and the treasure of their sacred technology.

The birth can only take place in democracy. In the Western world, there is a growing awareness of the body as sacred, of the value of freedom, of recognizing the power and potency of the Sacred Feminine, and seeing the blessing in human variety and diversity. There is also here tremendous scientific, biological, ecological, and economic knowledge that, if it were dedicated to divine love and to the re-creation of the world in and under God, could help a massive transformation take place really quite fast. That is really why this crisis is manifesting at this moment—to bring the West to a knowledge of its fundamental role in bringing about this potentially all-transforming birth. We really do have to dedicate ourselves to this birth seriously, with all our powers, if it is going to take place.

This is very much the time in which human history is going to be decided. It is going to take a real turning in the psyche toward the dark side of the feminine, toward the side that reveals the horror of what we have done, the cruelty the shadow inflicts, and the depths of the vastness of the major problems that threaten humanity. These are not simply terrorism but are environmental, psychological, spiritual, and political.

Only the Dark Feminine can open us up to the vastness of the suffering we all need to go through to become responsible for what the human shadow has inflicted both on the life of humanity and on the life of nature. We are going to have to open up to the necessity of suffering as part of the great, sacred, dark heart of the Dark Feminine, the dark heart that bleeds and suffers with all living things. We are going to have to be taught by the Dark Feminine how to go through what is about to occur, which is really the crucifixion of all of our illusions, fantasies, and beliefs in humanity as separate from God. We are going to have to turn to the Dark Feminine in order to be able to endure the various stages of deceit, disintegration, and disillusion that are about to be unfolded in meticulous and ruthless geometrical stages. We are going to have to turn to the positive Dark Feminine, the glowing, Guadalupe aspect of the Dark Feminine, because only that will reconnect us to the sacredness of embodiment. She will give us the blood knowledge, the green-heart knowledge, the connection to the living streams of life that we must recapture very fast if we are going to have a chance of birthing ourselves in all dimensions as a renovated divine humanity. We are going to have to turn to the transcendent aspect of the Dark Feminine, the one who goes beyond all dogma or religion, the absolute eternal marriage of all opposites, the final mystery of paradoxical grace that will be the only source of guidance and of stamina to take us through the process of annihilation into resurrection, the only one who could feed us the mystical awareness that we will need.

The clearer the individual sees the overall global reach of what is happening, the clearer the archetypal patterns will be understood. The more that people see, the greater the chance they will be able to turn to the Black Madonna and ask directly for help and start opening up in the ways She demands.

The Black Madonna is a very demanding archetype. She demands radical honesty about one's own motive. She demands total connectedness to the living glory of the world. She demands total submission to the mysteries of Her paradoxical dance. She demands total, passionate commitment to giving your life to serve justice and transfiguration in the real world. She really is asking humanity to kick away not only the material toys but also all of the religious divisions that have kept humanity from the heart of God and from each other's hearts. We need to kick away the dogmas and the crazy fundamentalist systems, whether they are Islamic, Hindu, or Christian, and to place ourselves in contact with Her naked heart, which transforms everything. That will take a massive breakdown on all levels. She is preparing us for that. I think we are going to be put through this because we have been given absolutely every chance to change for the last 150 years. We have been given extraordinary messages of warning and potential hope by the Divine Mother Herself as Mary at Fatima and elsewhere. We have been given extraordinary evidence of our destructiveness, revealed in, for example, two world wars, the creation of atomic bombs, the devastating information about the environment and worldwide diseases and the extent of poverty that threatens the world at the moment. We have paid no attention. Now what has happened is the divine Dark One has organized a crisis perfectly horrible in all of its aspects, perfectly tuned to drive us from every single illusion that we have held dear, every single dogma that we have clung to into the arms of Her own Kali knowledge and transcendent awareness. We can either go into those arms and become free, become one with Her heart and start giving everything to turn this lunacy around before it destroys the planet, or we can simply pretend it is not going on and retreat into denial and join the destructive forces and hasten the end of everything. Now, more than ever, the choice is ours. What I am certain of is this: the Black Madonna will give us all the strength and passion we need if only we can find the courage to surrender to Her.

These days I find myself praying continuously a prayer that came to me on September 12:

"Mary as the Black Madonna"

O glorious Dark One,
do what is necessary
to wake us up,
and give us
the strength and sacred passion
to bear our illumination.

"Mary as the Black Madonna" from *The Son of Man*

Perhaps the most powerful and all-embracing of all the symbols of the Virgin that are "returning" to our Christian consciousness to help us reimagine the power of the Divine Feminine is that of the Black Madonna. In its complex and majestic truth, I believe, all of the powers that need to be restored to the Mother in the revelation can be symbolized and worshipped. Seen in its full splendor, the image of the Black Madonna is one of the most moving and profound images of the Divine Mother ever imagined by humankind, and a perfect image on which to focus devotion for Mary, the full Divine Mother, in all Her aspects—as Queen of Heaven, Queen of Nature, Queen of Earth, and as a suffering, brave, dignified, mystical, and practical human divine being, who struggled and wept and prayed with us and who struggles, weeps, and prays with us and in us and for us still.

The Black Madonna is the transcendent Kali-Mother, the black womb of light out of which all the worlds are always arising and into which they dissolve, the unknowable mystery behind all matter and all events, the "darkness" of divine love and the loving unknowing the divine Child embraces when his or her illumination is perfect. The Black Madonna is also the Queen of Nature and Tantra, the blesser and agent of all rich, fertile transformations in external and inner nature, in the outside world and in the intimacy of the psyche. And She is as well the human mother blackened by anguish and grief, but ennobled and made adamant by the secret mystical knowledge She has won from agony and is representing with dignity and is "voicing" as a perpetual appeal for justice and true change on every level. All of the different energies and powers of Mary are present in the Black Madonna in all of their different levels and dimensions and inner relations.

And because the fullness of the Divine Feminine is represented in this image, when we contemplate it fearlessly, we are gradually initiated through it into the full nature of our Christhood in Her. The human, seared mother, the Maryam of the Magnificat, accompanies us in our worst anguishes and humiliations, representing that endurance and belief and surrender that are the clues to their transmutation into divine wisdom. The Queen of Nature and Tantra blesses us, and through our awed and grateful reception of that blessing, transmutes into bliss and gnosis all the movement of our nature, making them whole and rich with Her dark fecundity and strong with Her strength, which is rooted in the depths and mysteries of natural processes and rhythms, rhythms of creativity, transformation, and continual birth and rebirth. The transcended and glorious dark Queen of Heaven, dark as the virgin of Guadalupe but, like Her, wearing all the splendor of the sun and pregnant with the new, constantly inspires us and leads us forward and upward into the highest mysteries, while showing us in other of Her aspects, which are also simultaneously present, how to ground, root, demonstrate, live, and embody them with naked courage.

As the Christ-Children of so complete and absolute and empowered a Mother, holy and unifying energies will be graced us, and all aspects of life on earth can be transformed. In Her and His name, in the name and in the glory of the completely realized Father-Mother-Child, nature will be saved and preserved and human life in all of its aspects changed forever into a mirror of divine love and justice.

And the Cosmic Christ will be born on earth at last.

Chapter Two

The Language of Love–
The Eternal Renaissance of the Mystical Poets

Introduction

What humanity's greatest mystics offer us and what we desperately need to heal the long desolation of our separation from the Divine is the authentic, radical, passionate language of love. The mystical renaissance of the last thirty years makes available to us in our era of irony, nihilism, and despair, the language of our essential, divine dignity and possibility.

This language transcends all religious, social, political, and sexual barriers to speak nakedly and directly to the buried, divine heart in all of us. It can empower us with the splendor and courage we now need to become radical servant warriors of divine love in an exploding world.

To hear the words the mystics pour out to us with such high, wild intensity, we need to attune our whole being to the silence of the Divine, which Ramana Maharshi, the great Indian sage, called "unceasing eloquence." Just as the moon radiates the reflected light of an invisible sun, the words of Rumi, Kabir, Rilke, Whitman, and the other, more modern mystics that I celebrate in this chapter arrive to us, bathed in the unceasing eloquence and endlessly vibrant, initiatory power of the silence they are born from.

The love that the great mystics celebrate with such abandoned ecstasy is not the sentimental or possessive, self-absorbed love of our contemporary novels, magazines, and TV shows. It has nothing to do with the saccharine fantasies of the New Age, narcissistically addicted to a vision of God as a benign parent who will make everything right whatever we do and however destructive and suicidal we are.

The Language of Love

The love that Kabir and Rumi knew is a vast, divine fire that burns away all the games and illusions of the false self. It is as terrifying as it is radiant, as radically demanding in its majestic truth as it is unconditionally loving and forgiving, as ferocious as it is tender and ecstatic. To become one with it, as all true mystics know, requires a death of everything we have believed, clung to, and enshrined as real. It demands not only a ceaseless discipline of inner sacred practice and a stringent self-knowledge, but also a commitment to enact its laws of clarity and burning compassion in the core of life. As Angelus Silesius, the seventeenth-century mystic wrote:

> *Love is difficult because loving is not enough;*
> *We must, like God, ourselves be love.*

I would add that being love, we must act in love, as love, for love, urgently and fearlessly to prevent the destruction of humanity and nature and cooperate with the Divine to birth a new world.

Andrew Harvey

Introduction to *Songs of Kabir,* translated by Rabindranath Tagore

You have in hand a new edition of a book first published in English in 1915. In this terrible and desperate time—after the terrorist attacks on the World Trade Center and Pentagon permanently shattered a whole civilization's sense of security and began an international war on terrorism that may last for years and decide the future of humanity—it may seem frivolous, even shocking, to celebrate the republication of a famous translation by Tagore of the Indian mystic Kabir. With human history now being poured red-hot from the cauldron of terror and war, what use is there in reading and meditating on a hundred or so of the poems of an illiterate weaver from Benares? Some five hundred years have passed since Kabir wrote these poems.

He lived and worked in a civilization very different from our own and from a mystical vision that may seem irrelevant to us now, trapped as we are in a conflict whose impact is ever more unnerving and brutal.

Kabir wrote, "More than all else do I cherish at heart that love which makes me to live a limitless life in this world?" How in our world, increasingly limited by fear and violence, can we credit his claims, let alone believe they have any light to give to our situation?

Such a reaction is understandable, but it fails to realize that the root of the problems that now afflict us from every direction lie in a worldwide spiritual crisis that only the highest and deepest mystical knowledge and vision can cure. This worldwide crisis is essentially a crisis of human identity. Humanity as a whole has lost its sense of radical interconnection with the Divine and so with the creation. And, as individuals, we have lost that mystical connection with each other.

More than forty years ago, Teilhard de Chardin wrote, "We have come to the moment when we will have to choose between suicide and adoration." These words may have seemed unduly apocalyptic when they were first written in the 1960s. Now, to anyone who is spiritually awake to what is happening, they are nothing less than the clearest imaginable formulation of the choice that faces humanity. We can choose the suicide of an addiction to materialism and a materialistic vision of humanity or we can choose adoration of the Divine and the Divine in the creation and in the human. Such an adoration could engender a massive revolution of the heart and so a wholly new way of acting in every arena.

Are we as a race going to go on choosing division and separation, the passion to possess and dominate, the constant reaching after violence to solve our problems? Or are we going to listen to the drumbeats of apocalypse and undergo a vast inner transformation that would at last give us access to the Divine within us, as well as its force, stamina, and brilliantly refined knowledge of unity of all beings and things? This is what Kabir wrote of. He called it the "formless God that takes a thousand forms in the eyes of his creatures."

The Language of Love

It must be clear now to anyone who wants to see that the problems the world faces—not only of terrorism but also of environmental holocaust, population explosion, and the cruel domination of a world economic system that keeps a few countries living in decadent comfort while the rest of the world starves—cannot be dealt with using the consciousness at which humanity now finds itself. We must transform or commit suicide. We are going to have to take, in massive numbers and with great fervor, a leap into our inner divinity and into the "limitless life in this world" it alone can give us. If we don't do this, not only will we die out as a species, but we're apt to take the whole of nature with us in a bloodbath of unimaginable devastation and ferocity.

As we struggle—those of us who are awake and many more who will be awakened by the horror of what is to come—the testimony of the greatest mystics to our essential divine identity and to the powers, new life, energy, and vision that spring from it will be our central inspiration. These men and women from history will be our oxygen, the force and truth that keep us hoping and fighting and working and enduring through everything. In the all-testing times ahead, only a deep, mystical inner faith and knowledge will have the power to lift people to a plane of truth that no horror or cruelty can disturb.

As we take this new and unprecedented journey into our divine truth, the hundred or so poems of Kabir that are offered here in the sublime translations of Rabindranath Tagore will be of profound help to us. With Rumi, Jesus, Ramakrishna, and Aurobindo, Kabir is one of a handful of spiritual geniuses whose realization transcends all barriers of dogma, religion, country, and civilization. Kabir's God is at once immanent and transcendent and beyond either. He is both the uncreated Eternal Light and the cosmos constantly birthed and rebirthed from it. He is the eternal and glorious One and the friend directly knowable to all those who want to offer their hearts in love to Him, whatever their castes or faith. Only such a clear knowledge is of any use in the mystical journey for, as he wrote in one of his greatest poems:

Introduction to *Songs of Kabir*

It is a hard fight and a weary one, this fight of the truth-seeker:
*   for the*
vow of the truth-seeker is more hard than that of the warrior,
or of the widowed wife who would follow her husband.
For the warrior fights for a few hours, and the widow's struggle
*   with death is soon ended:*
But the truth seeker's battle goes on day and night, as long as life
lasts it never ceases.

Of Kabir the man, very little is known definitively. He was born in or around 1398, the son of a Muslim weaver, Niru, and his wife, Nima, who lived on the outskirts of India's holiest city, Benares. Kabir's name is a Muslim one, a Koranic title of Allah meaning "great," but in the poems of his that have best claim to authenticity, there is little to suggest that he was a Muslim in any conventional sense. He criticized Islam rather than embracing it. He had a sometimes ferocious contempt for the quibbles and nuances of Islamic theology. Nor can Kabir be claimed for Hinduism—he could be just as severe in his mockery of Hindu beliefs about the status of Brahmins, the unalterable authority of the Vedas, the necessity of pilgrimages, and the worship of idols. There are many legends of his life that suggest that, by his unconventional behavior, he outraged both the ruling Islamic authorities and the Brahmins. Like Jesus, he seemed to have the rebel of love's supreme gift of annoying everyone.

Many modern scholars believe that Kabir's radical genius was so threatening to his Hindu contemporaries that they concocted a false legend of him being the "disciple" of the great contemporary Hindu reformer, Ramananda. In the famous old story, Kabir as a boy "knew" that Ramananda was destined to be his master, although he was a Muslim and Ramananda a Brahmin. One day when Ramananda was coming down to bathe in the Ganges, Kabir contrived to hide himself on one of the steps along his path. Unwittingly, Ramananda placed his foot on the boy and cried out "Ram! Ram!" This was the name of the divine incarnation he worshipped. Kabir then sprang up and claimed that this constituted an initiation on Ramananda's part. Ramananda was so moved by his sincerity that he accepted him and taught him the truth of his eternal identity with God.

The only problem with this story is that it probably didn't happen at all and was fabricated as part of a Hindu plot to contain Kabir's wild and direct genius within the conventional patterns of Hindu "master-disciple" relationship. In truth, however, Kabir's realization was self-born and unmediated. The "guru" he mentions in his poetry is not the external master, but the inner divine voice and guidance. Kabir's whole path is a revolutionary one of direct access to God in the core of ordinary life—one that implicitly critiques and implodes two millennia of conventional Hindu practice.

There is one legend, though, that I would like to believe, because it acidly presents Kabir's transcendence of all religion and dogma. In his last years, Kabir retired from Benares to live in the small town of Magahar, some miles to the north, near Gorakhpur. He may have moved there either because he had offended the Islamic authorities of Benares or because he wanted to affront pious Hindu sensibilities that considered Magahar as unholy as Benares was holy (Kabir in many of his poems mocks superstitious "man-made" distinctions). Whatever the reason for his move, he died in Magahar, probably in the 1470s. His death, it is said, was witnessed by great crowds of people, among whom could be found equal numbers of Hindus and Muslims. When he at last passed away, these two camps set upon each other, each battling to lay claim to his body. Their struggle was as useless as it was absurd. After fighting one another to get to the corpse, they found instead two piles of flowers. A voice from heaven—Kabir himself?—told the Muslims to bury one pile according to their religious customs and the Hindus to cremate the other pile according to theirs. It is easy to imagine the irony in that "heavenly voice," since both the Muslims and Hindus so avid to claim him as one of their own on his deathbed had so harried and misunderstood him in life.

The universality, directness, and radicalism of his message that caused Kabir so much pain and trouble during his lifetime is precisely what makes him indispensable to us now. In a world ravaged by the strife between fundamentalist versions of the Divine, it has never been more important for human beings to dare to listen to the simplicity of Kabir, a simplicity that cuts finally through all barriers and distinctions.

> *O Servant, where dost thou seek Me?*
> *Lo! I am beside thee.*
> *I am neither in temple nor in mosque: I am neither in Kaaba nor*
> *in Kailash:*
> *Neither am I in rites and ceremonies, nor in Yoga and renunciation*
> *If thou art a true seeker, thou shalt at once see Me:*
> *thou shalt meet Me in a moment of time.*
> *Kabir says, "O Sadhu! God is the breath of all breath." (45)*
>
> *O friend! hope for Him whilst you live, know whilst you live,*
> *understand*
> *whilst you live: for in life deliverance abides.*
> *If your bonds be not broken whilst living, what hope of deliverance*
> *in death? (46)*
>
> *I laugh when I hear that the fish in the water are thirsty:*
> *You do not see that that the Real is in your home,*
> *and you wander from forest to forest listlessly! (91)*

Kabir's challenge to all of us—to go beyond all barriers of religion or belief or dogma and plunge here and now in the core of our lives into a passionate relationship with the Beloved, within and without, through adoration and service to others—mirrors exactly that of Jesus in logion 3 of the Gospel of Thomas:

> If those who lead you say to you "see the kingdom in the sky" then the birds of the sky will precede you. If they say to you "it is in the sea" then the fish of the sea will precede you: Rather the Kingdom is inside you and outside you. When you come to know yourselves, then you will become known and you will realize that

it is you who are the sons and daughters of the living Father. But if you will not know yourselves, you dwell in poverty, and it is you who are that poverty.

Kabir's and Jesus's great promises to those who are brave enough to see through the versions of God that place the Divine in a transcendent beyond is that coming to "know yourself" results in a wholly different life here on earth, one infused at every level with divine passion, knowledge, and love.

Kabir came to live this life not as a monk in a monastery or a hermitage, but as a husband, father, and weaver in a tiny shop in an alleyway in Benares. This fact is crucial for all of us who need to know how to live in the Divine in the core of a burning world. As he wrote, "Kabir says: the home is the abiding place; in the home is reality; the home helps to attain Him Who is real. So stay where you are, and all things will come to you in time. (88)"

Again and again, with ruthless wit and tremendous passion, Kabir tells us that it is not necessary to run from the world or go on ceaseless pilgrimages or, in fact, indulge in any of the sometimes ascetic and life-denying disciplines that the religions and mystical transmissions systems have decreed as essential to the true and holy life. What is essential is to wake up to the living presence of God in and as life itself and as the love and power constantly reinventing all creation, and to live in that sacred knowledge and bliss, radiating the power of that truth through all one's actions and choices. All things are holy when seen with the eyes of awakened love. Nothing less than this all-embracing vision of God and divine humanity will bring about the great transformation that is humanity's last and greatest hope.

If we are going to do everything in our power to preserve this planet, it will not be, I believe, in the name of some heavenly ideal nor in the name, certainly, of any one religion or even of a noble, political vision of democracy. Rather, it will be because more and more of us have dared to take the mystic journey into the heart of life and to find what Jesus and Rumi and Kabir and Ramakrishna and Aurobindo and countless others have found there—the living, divine fire creating and illuminating and inspiring all things, "the love that makes me to live a limitless life in this world." And with the living and growing experience of that fire and love to fuel all of our struggles and efforts, to give us passion and wisdom, true holy detachment and compassion, there is nothing, even at this late hour, that will be impossible for us.

In time, a tremendous paradox may well be revealed to us—that what we are experiencing now as a time of death is secretly a time of birth and that the crises that now seem insuperable will, in the end, occasion in us a transformation that will at last bring us into the glory of that simple union with the Divine. No other poet has sung of this with so precise a radiance as Kabir:

> O Sadhu! The simple union is the best.
> Since the day when I met with my Lord, there has
>   been no end the sport of our love.
> I shut not my eyes, I close not my ears, I do not mortify my body;
> I see with eyes open and smile, and behold His beauty everywhere:
> I utter His Name and whatever I see, it reminds me of Him;
>   whatever I do, it becomes His worship.

Introduction to *The Teachings of Rumi*

Jalal-ud-din Rumi, the greatest mystic of Islam, and many people believe, of the world, was born in Balkh, Afghanistan, on September 30, 1207, and died in Konya, Southern Turkey, on December 17, 1273. He left behind as the record of his extraordinarily intense life, lived on the wildest and grandest heights of the spirit, the *Mathnawi*, a mystical epic; 3,500 odes; 2,000 quatrains; a book of table talk; and a large volume of letters. The Mevlevi Order that he founded and that was continued by his son, Sultan Valad, spread his vision all over Asia and Africa and now has centers all over the world.

The Language of Love

In the last twenty years, through the pioneering translations of Coleman Barks, Robert Bly, Kabir Helminski, and Jonathan Star, among others, Rumi has become, as Bill Moyers pointed out in his recent television special on him, "the most popular poet in America," read and loved by seekers of all persuasions and creeds. For hundreds of thousands of people, Rumi's work, in its passion, honesty, and gorgeous imagery, has become a way of connecting directly with the Divine beyond the constrictions of religion or dogma. Rumi now commands in the West what he has long commanded in the East—an unassailable position as the most poignant and vibrant of all celebrators of the Path of Love and as a supreme witness, in a way that transcends all national, cultural, and religious boundaries, to the mysteries of divine identity and presence.

Rumi combined the intellect of a Plato, the vision and enlightened soul-force of a Buddha or a Christ, and the extravagant literary gifts of a Shakespeare. This unique fusion of the highest philosophical lucidity with the greatest possible spiritual awareness and the most complete artistic gifts gave Rumi unique power as what might be called a "sacred initiator" or "initiator into the sacred." Born out of the fire of a vast awakening, Rumi's work has an uncanny direct force of illumination; anyone approaching it with an open heart and mind, at whatever stage of his or her evolution, will derive from it inspiration, excitement, and help of the highest kind. Everything Rumi wrote or transmitted has the unmistakable authority of total inner experience, the authority of a human being who has risked and given everything to the search for divine truth.

As fears of an environmental apocalypse grow, and the terrible dangers that afflict humanity on every level become more and more inescapably clear, Rumi's work will become increasingly important for its testimony to the divine origin and purpose of human life, its overwhelmingly beautiful celebration of the truths and mysteries of divine glory, and its wise embrace of all paths and approaches to the experience of God. Increasingly it will become clear that Rumi is not only humanity's supreme mystical poet but also one of its clearest guides to the mystical renaissance that is trying to be born in the rubble of our suicidal civilization. What might be called the "return of Rumi" to the consciousness of humanity occurs at a time when the truths of Rumi's celebration of the Beloved are needed not only as revelations of the real purpose of human life but as essential inspirations and empowerments in the struggle to save the human race and preserve the planet. Unless the vision of Rumi and other great mystics from the major traditions possesses the spirit and hones the motivation of millions of human beings and initiates them into the sacredness of human life and the holiness of nature, humanity will destroy the world in a bitter frenzy of ignorance, pride, and greed.

If Rumi is to be given, as I believe, a central role in the awakening of humanity to its own divine truth and possibility, then it has never been more important to see his work and the teaching it enshrines in as lucid and fearless a way as possible. The New Age, in its narcissism, its lazy greed of appropriation, its ability to make over all sublime and demanding truth in its own hazy image, and its lack of any real or ennobling concern for political, social, and environmental issues, has created a limited vision of Rumi to serve its own ends; it has created, in fact, what I call "Rosebud Rumi," a Californian hippie-like figure of vague, ecstatic sweetness and diffused, "warmhearted" brotherhood, a kind of medieval Jerry Garcia of the sacred heart.

This limp and vulgar vision entirely omits an essential side of Rumi's spiritual genius—its rigorous, even ferocious, austerity. Rumi is indeed an ecstatic, the greatest of all celebrators of that ecstasy that streams from the presence of Love. He is also—as I hope this volume will make clear—the canniest, shrewdest, most unsentimental, and sober of teachers, very un–New Age in his refusal to deny the power of evil, his candor about the limits of all worldly and earthly enlightenment, his Jesus-like suspicion of all forms of wealth and power, and his embrace of the sometimes terrible and prolonged suffering that authentic transformation must and does demand. This rigorous, fierce, authoritative Rumi, the veteran of the wars of Love, is what our spiritual renaissance deeply needs to listen to and learn from, if the transformation that is trying to happen in our time is not to be diffused in a cloud of laziness, fantasy, denial, and occult charlatanry.

Rumi can be a complete guide for seekers now precisely because he combined the most extreme imaginable vision and experience of divine beauty and mystery with a sober and humble teaching of how to sustain, continually deepen, and integrate them with daily life. Unlike many of our contemporary teachers, drunk on partial awakening, Rumi—whose knowledge of the Path of Love was perhaps the most thorough that any human has ever had—never claimed total enlightenment; in fact, one of his most original contributions to the history of mystical thought is his intuition that evolution is an infinite process that never ends on any of the planes of any world, and that the journey into embodying and living Love is as infinite and boundless as Love itself. Unlike many contemporary seekers, Rumi's passion was not for sensational experiences, occult powers, or radically enhanced "self-esteem"; he was dragged deep enough into Love to know that divine life could only be found on the other side of an annihilation of self that demanded and cost everything and that authentic spiritual "lordship" was not the acquisition of any kind of power but a humble embrace of "servanthood"—of the life of the servant-slave of Love and so of every human and sentient being in the name, and for the glory of, God. Such a vision is simultaneously far more humble and more exalted than the pseudo-mysticisms being peddled everywhere in the New Age, and sometimes in Rumi's name. The laws of such a final vision of human truth and divine possibility are not tailored as are so many of the contemporary mystical "systems," either to flatter human weakness or to inflate human claims to divinity; complete experience gave Rumi an unfailing sense of balance and a fundamental and astonished humility before the always changing and always deepening experience of the Divine.

This balance and humility inform Rumi's teaching at every level and are the source of its extreme clarity about the dangers, temptations, fantasies, and various forms of inflation, hysteria, and pride that threaten the authentic seeker. They are also the source of perhaps its most challenging, even frightening aspect—that of Rumi's fearless and scathingly truthful embrace of the ordeals that true transformation demand. Rumi's own awakening was at the price of a vast suffering, or rather, a series of sufferings, that led to his death and rebirth in the dimension of resurrection. Rumi knew from bitter and glorious experience that the life of the real lover of God is often one of frightful ordeal and exposure to bewilderment and grief of every kind. Yet, because Rumi both lived and survived such appalling experience, he is able to speak with ennobling courage and hope about the gnosis that is born from it and about the glory of sustained divine human being that annihilation opens onto, the inner "rose garden" that only a pure-souled dying-into-Love can uncover in all its amazing rapture and loveliness.

All authentic seekers will, if they are sincere, come by divine grace to the test of the cross, of the Great Death in which the false self and all its fantasies and games are systematically destroyed to reveal the presence of the Divine and deathless self within. In this time of ordeal, when everything depends on a capacity for sustained adoration, blind and half-mad faith, and the ability to expose the heart again and again to radiant and sometimes murderous danger, Rumi's work will provide the most luminous guidance and a clear and holy encouragement to ever-deeper surrender. Such encouragement is especially important in a time like ours, when the entire planet and nature itself are passing through an experience of prolonged breakdown, even crucifixion. More than ever we need guides to ordeal and its hidden mystical meanings, and Rumi, of all mystics and teachers, is the most experienced in what might be called the "alchemy of agony." The splendor of his fearlessness, humility, and endless courage can help us all develop those powers of insight and trust that could enable us to transmute catastrophe into an opening for massive spiritual growth.

May the testimony of Rumi to the glory and power of Love humble, illumine, and embolden us all! May all of us know on earth and in a body the saving mysteries of our divine identity and enact them in the Real in works of justice and compassion to help transform and preserve our planet!

Nevada, August 15, 1998

Excerpt from *Sixty Seconds,* edited by Phil Bolsta

In 1997 my mother sent me a fax from Coimbatore in southern India, where I was born, saying that my father was dying and that I should get there as quickly as possible. I was living in San Francisco at the time. I managed to get a visa within two days and got to his bedside in the next week.

What followed was the most beautiful week of my life, because my father and I were able to communicate at a level and depth and true spiritual height that we had never managed before. All our political and personal differences were drowned in great sweetness and tender communication. And I realized how finely and absolutely he had always loved me and how much he had always held me in his heart. This was in itself a huge healing. But another healing on an even larger scale was going to take place.

During our time together, my father and I did not talk about anything that had ever happened between us. What we talked about was Jesus. My father spoke out of the depth of his passionate and simple faith in Jesus. Now that he was facing death, he was speaking inwardly to Jesus in Gethsemane—because, as he said, Jesus knows everything about terrors of the heart, and he accompanies us in whatever anguish and loneliness we go into.

"So now I am facing death as he faced it in the garden of Gethsemane," my father said. "I'm speaking to him as if he were in the garden, so that he can help me."

I was deeply moved by my father's faith and by the simplicity and purity and nobility of it. And I understood that my father's great qualities as a human being—courtesy, humility, generosity, tolerance—had been rooted in a lifelong spiritual friendship with the Christ. Many times as we spoke, I felt in the room the presence of an extraordinary power that enfolded us in wings of light. And he felt it too.

On his deathbed, I was able to teach my father a practice that I had learned from the Tibetan masters on how to visualize the divine Beloved in whatever form you love Him or Her so that you could enter into total relationship with the Divine. One of the greatest joys of my life is that, before he died, he said to my mother that he had practiced this visualization and that he had indeed seen the living Christ.

I had arrived in Coimbatore on a Tuesday. That Sunday, I went to services at a Catholic church called the Church of Christ the King. A small, plump Indian priest gave an utterly simple and heartbreaking sermon about how Christ is the mystical king of reality—not only because of the miracles that Jesus did or the enormous influence that he has had, but because of Jesus's abandoned service to all beings out of complete compassion and complete and final love.

These words absolutely pierced my soul. I had been utterly flayed by my closeness to my father's dying and had been completely opened by the bliss and heartbreak that passed between us. I heard the priest's words as if they were spoken to me directly to wake me up to the essence of the spiritual path—which is, I believe, service in all its forms in the spirit of absolute, tender compassion to all beings.

When the priest finished talking and sat down, I looked up at the statue of the resurrected Christ at the end of the church. To my absolute awe and astonishment, it became alive and began to emit radiant golden light. I knew beyond a shadow of any doubt that the living resurrected Christ was appearing to me and radiating toward me, burning an infinite passion. My whole being trembled and blazed in the exquisite, terrible, fierce, glorious force of intense, ecstatic passion flowing from him to me. As this force entered me, it seemed to hack my chest open and split open my heart so that from the depths of my heart a smaller, answering force started to radiate back to the great force emanating from the Christ.

And in those sacred moments, I understood the truth of what the great mystics of divine love of all traditions have been trying to teach us—that lover, beloved, and love are one, and that this oneness in the burning, tender communion of divine love is the absolute and final reality of the universe.

I was standing next to my brother, who is a banker, so I had to control myself. But tears of rapture and gratitude and infinite joy poured from my eyes. And I felt that one period of my life had ended and a whole new period was beginning. I had been in a savage and frightening dark night of the soul for many years, undergoing a stripping and searing and burning of all of my ideas and agendas. This supreme experience signaled to me the dawn of my own inmost, divine identity. I knew from a study of Christian mystical literature that experiences of the risen Christ such as this very often signaled the end of the dark night and the beginning of consciousness of divine identity.

The experience did not end with my vision, however. As I stumbled out of church into the blazing noon of an Indian morning, I saw a young man, without arms or legs, in a filthy shirt, squatting miserably and desolately in a puddle. He was one of the most beautiful human beings I had ever seen, with a face absolutely purified by extreme pain and extreme suffering. As I helped him out of the puddle, I realized that just as I had seen the living Christ in the statue now I was seeing him in this desperate being before me. And as I gazed into the eyes of the broken Christ, I heard a thunderous voice within me say:

> You have been playing with light for years now and have been using the mystical experiences that the Divine has given you for your own satisfaction, your own career, and your own self-aggrandizement. You must stop this, because the only purpose of mystical awakening is to make you a servant of divine love in the

world and help you to dedicate all of your thoughts, emotions, actions, and resources to the dissolution of those circumstances that create the torment, misery, loneliness, dejection, and desolation that you see before you. In this tormented world, threatened by extinction, it is time you realize, Andrew, that you must turn from every form of narcissism and self-absorption. It is time for you to dedicate your entire work to bringing about the revolution of Christ-consciousness in the world, so that human beings can transform themselves and the conditions they create, and so that nature can be preserved, because the world is in extreme and potentially terminal danger.

These words—and, of course, I am paraphrasing them and putting them into language, because they came to me in great blocks of fierce emotion—have been the guiding force behind all the work that I have done in these last years. My experience in the church has never died in me, and I don't believe it will ever die in me. In every moment of every day, I feel the presence of that flame of divine passion in the core of my heart. And I know that the one hope for humanity is to take up the challenge of the living Christ—to put divine love and divine compassion into radical, transformative action on every level and in every arena of the world so as to transform the world before the destructive power of humanity utterly and completely devastates it.

This Sacred Activism, which is how I express my vision of the Christ, is for me a fusion of the deepest level of mystical practice of stamina, strength, passion, peace, and clarity with focused, wise, nonviolent, radical action in the real world. I know that this work of Sacred Activism is the work of the Christ-consciousness and that this work is crucial for the preservation of the planet. I believe that everyone who is mystically awake and who is awake to the terrible destruction that is now happening in the world will be summoned by the Divine to this fusion of inner practice with radical action that I was summoned to on that November day in Coimbatore.

This revelation came to me in terms of the Christ because of my Christian background, but I know it is coming to millions of people all over the world in terms of their own religious traditions or symbols. And when it comes, it comes as it did to me, in a blaze of infinite joy and peace and rapture—and in a blaze of agonized compassion. This fusion of rapture and agonized compassion is the hallmark of what is known in the mystical tradition as the sacred heart, the heart-center, the heart-truth.

This experience has given me a tremendous faith in the next stage of human evolution. It was the beginning of a birth—a birth of the presence of the Divine inside my heart and mind and body. I know that this birth is not mine alone but is happening in the middle of the chaos and the madness of our time—and partly through that chaos—all over the planet. And it is this birth—this birth of a new, divine human that has a total focus on justice and on transformative sacred action—that offers the great hope for the future.

It is this birth, in fact, that is the secret meaning of the apocalyptic situation we are now going through. It signals that what we are dealing with is potentially not the end of everything but the beginning of a new divine humanity. And this apocalyptic situation is, in fact, the birth canal—the terrible, amazing birth canal—of a new divine human being capable of cocreating, in and under the Divine, a holy new world.

Preface to *Stèles,* by Victor Segalen, translated by Andrew Harvey and Iain Watson

Segalen is one of the most astute, astringent, and complex visionaries of modern literature, and one of the least well known. Born on January 14, 1878, in Brittany, he died in 1919, also in Brittany, aged only forty-one years, but exhausted from a life that had taken him to Tahiti, Japan, and China, and seen him in a bewildering variety of different roles—naval doctor, ethnographer, archaeologist, novelist, essayist, poet. It is only within the last twenty years that his oeuvre has begun to receive the attention it deserves: it is of a disconcerting range and includes novellas; a libretto, *Orphée-Roi,* for Debussy; a play on Buddha's life; the finest book on Polynesia, *Les Immémoriaux;* fragments of a study of Chinese statuary; as well as two indisputably major collections of poems, *Stèles* and *Thibet.*

In an early essay on Rimbaud, Segalen wrote: "Behind the actorish being, an essential 'I' lies hidden in its cave and its lair remains inaccessible." The whole of Segalen's life and work was a remorseless, brave, paradoxical search for this essential "inaccessible I," for that secret of identity, which he believed lay behind the shifting masks and "moving chaos" of the world. This search came to its crisis of revelation in China, where Segalen went in 1909, and where he wrote the works that have guaranteed his name—*René Leys, Le Fils du Ciel, Peintures, Equipée,* and *Stèles.*

Segalen's passion for China was not an exotic indulgence and had nothing dandyish about it. He learned classical Chinese and spoke it fluently; travelled the length and breadth of the crumbling Manchu empire, often in grueling circumstance; despised the boudoir exoticism of Loti and others; meditated with intricate thoroughness on all aspects of Chinese culture, from its literature to its sculpture and ancient architecture. Segalen recognized in China not only a field of study and source of aesthetic rapture but an image, constantly shifting, both radiant and disturbing, of his inner landscape. He came to China, he wrote to Debussy, "not for ideas, but to find a VISION." He found his vision. For the only time in his life, his inner search for the "essential I" and the world in which he found himself coincided; from this uncanny coincidence *Stèles* was born.

The China of *Stèles* is a metaphysical invented landscape, the "place and the formula," as Pierre Jean Jove put it, where an alchemical transformation of Segalen's self-understanding could take place. Segalen uses the imagery and philosophy of Chinese culture in an entirely and passionately idiosyncratic way—both to celebrate and preserve an ancient hieratic world in its essence at a moment when it was disappearing forever, and to deride the spiritual blankness, hypocrisy, and sterile egalitarianism of the West that he fled all his life. *Stèles* then is a "Western" book written with "Eastern" imagery about both the "East" and the "West" for a time when "East" and "West" were ceasing to have separate meaning. From this ironic and poignant inner stance derives the stark, many-sided power of these poems and their intellectual passion.

It is part of Segalen's continuing mystery—and the mystery of *Stèles*—that the secret of the "essential I" Segalen searched for so unremittingly is hinted at in *Stèles* but never named. Segalen called himself a "proud mystic" and by that he meant he belonged to neither sect nor church, followed no discipline, and accepted no dogma. All his life, he loathed the life-denying aspects of Catholicism and had hard things to say about Buddhism and its denigration of the flesh. Segalen could be said to be a kind of Nietzchean-Taoist: a celebrator—as many poems in *Stèles* testify—of heroic values, of nature, of eros, of noble friendship and courage; and also profoundly—if reticently—reverent before the mystery of what he described as the "world behind," whose empty immobile splendor and power he constantly alludes to. *Stèles* is born out of the struggle between these two incompatible versions, both held with real rigor, reconciled only in what Segalen called, in his essay on Rimbaud, "divinatory moments" that open unforgettably onto another reality but which do not, for him, last. Segalen's greatest quality as a visionary is to remain faithful to this tension, to the claims of both sides of his personality, refusing ever to "surrender" to an accepted mystic discipline or to overpraise the rapture of flux that he knew fragile and frequently tragic. It is this fidelity to almost intolerable contradiction that makes Segalen modern and gives his poetry its paradoxical range—of harshness and asceticism, erotic wildness and stoic withdrawal—and its protean power constantly, insolently, to evade any categorizing restraints placed on it.

Any translation of *Stèles* worth the name has to attempt to honor and match the laconic, often gnarled, succinctness of the original, and

Preface to *Stèles*

to mirror Segalen's dense hieratic diction and idiosyncratic syntax. These are not poems whose difficulties should be domesticated.

Hymn to the Resting Dragon

The Dragon couchant: sky void, earth heavy, clouds
incoherent; sun and moon throttle their light;
men bear the seal of a winter which no one
can explain.

The Dragon stirs: at once the fog lifts and the day
ascends. A nourishing dew assuages hunger.
Ecstasy dances as if at the edge of an unhoped-for
dawn.

The Dragon rattles his pinions and takes flight:
for him the scarlet horizon, his banner; the
wind for an advance guard, and the lush rain
for escort. Laugh with hope under the crackling
of his cutting whip: lightning.

Hey Dragon! Coiled-up sluggard! Lazy hero
asleep in each of us, unrecognized, sluggish
and unknown.

Here are figs, mulled wine, blood: eat, drink
and inhale: our rustling sleeves call you with
great beatings of wings.

Rise up, awake, it is time. Leap out of us with
one bound; and to affirm your brilliance.

Coil in us your serpent's tail, make us sick with a
wink of your beady eye, but blaze, blaze out of us.

Advice to the Worthy Traveler

Town at the end of the road and road protracting
the town: do not choose then one or the other
but one and the other in strict turn.

Mountain enveloping your view breaks down and
constrains that which the rotund plain frees.
Love to jump over rocks and steps; but fondle
the flag-stones where the footsteps smoothly level.

Rest yourself from the sound in silence, and, from
silence, deign to come back to sound. Alone if
you can, if you know how to be alone, occasionally
pour yourself even into the mob.

Take good care not to choose an asylum. Do not
believe in the merit of a lasting merit: rupture
it with some violent spice which burns and erodes
and gives a sting even to the insipid.

So, without a halt or a false step, without bridle
or stable, without merit or suffering, you shall
reach, friend, not the swamp of immortal bliss.
But the eddies rich with drunkenness of the mighty
river Diversity.

Introduction to *Peintures,* by Victor Segalen, translated by Andrew Harvey and Iain Watson

That Segalen is amongst the most sophisticated, astute, and disturb-ing of modern visionaries is one of the best kept secrets of twentieth-century literature. Just before he died, Borges remarked to a French poet friend of ours: "The French talk about Valery and even the preposterous Peguy with adoration—don't they know that in Vic-tor Segalen they have one of the most intelligent writers of our age, perhaps the only one to have made a fresh synthesis of Western and Eastern aesthetics and philosophy?" Our French friend had not heard of Segalen and said so. Borges hid his face in his hands and groaned. "My dear L," he murmured, "do not live another month before you have read the entire oeuvre." Then he started to laugh: "You can read Segalen in less than a month, but it might take you the rest of your life to begin to understand him."

Victor Segalen was born in Brest in 1878 and died in 1919, in a wood near Heulgoat in Brittany, of a mysterious wasting illness, with *Hamlet* open by his side. In the course of his relatively short life, he was a doctor, traveler, librettist, philosopher, poet, novelist, and archaeologist. He left behind him a work of astonishing diversity; his books include *Les Immémoriaux* (which remains the subtlest book ever written by a westerner about Polynesia), written at the age of twenty-four after a visit to the Marquesas; *Siddharta,* a libretto on the life of the Buddha which he wrote for Debussy; brilliant short studies on Rimbaud and Gauguin; and a cluster of masterpieces inspired by his long stay in China from 1906 to 1916: *Stèles, Equipée, René Leys, Le Fils du Ciel,* and *Peintures.* The scorched and fading photos that survive of Segalen show a haughty, lean, handsome face with the eyes of a mystic Apache, of a man of intricate disdains, drastic ironies, and just as drastic a capacity for reverence. To take Borges's suggestion and read Segalen's entire oeuvre is to undertake a metaphysical journey of great intensity and complexity. Segalen writes towards the end of *Peintures:* "Only the painter and those who know how to see have access to magical space." This "access to magical space" was Segalen's reward for his passion and long solitude, and his fierce gift to those willing to travel with him.

The blessing of Segalen's life, and the inspiration of his best and most exacting work, was his discovery of China, of a world as elaborate, hieratic, terrifying, and mysterious as his own deepest imagination. Late Manchu China, in its chaos and sumptuousness, its mystical cult of the "hidden" emperor, in the profusion and radiance of its still-existent schools of Buddhism and Taoism, was for Segalen the "place and the formula," the long-desired encounter with a landscape and history and spiritual tradition that fulfilled his wildest and most exalted fantasies. From the beginning of his stay in China, Segalen understood that the secret meaning of his life and the secret of China were inextricably intertwined. As he wrote to a friend: "In the end it was not a creation of China itself that I came to look for but a vision of China ... and I hold on to that with my teeth." China awoke Segalen's own visionary imagination because it constantly confronted him with the impenetrable both in the world and in himself: out of the excited but intellectually fastidious and precise meeting between his Western intellect, honed on Nietzsche, and the Buddhist and Taoist philosophies of China came the great work of his late period, work that is neither "Western" nor "Eastern," but a strange and haunting hybrid of both, a work in which the assumptions of Eastern and Western aesthetics and philosophy are flung against each other with expert savagery and recombined in startling ways. As Segalen wrote in fragments of an essay, "Exoticism" (an essay that was to sum up his vision of life, but which was never completed): "Exoticism is not that kaleidoscopic state of the tourist and of the mediocre spectator ... but the live and curious reaction to the *shock of a strong* individual against an objectivity it perceives and whose distance it savors." He adds later: "Exoticism ... is not an adaptation ... not the comprehension of a beyond-itself that one could then embrace into oneself ... *but the sharp and direct perception of something eternally incomprehensible*" [our italics]. To keep "sharp" and "direct" perception that is trained—relentlessly—on the incomprehensible demands the rarest and finest kind of intellect—one that is at once capable of protean reverence (each of Segalen's "Chinese" works is a different experiment in homage) and of an unwavering fidelity to solitude and detachment. Segalen said of himself, conscious, of course, of all the levels of paradox that he was playing with, that he was a "proud mystic," ferociously unattached to any kind of religious dogma, but "in awe of the indefinable" of that "China-behind and beyond-the-world" he refers to in one of his last letters. To keep alive this proud mystical self, to allow himself to be crucified on its continuing and continually fertile contradictions without allowing himself any of the ways out of its exposure that he might have taken—into less faith, less cynicism, or silence—was Segalen's courage as a human being; from that courage were born the powers of analytic ecstasy and sardonic exultation that inform and illumine his work.

Peintures, finished in 1916 after six years' labor, is in some ways the strangest of the "Chinese" works, and the one most completely and daringly informed by Chinese metaphysics, both in its subject matter and its aesthetic structure. Although Segalen had withering things to say about Buddhism's life-weariness and contempt for the body, and never in any "official" way became a Taoist, he had enormous (and very well-informed) curiosity about the higher metaphysics of both religions and felt temperamentally akin to Lao Tzu. The lightness of tone of *Peintures,* and its wild playfulness of structure, derive their depth and their intensity from Segalen's immersion in the Taoist and Buddhist vision of the universe. In Buddhism, as the *Prajnaparamita Sutra* puts it, "emptiness is form; form emptiness"; what the senses perceive—wrongly—as solid is, in fact, incessantly projected from a void, whose essential luminous emptiness is the true nature of all phenomena. In Taoism this universe—what Lao Tzu calls the "ten thousand things"—has its source in the Tao, the governing power of the cosmos, and is in continual movement within and against the Tao's rapt, immobile, but infinitely creative calm. Reality is a phantasmagoria, a rush of electric, transforming, transient energies that spring out of and flow back into a blissful vacancy. Both Buddhism and Taoism, then, view reality not as, in the Western sense, an architectural structure, but as a collection of phenomena perpetually oscillating between appearance and disappearance. For both philosophies, moreover, the "spectator" of the "play" is as unreal, finally, as the "play" itself. As Santideva says in the *Bodhicharyavatara:* "If that which is seen is as unreal as illusion, then so is the one who sees the mind." An unreal person is watching an unreal "parade" (to use Segalen's own description of *Peintures*) in which every possible combination of possibilities can—and will—occur, but in which nothing, in the final analysis, exists. Liberation for Taoist and Buddhist consists in the unwavering awareness of this essential unreality, and in the magical power, humor, and love that is released from this awareness and devastation of all possible clinging to appearances or to any of the vanities of a fictitious self.

It is this vision—of the fantastical flux of the cosmos and of the essential nonexistence of both "parade" and spectator—that *Peintures* is dedicated to "embodying" (the word in such a context has a more than ironic ring). Segalen's hills in *Peintures* are mobile, his fans are agitated by their own energy, the lacquers swim suddenly under the glare of hidden lights, the vicious empresses and their consorts reveal themselves as pioneers of bizarre virtue. The reader himself is exhorted, bullied, teased in frequently contradictory ways that compel him to give up the safety of considered judgment and force him into plunging—with the writer-creator's own abandon—into the hilarious and terrible dance of the world. *Peintures* has the same lack of structure, the same endless ambiguity, the same incessantly dissolving nature as reality itself—viewed through illumined Buddhist or Taoist eyes. In Segalen's work, as in Lao Tzu's or Santideva's, no irony is without its secret transcendent opposite; no transcendence without its shadow of derision or derangement; no vice without its inherent possibility of virtue; no object exists that cannot, under certain special conditions, melt into another, equally deceptive shape; no rhetoric of presentation can be paraded that does not disguise as much as it discloses, that does not disguise, in fact, by pretending to disclose. All is flux and fantasy, all is theatrical in the highest, wildest, saddest, and most liberating sense of the word. If there is any truth, it is in the cold, hard, blue autumn sky, perpetually unstained by such shenanigans as "human history," which saves (if it can be said to "save") by being blankly detached.

In *Peintures* all the standard securities of Western writing are dissolved, all nineteenth-century beliefs in virtue, progress, and the amiable and tractable solidity of reality are implicitly and explicitly derided, all traditional Western distinctions between "reader," "writer," "language," and "world" are collapsed vehemently into each other in an extraordinary and insolent act of metaphysical prestidigitation whose ingenuity is at once liberating and menacing, brilliant and vacant with the brilliance and vacancy of illusion itself spun endlessly, without any "interpretable" meaning, out of the void. *Peintures* is a mystic cabaret by a polymorphous, perverse, philosophic poet of genius. Nothing is safe from the irreverence of Segalen's mind—not even some of the most cherished beliefs of Chinese civilization itself—as in the parade of exuberant monsters in "Peintures Dynastiques" that savages all Confucian and conventional Buddhist notions of "virtue." But as with Lao Tzu and the highest Mahayana metaphysics, such relentless irreverence is itself a form of reverence, a merciless honoring of a truth that lies beyond dogma, beyond formulation, beyond all kinds of language, beyond society, in a limitless freedom that is the secret identity and only real glory of consciousness itself. The Buddha refused to define the truth in anything but the most negative terms, so as to preserve its perpetual virgin astonishment; behind the parade of *Peintures* there is a similar belief in a truth too high and too mysterious to be defiled by language, a truth that is barely even alluded to but that, as the work is read again and again, comes to be the one true, constant actor.

Translating such a work of resourceful mystic nihilism is an exhausting task. Style and meaning in *Peintures* are one and the same thing and Segalen's style can veer, in one paragraph, from grandiose vision to irony to frivolity and all the way round and back again through the various ornate and frivolous registers of French. To remain faithful to Segalen's "magical surface" and the philosophical intentions behind its shifting movements required endless revisions. What began as an act of love became something like a metaphysical journey into the heart of the English language—a language that had in some subtle ways to be remade to mirror Segalen's lapidary ferocities and quicksilver deracinations. We chose to preserve at all costs the strangeness of the original, and tried never to betray its electric perversities for simpler satisfactions. Nothing in our "re-creation" of *Peintures* has been smoothed out; no falsely "helpful" connections have been made; all abruptness of syntax and alarming jumps of thought and address have been preserved as far as possible. We have tried an English happily deranged at moments to mirror the derangement of the original to recreate an antic visionary prose-poem that compromises neither with "reality" nor the "reader."

Our inspiration throughout—sometimes badly needed—has been the hidden and mischievous center of *Peintures*—the figure of the Master Painter, who is always blind-drunk and who finds "the link of light uniting for ever joy and life." It is this link of light that for the Buddhist and Taoist runs under the entire play of life, that connects and binds together all Segalen's shifts and poses, and this link and its light we hope sparkles underneath and in our English version. *Peintures* is, as Segalen wrote, an "oeuvre réciproque," demanding of the reader (and translators) something of the writer's own power of abandon and "drunken clairvoyance"; over several years we tried to rise to Segalen's cruel and marvelous challenge. "One is one. Two even is one if you so desire it. Nothing of what you touch daily has solidity ... only the painter and those who know how to see have access to magical space."

Interview with Daniel Joseph Polikoff about *In the Image of Orpheus: Rilke: A Soul History*

Andrew Harvey: I consider Rilke to be the Rumi of Europe, our greatest and wisest and most poignant mystical poet and so immensely important to the great mystical renaissance that is struggling to take place in the middle of the chaos of our time. Who is Rilke for you, and why have you devoted twenty years of your life to this extraordinary book?

Daniel Joseph Polikoff: Yes. Well, I think Rilke and his work in some way answer to the deepest needs of Western culture. He's a poet of soul who engages the great Judeo-Christian tradition in a very profound way and yet transforms it in a manner that makes spiritual wisdom accessible to the modern individual. So many people have been touched by Rilke, people of all walks of life, and that is because he speaks with a unique intimacy and depth to our most troubling existential concerns as well as our deepest joys. When Rilke writes, or speaks—in poems, in letters—many people feel, somehow, directly addressed, as if he were writing or speaking to and for us.

Rilke is, too, a poet who undertook a visionary quest outside the precinct of any established spiritual teaching. Forging his own path, he explored the reach of his own individual psyche with a probity, intensity, and constancy that is very special. The fruits of that search are given to us in language of surpassing beauty; in poetry and prose of superb style and grace. Rilke is a writer who succeeded in translating the deepest and highest levels of spiritual experience into language adequate to convey those experiences, and that is a tremendous achievement. I really regard Rilke as a poet-seer, a spiritual teacher as well as a poet, and one whose teaching embraces not so much certainty about spiritual truths—because his life was assuredly not one of certainty—but ... well, his life was one of search and question, an odyssey. And that, too, comes through in his art, his literature. He is a poet that shares our deepest questions, and in so doing opens paths of exploration that invite us inward and onward.

AH: How did he come into your life, and why did he have such an enormous sacred importance to you?

DJP: Well, I was finishing up my PhD in comparative literature at Cornell University. I was not writing on Rilke. In fact, I had not spent that much time with Rilke. I had spent more time with the romantic poets and was writing my dissertation on Emerson. But as often happens in the pursuit of PhDs, I ran into hard times. I not only became blocked in my dissertation work, but I was going through a very difficult divorce. Many of the fundaments of my own life seemed to crumble at a certain point. That phase of vulnerability and darkness was a kind of "dark night of the soul" period for me.

You know, I had not been someone who had explored psychology deeply. I was always more interested in metaphysics and philosophy and literature, but I had entertained a kind of adverse relationship to many forms of psychology. Arriving at that dark place, I had to look inside in a very deep way, and was forced to confront my own personal suffering and existential questions with a kind of immediacy and urgency that I had not brought to such concerns before, and it was in that space, that psychic space, that Rilke's poetry—and not only his poetry, but his letters as well, which are such an important part of his work—seemed to offer me a path, a means of beginning to make sense of the darkness that I was experiencing. So even though I was in academia at the time, it wasn't really academic concerns that brought me to Rilke. It was his stature as a teacher who could shine a light into what was for me a very intense darkness.

AH: I'm sure he did so, too, in a way that spoke to your own individual psyche, did not put you into any cultural or dogmatic box. It gave you permission to sing the authentic song of your own soul.

DJP: Very much so. That is the key to Rilke. He has, as I mentioned, a deep relationship to Christianity and, as well, some relationship to Judaism and Islam, but he is altogether his own individual, not beholden to any preestablished code of Being and Becoming.

AH: I think that this path of forging a solitary direct relationship with the spiritual, with the mystical, with the Divine—is a path that millions are on now, because conventional religions have failed. There's a great explosion of mindless and destructive fundamentalism.

DJP: Yes, certainly that is an enormous part of Rilke's appeal. In the *Duino Elegies*, for example, there's a profound existential questioning; the poem addresses the human being, the human individual, as he or she stands alone in the face of a universe that may well appear void of spiritual meaning. In the *Elegies*, the angel— who is a kind of symbol and guarantor of the authenticity of spiritual life—is acknowledged initially, but is distant and unapproachable, and it is Rilke's genius to try to find a way to gain access to that spiritual reality by traveling a path that had never been trod before. There are, as you say, so many people today for whom the great religious traditions cannot supply such a path, such means of access, and Rilke's writing—the questions he asks, and multiple forms of his provisional poetic responses—can sometimes do so, because he speaks so immediately, so feelingly, and so perceptively to the crises, concerns, and potentials of the contemporary human soul.

AH: I think one of the greatest crises—that's one of the greatest aspects of this crisis—is the individual's longing for sacred connection, while finding it impossible to sustain that sacred connection in relationship to any of the existing religions or the patriarchal systems. What Rilke is inviting us to is an excavation of deep solitude in which the voice of the individual soul can be heard clearly.

DJP: Yes, very much so. And one point that you allude to there is the role of the feminine in Rilke's life and work. First of all, his relationships with women were central to both his life and his art. These were, of course, seldom easy or fully satisfying. His marriage to Clara Westhoff, for instance, was short lived—at least the time during which they lived together as a married couple was. Even so, Rilke had deep, lasting friendships with women throughout his life, and his work would be unthinkable without his relationships with women such as Lou Andreas-Salomé, Magda Von Hattingberg, or Baladine Klossowska—women who were, for the most part, themselves artists and intellectuals. But it's not only the relationship to women, but also Rilke's profound exploration of what you could call the feminine side of himself: his anima, his receptivity, his openness to vulnerability, his refusal to assent to any kind of conceptual superstructure or belief system or external authority, the tremendous receptivity of his soul. This is a hugely important part of his being, his character, and his art.

AH: Part of his enormous appeal to us now, I think, because the most serious seekers are really undertaking the work of the sacred marriage, the work of the marriage of the true masculine with the true feminine. And Rilke can be an extraordinary guide to this marriage, since it was this marriage that preoccupied him throughout his life.

DJP: Yes. It runs as a kind of a red thread through his work. I've been talking a little bit about Rilke's feminine side, but Lou Salomé, who was his lover and first great teacher, emphasized [his masculine side]. Despite his feminine middle name, "Maria,"—it's interesting that "Rainer Maria" can be heard, in German, to mean "the pure (or Virgin) Mary," which is a hardly irrelevant resonance—Lou stressed that Rilke's masculine side was also very strong. In that connection, the constancy with which he pursued his artistic goals, his unswerving dedication to his poetic vocation, may come to mind. In general, I do think there's a profound wedding of the masculine and feminine enacted in his life's work.

One of the matters that I explore in my book is the profound relationship between Rilke's life and work and the myth of Psyche and Eros as that story is told by the Apuleius in his book *The Golden Ass*. I use that myth as kind of a structure, a template, for understanding the evolution of Rilke's life and art. It's almost uncanny to what degree one can, I think, successfully look at his life and the development of his work against the background of that myth, which is all about the sacred marriage of the masculine and the feminine, the *hieros gamos* of Eros, the spirit of love, and Psyche, the feminine human soul. You can track different stages of that odyssey in the myth as well as in Rilke's life and work, and these correlations function as the scaffolding of my treatment of the poet.

AH: I think the most exciting aspect of the book—let's turn to the book now—is the way in which you marry your very profound, deep love of Rilke's unfolding journey to a very clear structure of archetype of psychology taken from James Hillman's work. How did this marriage of Hillman and Rilke suggest itself to you, and how do you work this marriage out in the book?

DJP: Yes, well, it was another instance of synchronicity, so to speak. I spoke a bit earlier about how I was drawn to Rilke at a particular time and how, at the same time, I had to look at psychology in a new light. It was at that very same time that I became very deeply interested in James Hillman's work. I was doing some studying at a place called Wisdom's Goldenrod Center for Philosophic Studies, outside Ithaca, NY, and there were classes there just starting up on Hillman. The confluence between Rilke and Hillman is very deep and not too difficult to discern. Rilke is a poet of soul and Hillman— as he himself repeatedly emphasizes—puts soul at the center of his psychology. Hillman's very much an iconoclast himself, in the Emersonian tradition, and the bases of his psychology are deeply consonant with Rilke's poetic vision. Hillman, for instance—in addition to probing many of the archetypes inherent in the soul's infinitely complex nature—stresses the importance of language in psychology—what he speaks of as "the poetic basis of mind"— and makes image and imagination central to his whole project of "revisioning psychology." Image, imagination, anima, dream, death, and the underworld ...

AH: *[in background]* Creative process.

DJP: Yes, creative process. I mentioned the myth of Psyche and Eros. Well, one of Hillman's most important books, *The Myth of Analysis,* develops the myth of Psyche and Eros as an alternative to the originally sovereign myth of psychoanalysis—the Oedipus myth— and, in connection with the imagery of the tale of Psyche and Eros, explores *creativity* as an indispensable feature of the soul's spiritual life. So my work with this myth is also very deeply informed by Hillman's work. Relatedly, Hillman's most seminal work is probably *Revisioning Psychology,* a book centered around the quintessentially creative project of "soul-making"—a phrase Hillman borrows from the romantic poet Keats. This too becomes part of the scaffolding of my book, because in *Revisioning Psychology*, Hillman details four basic modes of soul-making. In my book, I associate those modes with, on the one hand, the four labors of Psyche in the myth, and, on the other, the sequence of Rilke's four major, mature works: *The New Poems*, *The Notebooks of Malte Laurids Brigge*, the *Duino Elegies*, and *Sonnets to Orpheus*. So Hillman and Rilke came into my life as a package and have been pretty much inseparable from the beginning.

AH: One of the distinctions that Isaiah Berlin makes in his book *The Hedgehog and the Fox* is between those beings who've pursued polymorphous, multifarious initiatives, and those beings who have a very fixed trajectory all their lives. Hillman is very much a devotee of a polymorphous approach to the spiritual, isn't he?

DJP: Yes, he's a very polemical, exciting writer, but certainly one for whom strife and difference is native ground, and he takes great issue with the monotheistic tradition; he's a champion of the multiplicity of the polytheistic mythology of Greece and the great imaginative resources it puts at our disposal. His cultural project revolves around reopening the soul to the plethora of imaginative possibilities inherent in its nature, and he sees this initiative as a way of revivifying the human being's relationships with the outer as well as the inner world; and a way of opening new paths to the sacral dimensions of life. So yes, there's a certain distinct emphasis on multiplicity and diversity at the level of the Gods themselves—and most every other level too—that is very important to Hillman's soul-making project. Rilke certainly shares a similar breadth of interest. At the same time ...

AH: In Rilke, there's an intense focus on major themes that come back again and again. Perhaps this suggests that Rilke is a very strange mixture of both hedgehog and fox?

DJP: Yes, I think that's a wonderful way of putting it. If you look at his poetic oeuvre, you can see that the later works form a profound continuity with the very earliest one. One of Rilke's critics, Frank Wood, suggested a biological analogy: in the same way that a fetus develops into more complex forms that are nonetheless already visible in it, you can see Rilke's later works as metamorphoses of the earlier ones. In my book, I try to reveal that profound unity. At the same time, however, I don't think there are that many major poets who exhibit such a tremendous diversity in the nature and character of their chief works. Each of Rilke's most important works, *The Book of Hours,* the *Elegies,* the *Sonnets, New Poems, The Notebooks of Malte Laurids Brigge,* are, stylistically speaking, dramatically different from each other. Stefan Zweig, a German poet and contemporary of Rilke's, remarked upon how Rilke effectively revolutionized his style with each new work. To me, that is a mark of the depth of his spiritual exploration and shows that the One and the Many are well balanced and indeed equally potent forces in Rilke's work.

AH: Go to the title of your radical and wonderful book, *In the Image of Orpheus: Rilke: A Soul History.* People coming to your book will be very moved by the biographical unfolding of it, but I think they'll be even more moved by the sense of a growing soul and the history of the individuality that unfolds there. What is a soul history, and why did you choose to write a soul history about Rilke, something that has never really been done before?

DJP: Well, the term "soul history" is borrowed from Hillman. He introduced it in one of his earliest books, *Suicide and the Soul.* In that book he distinguishes a soul history from the model of the "case history" developed by Freud in his pathbreaking work in psychoanalysis. Now, a case history à la Freud involves going over all the biographical details of a particular psychological case. Hillman's idea of a soul history is one that, as the term itself indicates, focuses more on inner, less visible developments. That's certainly central to the book. It is not a traditional biography. The external biographical narrative is there, but it is the story of Rilke's inner life that is most challenging to trace, because it's not on the surface. That's where Hillman's archetypal psychology and the mythic structure of the Psyche and Eros tale are so important. It gives me a lens through which I can trace the subtle transitions that only appear in the biographical details once you grasp the understory. The idea of a soul history is thus very closely associated with the whole idea of soul-making and of individuation, which are basically one and the same: you're invested in charting the different stages and phases that the soul goes through in its striving to come to spirit. That is the story that I try to tell. There is the biographical surface, the record of events, and then there's the mythic, archetypal depths that inform and "secretly" plot and give shape to that surface.

AH: Is one of the intentions of your book to awaken, through Rilke's epochal, archetypal journey, our own expanded sense of the heroic, archetypal significance of our own journeys?

DJP: Very much so. Rilke's teaching is the teaching one might say not so much of a God, but a teaching of the human being.

AH: And human spirit.

DJP: The human spirit—in body, soul, and spirit—and the unity of that triplicity. He is, as Emerson phrased it, a kind of representative man, or representative human being, whose teaching is an exploration of the width, breadth, height, and depth of the state of the human being. He really does open horizons, new horizons in terms of our concept of who and what we are. He certainly is not an author invested in transcending, prematurely, the full complexity of the human condition; that is not the end of his "long path," even if a certain kind of transcendence remains one impulse.

Interview with Daniel Joseph Polikoff

AH: One of the poles of his nature.

DJP: Right, it's one of the poles of his nature, and naturally enough it's there more in force at the beginning of his career, in the youthful Rilke and even in *The Book of Hours*. Actually, my book is made up of two major divisions. I call them two "books." And the first "book," which treats the first half of his life, is called "Eternal Youth." The second half is called "Love's Labors." And in that first half, the crowning work of which is his *Book of Hours,* which came out of his trips to Italy and Russia, you very clearly see the energy of the eternal youth—archetypally, the *puer aeternus*—and its tremendous spiritual drive, its desire for unity with God. *The Book of Hours* is the one truly major Rilke work in which God is a central character. It's all about the dialogue of the self and God. So, it's a soaring work. But not long after Rilke's Russian journey, Icarus-like, he crashed. He went through …

AH: Crashed into embodiment.

DJP: Yes, the romantic relationship with Lou Andreas-Salomé, which was so important to him, began to fall apart, and his whole world darkened, and he went into the depths of an extended *nigredo,* which you could pretty much say lasted, in one or another form, for the rest of his life.

AH: He extended into the *nigredo* of a whole civilization collapsing in greed and violence and decadence.

DJP: In World War 1, most certainly.

AH: What was so significant, I think, about his *nigredo* is that it corresponded in its profoundest depths with the darkness of a whole world falling apart.

DJP: Right. And that's the role of the true poet. A culture-hero should reflect in their own individual psyche the lineaments of humankind at a given point in historical culture. Rilke certainly does that.

AH: I think it's one of the deepest reasons why his poetry is so moving to us now, because we're in a time in which, even more than his time, the world's falling apart. We're in a time of massive evolutionary crisis, environmental despair, world tribalism, horrible domination by the corporations, completely meaningless mash preached by the media. What Rilke is showing us is that disastrous though the situation is, there is a way through profound interiority, commitment to one's solitude, commitment to the voice of the soul, commitment to an ever-increasingly radical embodiment of the spirit in the body.

DJP: Right. And I think one of the things that's so compelling about Rilke is that he did live and work at the dawn of modernity, or at least a crucial, seminal phase of it. All the problems that we are facing—all those which you listed, and which are so overwhelming—can be understood to have been seeded or perhaps sprouted at that pivotal time.

AH: Well, I think the fundamental seed of all of these disasters is our radical dissociation from the sacred.

DJP: Yes, very much so.

AH: This radical dissociation that Rilke's whole work is poured out to heal, because he was trying desperately to heal himself and his own desperate need.

DJP: Precisely. And another compelling aspect of Rilke's accomplishment is that he looks for the springs of the sacred close by. He takes sustenance and inspiration from nature, his relationship to the woods and the fields and the sky and the water is very profound and is a source of great nourishment. And his human relationships— there is something of a paradox here, in fact. Rilke is esteemed as a sage of solitude. He certainly is that. Auden called him the Santa Claus of loneliness. But at the same time, you look at his life and work and his relationships with others—those relationships were so essential to his development. The evolution of his being would be unthinkable without his relationships with Lou Andreas-Salomé and Auguste Rodin and Clara Westhoff and Paula Becker and many other …

AH: Princess Marie von Turn-und-Taxis Hohenlohe.

DJP: Yes—his relation to Europe's old and dying nobility was crucial to him, materially and spiritually. So he is, in any event, an individual who is searching for the sacred. He has to deal with his own tortured relationship to Christianity and his mother's overweening piety, which he reacted against very strongly. And he looks at nature, at the world, and at the imaginative landscape of his childhood. He looks at his human relationships and loves as well as into the riches of great spiritual traditions—primarily for him the Bible and the great stories of the Old and New Testaments, but as well as the resources of Greek mythology that figure so importantly in his work, not to mention the Koran and traces of the Egyptian mysteries. He made a journey to Egypt at one point that actually is quite important to the *Elegies*. So he is a poet engaged in refurbishing a relationship to the spirit out of the depths of the individual soul and its own quests, and all the resources he finds available in nature and in human culture, which weave together in the crucible of his own unique, creative, heartfelt synthesis of life and human being.

AH: This brings me to the next question. You talk a great deal about the distinction between soul and spirit, and this is a distinction that Hillman makes, and is central to your book. It's a hard distinction to maintain. How would you want to express the difference between soul and spirit? How is soul different from spirit?

DJP: Right. This is a very tricky question. But, as you say, it is important in my book. I would first want to acknowledge that while I do invest in the difference between soul and spirit, it is true that soul and spirit are perpetually interweaving, so there's really no question of some kind of radical splitting of one from the other. At the same time, meaningful distinctions can and must be made. Hillman argues that the dominant stream of Western religion tends to suppress or repress soul in favor of the clarity, enlightenment, logic, and authority of univocal spiritual structures. Philosophy enters in here as well: reason is another kind of term that can be associated with the spirit. To put the relevant differences on a biographical basis, you can look, for example, at Rilke versus Ralph Waldo Emerson, another author whom I revere. Emerson was a Transcendentalist, a champion of the human spirit, and his vision continually lifts up toward the sphere of the ideal. Relationships with women—with the signal exception of Margaret Fuller—were generally not as important for Emerson as they were for Rilke. Issues of vulnerability, sickness, inferiority—these are all matters closely connected with the soul, the spirit's immediate liaison with the body—and are central to Rilke, but, at best, peripheral to Emerson's vision. Indeed, the whole sphere of image and imagination, which derives directly from the relationship to the sensible world and the body—this medial realm is the realm of the soul, and is very much Rilke's native milieu. As we've spoken of already, what is ultimately essential is the marriage of the masculine and feminine, which is also the marriage of the soul and the spirit. Even so, Rilke certainly shows a special openness to the vulnerabilities and the vagaries of being that are specific to the soul nature and especially its archetypally feminine character.

AH: Soul and spirit seem to be very different in one important respect, and that is that the soul is embodied and the body is in the soul. And the soul learns a great deal through loneliness, failure, betrayal, grief. It learns how to inhabit the body through those things. And to arrive in the place that connects it to everyone. Spirit, on the other hand, stresses a freedom from more material things. And asserts the victory and sacred prerogative of the Transcendent. And the relationship between the soul and the spirit is a particularly complex and difficult one, especially if you take, as Rilke did, the road of embodiment.

DJP: Yes, and that's the saga of soul-making that his life and work unfolds for us. You've put it very well, and really, the story of Rilke's life and work—a life that is lived *through* art—is a dance of the nuanced and multiple phases of this relationship between the embodied and embodying soul and the spirit. This is another reason for the importance of the Psyche-Eros myth in my book, because the interaction of Psyche and Eros is also the interaction of soul and spirit. Different works of Rilke represent different stages of the ongoing dramatic interplay of soul and spirit—indeed, different moments within the complex weave of a single work, say the *Elegies*—dramatize that interplay. I go into this in great detail in the book.

Rilke, after all, is a poet of distance and departure ("Be ahead of all parting" he writes in one famous sonnet); and the moment in the Psyche-Eros story when the wounded Eros flees the overanxious Psyche's grasp is relevant in that connection. But those moments of splitting and difference are ultimately in the service of a higher fusion, the sacred marriage, that takes place both at the end of the Psyche-Eros story, and in similar unions (for example, between Orpheus and Eurydice) inscribed in Rilke's poetry.

AH: And doesn't this journey toward ultimate union find some reflection in the plotting of your book? Because, really, there are two books. There's "Eternal Youth: Prague to Paris" and then "Love's Labors: Paris to Muzot." Why did you choose this structure?

DJP: It reflects on one level the archetypal dominance that one can discern in Rilke's early life, on the one hand, and his later life, on the other. As I mentioned, in Rilke's youth, up to roughly age twenty-five, the archetype of the eternal youth, or *puer aeternus,* is very powerful in him and can be seen as the archetypal dominant. This first period culminates in the first part of his *Book of Hours,* "The Book of Monastic Life." And then he goes through this dark period, this *nigredo,* or dark night, and plunges into a psychological abyss in Paris. From that time on, it's a matter of trying to recover or refashion a spontaneous relationship to spirit that he in some ways feels he has lost. And that phase of his journey, that latter phase in the book, I associate with the four labors of Psyche. And that's why the second part of my book ("book 2") is called "Love's Labors," and I see each of Rilke's major works as a distinct stage of that laborious struggle to rediscover a relationship with the spirit of love that seemed to have been present early in his life, but has flown away, like Eros in the myth, and become inaccessible.

In Paris, Rilke writes his *New Poems,* and, as well, his unique novel, *The Notebooks of Malte Laurids Brigge.* Work on those projects occupies him for most of the first decade of the new century, and correlates with the first two of Psyche's labors, and Hillman's first two modes of soul-making, which he calls, respectively, *personifying* and *pathologizing.* But it's only after the tremendous spiritual odyssey involved in Rilke's attempt to complete his *Elegies,* which he begins in 1912, just before World War 1, that Rilke nears the end of his poetic quest. He doesn't finish the *Elegies* until a decade later, 1922, and it's not until he completes those *Elegies,* and in the same miraculous poetic breath composes his fifty-five *Sonnets to Orpheus,* that he reestablishes that relationship to spirit, and does so on a new, higher level that integrates the soul-challenges that deepen his story: the travail, the grief, the inveterate yearning for impossible love, and (above all, perhaps) the decisive, initiatory confrontation with death so basic to Rilke's oeuvre. All these aspects of soul-being, of Psyche, contribute to and enrich the ultimate union with the immortal spirit symbolized by Eros. And that's the brilliance and genius of the late works of Rilke, the *Elegies* and the *Sonnets,* that this marriage is in some ways achieved and displayed for us. Rilke finally enacts what Jung might call the mystery of the *coniunctio;* he is, too, a poet who travels the classic initiatory path described by Joseph Campbell in his famous book *The Hero with a Thousand Faces.*

AH: Of course, a great deal has been written about Rilke already. In writing your book, did you feel you were breaking new ground most especially in this or that chapter, in writing about one or another particular topic?

DJP: Rilke's early *Visions of Christ* is a relatively little-known work. It wasn't published during his lifetime. I feel it's a very important work in his development, because it really does stage his confrontation with his childhood religion in a quite remarkable way. I devote a whole chapter to that cycle of poems ("epic-lyric fantasies," as Rilke himself called them), which, as I say, has received scant attention. In general, the way Rilke's early work prepares the foundation for his later work is a domain that hasn't been as thoroughly explored as it might have been.

AH: A very important aspect is his relationship to Lou Andreas-Salomé, not just as a sexual and artistic muse, but as a very formidable thinker about religion. You bring this out in great detail in the book in a wonderful way.

DJP: Yes, I feel this is one of the most important contributions to Rilke criticism, so to speak, in the book. Lou Andreas-Salomé's role as an emotional partner to Rilke is everywhere recognized, but it is nowhere adequately documented how formative her *ideas* were for his development. Most of her work remains untranslated, and one can understand why, because her essays, for example, on the psychology of religion or Russian culture—which are so important to Rilke—well, let's just say her prose style does nothing to impede the tendency toward turgidity and complexity inherent in German grammar. Nonetheless, those essays really provide the foundation for the philosophy of art, religion, and psychology that ground Rilke's vision, intellectually speaking, for the rest of his life. I do try and delve into the content of some of those essays, because those essays are so little known, yet at the same time their contribution to Rilke's thought is so profound and pervasive.

AH: What do you think the main aspects of this contribution are?

DJP: Lou Andreas-Salomé gave intellectual depth to Rilke's own very personal meditations about the relationship between the individual and God. Writing extensively on the psychology of religion, she investigates various ways that the concept of "God" is fashioned and operates within the context of religious constructions. She also wrote about the psychology of aesthetics. These two are related in a very intricate and an important way. If you read *Book of Hours,* in which Rilke constantly speaks of and to God, without the background of knowing what Lou Andreas-Salomé has written about the psychology of religion, you may well find yourself at a loss as you try to figure out where Rilke is coming from, theologically speaking. But when you understand something of what Lou has laid out about the dynamic through which an individual soul generates a God-image in and through its own yearning, and then—through what she calls the logic of the *back-effect*—that God-image takes on a kind of objective reality.

AH: An archetypal force.

DJP: Yes, and the way that this God-image then works back upon the individual, and the intricate relation of these two dynamics, you have what is really the paradigm for the relationship between the poetic self and God that is unfolded in the *Book of Hours.*

Interview with Daniel Joseph Polikoff

AH: And throughout his work?

DJP: And throughout his work, very much so.

AH: There's a very profound and strange and mysterious relationship in his work between self-discovery and discovery of the Divine, and the deep, strange, and penetrating rhythms between the two. The focus of this is in his vision of Christ, isn't it—the changing vision of Christ that dominated his whole work. Because it's very clear from the early work that he's deeply drawn to the figure and the passion and the consciousness of the Christ, while appalled by the betrayal of that in contemporary religion.

DJP: Yes, certainly, and this is one of the most important strains in Rilke's work. In fact, my book is divided up not only into two main sections, called books 1 and 2, but there's also a four-part division. Each of the two "books," so to speak, is divided in half, so there are also four parts, which cover four major sections of Rilke's life. The first section is called "Realism in Religion," which is, in fact, the title of a very important essay on the psychology of religion by Lou Salomé. In that section I go in some depth into Rilke's relationship to the Christ as it is first worked out through his early *Visions of Christ*—a work published, by his own choice, only after Rilke's death. As you suggest, though, this relationship to the Christ remains important to Rilke throughout his life. In fact, when he begins working on the *Elegies* in 1912–1914, he visits Lou Salomé in Göttingen and he makes a point of giving her another copy of the *Visions of Christ*, because he is very keenly aware of how his work on the *Elegies* is taking place against the background of this early confrontation with this spiritual figure who is so central to the religious imagination of our culture and with whom he certainly has a kind of love-hate relationship. In certain sections, for example, of the *Visions of Christ*—well, I think one can say that in general the image of the Christ there is not a very flattering one. In Rilke's

Visions, Jesus is cast in a tragic light; he ultimately has little to offer humanity; his hands are spiritually empty. But, as you say, Rilke makes quite clear that it is not so much Jesus, the individual, who is spiritually false and impoverished, but the doctrine and dogma that has been built up around him by his followers—though Rilke also takes strenuous issue with Jesus's own claim to divinity. I'm not implying that the historical Jesus actually made such claims, but that it's the way it has come down to us. And Rilke took great issue with that. His primary difficulty with the image of Christ as it's conveyed through the church is that Christ does not become so much a conduit for the individual to their own spirituality, but an obstacle, an idol, a blockade. And that was intolerable to Rilke. He felt in some way that his own access to his own spirituality was obstructed by this figure that, so to speak, stood there in the way of his own path to God.

AH: This was Rilke's tremendous critique of Christianity—that the church created in Jesus a savior icon that acted as a force that depressed everybody else's direct relationship to the Divine. It was created especially by an authoritarian boys' club to keep people enslaved to the priest class. And this made it impossible in Rilke's vision for human beings to "Christ" themselves. And Rilke's whole enterprise is a self-Christing on a most profound level.

DJP: Exactly, and one of the things that I detail somewhat in the book is how one can look at the *Elegies* as a process of that Christing, so to speak. The *Elegies* do not refer to any explicit Christian imagery at all. There is no reference....

AH: It becomes totally serious. There is no mention of Christ because the Christing is taking place in the archetypal depths of human nature.

DJP: Precisely, and that's what's unfolding in Rilke's *Elegies.* You can feel very palpably how there's a crucifixion of consciousness in the *Elegies,* how there's a kind of entombment, a descent into the grave, how there's a carrying of the cross, the burden of humanity is squarely upon the poet's shoulders, the poetic soul's shoulders, in the *Elegies.* So there is a kind of replaying of the archetypal motifs that are inscribed in the Passion. But it is done in an entirely interiorized way, so that there's an enactment in and through soul consciousness of the fundamental stages of the passion. There is, of course, also more than a hint of resurrection in the later *Elegies.*

AH: Yes, in the ninth elegy there is a complete vision of resurrected experience.

DJP: True. So, there is, on an archetypal level, a profound relationship to the formative motifs of Christianity, but ...

AH: You might say, in fact, is that Rilke couldn't stand official Christianity and the official Christ myth because it blocked him from the work that he knew that he had to do, which was the work of descending into the same depths and ascending to the same heights that the Christ had done in his journey of Christ-consciousness.

DJP: Yes, very much so. I mean, in one sense one could say that Rilke performed the imitation of Christ in the deepest, most genuine manner. And, indeed, he was not unaware of that at some level. At the beginning of the war, Rilke was abroad—he had been living in Paris—and most of his belongings were there, and they were lost to him, because when the war broke out, they were confiscated, and he could never recover them. And he said that for the most part that didn't matter to him. But there were a few things, a few treasures that (as we know from his correspondence) he terribly regretted losing. One was an image of his father, and another was an image of Christ that he said he had had with him his entire life. So, there was this current of an individualized relationship to this great spiritual figure that Rilke took in and interiorized and lived with throughout his life.

The Language of Love

AH: One of the things that I found most compelling about your book is not only your exploration of Rilke's relationship with the Christ at this archetypal, painful, poignant, deeply transformatory level, but your very brave and very original exploration of Rilke's relationship to Islam. And I think that this is very, very important, also, for the later work. Could you sketch it for us?

DJP: That's a tall order. I actually deal most extensively with it in connection with Henry Corbin's work, *Alone with the Alone— Creative Imagination in the Sufism of Ibn Arabi*.

AH: It's a crucial piece for the understanding of the role of the angel in the *Elegies*. You make the most clear and precise rapprochement between Corbin's understanding of the role of imagination in the imaginal world, in Sufi mysticism, and Rilke's own eruption into the imaginal world in the figure of the angel.

DJP: Yes, and another element of that which is fascinating is individuation. Corbin himself mentions the Jungian idea of individuation in his discussion of the angel, and elaborates how a relationship to the angel, rather than kind of lifting the soul out of itself, so to speak, is actually the higher agency directing our individuation. It's the relationship to that spiritual being, the angel, which acts as a kind of pole star that guides and forms the evolution, the development, of the soul. So, there's this fascinating coincidence or connection between Ibn Arabi's Sufism, Jungian ideas of individuation, and Rilke's embodiment of these ideas through his poetic oeuvre.

AH: I think also that the relationship with Islam excited him in two very fundamental ways. And both these ways are brought out in your book. The first is that he met in the Koran a consciously, ecstatically, sometimes terrifyingly prophetic book with a consistent prophetic voice. And this consistent prophetic voice was something he was looking for and found it in unmitigated majesty and clarity in the Koran.

DJP: Yes, though he didn't really involve himself with the Koran very much until somewhat later in his life. Again, it was in the period when the *Elegies* were gestating, and he makes a journey to Spain and sojourns for extended periods in both Toledo and Ronda. It was there, in that Islamic setting, that he first read the Koran with great attention and found the overwhelming presence of the Divine, of Allah, that resonates in the Koran reflected in his experience of the landscape and culture. Rilke was always looking for ways to enter into a more direct experience of the sacred, of God, and both the Koran and the Old Testament (which he also read assiduously at this time) served that purpose for him; they provided byways around the too familiar, too conventionalized, and too mediated images of divinity transmitted to him through his Catholic background.

Not that Rilke did not continue to draw upon Christian inspiration as well! His relationship to Christianity is perpetually double edged. That very Spanish journey, in fact, was motivated by his avid interest in El Greco's art. That's as an interesting digression. I have a whole chapter in the book pretty much devoted to the relationship between the *Duino Elegies* and El Greco's painting *View of Toledo*. This chapter looks at that painting as an archetypal image that in some way represented for Rilke a spiritual picture of the relationship between the heights and the depths that he was trying to find in himself.

AH: In a sense it also represents the tension in the Koran itself between this overwhelming majesty of transcendent presence and the way in which it expresses itself convulsively in history and in nature. Because the El Greco painting is at once realistic and shatteringly mystical in its portrayal of a force of presence so convulsive that it distends all geometric and realistic relationships.

DJP: Yes, it's a quite unique painting in El Greco's oeuvre. I think it may be, if I remember correctly, the only real landscape in the canon of El Greco works. El Greco, of course, was a painter of the Counter-Reformation and angels are more common that trees in his work. But *View of Toledo*—by the way, there are over forty images in the book, including this painting, Rodin sculptures, photos of Rilke and Lou, and so forth, so the visual is well represented in the book itself—well, one could call *View of Toledo* an expressionistic or protoexpressionistic work and stylistically it's very exceptional in that way. It's like a Sturm und Drang.

AH: A storm of the absolute energy within the soul and its world.

DJP: Right, and, as I mentioned, Rilke looked to both Judaism and Islam as kind of antidotes to Christianity in a way that is related to what you are speaking about. There is the kind of direct, unmediated relationship to the godhead provided by the great prophets. The shattering experiences of the prophets in those traditions—most notably, Muhammad and Moses—seemed to him to offer an image or a picture of a direct, unmediated relationship to the godhead that he himself sought.

AH: Well I think one of the astonishing affinities between the *Elegies* and the Koran lies in precisely the nature of both the Prophet Muhammad's relationship to the Divine and Rilke's. They share an overwhelming sense of the majesty of the divine presence, a deep fear and awe at that majesty which terrifies them. The prophet Muhammad was overwhelmed when visited by the angel that bore his prophetic commission, and, in the opening of the *Elegies*, the poet too envisions the angel as terrifying, the angel's sublime beauty inspires terror that "serenely disdains to destroy us." In both, too, there's a sense of being inadequate to the divine vision and the task that comes with it, an incommensurability between the human vessel and the Divine; this is another key dimension of the vision and of the prophetic agony. And it's shared by all authentic prophets. And a third real parallel between Rilke and the Prophet is that the Prophet had to endure tremendous loneliness in the unfolding of his vision and years of strife and suffering and betrayal. And Rilke, I think, resonated with this at the deepest level.

DJP: Yes. There's a key poem that Rilke titled "Muhammad's Calling," which gives Rilke's own poetic rendition of Muhammad's formative experience. I'll read it in my translation as it appears in the book in that chapter on the genesis of the *Elegies*.

Muhammad's Calling

Such majesty could not be mistaken.
Yet, when the angel stepped into his hideout,
erect and pure and radiant as flame:
He put off all his old ambition and begged

to be allowed to remain what he was—a merchant
inwardly confused by his travels.
He had never read before—and now
such a word, too much even for a wise man.

But the angel, commanding, pointed again
and again to what was written on his page,
and would not yield and once more beckoned: read.

Then he read: so deeply, the angel bowed.
And he was already someone who had read.
And, obeying, could and did fulfill the Word.

I think another dimension of why this was so important to Rilke was a call to vocation. And he saw his poetic vocation as …

AH: As a prophetic one, one that carried the hidden freight of the whole shattered civilization.

DJP: Yes, certainly, and that's why the accomplishment of the *Elegies* weighed so heavily on him. He conceived the *Elegies* in a burst of inspiration in 1912, but only accomplished a fragment of the work, even though he had a vision of the whole cycle of ten already at that early time. Then the next decade of his life was preoccupied with the desire to fulfill what he felt was his own prophetic mission. There were many points at which he felt that he would never get there. And, in fact, at one point he wrote a last testament, explaining and exonerating himself in case he didn't manage to complete this prophetic mission that he had embraced. But there's a happy ending to that story because, of course, he did complete it.

AH: The other side of his absorption with Islam, I think, is also important and less completely worked out in his life. What Islam showed him in his visit to Egypt and in his other experiences of Islam was that an authentic spiritual culture can also be embedded deeply in ordinary life. Because, after all, there are five prayer stations during the day in Islam. And he was especially moved by the way in which the calls to prayer unfolded and interpenetrated the din of the marketplace in Islamic cultures. And this is, in a very grand way, an image of what he is offering us, the *Elegies*. Because as you say, the ninth elegy is an elegy of resurrection. But it isn't a resurrection into a bodiless, transcendent light. It's a resurrection into a living, pulsing, natural world that is utterly and completely saturated with sacred presence.

DJP: Right. And this is something Rilke had been looking for his whole life and found earlier as well—and powerfully so—in Russia. When he traveled to Russia with Lou he arrived right around Good Friday, and on Easter Sunday he heard the bells ringing in the Kremlin amidst the throngs of the people in worship: that was one of his most important experiences, and indeed acted like a kind of a mystical bell that rang throughout his life. And he was always trying to hear the tones of that mystical bell. In line with what you are saying, what drew him to Russia was his sense that God was so deeply embodied there, in both the land itself—the vast sky and spreading earth—and in the people. Of course, this experience was in large part mythic—reflected Rilke's myth of Russia as much as or more than historical truth, and in the book I discuss the phenomenon of "Russomania," the widespread infatuation with Russia that took hold in Europe toward the end of the nineteenth century. Be that as it may, it is true that places such as Russia and Islamic cultures did project and image, for Rilke, the kind of embodied spirituality he sought his entire life; the kind of living and glowing spiritual culture he often—despite all its cultural brilliance—missed in Europe.

AH: Something he never really found, because I think while Rilke's poetry is a supremely gifted poetry of the individual soul's search for reality, there is very little sense of a communal reality in it. I think he's facing one of the major aspects of our crisis, which is its chronic disintegration of any embracing spiritual reality, or larger sacred context.

DJP: Yes, and that's played out in his novel, *The Notebooks of Malte Laurids Brigge,* which is by no means a traditional *Bildungsroman,* or "novel of education." We've spoken about soul-making and the individuation process, and you might think that Rilke's one major novel might follow that romantic model; or might—given Rilke's reverence for the childhood imagination—unfold more like Wordsworth's *Prelude,* an epic autobiographical poem in which the soul goes through a process of education comes to some kind of provisional consummation. Well, *The Notebooks of Malte Laurids Brigge,* both in terms of content and its collage-like form, is really a novel of disintegration, of falling apart. I associate it with Hillman's second mode of soul-making, which Hillman in fact (in the chapter devoted to the subject) calls "Pathologizing, or Falling Apart." *Malte* is reflective, certainly, of the existential crisis of the modern, especially European, individual at that time in history. What had been, for centuries, that kind of communal myth for the West, for Europe, had been provided by Christianity, and it was precisely the institutions of that tradition and its associated doctrines that Rilke could no longer embrace or endorse. So, that kind of community wasn't really available to him in his culture. He is part of a larger movement that I think we may well be part of as well; a movement aimed at reestablishing genuine relationship to spiritual community, which aim requires, however, that the members of that community all pass through the eye of the needle: the individual soul in all its irreducible particularity.

AH: This is the great challenge of our time. To combine a very fierce, rigorous individual search for reality with a commitment to communal service and justice. Rilke is a pioneer of this very difficult fusion.

DJP: Yes, and I think at some level the legions of people who love and honor Rilke and his work form a kind of an unseen community, one unseen community of many who are drawn together by ideals that find such intimate and powerful expression in his work. And it's in part through becoming more conscious of the premises of the work of someone like Rilke that such a community of individuals may become more conscious of itself. What impulses, what vision, is embodied in Rilke's complex and multifaceted and symbolically rich work? Reading him more deeply, and so bringing those ideas to greater consciousness, so that they can be cultivated at another level in our own spiritual practices, in our own literary endeavor, in our own ordinary lives—it is by tracing and traveling this path that I think Rilke can emerge as not just a beloved poet with a tremendous international readership, but as well a teacher of humanity, one whose essential inspiration and vision can work all the more powerfully in us the more they are understood. And that's part of the project of the book—to unearth, to discover the wisdom that is pervasive in the form and content of Rilke's oeuvre, and yet really hasn't been elucidated as a kind of coherent whole, as a kind of comprehensive vision, or *Weltanschauung*.

The trick, of course—and this reflects yet again the myth of Psyche and Eros—is to elaborate the premises of Rilke's vision without reducing the poetry to conceptual frames of reference, to read Rilke in such a way as to allow his symbolic, his poetic language to speak and to resound, to permit his poetic voices and images to excite and inform our own creative imagination, our own soul-work. Rilke, after all, was the quintessential poet—thus the centrality of the figure and myth of Orpheus in his life and in my book; in the last chapter, in fact, I compare and contrast the myths of Psyche and Eros and that of Orpheus and Eurydice. In any event, the archetypal essence of poetry—which always unites spirit and body in soul-gestures enacted in language—remains at the core of his, of Rilke's vision, and provides the vehicle of embodying and realizing the mystical elements of that vision.

AH: The appearance of your book coincides with the intensification of many major questions that are troubling all of us right now. And a book like yours could only have been written now because it addresses the fundamental needs of our times through the exploration of someone who pioneered the expression of those needs, and whose quest unfolded responses to them.

DJP: Yes, it's interesting that we're about a hundred years from the time at which Rilke began the *Elegies*. That was in 1912, so in one year we'll be at the hundredth anniversary of their inception. This is also the time, give or take a few years, when Jung's *Red Book* was written, or at least initiated. I think that too is not entirely coincidental, for Jung is also a teacher of the spirituality that's implicit in the individual soul and the exploration of its spiritual estate. And there's a deep kinship, of course, between Jung, who is the godfather of archetypal psychology, and Rilke. My book certainly reflects that. But, as you're implying, there's something historically resonant, too, in the fact that we're coming to the hundredth anniversary of this time in our history. Sometimes at that hundredth year (that is three times thirty-three and a third, which has relevance to the Christ archetype, as that was Jesus's age at the time of his Passion), there's a new level of consciousness that's available for understanding great works. That is also true with Rudolf Steiner, whose mystery dramas and much other formative work (for instance, his *Outline of Occult Science*) was also written at precisely this period—between 1910 and 1915. There's a kind of resonance between these great teachers, all of whom have their own angle, but all of whom are guides of this project of renovating a relationship to the sacred, building upon the accomplishments of spiritual traditions, but forging new avenues that are rooted in the unique character of the modern individual soul.

AH: And this reflects something that is really at the core of our current spiritual and mystical adventure, which is how to fuse together a very radical vision of the impersonal transcendent—reality beyond the concepts and dogmas—with a predominately Western vision of the absolutely sacred role of individualists.

DJP: And it's in this respect that art, as a form of expression and a way of being, can play an especially vital role, because it is precisely in poetry and art that the kind of tension that you just elucidated—well, that tension indwells and energizes the very nature of art, constitutes its essential character. Any successful poem or piece of art of any kind must reconcile the universal and the individual. Otherwise, it's not a piece of art. The nature of art in that respect is inseparable from the nature of the psyche, of the soul, which in turn is inseparable from the nature of image and the relationship to body or sensible reality implicit in image.

AH: Central to the fusion of the impersonal and the personal, which could be said to be making your whole life a work of unfolding, sacred art.

DJP: Yes, which is exactly what Rilke does. And, of course, those poles of the impersonal and the personal are exemplified in his life and art. The tension between them, but also, at some level ...

AH: Their ... fusion ...

DJP: Yes, it is so clear in Rilke because you have, certainly, the sage of solitude, the poet who pursued the Plotinian path of the alone to the alone, the cosmic hermit. This is the Rilke we all know and recognize. And yet, at the same, as Robert Hass elucidates so movingly in one of his essays on Rilke, there are few poets who generate a greater feeling of intimacy with their reader, who touches us so deeply on a very personal, human level as does Rilke. Now, this is a paradox. How can the same poet be the cosmic hermit who is singing the angel in his terrible spiritual inaccessibility (and who often appeared remote and inapproachable in his personal life) be the same poet whose words weave themselves into the most intimate and personal recesses of our being and consciousness?

AH: An analogy is Beethoven's last quartet, isn't it? It has the same extreme, strange impersonality and radical, poignant individual tone.

DJP: Yes, that's interesting, though Rilke didn't have such a deep relationship to music; it was far more his relationship with the visual arts that constantly fed his poetry, as can be most clearly seen in connection with his sojourn in the Worpswede art colony, where he met the sculptress Clara Westhoff (who later became his wife) and the painter Paula Becker, a formative period which I deal in part 2 of my book, "Death and the Maiden." That connection with the visual arts continues too, in Rilke's enormously important relationship with Rodin—his second greatest teacher, after Lou Andreas-Salomé—which finally issued in the first great work of Rilke's maturity, his *New Poems,* which I discuss (along with *Malte*) in part 3, "By Beauty and by Fear." Even so, Beethoven is a figure who earns a very moving portrait in *The Notebooks of Malte Laurids Brigge,* and was, for Rilke, a kind of an image of the cosmic hermit, the artist, who was playing on a cosmic instrument and ...

AH: Being played.

DJP: Being played, exactly. Another theme of many of Rilke's poems.

AH: So, just let me end with one question. Everybody, when they create a work, especially when it takes them twenty years, has in their heart and mind an ideal reader. What would you want your ideal reader to be like and how would you like your ideal reader to approach this book?

DJP: Hmm. That's an interesting question. Well, my ideal reader would be somebody who's drawn to Rilke and the spiritual questions that Rilke engages. He or she could be someone who has some interest in literature and psychology, some interest in the tremendous cultural history that informs the background of the work of somebody like Rilke. My ideal reader is not necessarily a scholar in the narrow sense of the term (though Emerson's essay *The American Scholar* is one of my favorites!) but is someone who brings the intensity of his or her own searching to the reading of this book and is willing to exercise some of the patience that it took to write the book, which I like to think is kin to the patience Rilke needed to achieve his poetic goals over the course of his decades-long poetic career. While the book, I think, is very engaging, it also is challenging. So a reader would have to be willing to climb those mountains with me and to plunge into those valleys. It's somebody whose heart and mind are open to the vistas that Rilke and his poetry can open for us.

AH: When I hear you speak, I think of the line from the *Sonnets,* "Sei für die Flamme begeistert" (Be inspired by the flame).

DJP: Yes.

AH: That you're really asking for someone who is prepared to put their whole lives into service of a troubling, precarious, extreme, and endless transformation.

DJP: Yes.

AH: And to do so out of a leap of courage, the courage that it requires to be enraptured of the flame, knowing that the flame will burn you.

DJP: Yes.

AH: And will turn your agendas to ash.

DJP: [*reciting Sonnets to Orpheus*, II, 12]
> *Desire metamorphosis. Be inspired for the flame*
> *within which a thing withdraws, resplendent with transformation;*
> *that creative spirit, which masters our earthly frame.*
> *loves nothing more than the figure's turn; its endless variation.*

Foreword to *The Seasons of the Soul: The Poetic Guidance and Spiritual Wisdom of Hermann Hesse,* by Ludwig Max Fischer

As the great deciding crisis of our civilization continues to explode, the wisdom of voices like Hermann Hesse's—wisdom like a dry but rich old red wine—becomes ever rarer and ever more important. Hesse's voice is particularly necessary because it speaks with deep sincerity of one of the key spiritual adventures of the last hundred years, that of fusing together the best of the Western philosophical and mystery traditions with the highest understanding of unity and divine identity of the East. This is an adventure that many of us believe provides the fuel for the next evolutionary stage of humanity and for the birth of a universal mysticism that can lead to a wholesale transformation of all form of earth life.

The problems and opportunities such a fusion of East and West arouses are explored with complex and laconic elegance in Hesse's great novels, especially *Siddhartha* and his masterpiece, *The Glass Bead Game,* which many consider the greatest philosophical novel of the twentieth century. But it is in his poems that you meet most intimately Hesse the man in all his emotional intensity, sometimes scalding self-knowledge, and fierce spiritual struggle, and so experience most completely the inner turmoil and revelations that led to his becoming one of the philosopher-sages of our tumultuous transition.

Perhaps the most moving quality of the poems that Ludwig Fischer has selected and translated with such magisterial ease is their absolute lack of pretension, their hard-won and wonderfully humane simplicity of approach. Hesse is the least pompous and gnomic of sages; he does not attain, or want to attain, the prophetic heights of a Nietzsche, or the ecstatic complexity of a Rilke, or Goethe's all-embracing philosophical range. Hesse speaks to us nakedly, without artifice, from his profound fatherly heart, without any need to exaggerate his realization or play down or excuse his own faults and shadows. That is why we come to trust him, knowing that he has no need to convince us of his own uniqueness or seduce us to marvel at his achievement. Such wry and radical humility is rare in the Western tradition and comes, I believe, from Hesse's deep immersion in Eastern, especially Chinese, thought, with which his reclusive temperament had the greatest affinity. Hesse is closer to Li Po or Wang Wei than he is to the earlier German romantic or landscape poets to whom he has often been compared. Hesse's best poems radiate a secret, timeless knowledge of the mystery of cyclical change, the interconnection of "the ten thousand things" that comprise phenomenal reality, and the profound empty peace that bathes and underlies all life's fervid dramas, revealing just how deeply the discoveries of Chinese spirituality penetrated his soul.

In an age as chaotic and noisy as ours, such a clear, humble voice could easily go unheard. But that would be a grave mistake. It is at times of ferocious change that we most need sensibilities attuned to the changeless; it is in an age of wild bombast and nihilistic irony that a temperament like Hesse's—grounded, reverent, serious without being earnest—has the most to offer those who, like him, look to the order of the cosmos and to ageless, timeless truths for consolation, inspiration, and strength of soul. The struggle ahead to secure any kind of sustainable human future is bound to be a heartbreaking and brutal one; we will all need the reminders that Hesse's holy and sober poems give us of the necessity to trust and surrender to nature's slowly unfolding healing rhythms and the eternal mother's cosmic laws of death and rebirth.

Ludwig Fischer is an old and beloved friend of mine, whose heart and intellect I draw deep inspiration from. I salute his selection of Hesse's poems, the honed purity and lyrical directness of his translations, and the wide-ranging depth of his introductions to each of the sections of *Seasons of the Soul*. May this wise, grand, radiant book find the loving army of devoted readers it deserves.

> Andrew Harvey
> Oak Park, Illinois
> May 20, 2011

Interview with Ludwig Max Fischer

Andrew Harvey: I'm so honored and so delighted to be sitting here with one of my greatest friends, Ludwig Max Fischer. It's very difficult to describe Max, and I'm not going to attempt to do so because you're going to experience him. But the reason why we're having this conversation is that Max has just published a very, very important book called *Seasons of the Soul: The Poetic Guidance and Spiritual Wisdom of Hermann Hesse*. And it's been one of my dreams for a long time to get Max in a room and to speak to him about Hermann Hesse and the great and sacred themes that are evoked by his poetry. And here we are, sitting in his house in Toronto. Max, I thought that as we entered this radiant labyrinth of Hesse's poetry, that we begin really by reading a favorite poem of each of ours. So please.

Ludwig Max Fischer: I'm glad you ask to start with a poem, because most of the time we talk about poems before we actually focus on the poems themselves. So my favorite, or one of my favorites, is called "Pruned Oak." And this is how it goes:

Pruned Oak

Oh oak tree, how they have pruned you.
Now you stand odd and strangely shaped!
You were hacked a hundred times
until you had nothing left but spite and will!
I am like you, so many insults and humiliations
could not shatter my link with life.
And every day I raise my head
beyond countless insults toward new light.
What in me was once gentle, sweet, and tender,
this world has ridiculed to death.
But my true self cannot be murdered.
I am at peace and reconciled.
I grow new leaves with patience
from branches hacked a hundred times.
In spite of all the pain and sorrow
I'm still in love with this mad, mad world.

It's mad isn't it, Andrew?

AH: This world certainly qualifies as mad and it's getting madder. And our conversation is going to unfold in the full presence of the world going crazy and falling apart. But I wanted to read a poem that gives me great peace in all the madness. A poem that really convinces me that even in this madness, or, perhaps, especially in this madness, we are being nourished and protected and held by the great love of the Divine. And the poem I chose was "Contemplation."

The spirit is divine and eternal.
Our paths lead toward it.
We are its mirror and instrument.
Our innermost passion is to become spirit,
to shine in its light.

But we are made of earth and are mortal,
feel heavy, and carry the burden of creatures.
Mother Nature nurtures and nourishes us,
nurses us along from cradle to the grave,
and yet she cannot give us peace.
The mythic Mother is ruptured
by the eternal spark of the spirit.
The heavenly father turns the child into man,
leaves innocence behind,
and summons us to conflict and conscience.

Torn between mother and father,
torn between body and spirit,
we, the most fragile child of creation, hesitate.
We, who are able to endure in our souls
suffering like no other being.
We, who are capable of the most noble achievement:
love fueled and filled by faith and hope.

The path is thorny, sin and death its food.
We often stray into darkness and feel
it had been better never to be born.
But our yearning always calls us
toward our ultimate calling: to light and spirit
and we do feel it deeply: God loves this fragile creature
with a unique tender blaze of affection.

The Language of Love

Therefore love is ever present and possible
when we brothers get confused in conflict.
We know neither condemnation nor hatred
will bring us closer to our most sacred goal,
but only patient love and loving patience.

I love those lines, "God loves this fragile creature with a unique, tender blaze of affection." Max, what made you devote so many years and such deep, deep heart time to the translation of Hesse's poetry? What sustained you in your search for the way to convey these extraordinary poems in English?

LMF: Well, Hesse didn't actually come to me very early in my life, in my rebellious phase. Actually, Hesse came to someone who was born and grew up in Germany via America. It was when I was hitchhiking across Europe, and Americans were also hitchhiking and wanted to explore Europe. They had "Hess" in their backpacks and they would always ask, "Have you read 'Hess'? *Siddhartha?* Have you read *The Glass Bead Game?* Have you read *Demian?* And have you read *Narcissus and Goldmund?* Have you read *Steppenwolf?*" I mean, even a rock band called themselves after *Steppenwolf,* so it was sort of obligatory. I actually at the time was into the Beat Generation, you know, and read Jack Kerouac's *On the Road* while I was sticking my thumb out and hoping that a car would stop.

AH: Was this during the time you were a member of a rock band?

LMF: That's when I was a bass player, and in our culture at that time in Germany, we were very much looking toward America. I grew up with Bob Dylan or British bands, that's what our orientation was. And our whole German heritage was sort of something we hoped to forget. So "Hess" actually wasn't quite up there for us.

But it was not until my forties, actually, when I was offered an opportunity to teach a seminar on *The Glass Bead Game* for a whole semester, and I found in *The Glass Bead Game* a poem called "The Glass Bead Game," which is actually in this volume. And I thought, "this is a really good poem." So I found out Hesse wrote poetry too. All the people talking to me now about Hesse and *The Season of the Soul,* they always say the same thing: "I didn't know that 'Hess' wrote poetry! How did I miss that?"

So I went through all the works of Hesse in German, and there were over a thousand poems. I thought, "well, they all have been translated for sure." I did my research and I found one very small little volume, bilingual, by a great American poet—really the poets' poet, and there are festivals for him, and anybody who knows anything about poetry knows James Wright. But it was just twenty-two poems in a bilingual edition! It was published in 1970, and I thought, "nothing ever since?" I thought, "Well maybe, if nobody has done it, it definitely needs to be done! How about if I do it?"

So then I got myself into it, but it took some while, actually. It was like the poems did want to have their own long incubation time. I did a first version, a second version, then I put it aside. Being an academic, I had some professorial obligations, where I had to do some publications with lots of footnotes. But it came back, it came back to me, again and again. For some reason, because often in life we get signs, actually years after, I got really deep into translation, and I was thinking this really should be brought to the English-speaking audience. I noticed that I had for years, a big poster of Hesse in my office.

AH: And you'd never seen it? You'd never really taken it in?

LMF: In some discreet way actually he was looking at me and saying, "he will eventually get it." It had a wonderful inscription, which I did understand and used quite often in my life. It was about three virtues that you need to have in order to succeed against the infamies of life. And they are courage, willfulness, and, as you just mentioned, patience. Courage gives you strength, willfulness is fun, and patience gives you tranquility. These are really very, very helpful qualities, because they don't require you to follow a certain code, and I think this is one of the basic ways why Hesse becomes so close and so familiar. Because he never takes the stage in order to preach for any specific ideology: for something that if you do this and then you do that and then you achieve another level, and then another level. You constantly improve yourself. It is very important that if you do *not* improve yourself, these are the punishments that will follow all the way down, purgatory and eternal fire.

AH: There's no dogmatic religiosity in Hesse?

LMF: There is no hell there. There is also no promise: "I will be full of bliss. I will be totally enlightened." He doesn't build a throne for anybody either. No: "I will be the archbishop" of this new church he builds.

AH: It's a very special kind of tone, isn't it? It's a tone that isn't prophetic and ecstatic like Nietzsche, doesn't have the self-conscious rightness and richness of Goethe. It's a very tender, sober, humane, human tone forged in the fires of real life and constantly turning back to real life for its evidence and for its inspiration. I think it's a tone that is particularly suited to our time, a time in which all ideologies are failing, all agendas are crumbling. It's a tone we can trust, it's a tone we can rely on. I wondered if you'd like to read the wonderful passage Hesse gives us that really describes what a poet is and what kind of a poet he is.

LMF: We all now live with a terrible case of poetry deficiency disorder. The poetic life and the value of the poet has been put so far on the periphery. With all the texting and with all the devaluation of the word—I'm thinking of Jacques Ellul, "the humiliation of the word." I'm thinking that there are plenty of thinkers that realize the price we pay for commodified language and what we have gained on the horizontal level. We can send something that isn't really a word anymore, isn't really a message anymore either, but it is sort of a word item that we can send within seconds across the planet. But we have forgotten about the vertical axis of language. We are almost unable to access real language anymore. We are so obsessed with the quantity of text, we can send so fast and so much, we forget about the roots and the blossoms of the words. The vertical axis where the meaning comes out of the rhyme, comes out of the sound, comes out of the rhythms, comes out of the spoken word. You need a bard to bring the spoken word into the community. That is then the live prophet. The blossoms, of course, are the metaphors, are the analogies, then you have a full word where the horizontal axis and the vertical axis are fully present.

AH: And a word that's pregnant with new possibilities and that engenders deep, deep feeling and thought. That creates a kind of sacred intimacy between beings.

LMF: Then you have messages that can find a crack between whatever has been hardened as an ideology, what has been dogmatized, what has already been established, categorized, classified, functionalized, has been abused with the terrible word—the ultimate "efficiency." Whatever the original inspiration was, it has been totally used up in complete efficiency. Then you look at these empty words. I like the Canadian author Robert Bringhurst and a number of other people and the way they speak. Now people speak like the air is out of the word. When Hesse talks about what is the appointed office of a poet—it is a very, very important office. But it doesn't come with some PhD certification.

AH: Or a title.

LMF: Where you can talk from an authoritarian point of view that other people have to obey, because you have basically cornered the market. It is like—whatever you say someone has to obey it in your sphere of influence. This way of thinking is about another kind of authority, it is actually the authority of the one who listens deep into the word and then gets in touch with his or her own imagination. Relying on the imagination, which is hopefully not polluted with a lot of fake metaphors—fake and abusive analogies as in advertising, where you have charged images like the beauty of a young woman.

AH: Addictive images?

LMF: That's right. But it is a completely different "reaching in to"— what Rilke says at one point—"what has not yet been said." Rilke once said, "I am proud of listening to what has not yet been said." And that is the job, really, that is the profession, that is the vocation. That becomes the invocation of the poet, to bring forth the unsaid. That to bring forth the unsaid and unsayable.

AH: The poet does that on the behalf of everyone. To keep alive the mysterious creativity of the poet, poetic force, the holy force, the poetic spirit, is constantly evolving forms to release us from the agendas that keep us captive.

LMF: The poet is the one who digs the new water well, goes to the source, and finds incredible treasures, because the body of language itself is actually infinite, and there's so much wealth in there. That is the wealth of the soul, and it is bestowed freely by the soul if a person is willing to take this wealth. Most of the time it means you have to separate from a well-established community, or I would rather call it a pseudocommunity, where categories have been established, ways of doing things normal and regular. Someone who offends the norm is either a rebel or is weird. The norm goes after these people. A poet usually goes through a long period of solitude; Hesse has a number of poems on that. It is something that, over the long run, though, gives you a very rich harvest. But initially you don't get invited to the next party. You are the person who is all by himself or all by herself.

Interview with Ludwig Max Fischer

Let me quote Hesse a little bit here, because this book, *Seasons of the Soul,* I didn't want it to be just a poetry book. I wanted a book that really offers food, nourishment for the soul, for the person. I brought in some quotes from Hesse's prose. Like in the second chapter of the book, which is entitled "To Imagine Is to Inspire," he says, "Today I am more aware than ever that I stand alone in my role as a dreamer. I am conscious of this fact, and I see it not only as a curse, but an appointed office. I am neither a minister nor a therapist, and I act without authority or entitlement, but I strengthen each and every individual, to the extent that I am able to understand him, in those aspects which distinguish him from the norm, and I try to show him the meaning of his uniqueness."

AH: So beautiful that it's all about "the other" for Hesse. He goes deep into himself not to advertise the glorious riches of his own imagination, but to offer things to others with a simplicity and a tenderness that evokes what is most unique in them. And this is a dangerous activity! You remember that other quote in which he really does go to the heart of why great poets are so, so important, but also dangerous. Dangerous because, if the enterprise of poetry succeeds, it does create unique individuals. It does create people who cannot be tamed or disciplined into an adherence into mass psychosis. It would be wonderful if you could read that.

LMF: Hesse says:

> In the end all art, and especially poetry, has only raison d'être if it offers more than entertainment, and has a direct effect on life, provides solace, clarification, counsel, aid, and fortification in life's struggles, and helps overcome what is difficult in life. Great poets feel into the future with most sensitive antennas, and live out ahead of us, a piece of future development, a yet unrealized potential. Poets and philosophers, if they do not sell out to please, but have the courage to be themselves, represent the most precious

145

and dangerous models a culture can have. They don't supply a ready-made set of duties and doctrines to be followed, but they show and teach the opposite: the path to individuality and personal conscience.

AH: Magnificent! You know, this year is going to be the fiftieth anniversary of his death.

LMF: August 9, 2012.

AH: Right. And one of the things that we're so hoping is that there can be and must be a Hesse renaissance. And I believe this book is going to play an enormous part in that renaissance. But in that quotation there is a very, very important phrase for me—and I know for you—which is that great poets have the sensitive, clairvoyant antennas to see into the future and to live out a part of the future. And this is certainly true of Hesse, because he lived out, in the very deepest sense, the East/West adventure that has proved such an important and fertile and fecund ground for our own evolution. I was born in India and my whole life has been dedicated to creating, in my work and in the way I teach, a bridge between East and West. And I know this is true for hundreds of thousands of philosophers and seekers all over the world. How do you see Hesse's East/West adventure as providing great guidance for us now as we continue with this crucial dialogue that may well contain the secret of the future? Because what is being brought together in this dialogue is the deepest knowledge in Western traditions of the sacred importance of the individual, with the profoundest knowledge of the Eastern traditions of the divine identity of the Atman, which is always one with Brahman of the nondual consciousness. How do you see this marriage happening in Hesse and how do you see his particularly wise and gracious way of going through and undergoing this dialogue? What do you see this way has to teach us?

LMF: Well, Hesse grew up in Wilhelmine, Germany, and that was when Germans had their ideas of world rulership. It looks like every European nation had its own turn.

AH: And now it's America's turn, yes?

LMF: He was aware very early that, particularly the successful domination fantasies, at the end they would collapse and cause more damage than the initial benefits. But in this whole devaluation and secularization process in the nineteenth century, when basically the next ideology was science and technology, and "we will be able to defeat nature," "the Divine is useless and unreliable anyway." I think people already in the 1890s, the 1900s, at that turn toward modernity, had a sense that the traditional churches really are not offering the anchor anymore.

AH: Right. Or the inspiration. And Nietzsche had really started this in German thought. It had to do with a huge German ferocity.

LMF: The church was another establishment with its own palaces, with its own hierarchies, where you could ascend if you obeyed. But the actual original inspiration was in many ways traded against power and privilege. What happens in sensitive souls, particularly in poets, but in other artists as well, is that they search somewhere else. There were already around 1900 two big movements. One was "let's go into nature again." Hesse was very much a part of that, when he went to Monte Verita and joined the people. There was this "we have moved away from something," where actually the escape in itself does not lead us to somewhere that is fruitful. The other one was an awareness of other religions.

AH: This had come quite early in German literature because in the nineteenth century you had these very great beings like Schelling and Hegel who had been very deeply influenced by the Upanishads. Schopenhauer's whole philosophy had been transformed by his plunging into the depths of both Buddhism and Hinduism. And even Nietzsche had read a lot of the Hindu philosophers and Goethe himself was very excited by Sufism, so there was a preparation for the moment when people like Hesse would really plunge into a deep exploration of the East and a kind of philosophy that could sustain human life.

LMF: He had access to excellent translations of those texts and we have those great German Indologists like Max Müller ...

AH: Who was a professor at my old college at Oxford! I had his room for a while!

LMF: With the catastrophe of World War 1 with the hierarchy of the aristocracy falling, there was a real, deep crisis of Western values. I think it was natural for people to say, "Couldn't there be somewhere else? A new anchor?" Which actually turned out to be an ancient anchor for people who want to replace or find other ways of living a meaningful life.

AH: Hesse went to India, Hesse went to Ceylon, Hesse plunged into the Indian classics, Hesse plunged into the Chinese classics, but one of the things that has emerged in our conversations about him is Hesse's plunging into Eastern philosophy did not mean his abandonment of Western literature or the tradition of his own world. And I think you and I agree that shows a very deep maturity, and also a very important guidance for us in our time, because we have seen in so many ways, both the benefits of the Eastern traditions to us, but we have lived through the catastrophic follies of the corruption of the guru system, the follies of imitating too deeply the Eastern systems, and jettisoning too completely the wisdom of the Western. The Dalai Lama always says, and he says it again and again, "don't forget your own traditions in your passion for Buddhism! Use whatever you can in your understanding of Buddhism to deepen your experience of your own tradition so each of the different traditions can come into their maturity and each play a different part in this redemption of the global soul that now has to take place for the transformation of the world." Hesse's a great guide in that, isn't he?

LMF: He understood you cannot cut off your own roots and replace them and craft a completely different worldview that has grown over many centuries. You know, Gandhi at one point said, "In my house of spirituality, I have the windows wide open, and so the winds of all different directions can blow in. But I make sure none can blow me out of my house."

AH: And Gandhi is such a good example on the other side, because Gandhi married the deepest Indian wisdom with the prophetic passion of the Gospel. He was profoundly influenced by Tolstoy, he was deeply, deeply moved by Jesus, and in his own philosophy he fused together the peace of the East with the social transformation at the core of the Western ministry tradition. And Hesse did exactly the same thing!

LMF: That was one of the big problems in the 1960s and 1970s. There was a quick, naive, and in some ways, arrogant adoption of, "well tomorrow I think I'll be a Jew, but maybe next week I'll take another workshop and I'll be a Tibetan Buddhist. But then I have this other friend who said go this third workshop and ... I'm a Sufi now, did you know that?" It's like you ask, "what are you today," you know? Are you still the same religion? But in other ways there was a sweetness to this naivety, because it was another time when something had to break open.

AH: It was sweetness but it was also tremendous danger because many of us, and I include myself, bought the Eastern idea of the guru hook, line, and sinker, which came to a tragic end, because of all these exploding Buddhist scandals.

LMF: Instead of looking at what was missing in our world, and looking at how did we get so far into hedonism, how did we get this idea that the world is here to please us? Let's look at what the people are really teaching us, the exotic imports. They were all focusing on devotion, and devotion—dedication—was at a very low level in the Western societies. The other thing they were offering was discipline.

AH: Spiritual discipline, my God, yes!

LMF: People were doing their evening prayers for a long time, they were doing all of this prostration and all these practices regularly.

AH: And this was a valuable discipline, wasn't it?

LMF: Yes, but what about looking at where you came from? What are you doing with a tradition that has been in your culture for maybe a thousand or more years? You cannot just throw it out!

AH: If you do throw it out, you forbid the real marriage that is trying to take place in our time which is between the Eastern vision of divine identity, this extraordinary understanding of the innate nonduality in our self-consciousness, with the Western evolution of the notion of the individual and of the necessity of putting justice and compassion into action! The shadow of the East has been its passivity and its acceptance of many terrible injustices in a world that it calls illusion. The shadow of the West, of course, is that it is being driven by the ego rather than by the divine person. But if you bring the best of the West together with the best of the East, then you have the potential creation of a divine human being that draws on the full strength of divine identity, but also focuses it through a mature individuality.

LMF: Hesse came back in 1911 from India essentially saying, "this was a humbling experience." He looked at the social and political situation there, and he also realized his own limitations. But realizing his own limitations in this world didn't make him stop exploring it or throw it out. But you have to stand on two legs and you have to be at home in your tradition while an integration and a meeting between whatever it is at a certain time, exotic or dismissed or devalued, happens. And I think it is a very similar situation today with Islam and the Western world and the Christian world. In Islam, "they live in our shadow," there is a tremendous amount of devotion.

AH: And courage! And focus! And deep faith! All the things we lack so terrifyingly.

LMF: To be at home in the world that you came from, to open abandoning or condemning your own world, that is where the meeting happens. Actually, I want to give you one more quote here about the poet. Hesse says, a poet is an explorer, a visionary, imagining what convention censors. Because convention always tells you, if you believe these things that these other people from this other terrible religion tell you, you will be a traitor and we will persecute you, or we will actually expel you. You're not a part of us anymore. But Hesse says, "A poet is a messenger between the familiar and the unknown, as if he were at home in both places." It is that being at home in both places.

AH: And slowly growing a universal soul.

LMF: You don't have to throw out where you came from because we have beautiful saints in Christianity, we have beautiful mystics. I wouldn't even want to start mentioning them. It is a long list!

AH: Could you read that beautiful poem Hesse wrote to the ancient Buddha? The wonderful poem in which he describes—like no other

Western poet has ever described—the true depth of Eastern wisdom and what it can offer us.

LMF: "An Ancient Buddha Decaying in a Japanese Forest Ravine"
> *Long rain and cold nights of frost*
> *unveil your shape, soft and worn away.*
> *Covered with moss, your face still shines serene.*
> *Your half-closed eyes still reveal*
> *your calm focus on eternity,*
> *your tranquil yes to the changing over*
> *into the formless void of the unlimited.*
> *The slowly withering features of your face*
> *still speak of your noble mission,*
> *but dampness, mud, and soil*
> *are finishing the fate of form, completing its purpose.*
> *Tomorrow, you will be root and rustling leaf.*
> *Tomorrow, you will turn into water mirroring clear sky.*
> *You will curl as ivy, grow as fern and algae,*
> *become symbol of all transformations,*
> *and show the eternal oneness behind all change.*

AH: "The eternal oneness behind all change." That is the great gift of the East to us. Because you can only make effective and truthful and transforming change, which we need to do on every level, if you also paradoxically know, and feel, and are grounded in the oneness behind all change.

LMF: For me, every person is that decaying figure in the forest, in nature. And so when you meditate, you look at how time works on you. At one point everyone has the opportunity to reach a point of stillness inside, where the war against time, which rules our society today, becomes ridiculous and really is palpable and is an illusion.

AH: And the war against death! You remember the great poem, "Ich bin ein Freund und komme nicht zu strafen" and that says "I am your friend and don't come to punish." Death and time are actually friends, because they are cocreators of a masterpiece.

LMF: Those phases assure progressions and not necessarily our ideas of progress, because that is basically what we traded in the West, instead of going with the progressions as they happen and as they inform us and as they outform us.

AH: What is so important about Hesse's work and why it's so essential for us now, is that I think there's a second wave for a profound hunger for the soul beginning. We had the first wave in the 1960s and that played itself out in the 1980s and 1990s and the whole New Age movement. But I think many of us are now feeling that that initial stage, that first wave, was very naive. It was not disciplined enough, not focused enough, didn't go deep enough, and didn't have enough passions for the higher transformation of society. It was a kind of narcissism, another narcissism, not a healing of narcissism. And one of the things that strikes me so much about Hesse's poetry, especially his spiritual poetry, is how deeply grounded and sober and realistic it is. Realistic about the suffering that the path entails, realistic about the failures that you will have and continue to have on the path, and realistic too about the loneliness the path can lead to and the sense of bewilderment and estrangement. And realistic too about the responsibilities that evolution places upon the seeker. Not just of his own or her own joy and bliss but putting that into action. So one of the ways I think Hesse guides us into this second wave, just as he came into this first wave to open up the wonders of Buddhism and Hinduism and this potential union. Now when we're maturer and really hungry for an authentic spirituality, which we desperately need to be able to deal with the chaotic crisis that is exploding everywhere around us, Hesse's poetry is coming to us in which you can truly hear this note of acute, humane, sober, no-nonsense realism, which is the key to the transformations ahead.

How do you feel this? How do you relate this peculiar note in Hesse?

LMF: The rebellion against the norm was a necessity in the 1960s with the Cold War, we tried to eliminate an "evil system." This kind of thinking had to be replaced with something else, because this worldview was just not satisfying.

AH: Well, it was corrupt and destructive.

LMF: It turned out, actually, that to reach a mature spirituality, you pay a price. Pretty much every novel that Hesse ever wrote shows you that it will not be free. Stages are following stages, are very difficult. And many people escape into another illusion of the free ride, which all the addictions provide: alcohol will make it go away, some drug (whether legal or illegal) will make it go away. "I will not have to go through the growing pains to get to the mature personality." In a way Hesse possibly played less of a role in the 1980s and 1990s and in the first decade of the twenty-first century, because that was a time when political ideologies promised that you will not have to pay a price, that it will be easier.

AH: Well it's not just that, it's when New Age spirituality became ascendant and when New Age spirituality was just a masterpiece of tragic narcissism, saying "you can have it all, you can be it all. You can be thin, rich, fabulous, and enlightened very, very quickly simply by deciding to be so."

LMF: But Hesse, as we said earlier, said "your branches will be hacked a hundred times." But then you will grow new leaves on these branches.

AH: Yes! That's the ancient wisdom of both the West and East! It's the wisdom of Rumi and it's the wisdom of Lao Tzu and it's the wisdom of Goethe and it's the wisdom of life!

LMF: And that takes a lifetime. And you will not get it at eighteen or at twenty-four.

AH: I don't think you ever get it, do you? I think you're always grasping for it. One of the things I've noticed from the great beings that I am privileged to be close to—the likes of Father Bede Griffiths—is that on their death beds, the death beds of these great masters, part of me was expecting them to sit in the lotus position, just serenely floating through death, so I was shocked to see that they were really struggling with death. In their teachings they would constantly pray, constantly going deeper, constantly opening up. Older men should search for a deeper intensity. Could we look at the poem that we chose for this section? That extraordinary poem, which you wanted to read here to really express this vision of the soul that Hesse has.

LMF: This poem is called "Confession."

AH: I'm glad you chose this one, because you could have chosen a more airy poem, but this is the real thing.

LMF: "Confession."
> *The games of glamor and glitter*
> *I have played with gusto.*
> *Let others have goals and ambitions,*
> *for me, living is enough.*
>
> *Whatever has moved me*
> *has all become a symbol.*
> *I always feel the power of this moment,*
> *the presence of boundless oneness in my life.*
>
> *To make my life inspired and abundant*
> *I read in life's open book of symbols*
> *because now I have that depth within me.*
> *My eternal, changeless essence is at peace.*

AH: "My eternal, changeless essence is at peace." But what's so moving about the poem—and it's called "Confession"—is that that cannot be arrived at until you've played out all the illusionary aspects of your nature. You have to live, sometimes very darkly and difficultly, to be able to understand the nature of illusionary.

LMF: It doesn't mean your body has no pains. It doesn't mean you haven't lost people that were very close to you and very precious to you. But that journey toward the center is a long journey, and it isn't a journey that is filled with solutions, but it's filled with trials and tribulations. But the trials and tribulations are the waves on the water. Those are the storms, but the ground underneath is something that you have come in contact with, and you don't come in contact with it by hurrying, by amassing or accumulating or fulfilling desire, because in these fulfillments of desire you forget what you need and who needs you. Only through these stages of moving beyond what you desire, as Hesse says in another poem, the poem "Happiness," do you realize what life is wanting from you. Another line in one of these poems in *Seasons of the Soul* is Hesse's short, three-word line that says, "trust your life."

AH: Don't force your life, don't shape your life, don't project some fantasy life onto the Divine and expect them to give it to you. Trust them.

LMF: Once you get what you want, there is only one thing for certain: that you want more. And once you get more of the more that you want, there is only one thing certain: you want more.

AH: Oscar Wilde said, "If you want to punish somebody, give them exactly what they want." Because whatever you want from a consciousness that isn't awake is actually going to trap you forever. You want fame, you get fame, and then you find out that fame is a horror. So you want money, you get money, then you find out that everybody's jealous of you, so you want beauty! Then you find out that beauty has a tragic edge, or that all the things that the ego wants actually involve the ego in disastrous dramas, and play themselves out, and end in terrible disillusionment and death.

LMF: And the goal is fulfillment, but the glass you are trying to fill becomes bigger and bigger and there's more space you need to fill. *Satisfaction* in Latin *[satisfactio]* is that something is enough *[satis]*. That is something we don't have anymore. We have no notion of sufficiency.

AH: I was sitting in my log cabin the other day listening to Bach, listening to "Ich habe genug," "I have enough," sung by Matthias Goerne, and an overwhelming wave of peace swept over me and I understood how the old, ancient, spiritual culture of Europe was rooted and its vision of contentment, and how tragic our loss of this spacious peace has been, and how deeply now we need it as we begin to face the biggest storm in history. You cannot begin to face this storm with a hysterical reaction to it. The only way you can hope to stand strong in this storm is the place of essence, the place of peace, the place of trusting your life beyond any kind of reason.

LMF: The big confusion, or the big temptation, is that we confuse contentment with complacency. At the very end of that poem, "Stages," he addresses the stages precisely.

AH: Well we're going to get to "Stages," but one of the things that is very clear from everything we've been saying and is very, very important, is that Hesse's vision was founded, not only in a very profound love of the Spirit, and not only in a very high dedication to the calling of the poet, but it was founded in a very dry-eyed analysis of modernity. Because he understood, at a level that I think only Rilke understood so deeply, that modernity was tragic and was destined to self-destruct, and all the technological progress that his own family was celebrating with such exuberance, was actually tragic and would end in the devastation of the planet. And now in 2012 we see that all of our technological advances have only created a vast, stinking, ash pit of a wasteland, Hesse's very sober voice is more important than ever, isn't it?

LMF: There are these magic words like "faster," "more," "easy." Since there are so many time-saving devices that everybody has. People today talk about when their computer is slow, how they have to wait for information maybe three seconds instead of half a second, they get irritated because their computer is "so slow." But with all this saved time, there should be a huge bank of "saved time"somewhere and everybody should have more time.

AH: But nobody has time because our lives have sped up unbelievably, we're multitasking, people are like hamsters on a wheel!

LMF: It's a totally silly spiral. There is a book about frenetic stagnation by Paul Virilio, *Speed and Politics*.

AH: Frenetic stagnation. But it is not just silly, I actually think it is one of the real disasters of our time because the only way in which profound spiritual discovery can happen is from stillness, silence, peace, and leisure for the soul.

LMF: Then the managers of today, after their first heart attack, after the increased activity and being incredibly productive and getting more done, they go on the pilgrimage of Santiago de Compostela. Or they go to a Buddhist meditation center, and it takes them an hour to walk around the circle in very slow, deliberate steps. So why not in the beginning bring natural movement back into the way we operate in this world. Why do we have to get there first and do an incredible amount of damage in order to dramatically slow down? People speed up and I think that has to do with a very amazing illusion that eventually—just like science has the illusion—that we can eliminate the unknown. There is a kind of attitude, we haven't used enough thinking, enough research. "There is still this terrible, evil virus, but we will catch it. Then we will find a way so it will never mutate." This fantasy of eliminating is like a chain around all causalities. We have banned anything that is sacred and divine in our lives. That horrible, horrible nature that does with us anything it wants and gives birth any time it wants to give birth, it should be finally controlled.

AH: Underneath this speed is a devastating panic. What I see in the eyes of almost everyone as I travel the world is panic. Extreme panic. And people speed up their lives, do more and more, as a way of assuaging this deep dread, this hysteria of what's happening, this terror of death, this terror of the world disintegrating. And, of course, that only creates more disintegration and destruction and doesn't heal anything.

LMF: Because really it is driven by this idea that at one point, I move so fast and I get so much done that I have sort of have it all.

AH: You are maybe six feet ahead of death, six feet ahead of the destruction. Or that in some way you'll have done so much that you'll have earned God's grace and that you'll be protected, you'll be safe, you'll be a good person.

LMF: Whatever threatening monster comes into my life, I just push the delete button.

AH: Right. You could just cyberattack your own demons.

LMF: It will vanish.

AH: It's very scary, very frightening, and very sad.

LMF: Then the countermovement, which was very necessary, is still very necessary, is very useful in terms of people going on retreats and people doing meditation practices. But eventually the natural course of life needs to become a continuous interaction and move between the *vita contemplativa* and the *vita activa*.

AH: It's like in music, you know. When you're talking, I had this vision inside of being at a great concert in the music with Ravi Shankar. And this wonderful, plump woman came and sat down first. And she was just plucking one string continuously. And then the *tabla* can do whatever it wants and the *sitar* can do whatever it wants, but it's held together in the embrace of the steady pulse of attention and of peace. So you're uniting, so being peaceful doesn't mean that you don't act, that you don't create. But that those actions and creativity spring from a fountain of deep, peaceful strength. And that's the key to everything.

LMF: You're aware and you're in the presence of the ground tone that carries it. You move your little boat with great effort, maybe, at certain times, but you still know that you're on the river. That the main current is the river, and it will reach the ocean, and it will dissolve in the ocean. And it doesn't help if you stand at the banks and you do research on water by getting a fish out and cutting it up, which is modern science. It's all a process of separation. And you take the water out and you analyze it.... No, you have to get wet and you have to swim or you have to get in your boat and then not fight the current, but swim with the current. And there's still plenty for you to do! In the story of Tristan and Isolde, Tristan at one point is in the boat without oars and is then carried to the right place.

AH: Yes! In fact, only then can he be carried to the right place. That's the paradox.

LMF: Which is a beautiful metaphor, but it doesn't mean that he didn't have to do a lot of work beforehand. And it doesn't mean that he doesn't get out of that boat, and that the next challenge will not be waiting for him.

AH: It is one of the experiences that's most difficult for oneself and also most difficult to teach, is the necessity of surrender. Surrender is not actually weakness or passivity, but it is the strongest thing you ever do and it requires infinite amounts of inner experience and profound spiritual discipline before you can truly, with trust and with faith, say to life, "I trust you, I love you, I give myself to you, I rely on you, I rest in you, and I know that whatever happens, something far deeper, wiser, more intelligent than myself is going to carry me home." And that is the only way to live a truly open life and that is the only way to live in a time like this. And I wondered if you'd like to read the poem we chose for this particular section.

LMF: We are again at "trust your life." As the Arabs would say, "And tie up your camel." Actually they would say "Trust God and tie up your camel." In the year 2012 I would say, "trust your life and get off-line!"

AH: You are speaking to the converted.

LMF: "Devotion."

AH: I love this poem.

LMF:

> *What people desire so furiously*
> *leads to battle, blood, and guilt.*
> *Once you find your home in nature,*
> *the earth becomes your holy home*
> *and every person is your kin.*

Everywhere throughout this world
winds blow and water falls
and blue skies and precious jewels
greet you from everywhere.

My treasures are the golden clouds at dusk,
the soft gleam of the rising moon,
birds calling and the cries of creatures in the woods,
birch trees, long sandy beaches,
rolling hills, and mountain paths.

These are my heart's possessions,
the comforts of my soul, in which it safely rests.

Don't pit one fault against another,
just gauge yourself in every step
by the timeless, patient laws of nature.
It is she who carries you through life.
May she be your real home.

Then every morning and evening
will find you safely sheltered
in your father's house.

AH: This guides us so beautifully into the next part of our conversation, which is about Hesse's deep, abiding love of nature. We have talked a great deal about the catastrophe we are in, about the appalling world crisis, about the craziness of our culture, but one of the reasons Hesse is so important to us is that he is really giving us deep guidance toward the sources of health that can heal us and strengthen us. And the deepest and richest of these is nature. How do you experience Hesse's vision of nature and how does it feed you and what do you believe we need to establish in our new relationship with nature, which is really a revival of an ancient bond.

LMF: The idea we should somehow rise above nature is the first thing we need to sacrifice. Then it is really trusting our senses again. At this moment in our times we are doing a lot of interacting with substitutes. Jerry Mander said, "television is sensory deprivation." Instead of getting information through immediate and direct perception, where all our senses are involved, like when we do gardening or when a painter looks at a tree for a very long time.

AH: Or walking through a field and smelling the rain and the mud! And seeing the cows and watching the birds fly.

LMF: We have a kind of sensory poverty, perceptional poverty. We are completely in denial about it, because that pseudo-richness, which is really no richness at all, what a screen can give us, what is far away is seemingly close. The word *television* in German is *Fernsehen*. *Fern* is the word for *far* and *sehen* is the word for *see*. So you see something and you hear it a little bit too, even though the frequency that comes over the loudspeakers gives only a fraction of the frequency that a human voice gives. But this idea that there is more that comes to me from far away. That is actually taking huge possibilities and potentials away that my senses could give me in the moment, when I plant something, whatever it might be: carrots, or vegetables, or herbs, when I tend my garden, or when I walk through the woods.

Even the way we deal with nature in sports today. There are huge amounts of equipment necessary and very specific kinds of equipment. It is not possible that you just walk along a river on a path. No, you have to make it into a competition. You have to have a very special, incredibly expensive bicycle or all kinds of other equipment. Then, the most important thing is that you are the winner of this race. But you actually miss all this when you have a speedboat and you jet across the lake. Maybe you are the fastest one, but you need to maybe row, and let the boat stop in the middle of the lake. Then the fish will come close and the birds will come close, and you will hear again the symphony of nature. It will carry your senses to a bliss.

The success of being crowned, being the king of a specific competition, is ridiculous, because it only lasts a very short time. And it is extremely exclusive, because everybody else is the loser. Sometimes you have a hundred thousand people or whatever, competing in the various races, until you become the regional, the national, the international, and then you are the world champion, and the rest feel "well, I didn't make it." What does that leave all the ones who didn't make it?

AH: It is even more serious even than that, because as long as we are in this hectic, mad, desire to dominate nature, we're also in the death machine that is on the verge of destroying nature and on the verge of complete matricide. Slowing down, savoring, realizing that we *are* nature, that we are one with nature, is not something only that will heal us, but also potentially something that will save us, because it will suddenly wake us up to where we are in a divine world, in a creative masterpiece, in an endlessly unfolding symphony of love and tenderness and power and wisdom! And that will breed in us a sacred passion to protect the Mother instead of ravaging and raping and destroying Her. Unless we really listen to the words of the great mystics and philosophers and the great poets like Hesse, who really speak of this salvific power of nature, unless we not only listen to but experience this, we are going to commit mass suicide. I think Hesse understood this very deeply, because Hesse was living in a time when the first wave of romantic poets had already screamed with outrage against what was being done to nature in the name of industrial progress. He had seen Europe and the United States go on a long, brutal orgy of the beginnings of capitalism. Now we're living at the end of the capitalist orgy, seeing what it has actually created and now, more than ever, we need to listen. To listen to the shamanic traditions, to listen to the great nature poets like Wordsworth, to listen to Hesse. Let's read the poem you chose for this particular section.

LMF: I want to bring one more aspect in here: we have created an artificial kind of notion of success and therefore happiness. I would love to read this poem, "Happiness," because it illustrates this competitive, "there will be one winner" idea, and "eventually one of us could be this winner." And we sacrifice all peace and all natural progressions for this illusion, which is, of course, reserved for very few, and essentially only for one, who reigns then as a pseudo-king for that particular skill that everybody else tears their body apart for and is really in constant stress and poverty. And Hesse offers a different kind of idea of happiness, which I would like to introduce.

Happiness

As long as you chase happiness,
You are not ready to be happy,
even if you own everything.

As long as you lament a loss,
run after prizes in restless races,
you have not yet known peace.

But when you have moved beyond desire,
become a stranger to your goals and longings,
and call no longer Happiness by name,

then your heart rises calmly
above the ebb and flow of action
and peace has reached your soul.

So we are not pursuing happiness actually. We're pursued by happiness, and by a notion that is so self-condemning, with the exception of these few moments when we have defeated somebody else.

AH: So tragic, when happiness is actually lying in wait in every moment for you and every situation even.

LMF: It makes most games into brutal elimination rituals. There is team playing against another and they play great, and at the end one is one point or goal ahead of the other, and the other team is going home with nothing except being losers.

AH: It is tragic, and it actually is against the deep, healing rhythms of nature.

LMF: That's right.

AH: So read us the next poem.

LMF: "Autumn Takes Hold of My Life."

AH: I love this poem. This is such a wise poem.

LMF:
Autumn rain has drenched the great forest.
A brisk morning breeze blows through the valley.
The chestnuts crack hard, tumbling from the trees.
They burst open, moist, brown, as if full of joy.

Autumn takes hold of my life.
Gales split and tear my leaves.
My branches are shaking—did I bear fruit?

My flowers of love bear the fruit of suffering;
My flowers of faith bear the fruit of hate.
The wind rattles my brittle branches, but I laugh.
I still stand strong in the storm.

What do I care about bearing fruit, about achieving goals?
I blossomed and flowers were my purpose.
Now I am wilting and nothing but wilting is my aim.
Hearts don't beat for distant goals.

God lives in me, God dies in me,
God suffers in my soul: that is enough purpose.

Right or wrong, flower or fruit,
nothing but names, it is all the same.

A brisk morning breeze blows through the valley.
The chestnuts crack hard, tumbling from the trees.
They burst open, I too break open, burnished with joy.

AH: "I too break open, burnished with joy!" And yet he has described so much difficulty and suffering but he is still accepting wilting, which is part of nature! So from nature you can learn both how to blossom and how to accept winter, how to accept lying fallow, how to accept all the periods of what seem so boring, so unproductive, because they are actually preparing whole new levels of creativity.

We are coming to a close in our conversation, and I think everything that we've said really focuses on one essential theme in Hesse. This perhaps is the abiding theme. and that theme is grounded in the question: How do we become the deepest, most mature, most creative, and most useful kind of individual? How do we become someone who is so grounded in the truth of life that we become an instrument of life's most holy purpose? From my point of view, this is what I call *Sacred Activism,* because I believe that at this moment in the history of the planet we can only move forward if we fuse together the deeper spiritual awareness with wise, compassionate, clear, just, radical action on every level. Because mysticism alone isn't going to do it and activism alone isn't going to do it, but there is a deep truth in both that can be united and can create in each of us the deep, rich, mature individual that can then act from that wealth of inner awakening to help and serve and transform the world. How do you see Hesse's poetry as helping us in this tremendous adventure? Because I know this is very sacred to you, and I know that you feel that he has an enormous role to play in helping us shape ourselves to become these gentle warriors of loving action.

LMF: Hesse, in his indirect way of teaching, without preaching, without any kind of missionary purpose, and he was very aware of what missionaries can do in order to save a soul toward the right way.

AH: As a poet. As a loving mother of the soul, not a dictator, yes.

LMF: At one point he is giving an invitation. An invitation toward letting go of the "how" and of the "why."

AH: What do you mean?

LMF: We simply pay attention to "who" and "what" is in front of us. That gives us the "because." That is the gift and that which asks something from us. When we are in the presence of authentic and natural interaction with real people, interaction with what is happening in nature, at a particular season in our life, we will be at rest. We don't have to send a thousand emails. There is another kind of continuous flow of messages calling us, inviting us. If we respond in a loving, patient way, with patient loving, then that current of life does not need our direction. It does not need to be put on the right path or the right course.

AH: It is already everything.

LMF: It is! Giving us a gift, our own presence. Then we can live with a kind of being involved, that means turning with it, without resisting any particular turn or progression, which are just different kinds of invitations. That is why at the end of one of his poems, he has these profound lines that "the call of life toward us will never end." And it certainly will not end when our heart stops beating physically, and that is much more than a liberation, because it is not another overcoming.

AH: You are not being liberated from anything. You are being liberated into something that is endlessly unfolding and will always protect you and hold you and nourish you and sustain you, yes.

LMF: That is right. And it doesn't mean replacing one fantasy with another one, with a better one.

AH: It doesn't have to because it recognizes the call of existence is love and peace and immeasurable intelligence that is guiding everything, that is the Tao. It is fundamentally a very Chinese position, I always think of Hesse as a Chinese poet writing in German, because he has this tremendous faith.

LMF: He was very influenced by Richard Wilhelm, a great German Sinologist. He did read and study the classics, whether it is the Tao Te Ching or the I Ching.

AH: And the *Secret of the Golden Flower* played a huge role in his evolution, as it did in Jung's!

LMF: You go with the Tao, you do not fight it. If you fight it ...

AH: You will lose.

LMF: You will not even be a loser, because the presence ...

AH: Will help you out, will guide you when you need to become more sane. Let's end with this wonderful poem, "Stages."

LMF: "Stages." It is one of my favorite poems of all poets.
All blossoms will wilt,
each youth, fold to the mold of age.
Wisdom and virtue never last forever.
Your heart must always be ready to leave
and ready to begin again,
must form new bonds,
with courage and without regret.
Every beginning offers a magic power
that protects us and helps us to endure.

This journey through the realms of life
was not meant to end in one home only.
World spirit does not want to tie us down,
wants us to soar into the open.
When we stay too long in one place,
get stuck in norm and habit, we wear out.

Only embarking on new, unknown journeys
can free us from the prison of stagnation.

Maybe the moment of our death too
is just another gate to new dimensions.
The call of life to us will never end.
Well then, my heart, take leave and heal.

AH: Max, thank you so, so much. It was a great, great joy. I'm so glad we could do this.

LMF: My pleasure. And we thank Hermann Hesse.

Foreword to *Black Sun: The Collected Poems of Lewis Thompson*, edited by Richard Lannoy

It has been an insistent dream—even mission—of mine to help to get Lewis Thompson's profound and passionate poems into print ever since I read them, in Richard Lannoy's exemplary typescript edition, over twenty years ago. I consider Lewis Thompson to be one of the most original, brave, brilliant, and prescient of the pioneers of our contemporary mystical renaissance; his life and work exemplify what he called the "rarity of complete risk": his courage both as a person and as a writer; his acumen; the pure, fierce rigor of his spiritual intellect; and his iconoclastic honesty in the pursuit of illumination have been a constant source of inspiration and challenge to me. For twenty years, Lewis Thompson has been my heart-companion and soul-friend, a touchstone of the kind of integrity and astringent refinement of spirit anyone who dares to write about the mysteries of the inner life has to pursue and honor. I salute Hohm Press for their willingness to make this poetic opus available at last, fifty-two years after his tragic death from sunstroke in Benares in 1949. And, with all my heart, I thank Richard Lannoy for his unwavering loyalty to the cause of getting Lewis Thompson into print, and for the wise and patient ways in which he has followed it.

The first work of Thompson's I read was not his poems but his prose masterpiece *The Mirror to the Light*—a linked collection of brilliant aphorisms and short meditations on the authentic mystical life, edited by Richard Lannoy (who discovered the manuscript stashed in two shoe boxes). I was still, at twenty-nine, a fellow of All Souls; Richard had just read my *Journey in Ladakh* and knew instinctively that I would feel a kinship with Thompson's work. I can still remember the ecstatic, visceral excitement I felt when reading *Mirror:* Thompson's seared and searing directness, ferocious clarity, and unmistakable authority of lived experience shook me to my core, as did the poetic originality of his style, which seemed to fuse the gorgeous precision of the seventeenth-century masters of religious prose like John Donne and Sir Thomas Browne, the incendiary brilliance of Rimbaud's *Illuminations,* and the laconic compacted intensity of the Hindu and Buddhist mystics. I realized that I was in the presence of a true spiritual adept and adventurer of the soul with a God-given gift for the description of the highest spiritual states and the all-transforming, subtle self-discoveries that arise from them, and of someone whose bringing together of the richest and most sophisticated Western aesthetic standards with the mystical wisdom-seeking of the East offered me a galvanizing sign of what I wanted to achieve in my own writing. After finishing *Mirror to the Light,* I rang up Richard Lannoy in a daze of gratitude for having rescued and presented such an original writer; a few weeks later, on a fragrant midsummer evening, Richard and I dined together at my college and began a friendship that has become one of the delights of my life.

Two years later, when I was living in Paris, I had the joy of meeting someone who had actually known Lewis Thompson in Benares, Deben Bhattacharya, the translator and musicologue who had collaborated with Thompson on a set of translations of the Bengali *bhaki* mystic Chandidas. Deben is a man of luminous, great-hearted charm. Whenever he spoke of the Lewis he had known well as a young man forty years before, his face would shine and his eyes glitter with tears. Once, walking though Montmartre, he turned to me and said softly, "I have met many brilliant people and some holy ones, but never anyone like Lewis. He was uniquely clear and terribly, even frighteningly, uncompromising and brave. I hope to live to see him recognized as the spiritual and artistic genius he was."

When I was thirty-four and living for the summer in New York, I traveled to a dingy suburb of Long Island to interview the English writer and poet Lawrence Durrell. Durrell was wild, drunk, and hilarious, and the afternoon passed in attacks on Freud, the British national character, T. S. Eliot, and the "pallid, good girl" singing of Renata Tebaldi. As I was preparing to return to New York, I suddenly remembered that Durrell had praised *Mirror to the Light* on its dust jacket, calling it "a book of the highest distinction, self-scrutiny pushed to the point of anguish and described in poetic aphorisms of great density and beauty." I asked Durrell if he had seen any of Thompson's poems and what he thought of them. He drew himself up to his full height: "I have read 'The Black Angel,'" he said, "and would give five years of my life to have written it. If Thompson wrote other poems as explosive and majestic as this one, he would rank amongst the greatest spiritual poets in English. And not just of this godforsaken century, either."

Now, with nearly a hundred of Lewis Thompson's poems presented here, with superbly insightful and accurate notes by Richard Lannoy that help illuminate the spiritual and mental world they were born from, the world can judge for itself. In *The Future Poetry,* his great prophetic invocation of a new divinely inspired art, Sri Aurobindo wrote: "The intimate and intuitive poetry of the future will have on the one side all the inexhaustible range and profound complexities of the cosmic imagination of which it will be the interpreter … and, on the other side, it will reach those bare and absolute simplicities of utter and essential sight in which thought sublimates into a translucidity of light and vision, feeling passes beyond itself into sheer spiritual ecstasy and the word rarefies into a pure voice out of the silence (250)."

Aurobindo might have been describing Lewis Thompson's poetry, its ecstasy and the still strange and startling freshness of its "pure voice," honed by years of the deepest inner experience and rigor.

Whether it is immediately recognized as such or not, the publication of *Black Sun* will undoubtedly be one of the main spiritual events of the early twenty-first century, one whose repercussions and magical influences will be felt for a very long time, especially among those seekers who aspire to be vessels or instruments of sacred creativity. These are poems of permanent value, works of the utmost spiritual grandeur and passion, diamantine crystallizations of the dazzling flux of mystical knowing and feeling, telegrams from absolute consciousness whose electric directness will never dim. In at least ten poems—"Black Angel," "Poison," "Gold," "The Mango Trees," "The Glass," "The Eternal Man," "The Heart of the World," "The Silence of the Heart," "The Double Lips," and "Golgotha"—Lewis Thompson achieves the rarest and most charged dynamic fusion of spiritual insight, linguistic clarity, and metaphysical density, and embodies those characteristics of authentic poetry that he described in *Mirror to the Light:* "Poetry is the dance of truth among limits and which it explodes. It is absolute Intensity, Act, Illumination; it is always the Word, as Alpha and Omega, the lightning flash in which all is timelessly created, revealed, absorbed." Each of Lewis Thompson's finest poems is like the sound of a temple bell or gong, which he described in *Mirror to the Light* as "so denuded and luminous a shell of sound it continues indefinitely in the mind; you must listen again and again before you can believe it has really stopped."

I dedicate this foreword to my beloved friend, the wise poet

Dorothy Walters, who knows what Lewis Thompson means by "the singing light," and, like him, knows how to sing in unison with it.

Foreword to *Unmasking the Rose,* by Dorothy Walters

Near the end of *Unmasking the Rose,* her extraordinarily clear, poignant, and magisterially written memoir of her kundalini awakening, Dorothy Walters writes, "Our world today is at once a theater of disaster and a stage for universal transfiguration. We are at once Christ hanging on the cross and the splendor of the reawakened self." A few lines later, trying to sum up her whole journey, Dorothy writes, "I realized that mine was not merely a private experience but part of a larger process of planetary awakening, of bringing the body and spirit into alignment with divine love unlike anything humanity has previously known. This, I sensed, was the moment in history we had awaited so long. I felt deeply privileged to be a participant in this difficult but immensely significant process of human transfiguration."

In her characteristically humble but direct way, Dorothy Walters is pointing both to the inner meaning of the apocalypse we are living through and to the possible outcome of its agonies. Our world crisis is at once a horrible and protracted death of all ancient institutions and ways of thinking and a potential birth, on a massive and unprecedented scale, of a new humanity, divinely conscious and divinely inspired, whose creativity and sacred passion could transfigure everything we now understand abut human life.

Dorothy Walters knows that this "birth" is by no means certain: the forces of darkness and ignorance ranged against it are immense and immensely powerful and will not be beaten back or transformed except by an unprecedented effort of will, love, and surrender to divine wisdom and force in all arenas and all dimensions.

Dorothy Walters also knows that amidst all the chaos and horror of our time, humanity is being given a unique and possibly final opportunity to wake up, not only to its ethical and moral responsibilities toward all life, but to the possibility of living a wholly different, divinized life on earth, cocreating with the Divine and for the Divine a new world. The Divine, Walters knows, is flooding our world with grace, revelation, and power to awaken and transfigure humanity and help it transcend the destructive dualism both of materialism and of a religiosity addicted to transcendence and an otherworldly vision of God that degrades the body, sexuality, and the creation. In the middle of a crisis that seems to threaten everything, the Divine is holding out to humanity a challenge—the challenge, here on earth and in a body, to embrace astounding possibilities of incarnating the divine energies and working with them to transform the earth into the living mirror of the love and justice of the One.

Dorothy Walters knows these things not from book-learning or from mystical piety but because she has experienced them. She has experienced them in the core of her life and in the cells of her body. She has experienced both the apocalyptic terrors of our time and the glorious ferocities of what she calls divine love's "relentless alchemy." In her fifties, her entire life changed when she had a sudden, completely unforeseen, and transforming kundalini awakening. As *Unmasking the Rose* shows, this initiated a long period of struggle and sometimes bewildering and excruciating integration and adaptation. For, as Dorothy writes, "This, like all human experiences, is mixed. We falter, we lose 'control' (which is by way of not controlling). Our energies go awry, we feel pain where before we sensed ecstasy…. we walk always on a tightly drawn rope, swaying now this way, now that, occasionally catching our balance and holding it for an interval as our body moves across the immeasurable chasm below." Despite all the complexities and obstacles she encountered, however, Dorothy never lost hope or the passion to explore in ever deeper and ever more precise ways the mystery that had claimed and possessed her. Now, in her early seventies, she radiates a gentle serenity and strength that give her witness to the workings of Love's "relentless alchemy," the unshakable authority of lived and lived-through truth.

This witness is Dorothy Walters's extremely precious gift to all of us. She shows us not only *what* she knows but all the different stages and nuances of *how* she came to know it. Such a gift is priceless, for what we all now need is not more "mystical writing," or more "inspired utterances" (the bookshelves of our libraries are already groaning with both the radiant and fake versions of these) but no-nonsense, tough-minded, and generous-hearted *accounts of how* the process of transfiguration actually works—as far as that can be described in words—how it demands and tests and how, slowly and mysteriously, it comes to change everything, and go on and on changing everything.

This is what *Unmasking the Rose* so wisely, carefully, and reverently gives us, in a form ideally variegated so as to negotiate and reveal all the different levels of experience and in a prose (and occasionally verse) of exemplary clarity and lack of pretension. Dorothy's journey was a lonely one; for many years there was no one she could turn to for understanding or advice. It is just this extreme solitude, however—and the wild inner courage that it required to pursue so profound an awakening—that give Dorothy's meditations and descriptions their sense of vivid discovery and their bright, fierce, fresh truth. What Dorothy has learned, she has had to learn for herself and test repeatedly in and on herself; books and, later, certain friends and spiritual mentors helped, but essentially, like most mystical pioneers, Dorothy has been the chemist, under God, of her own transformation in the laboratory of her life. What must have been intensely difficult for her was, however, the condition for finding and testing those truths she is able to share with us, clear diamonds brought up from a depth of fire-streaked darkness shaped by prolonged, sometimes even intolerable, pressure.

Hold these diamonds now in the palm of your heart and turn them so their light can pierce and irradiate you. Let their dazzle remind you of the infinite wealth of your true nature and your infinite capacity for growth in and under God. Let them inspire you to join the hundreds of thousands of others who now know both the depth of the desperation of our time and the truth of the birth that it is struggling against vast odds to prepare. Let them give you too the courage to risk the great adventure of bringing your soul and body "into alignment with Divine Love." As Dorothy Walters so beautifully and accurately writes, "Constantly, we must turn up our limited receivers to admit higher and higher frequencies, to allow entry to ever more intense vibration streams from the infinite source.... Everything is a dance of light and within that dance we find our world of appearances—our visual imagery, our sounds, our inner sensations. And underlying all this is the source, which will speak to us and move us if we pause to attend."

June 26, 2001, Nevada

Chapter Three

The Body of Love—The Embodiment of Love in the Mystics from All Spiritual Traditions

Introduction

In this chapter, "The Body of Love," I honor the mystical systems and visions in which I myself have encountered the embodiment of divine love most powerfully: Hinduism, Buddhism, Sufism, the Jewish kabbalistic tradition, and Christian mysticism, with its core vision of the transcendent and immanent Christ.

One of the deepest beliefs that has driven my outer work and inner search has been the belief that this chaotic era is preparing for the birth of a Second Axial Age, which will correct the First Axial Age's noble obsession with transcendence. This addiction to transcendence must be balanced with a radical emphasis on the Sacred Feminine, the sacredness of the body, the holiness of consecrated tantric sexuality and sacredly inspired action. This Second Axial Age, I believe, will see the birth of a universal embodied evolutionary mysticism that will marry the transcendent and immanent aspects of God, and so give the whole of humanity direct access to a new level of sacred passion for nature, life, the world, and justice for all sentient beings.

This universal mysticism will not negate the extraordinary and brilliant achievements of the classical mystical systems and the indigenous revelations. It will, I believe, fuse together, in a uniquely potent revolutionary force, three of the most powerful streams of initiation with which humanity has been graced. These streams include the vision of the transcendent source that is so magnificently laid out in the mystical systems of the First Axial Age: Taoism, Buddhism, and Hinduism. Also included is the Mother vision of the indigenous tribes, with their sacred, precise knowledge about unity with the natural world, and finally, the great tantric revelation, hidden in the recesses not only of Hinduism and Vajrayana Buddhism, but also in the esoteric core of the Kabbalah and of Christianity.

It is, I believe, the grace of the Divine Feminine that will integrate these three initiatory strands of power so that humanity, at the time of its greatest dereliction, can be renewed by an all-embracing sacred vision that honors the transcendent light source; the creative forms it lives in; and the holy spiritual, psychological, and sexual diversity of the lives of human beings, inspired by its majesty, passion, and compassion.

Everything I have lived and written has been in service to the birth of this universal, integrated, evolutionarily embodied mysticism that I believe is central for the survival and transformation of humanity. Toward the end of this chapter is the introduction I wrote for *The Essential Gay Mystics*. As a gay mystic myself, I had the honor of, for the first time in history, bringing the mystical voices of gay men and women together to demonstrate the radiance and wisdom of what Native Americans sometimes call the Third Sex. The next stage of human evolution will make available to men and women, whatever their sexuality, the empowering mystery of sacred androgyny, the fusion of transcendence and immanence, masculine and feminine, soul and body that grounds and embodies the sacred marriage. In our communal historical journey into this radical new fusion, the testimony of those male and female gay mystics who have experienced their own mysterious and potent androgyny will be a profound grace and inspiration.

Andrew Harvey

Introduction to *The Essential Mystics*

At the beginning of his classic spiritual autobiography Bede Griffiths tells of the mystical experience that transformed his life:

> One day during my last term at school, I walked out alone in the evening and heard the birds singing in that full chorus of

song, which can only be heard at that time of the year at dawn or at sunset. I remember now the shock of surprise with which the sound broke on my ears. It seemed to me that I had never heard the birds singing before and I wondered whether they sang like this all the year round and I had never noticed it. As I walked on I came upon some hawthorn trees in full bloom and again I thought I had never seen such a sight or experienced such sweetness before. If I had been brought suddenly among the trees of the Garden of Paradise and heard a choir of angels singing I could not have been more surprised. I came then to where the sun was setting over the playing fields. A lark rose suddenly from the ground beside the tree, and then sank back still singing to rest. Everything then grew still as the sunset faded and the veil of dusk began to cover the earth. I remember now the feeling of awe which came over me. I felt inclined to kneel on the ground, as though I had been standing in the presence of an angel; and I hardly dared to look on the face of the sky, because it seemed as though it was but a veil before the face of God.

Up to that time, Bede Griffiths tells us, he had lived the life of a normal schoolboy, quite content with the world as he found it. He goes on:

I was suddenly made aware of another world of beauty and mystery such as I had never imagined to exist, except in poetry. It was as though I had begun to see and smell and hear for the first time. The world appeared to me as Wordsworth describes it with "the glory and freshness of a dream." The sight of a wild rose growing on a hedge, the scent of lime-tree blossoms caught suddenly as I rode down a hill on a bicycle, came to me like visitations from another world. But it was not only my senses that were awakened. I experienced an overwhelming emotion in the presence of nature, especially at evening. It began to have a kind of sacramental character for me. I approached it with a sense of almost religious awe and, in a hush that comes before sunset, I felt again the presence of an almost unfathomable mystery. The song of the birds, the shape of the trees, the colors of the sunset, were so many signs of this presence, which seemed to be drawing me to itself.

Mystical experience is the direct, unmediated experience of what Bede Griffiths beautifully describes as "the presence of an almost unfathomable mystery ... which seems to be drawing me to itself." This mystery is beyond name and beyond form; no name or form, no dogma, philosophy, or set of rituals can ever express it fully. It always transcends anything that can be said of it and remains always unstained by any of our human attempts to limit or exploit it. Every mystic of every time and tradition has awakened in wonder and rapture to the signs of this eternal presence and has known its mystery as one of relation and love, for in every tradition the presence is represented as hungry to reveal itself and to enter into ecstatic and intimate communion with its own creation. The awe and adoration that such an experience of love brings is the hidden foundation of all authentic religion, and to deepen and re-create more and more profoundly that awe and adoration, the wisdom they awaken, and the initiation into reality that they make possible is the goal of all authentic mystical discipline. As the great Islamic mystic Rumi tell us: "Generation upon generation have passed, my friend, but these meanings are constant and everlasting. The water in the stream may have changed many times, but the reflection of the moon and the stars remains the same."

The word *mystic* may mislead or intimidate some people—the prestige accorded to it has traditionally been so exalted that they feel such heightened perception and joy belong to and are attainable by only a few chosen human beings. This is far from the case. Mystical experience is always available—like the divine grace it is—to any who really want it; and all human beings are given in the course of their lives glimpses into the heart of the real, which they are free to pursue or forget. As Bede Griffiths writes of his illumination in the field at sunset:

Any experience of this kind is probably not at all uncommon, especially in early youth. Something breaks suddenly into our lives and upsets their normal pattern and we have to begin to adjust ourselves to a new kind of existence. This experience may come, as it came to me, through nature or poetry, or through art and music; or it may come through the adventure of flying or mountaineering, or of war; or it may come simply through falling in love, or through some apparent accident, an illness, the death of a friend, a sudden loss of fortune. Anything which breaks through the routine of daily life may be the bearer of this message to the soul. But however it may be, it is as though a veil has been lifted and we see for the first time behind the façade which the world has built around us. Suddenly we know we belong to another world, that there is another dimension to existence.... We see our life for a moment in its true perspective in relation to eternity. We are freed from the flux of time and see something of the eternal order that underlies it. We are no longer isolated individuals in conflict with our surroundings; we are parts of a whole, elements in an universal harmony.

Mystics in all world traditions testify to what Bede Griffiths is here telling us of the scope and effect of the mystical experience. From them we come to know that what any authentic mystical opening brings us is a sense of wonder, a freedom from time's fury and anxiety, and a growing revelation of a far larger and more marvelous universe and a far vaster identity than anything we could begin to intuit with our ordinary senses and consciousness. When we are touched by mystic grace and allow ourselves to enter its field without fear, we see that we are all parts of a whole; elements of an universal harmony; unique, essential, and sacred notes in a divine music that everyone and everything is playing together with us in God and for God. And if we work patiently with what we come to know, through prayer and meditation and loving service to other beings, we will, all the traditions promise us, come to understand what Christ meant when he said, "the kingdom of heaven is within you," and what

Sultan Valad, Rumi's son, is trying to transmit to us when he writes, "A human being must be born twice. Once from his mother and again from his own body and his own existence. The body is like an egg and the essence of man must become a bird in that egg through the warmth of love, and then he must go beyond his body and fly in the eternal world of the soul."

In *The Essential Mystics* I have collected what I believe to be the most precious testimonies to this "eternal world of the soul" from all the major world traditions. I have chosen to present these testimonies not individually but grouped together in the traditions they come from, because each revelation, however personal, is always partly conditioned by the time and tradition it occurs in. Each tradition, moreover, has a different way of approaching the "unfathomable mystery," its own particular truth of insight, and represents a different way of playing the "divine music" that, Rumi says, "Love, the Supreme Musician, is always playing in our souls." Structuring the book by tradition is designed to help readers to savor in depth these different kinds of mystical music and to appreciate richly how they all echo, inspire, illumine, and complete each other.

Such an approach respects the uniqueness and integrity of each tradition while also revealing its relatedness at the deepest level to all the others. As Ramakrishna, one of humanity's greatest mystic pioneers, tells us with complete authority of experience: "I say that all are calling on the same God.... It is not good to feel that my religion is true and the other religions are false. All seek the same object. A mother prepares dishes to suit the stomachs of her children. Suppose a mother has five children and a fish is brought for the family. She doesn't cook the same curry for all of them.... God has made religions to suit different aspirants, times, and countries. All doctrines are only so many paths."

Ramakrishna speaks of God as a mother who cooks the white fish of revelation for children in different ways; in my selection and presentation of the sacred texts in this book I have chosen to pay special attention to the Sacred Feminine, the motherhood of God, as understood in the different traditions. It is my belief that without the knowledge of God as Mother as well as Father and without the conscious incorporation of the healing and balancing wisdom of the Sacred Feminine into every part of life and every area of our understanding of the world and our relationship to it, the human race will die out and take a large part of nature with it.

Only a race in drastic denial of its interdependence with all things and beings could be devastating the environment as blindly as we are. What a recovery of the wisdom of the Mother brings to all of us is the knowledge of inseparable connection with the entire creation and the wise, active love that is born from that knowledge. Unless the human race realizes with a passion and reverence beyond thought or words its interbeing with nature, it will destroy in its greed the very environment it is itself sustained by. Unless our fundamental sacred connectedness with every being and thing is experienced deeply and enacted everywhere, religious, political, and other differences will go on creating intolerable conflict that can only increase the already dangerously high chances of our self-annihilation. The Mother's knowledge of unity, Her powers of sensitivity, humility, and balance, and Her infinite respect for the miracle of all life have now to be invoked by each of us and practiced if the "masculine" rational imbalance of our civilization is to be righted before it is too late.

Coming to know the hidden and forgotten Mother and the marvelous wisdom of the Sacred Feminine, as revealed from every side and angle by the different mystical traditions, is not a luxury; it is, I believe, a necessity for our survival as a species. Knowing Her, we will know that we are Her divine children in a relationship of complete, unconditionally loving intimacy; we will know that nature is holy in all its sacred particulars because it is everywhere vibrant with Her light and Her love; we will know that we have come to this earth not, as some of the patriarchal mystical traditions have implied, to escape it, but to embrace it fully, not to "transcend" it but to *arrive* here in full presence, gratitude, and love.

What knowing the Mother means above all is daring to put love

The Body of Love

into action. The Mother Herself is love in action, love acting everywhere and in everything to make creation possible. Coming into contact with the Mother is coming into contact with a force of passionate and active compassion in every area and dimension of life, a force that longs to be invoked by us to help transform all the existing conditions of life on earth so that they can mirror ever more clearly and accurately Her law, Her justice, and Her love.

The universe, as many mystical traditions tell us, is the "child" of a sacred marriage between the feminine and masculine forces within the One, what Taoists call yin and yang, what Hindus name Shiva and Shakti; it is the constantly self-transforming expression of their eternal mutual passion. For the human race to have a chance to survive, this cosmic sacred marriage has to be mirrored and enacted in our being at every level. At every level there has to be a fusion between our masculine and feminine energies, a fusion between those polarities we have been taught to keep apart—between our vision of "heaven" and our vision of "earth," between what we have called "sacred" and what we have called "profane," between our innermost mystical awareness and our political, technological, and economic choices. Only such a fusion and "sacred marriage" can produce in us the clarity, knowledge, and force of active love necessary to preserve the world. There cannot be a sacred marriage, however, without a bride; until the bride, the Mother, is recalled in all Her wise splendor, the fusion of full mystical knowledge with the most committed economic and political action that alone can help us now cannot take place.

It is with the intention of helping us recall the bride in Her wise splendor that I have structured *The Essential Mystics* in the way I have. I wanted this anthology not merely to be a feast of the greatest and wisest mystical texts, but also a *practical handbook* for anyone who wants to serve as effectively as possible the new balanced humanity that is trying to be born.

Teilhard de Chardin, at the end of his life, wrote, "Humanity is being brought to the moment when it will have to choose between

188

suicide or adoration." We must wake up in massive numbers, and very fast, to the sacred glory of life and nature and to our sacred responsibility to preserve both or be destroyed. In this waking up the great mystics of the world are our truest and deepest and bravest friends, for together they give us the full visionary information we now need as urgently as oxygen. Armed with the highest, most balanced, and most focused insights of all the different approaches to the "almost unfathomable mystery," we still have a chance to solve our and the planet's immense problems together.

There is very little time left. Now, more than ever before, everything depends on us.

Introduction to *Teachings of the Hindu Mystics*

Max Müller, the pioneering Indologist of the nineteenth century, wrote, "We all come from the East and in going to the East everyone ought to feel that he is going to his 'old home' full of memories if only he could read them." Those words have a specially poignant meaning for me, since I was born in India of parents who themselves were born in India, spent the first nine years of my life there, and have returned as often as possible since, always to try and drink deeper from the still-living springs of its ancient passion and wisdom. The texts that I am offering in this anthology have been intimate companions for many years; India, in all its faces and powers, has been at the core of my life and search. India is, and always will be, the "old home" of my heart and of my soul.

One of the first things I learned as a child about Hinduism is that the word itself is inaccurate. An old Indian scholar friend of my parents explained to me patiently one morning that *Hindu* was originally a geographical rather than a religious term, used first in the Persian empire and then by the Greek soldiers and historians who followed Alexander as he swept across the world for those who lived on the banks of the Indus River, in what is now the Punjab. "We Indians do not use this name," my friend said gently. "We call our religion the Sanatana Dharma—the 'Eternal Way.'" He spelled out the magical Sanskrit syllables slowly for me and then wrote them out in big letters in my red school notebook. Being an inquisitive seven-year-old, I asked, "Why do you call it the Eternal Way?" He looked a little startled and then almost whispered, "Because, my dear Andrew, it is eternal. The Sanatana Dharma, we believe, began when the universe was first unrolled out of the mind of God. It and creation began at exactly the same moment." Those words, with their sense of a clear, majestic, changeless order, thrilled me, and I repeated them to myself for years.

As a child, what I knew of this Sanatana Dharma was at once exotic and ordinary, homespun and picturesque. Hinduism for me was visits to temples where plump, smiling priests fed me sweets and introduced me to various gods swathed in brilliant yellow and purple silk; it was the garish shrines to Shiva and Vishnu by the side of the road, reeking of rancid butter; the festival of Holi with thousands of wild shriekers in the streets flinging fresh paint at each other; comic books with the stories of Krishna luridly fleshed out for children; the sound of temple bells echoing across moonlit fields; the tang of incense from our cook's tiny altar in the corner of his room. Once, as I was walking alone by the Jamuna River near our home, I saw an old holy man, a *sadhu* wrapped in a flame-orange robe, standing silently in prayer, his hands lifted in adoration to the rising sun; on his face I saw a look I had never seen in church, a look of still and incandescent devotion and tenderness; he seemed to be whispering to someone he knew very well and deeply. That afternoon I told my mother that I had seen a saint talking to God.

Later, when I came to discuss Hinduism with one of my colleagues at All Souls College, Oxford—Robin Zaehner, the brilliant and eccentric translator of the Upanishads and Bhagavad Gita—I learned that in many ways Hinduism is nothing like what we normally think of as a religion. The Sanatana Dharma is a gallimaufry of the most extravagantly varied faiths, rituals, customs, and beliefs; Hinduism has no single dogmatic authority and, until very recently in its history, no "missionary zeal" to convert others, since it has never seen itself as the one true religion or the only hope of salvation. Zaehner was, when I knew him, a fervent Catholic convert, but he loved to exclaim, "If only the church had had the sense to allow so many different and seemingly contradictory approaches to God, how much saner its history would have been!"

It was this sublime ancient tolerance, Zaehner stressed often, that was the true proof of the wisdom and mature dignity of the Hindu tradition. "In the family of religions, Hinduism is the wise old all-knowing mother," he would say. "Its most sacred books, the Vedas, claim, 'Truth is one, but sages call it by different names.' If only Islam, and all the rest of the monotheistic 'book' religions, had learned that lesson, all the horror of history's religious wars could have been avoided. Which other religion has its God say, as Krishna does in the Bhagavad Gita, 'All paths lead to me'?" And here Zaehner would delight in repeating an anecdote he loved about a Protestant evangelical missionary trying to convert an old sage in Calcutta:

> As you can imagine, the missionary pulled out all the stops. He wept and shuddered and shook and pleaded and implored and threatened hellfire and then evoked ecstatically all the joys of paradise. The old Indian sage listened quietly and, when he had finished, said "I accept wholeheartedly, dear honored sir, that Jesus Christ was a very great divine master whose life and teachings are of permanent sacred value to humanity. But the Buddha was also such a divine master, and so, I might add, was my dear swami, Sri Ramakrishna. Why would God, after all, be so mean as to give humanity only one divine master and that one only for the white people?" At that the missionary flung up his hands in horror and fled the room.

The sage in Zaehner's story was, it seems, a disciple of the great nineteenth-century Indian saint Ramakrishna, and it was Zaehner, in fact, who first read to me the following passage from *The Gospel of*

The Body of Love

Ramakrishna, which enshrines the Sanatana Dharma's "motherly" embrace of all ways to the Divine:

> God has made different religions to suit different aspirations, times and countries. All doctrines are only so many paths; but a path is by no means God himself. Indeed we can reach God if we follow any of the paths with whole-hearted devotion. One may eat a cake with icing either straight or sidewise. It will taste sweet either way.
>
> As we can ascend to the top of a house by ladder or bamboo or a staircase or a rope, so diverse are the ways to approach God and every religion shows one of these ways.
>
> People partition off their lands by means of boundaries, but no one can partition off the all-embracing sky overhead. The indivisible sky surrounds all and includes all. So people in ignorance say, "My religion is the only one, my religion is the best." But when the heart is illumined by true knowledge it knows that above all of these sects and sectarians presides the one indivisible eternal all-knowing bliss.
>
> As a mother, in nursing her sick children, gives rice and curry to one, and sago and arrowroot to another, and bread and butter to a third, so the Lord has laid out different paths for different people.

For all its tolerance and variety of faiths and beliefs, however, there *are* certain essential beliefs and attitudes of spirit that bind together all those we call "Hindus." Nearly all religious Hindus share a profound faith in rebirth and karma, in the cyclical nature of time, in the transcendent and immanent presence of the Divine, in the ultimately delusory and unsatisfactory nature of a life lived in ignorance of eternal truth, and in the supreme value of *moksha,* or liberation from all inner and outer limitations. Moreover, the different schools of Hinduism—while they may disagree even within themselves on such seemingly crucial issues as the nature of absolute reality, the status of the individual self, and the reality of the world—all derive their authority from the most ancient body of texts, the Vedas, which contain not only the great hymns of the Rig Veda (which begin my anthology) but also the Upanishads, the multifaceted core of Indian mysticism. While there is no one "exclusive" dogmatic Hindu tradition, then, there is, very definitely, a spirit of inquiry and of revelation that is so consistent that we find one of the greatest of modern Hindu mystics, Ramana Maharshi, speaking in ways and with images that echo exactly the terminology of the anonymous seers who wrote down the Upanishads more than two thousand years before him. It is this consistency that gives the Hindu mystical tradition its timeless purity, weight, and grandeur. It is as if one eternal voice is speaking in and through a myriad different voices, tirelessly exploring different registers of its own majestic range, as if all the tradition's poems and meditations and philosophical texts are, as Zaehner once said to me, "different-shaped peaks in one vast, grand, interconnected mountain chain, like the Himalayas."

What I have wanted to do in this anthology is to honor this consistency of vision and to present it in the way most relevant to all seekers on all paths today and most pertinent to the dangers and challenges facing our world. I wanted to create an anthology that would—in the spirit of the Gita and Ramakrishna—inspire all readers, whatever their religious background or lack of it, to plunge into the uncovering of their eternal nature and then enact its sacred laws in loving action in the world. As it is written in the Svetashvatara Upanishad, "What use are the scriptures to anyone who knows not the source from which they come?" And as the Yoga Vasishtha warns us, "If you conceptualize these teachings for your intellectual entertainment and do not let them act in your life, you will stumble and fall like a blind person." For all its metaphysical loftiness and joy in speculation, the Hindu mystical tradition, like all true mystical traditions, is essentially practical, concerned with teaching, inspiring, and guiding authentic transformation. Whatever path you are on, then, use these texts not as intellectual puzzles but as signs of your essential splendor; pray, meditate, and serve others so that the wordless truth behind these truths can be revealed to you in your own life.

What, then, is the core truth of the Hindu tradition? It is the truth of the mystery of a spirit that pervades, creates, and transcends all things and of each soul's conscious identity with that spirit beyond space and time. In the Upanishads, this all-pervading, all-creating, all-transcending spirit is named Brahman. In parts of the earlier Vedas, Brahman—from the Sanskrit *br,* "to become" or "to breathe," and *brih,* "to be great"—means "that which is powerful and great" and most often refers to the force inherent in sacred hymns and sacrifices. In the Upanishads this concept widens, and Brahman becomes the presence underlying, creating, and sustaining all of existence. For the Upanishads and all the later teachings rooted in them, every human being is naturally one with Brahman in his or her Atman, his or her "soul" or "indwelling core of divine consciousness." The aim of human life and the source of liberation from all the chains of life and death is to know, from inmost experience, the Atman's identity with Brahman and to live the calm, fearless, selflessly loving life that radiates from this knowledge.

There was a danger inherent in the tradition's celebration of the transcendent Brahman and of freedom from the world—the danger of what might be called an "addiction to transcendence" and a corresponding subtle but devastating devaluation of creation and life as "unreal." Many developments of the Hindu tradition did not escape this danger, but it is important to recognize that it was recognized and dealt with at the very beginning of the tradition's unfolding—both in the Vedas, with their celebration of the glory of the creation, and in the crucial and exalted statement of the necessity of "sacred balance" between immanence and transcendence, Being and Becoming, contemplative awareness and just action, that we discover in the Isha Upanishad:

> *In dark night live those*
> *For whom the world without alone is real;*
> *In night darker still, for whom the world within*
> *Alone is real. The first leads to a life*
> *Of action, the second to a life of meditation.*
> *But those who combine action with meditation*

Introduction to *Teachings of the Hindu Mystics*

Go across the sea of death through action
And enter into immortality
Through the practice of meditation.
So have we heard from the wise.

It was this mature and practical sacred balance between transcendence and immanence, meditation and service, that the Bhagavad Gita, composed several centuries after the Upanishads, brought to a marvelous depth of richness in its central vision of "selfless action."

In the Gita, Lord Krishna teaches his disciple Arjuna the timeless secret of an action inspired by divine will, wisdom, love, and knowledge, performed for its own sake and without attachment to results: only such action, Krishna tells Arjuna, can free a person from the chains of karma and also allow the Divine to use him or her for its own purpose without any interference of the false self, and so secure the triumph of sacred law and justice in history. Many modern mystics—I am one of them—believe that it is such a vision of "selfless action" that can most richly inspire the kind of "mystical activism" that is necessary in all arenas if we are going to preserve the planet. Activism without mystical inspiration and the strength, stamina, and passion that spring from divine love and divine knowledge will inevitably cause us to grow jaded and despairing in the bitter, fierce world of reality; mysticism without a commitment to enacting justice and truth in life will degenerate into what Gandhi called "the higher narcissism" and what Vivekananda derided as "heartless escapism masquerading as illumination." Krishna's revelation to Arjuna, then, of a middle way that fuses the deepest insights of contemplation with tireless service of the Divine in the Real may well hold the secret to our survival as a race, and to the survival of the natural world.

Lord Krishna's teaching in the Bhagavad Gita also suggests another holy secret that has inspired some of the greatest mystics of the Hindu tradition. Simply stated, the human being only achieves union with God in all of His aspects through a fusion of contemplation and action. God is after all both eternal Being *and* eternal

Becoming; in contemplative knowledge of our eternal identity with Brahman, we rest in God's being, like a drop of water in the all-surrounding ocean; in enacting the Divine will selflessly, we participate in the transforming activity of God, in what a great mystic of another tradition, Rumi, called "God's perpetual massive resurrection." Both aspects of the godhead, then, are open to us to taste, savor, celebrate, and enshrine, and life itself is the dancing ground of this divine human dance of opposites; the site of a perpetually evolving sacred marriage between matter and spirit whose potential possibilities and glories are boundless. What could a humanity attuned intimately to the Divine and selflessly transparent to its will not achieve?

The Hindu tradition provides exquisite, firm guidance toward this attunement because it has always recognized that different temperaments take different paths into the sacred marriage. It has not only recognized the validity of other religions but has also acknowledged within itself a variety of paths. Of these, the four main ways to *yoga* (union with God) are *jnana yoga,* the path to the Transcendent through direct intuitive knowledge; *bhakti yoga,* which focuses the powers of imagination and passion on a path of devotion, usually to a personal God; *raja yoga,* the path of "royal *(raj)* integration" through psychophysical exercises; and *karma yoga,* the path of works and action dedicated selflessly to the Supreme. None of these yogas excludes the practice of any of the others. Each temperament, however, finds in one or another of the paths its own door into that experience of the living presence most natural to it; and as this experience deepens, the chosen path opens to the realization of all the other paths and gradually fuses with them to birth a mature, divine human being. No other mystical tradition has had so broad and wise and all-embracing a vision of the different aspects and faces of the path. Robin Zaehner used to say, "If anyone feels excluded from the Hindu embrace it is by his or her own perverse choice."

In this anthology, I have chosen to emphasize—but by no means exclusively—the sacred texts devoted to *bhakti yoga,* the yoga of devotion or adoration. Sri Ramakrishna never tired of repeating that *bhakti yoga* is the path suited to the most people, the easiest to keep performing in the heart of the world, and the yoga most apt for this dark age, when religious culture is everywhere in decline and the exigencies of work make the time for more elaborate spiritual exercises hard to secure. *Bhakti yoga,* of course, opens onto all the other yogas: as Ramakrishna said, "The more you love, the more you know; the more you love and know, the more deeply you plunge into sacred action born from love and knowledge."

The great *bhakti* river of Hindu mysticism has its origins in the Vedas, where many gods—all of them different aspects of the One—are celebrated. In its more identifiable modern form, however, it began around the fourth century BCE, when several religious groups made their appearance worshiping a supreme God in His personal aspect as Vasudeva, Narayana, or Hari (later all three would be identified with Vishnu). During the next two thousand years, other streams of devotion—to Shiva, god of destruction and renewal; to the Goddess in all Her different forms and names; and to Krishna (an embodiment of Vishnu whose devotion began to flourish in the sixth century)—also joined this vast river.

It is vital to remember, however, that despite this plurality of divine names and forms and objects of adoration, Hinduism is not polytheistic; the different "gods" each represent different aspects of the Supreme. As Huston Smith writes in his *World Religions:* "It is obtuse to confuse Hinduism's images with idolatry and their multiplicity with polytheism. They are runways from which the sense-laden human spirit can rise for its 'flight of the alone to the Alone.'"

In traditional Hindu metaphysics, Brahman is recognized as having two faces: the Nirguna Brahman of many of the early Upanishads, the self without qualities and beyond all concepts and form, and Saguna Brahman, the spirit as form or forms, with qualities that can be approached and adored. In practice, many Hindu mystics moved between these two aspects of the Absolute with natural delight; even so austere a lover of the Nirguna Brahman as Shankara, the great philosopher of nondual Vedanta, also wrote ecstatic devotional hymns to the Saguna Brahman as Shiva or the Divine Mother. And Ramakrishna, in the course of a single discourse, can veer between the formless absolute and "the Mother" and back again, knowing their identity in the mystery that transcends all names and concepts. The face the Divine wears in the *bhakti* tradition always has the majesty of the Formless in and behind it; when baby Krishna's foster mother, Yashoda, looks into his mouth after scolding him for eating mud, she sees the whole universe ablaze in divine fire.

The glory of the *bhakti* tradition—in Mirabai's hymns to Krishna, as in Mahadeviyakka's to Shiva and Ramprasad's to the Mother—lies in its fierce emotional courage and passion. As the French thinker Simone Weil remarked to an atheist philosopher who was mocking the erotic language of certain Christian mystics and of the biblical Song of Songs: "The language of love belongs to mystics by right; other kinds of lovers merely borrow it." That God is Love—eternal, boundless, fiery, ecstatic Love—is known and experienced by mystics of all traditions: it is this Love that is the energy and force that creates and sustains all things and worlds.

In the *bhakti* tradition the "language of love" that such a Love inevitably arouses in its passionate devotees is explored in all its nuances of coquetry, agony, and sometimes even molten rage at divine "cruelty." In shamelessly exposing all possible responses to the Divine—imaged as friend, mentor, mother, child, and especially lover—the *bhakti* tradition helps all seekers on all paths to dedicate the full range, passion, and power of their emotions to God, and so enter into a nakedly intense, personal relationship with the Divine. Mirabai, Mahadeviyakka, Ramprasad, and the other great poets of the *bhakti* tradition bring their entire, tumultuous, complex selves to the encounter with the Beloved, censoring nothing and leaving out no part of their being; their huge pains and ecstasies challenge us to expose ourselves also to the irradiation of Love and its often ferocious alchemy.

For those who find the Nirguna Brahman too cold an object to pursue, adoring God-in-Form is a marvelously powerful way of keeping the whole being in the crucible of transformation until all of its ignorance and folly are burned away and a new being is ultimately forged in gold from the ashes of the old. As its crowning grace, adoration reveals the whole of creation as a nondual, interdependent dancing ground of Love; as the Baul poet Fikirchand sings so movingly:

> If I look at the clouds in the sky,
> I see His beauty afloat;
> And I see Him walk on the stars
> Blazing my heart.

This revelation of all beings, things, and events, being swept up in an infinite, interconnected, nondual dance of bliss—consciousness sources the second great stream of Hindu mysticism I have chosen to celebrate in this anthology—that of the tantric tradition. The word *tantra* is derived from the Sanskrit *tan*, "to stretch and expand"; *tantric* signifies that by which knowledge and consciousness are stretched and expanded so that the full, sublime passion and power and wisdom of the dance can infuse and illumine them. The tantric tradition is reflected in Jnaneshwar's "Hymn to Self-Awareness," the Devi Gita, Kabir, the songs of the mystic minstrels known as the Bauls, and the excerpts from the works of Ramakrishna and Aurobindo.

This magnificent tradition first made its literary appearance toward the middle of the first millennium CE. From the beginning, it celebrated, with enormous fervor, the feminine aspect of the godhead, the Shakti, the fire-energy that streams from the source to engender the creation and live in it. By honoring the Shakti, the tantric devotee would make himself or herself open to the Shakti's transforming power, to the all-healing revelation of Her presence in and as all things and beings. The great tantric formula (fundamental also to Mahayana Buddhism) is *"Samsara* equals *nirvana"*—which reveals that the world and the creation in all their holy particulars are coessential with the transcendent Being-Consciousness-Bliss. Everything, in its inherent bliss-nature, is divine and holy; there is nothing but God in us and around us at all times. For the tantric schools, *moksha,* or "liberation," does not come from renouncing reality, leaving the world, or killing one's natural desires. Rather true freedom arises naturally and sumptuously when what has been categorized as the "lower" reality is seen and known as contained within and always melting into the "higher," and when the "higher" is constantly invoked to penetrate and transfigure the "lower" at ever-greater depths of power, presence, and rapture. To the tantric mystic, the entire universe is the site of a constantly consummated, explosively and boundlessly fertile sacred marriage between the transcendent Source and His immanent Shakti, between the self and the Self, matter and spirit. For the tantric, the aim of human existence is to participate in this dynamic marriage, and to make all aspects of life radiant with its holy truth and joy.

Georg Feuerstein writes in *The Yoga Tradition:*

> It is important to realize that the Tantra revolution was not the product of mere philosophical speculation. Though connected with an immense architecture of old and new concepts and doctrines, Tantrism is intensely practical.... Historically, Tantra can be understood as a dialectical response to the often abstract approach of Advaita Vedanta, which was and still is the dominant philosophy of the Hindu elite. Tantra was a grassroots movement, and many if not most of its early protagonists hailed from the castes at the bottom of the social pyramid of India—fishermen, weavers, hunters, street vendors, washerwomen. They were responding to a widely felt need for more practical orientation that would integrate the lofty metaphysical ideals of non-dualism with down-to-earth procedures for living a sanctified life. (456)

Of all the different streams of the Hindi mystical tradition, it is, I believe, the tantric that offers most to us today. At a time when the natural world is itself in danger, the last thing the human race needs are mystical theologies addicted to transcendence. It is this addiction to otherworldliness, to a vision of freedom or "heaven" that lies outside the body and matter and time that has, in all the major religions, abetted our coma of denial about our connection to our bodies and the world around us, a denial that is now lethally abetting our destruction of the environment. The tantric vision of a *samsara* that is also *nirvana*, of an earth that is also heaven, of a body ensouled and a soul embodied, can help us live in the creation as in a temple, transfigure banal desire into holy celebration, and love our lives with sacred passion and so gather our powers to protect and honor the lives of all beings with courage and wisdom. Only such a passion, courage, and wisdom—and the hope born from them of a divine life in an increasingly divinized world—can give us now the fire and the strength to save our world from disaster. The great German poet Hölderlin wrote at the beginning of the nineteenth century that "at the time of greatest danger, salvation arises." In our contemporary danger, "salvation" is a vision of the world, creation, and our lives as inherently blessed and potentially divinely empowered, just, impassioned, and creative. From such a vision—that of tantra at its highest and richest—can spring astonishing powers of sacrifice and invention, stamina and hope. If we are going to find the strength as a race to band together to save the planet, it will be in the name of a world and a creation seen and known as holy, not "unreal"; as the sacred ground on and in which miracles of divine human evolution can still unfold, if we can only honors its laws.

The key to an integration of the tantric vision into every aspect of our lives and actions is, as I have already hinted, an exaltation and adoration of the Sacred Feminine in all its forms and powers. It is this exaltation and adoration of the Mother aspect of God, the tantric mystics assure us, that will restore to our deepest understanding the divinity of creation and enable us to flood our lives with sacred tenderness, joy, and power. Kabir wrote, "The formless Absolute is my Father, and God with form is my Mother"; for Jnaneshwar too, as his glorious hymn to Shiva and Shakti proclaims, the universe and every human being are the sites of a marriage between Shiva and Shakti. There can be no marriage, however, without a bride. In nearly all the major mystical systems, the Sacred Feminine has been lost or suppressed: it is this drastic loss and suppression that has prevented the birth on a large scale of a divine humanity. Without conscious awareness of the Sacred Feminine, of the feminine as sacred, the marriage—of immanence and transcendence, heart and mind, body and soul, masculine and feminine powers—that is meant to take place at the core of every human being to birth him or her into the authentic, divine human reality, fully empowered, and fully creative in all arenas of life, simply cannot take place.

Perhaps the supreme gift of Hinduism to the world is that its tantric traditions have kept the truth of the splendor, majesty, and power of the Bride vibrant and alive in all Her unbridled fullness. Worshiping Her as Devi, Ambika, Durga, Lakshmi, or Kali, the Hindu tantric mystics have known how to adore Her both as Queen of Transcendence *and* Earth Mother, and love Her both in Her terrifying, life-devouring aspects and as infinitely benign and tender. Their triumph has been not to water down or domesticate or "masculinize" the Mother but to allow Her to be Her full, gorgeous, wild, unpredictable, menacing, miraculous self, in all Her paradoxes and seeming contradictions, and to find the way to connect directly with Her all-transforming power through an embrace of Her in an adoration without conditions.

Ramakrishna described the Mother as a "spider who has spun the universe out of her entrails and gone to live herself in each shining strand of her web." In his last years he had a vision of Her, at once magnificent and appalling, as a beautiful pregnant woman arising out of the waves of the Ganges, birthing her child on the shore, tearing it to pieces, smiling, and then, with blood all over her face and mouth, walking serenely back into the waves of the river to merge with them. Ramakrishna's abandoned and unconditional love of the Mother gave him the heart-power to embrace Her in *all* of Her moods and facets, as destroyer as well as preserver, and so to share in Her timeless bliss-dance, beyond space and time and matter and beyond all conventional—or convenient—religious or moral categories. Such an unconditional embrace of the Mother aspect of the godhead as "naked reality" in its extremes of life and death, "good" and "evil," horror and bliss leads to the highest nondual realization, a realization that sees, knows, feels, exalts the Divine in all things and events, with a sublime outrageous fearlessness, in a rapture of freedom. This ultimate realization, Ramakrishna made clear, is always the gift of the Mother, for only the force and love of the Mother can forever explode and rubble all possible distinctions between "here" and "there," "eternity" and "time," "body" and "soul," and so finally birth Her divine human child into deathless Presence, alive with the Mother's own miraculous power of healing and creativity. And in his extraordinary life, Ramakrishna gave us sign after sign that he had truly become Her child, the founder-father-mother of a whole new world of children waiting to be born.

The tantric embrace of all the powers and aspects of the Divine Mother and of the miraculous transformations it makes possible infuses the extraordinary evolutionary vision of the greatest mystical philosopher of Hinduism, and perhaps of all human history: Sri Aurobindo. In his astounding series of books, from the *Foundation of Indian Culture* to *The Synthesis of Yoga* and *The Life Divine,* Aurobindo gathers masterfully together all the various strands of the Hindu mystical tradition, all the deepest truths of the Upanishadic, *bhakti,* and tantric traditions, and fuses them at diamond-pure heat with the most advanced Western understanding of historical evolution and progress. Out of this fusion of the deepest, broadest, and richest knowledge of both "sides" of the world's "mind" arises what many people consider to be the map of the possible future of humanity—a future that could see the whole of earth-life transfigured consciously by the descending power of the Divine Mother and of that initiatory "supramental" light-force that is in Her gift and control.

Other mystical systems have had a vision of what might be called "radiant apocalypse." Gregory of Nyssa and other Christian mystics envisaged all of the creation being transfigured by divine grace into the Pleroma, the divine fullness or glory, and Mahayana masters in Tibet and China taught and wrote about the coming reign of Shambhala, a heavenly kingdom on earth that would spread its rays of peace, health, and illumination everywhere. No one, however, in human history has had so precise a vision of transfiguration as Aurobindo; to call it a vision, in fact, is to limit its significance, for it was a living, "scientific" experience he underwent himself and described in meticulous detail up until his death, leaving behind, in his letters especially, very direct practical advice for anyone who wanted, like him, to be a pioneer of the Mother's new reality.

It is not a coincidence, I believe, that such an all-comprehensive, both dazzlingly inspired and dazzlingly lucid vision of the evolutionary possibilities of humanity should have arisen at the very moment during the first two world wars, when the future of humanity was first revealed as dangerously fragile. Just as the battles of the Somme and Marne and later the rise of fascism and the explosion of the atom bomb at Hiroshima were ushering in our age of tragic despair and violence, so, in Aurobindo, the genius of the Hindu mystical tradition was bringing to birth one final, believable, potentially all-transforming vision of the possible human future. Mystics of all traditions know the sacred, mysterious law by which the darkest midnights birth the most resplendent suns; the annihilation of all old forms with their attendant institutions and illusions is sometimes necessary before the full glory and outrageousness of the new can flash out. One world is clearly dying in agony around us; another is trying to rise, phoenix-like, from its ashes.

Although Aurobindo knew that his vision of a new, gnostic human race was real and possible, because he was living it, he also knew that its birth on a large enough scale to influence the course of history was far from inevitable, however great the divine powers gathered by the Mother to help it. Divine lights and initiations, dark and brilliant, may stream toward us, but the future will always depend on how profoundly receptive we are to them and how radical and brave we are in enacting the miraculous possibilities they open up to us.

Time is running out. As George Trakl, the great German prophet-poet, wrote in an unnamed poem during the First World War, "The hands of the clock are climbing toward midnight." Will the extreme danger of our time lead to birth or apocalypse, to a new, mystically inspired, universal humanity or our death and the death of most of nature? In our time, the Divine stands before us, nakedly offering us two mirrors in which we can see two contrasting destinies. One is a black mirror in which the last tree of the last forest is being burned down as the last whales and dolphins die in finally polluted seas and the entire planet becomes, in the environmentalist David Brower's words, "a vast stinking hospital of the dead and dying." The other is a golden mirror, in which we can also see clearly, if we dare to look at what our inner glory and divine power and beauty could create with divine grace, wisdom, and a transfigured world, a mirror of love and justice, a place where the sacred marriage becomes real in all its holy laws and potentials in all arts and sciences and institutions and technologies. It is our tragedy and our magnificence that both destinies should now be possible and within our grasp.

Which of our fates will we choose? No one knows, and all prophecies in a time like ours are straws thrown into a whirlwind. I have chosen the world I see clearly in the golden mirror. And in my own struggle to realize its laws within my own heart, mind, body, and soul, I find that the testimony of the Hindu mystical tradition to the divinity within us all and the powers that stream from that divinity is of priceless, practical usefulness and inspiration. On dark days, I try to remember what Aurobindo writes in one of his last letters: "In the way that one treads with the greater Light above, even every difficulty gives its help and Night itself carries in it the burden of the Light that has to be."

Introduction to *Perfume of the Desert*

In my early twenties, I read a Sufi story in a book on Lawrence of Arabia that has haunted me ever since. This is how I remember it:

The Body of Love

A group of wild young Bedouins were riding in the desert with their chief, who was a religious man as well as a great leader. They came in the course of their wanderings to a vast ruined palace. The young men rode through the deserted rooms, breaking off bits of the plaster and brick to smell what had gone into their making. One cried out, "In this clay are mixed the oils of rose and orange-blossom." Another exclaimed, "In this dirt I smell jasmine! How beautiful!"

The chief stood apart and said nothing. When the young men had ridden through all of the rooms, savoring the various fragrances that could still be smelled in the clay of the ruined palace, they asked the chief, "And what is your favorite perfume?" He smiled and leaned as far as he could out of one of the palace windows into the empty desert wind. He reached out his hands and cupped them. Then he held out his cupped hands to the young men and said, "Smell this! The best perfume of all is the perfume of the desert, for it smells of nothing."

A decade later I was sitting in Paris with an old Sufi friend—a great translator, scholar, and seeker with whom I was working on translations of Rumi. I told her the story and asked her what it meant for her. She did not speak for a long time and then she said: "For me, whenever I think of the Sufis and of Sufism, I think of the desert. I think of the desert's wildness, its gorgeous and terrible loneliness, its silence, its purity. I think of how in the desert you feel at once annihilated yet totally alive and present in all things around you and above you, as if you had become at once the sands stretching from horizon to horizon and the sky, so vast and empty and still. And I think too of what is written in the Koran, 'All is perishable except the Face of God.' The desert is the Face of God, the final mirror in which human beings see their nothingness and their absolute splendor-in-Him. The Sufis are those who spend their lives looking into the mirror of the desert, and in holding up the purity, glory, and rigor of the desert to their lives. And in the greatest Sufi philosophers and poets you smell what the chief in the story calls the 'best perfume of all'—the perfume of the desert, the fragrance of the void, the ecstatic sweet inebriating perfume of the Presence that is at once Everything and Nothing."

I was moved by what she said but I wanted her to speak about the story itself. So I asked her to tell me what the story had told her. "To me it is clear," she said. "Perhaps being in my early eighties helps it be so clear. The ruined palace is the world and all its games and desires and projects; each of them is made from some 'aromatic' desire that leaves a lingering trace. A line from T. S. Eliot's 'Four Quartets' comes back to me: 'Ash on an old man's sleeve / Is all the ash the burnt roses leave.' All the world's joys, however beautiful, are passing and cannot be kept long. The one eternal perfume is the one that smells of the Nothing of God; it is this 'perfume'—this gnosis, this bliss and ecstasy—that all mystics seek to 'smell' because they know it makes them drunk on the Beloved and lures them on to realize their identity with Him."

She paused and looked at her old, arthritic hands, smiling wryly. "And once you have smelled that perfume, your life is ruined, because nothing else will ever be as fragrant and your whole being becomes longing."

And then she told me a Sufi story. "You have told me a story that moves you; now I will tell you one I love. I think they are linked, and that if you listen to your story and my story together, you can hear almost the whole music of Sufism in them.

"I heard this story on my first visit to Konya, where Rumi, lived and when I heard it something changed in my heart forever."

There was an emperor who had a slave he loved passionately and who, he believed, loved him with his whole self. But the emperor wanted to be certain. So he filled ten rooms with heaps of every kind of treasure imaginable—rubies and emeralds, strands of large black pearls, chests full of the richest cloths and rarest, most marvelously illuminated manuscripts, large leather wallets with deeds in them to houses and country estates. When the rooms were full of this treasure, and the walls of the rooms seemed to glow and shine in the radiance of so much glory, the emperor summoned everyone in his court and all his servants and slaves and said, "Today I am releasing you all from my service. You are at perfect liberty to take anything you want from any of the rooms before you." You can imagine what pandemonium broke out! Even the chief vizier, normally a rather austere kind of man, started to dance a jig and to cram under his arms as many jewels and house deeds as he could find.

She paused and gazed out of the window, and the noise from the Parisian street below seemed to subside. "But the slave whom the emperor loved so did not move," she said, her voice trembling slightly.

He stayed standing where he was, silently, his face gazing at the emperor until all the treasure was gone and only he and the emperor were left in a desert of empty rooms. The emperor said quietly, "And you, who have stayed and not sought for anything for yourself, what is it you want? You can have anything you want in any of the worlds I own." The slave still said nothing, and then the emperor almost shouted, "What is it that you want? I order you to tell me!" And the slave said, "I want you." He repeated very slowly, "I want you. I want you." That was what he, the real Sufi, wanted—not the palace, or power, or any of the jewels and other gifts of the emperor—but the emperor himself.

She leaned back into the shadow of her chair and recited a poem by Rumi:

> *You are a sea of gnosis hidden in a drop of dew.*
> *You are a whole universe hidden in a sack of blood.*
> *What are all these worlds, pleasures, and joys*
> *That you keep grasping at them to make you alive?*

A profound silence fell between us. Then she said, "To smell the 'perfume of the desert' you have to learn to love like that slave loved his emperor. People ask me all the time what I think Sufism is. Sometimes, when I am lazy, I tell them it is the 'esoteric side of Islam' or trot out the quotation of some Sufi sage or philosopher. But when I am feeling reckless I just say, 'Sufism is the ancient wisdom of the heart. It predates Islam as eternity predates time. It has always been there from the beginning of human adoration of God. Sufism is the ancient wisdom of the heart and the science of love born from that wisdom, a science as precise but far more beneficial than the external sciences, perfected over centuries of brave exploration of the desert of the Absolute.' Did you know that the word for mystic path in Sufism—*tariqah*—means the path in the desert that the Bedouin takes to travel from oasis to oasis? Obviously such a path is not clearly marked like a highway and isn't even a visible road. But it is there to those who know. To find your way in the trackless desert you need to know the area intimately. Sufis are those who know the area intimately."

In the decade since that conversation, Sufism has come to attract ever-growing numbers of seekers and to enjoy an extraordinary renaissance throughout the Western world.

The main reason for this, I think, is that the Sufi approach to reality and to the quest for God is extremely passionate. The passion that the Sufi mystic prays for is one that embraces all of reality as a manifestation of the Divine and longs to burn itself out in the fire of love. Such a passion devours everything, is a furnace into which all other passions, desires, and agendas are quickly incinerated. Such a passion also costs everything, for the whole being and all its powers have to be strenuously devoted to it at all moments and in all circumstances to keep it alive and aflame. Rumi speaks in his Odes that this passion is a "howling storm in which all the houses of the false self are flattened forever."

In a passionless and psychologically devastated time like ours, the witness of the great Sufi saints and philosophers to this highest, noblest, and most devastating of all human passions—that of the soul for the Beloved—has an enormous force for awakening. Our modern addictions to reason and the games of irony and control have drained our psyches and souls of the heart-blood that keeps life abundant and miraculous; the Sufi lovers pump back that blood into us, fill us, in fact, with their blood, that long adoration and gnosis has turned into the purest—and most inebriating—mystic wine. The passion of the Sufi witnesses to the always shattering glory of the Beloved and to the splendor of the journey toward Him that restores us to the greatness of our real life, its vast capacity for suffering and joy, and the measureless growth of spirit that we are capable of if we let ourselves be possessed and devoured by divine love.

All authentic passion has great rigor, and true Sufi mysticism is nothing if not rigorous. The way of love demands from all who take it a terrible sincerity of being and a commitment to die again and again into the Nothing of the Divine. The Sufi mystical philosophers and poets face unsparingly all the ordeals and devastations of authentic transformation: their work has the "sear-marks" as well as the perfume of the desert. As my friend said that afternoon in Paris, "They know the area intimately," and we know that they know, because they speak to us with the broken-hearted authority of real lovers. They tell us in the most naked, arresting, and human way exactly what Love demands of us and what its multiple deaths feel like. Because they have so extreme and gorgeous a vision and knowledge of Love's glory, they never pretend that it is not worth all the horrors and ordeals of the journey towards it, and they never sell short the dangers that every soul must face on its voyage to the Absolute. They are reliable guides to the *tariqah* that crosses the desert of the Absolute and take us from oasis to oasis of gnosis and revelation with an effortlessness—and above all a purity of address—which will astonish and hearten all those who turn to them for help.

The greatest Sufis speak to us with a voice that is as practical as it is passionate, and this mixture of passion and practicality is one of the peculiar greatnesses of Sufism and another deep reason for its modern appeal. There is, of course, a strong ascetic tradition within Sufism: many of the greatest Sufi saints—particularly in the early period of the development of Sufism—were, like Rabia, seekers who abandoned the world to concentrate wholly on God; but the majority of the greatest Sufis have been men and women who lived in the world and who used its frictions, terrors, and tensions as ways of deepening their practice of Presence and as constant tests of their stability and sincerity. The highest ideals in Sufism, as in Christianity, are ones not of flight from the world but of living with divine peace, truth, and sobriety in it, and in a state of servanthood toward all beings and creatures. The Sufis are extremely wise guides to that integration that must happen on every level of our being if we are not only to glimpse the Absolute but also to live it at the heart of the inferno of ordinary life with all its distractions and worries. The Sufi tradition offers us not only a vast and complex witness to the ecstasy and passion of the path of love, but also a practical guide on how to integrate ecstasy and passion with the demands of everyday life. This fusion of drunkenness and sobriety, the highest and wildest kinds of gnosis with the most considered understanding of how to infuse dailiness with divine truth, is what makes Sufism one of the world's indispensable mystical traditions, one that seekers of all kinds have everything to learn from, especially in an era as deranged as ours.

In the hope of awakening the sacred heart in all of us and infusing its passion into all the choices of life, I have created this anthology. I have chosen to include only those poems, stories, or philosophical fragments that have directly inspired me; I wanted each selection to "smell of the desert" and to inebriate with its fragrance. Sufi talk or instruction is never linear; Sufi poets and sheikhs will try almost anything to shock their listeners awake, will swerve from the highest philosophy to the fragment of a great ode of Hafiz or Rumi, to a story in yesterday's newspaper, to a joke from Nasrudin. I remember hearing one old sheikh from the Mevlevi order speak in Paris for two hours and keep everyone preternaturally awake, because everything he said was clear, fierce, and vivid—and no one had the slightest idea what he would come up with next. It was like listening to life itself at its most exciting, precarious, and transformatory. I have tried to maintain this electric flow by alternating throughout the anthology poems and fragments of prose, stories with flights of ecstatic philosophy, jokes with diamantine definitions of awareness. I want to invite the reader to stay totally alert and to participate in the making of this anthology by diving deeply into its charged silences and empty spaces filled with the perfume of the desert wind.

There is a structure to *Perfume of the Desert*. It is really a five-part mystical symphony in words that I have designed to take the "listener" from the soul's first awakening to God, through all the splendors and rigors of its journey through the Desert of God, and to the glory and stability of union with the Beloved. Each part has a simple introduction that will initiate the reader into the main themes of what is to follow. In each section the selections are placed in a "musical" order that mirrors what I have come to understand of the journey into Love itself. I hope to communicate the authentic rhythm of awakening, with its alternating, mutually illuminating periods of expansion and contraction, passion and discipline, ecstasy and integration.

Whatever path you are on, let these Sufi heart-friends and their words and visions take you deeper into your heart, set you afire with holy passion for the Absolute, awaken you to the sacred necessity of suffering, enable your acceptance of ordeal, humble your power of adoration. And with their help and the grace of God, may we all come to serve the Real as they do—with the rapture and precision of the One whom Love has killed and remade!

Foreword to *The Way of a Pilgrim*, translated and annotated by Gleb Pokrovsky

Some books come to mean so much to you that you never forget the first time you read them. The first time I read *The Way of a Pilgrim* was over twenty years ago. I was then an academic, a fellow of an Oxford college; I had just returned to England after a life-changing year-long stay in India, where, for the first time, I had become aware of mystical reality through a series of experiences I could neither explain nor deny. I came back to Oxford convinced that spiritual truth could only be found in India and the Eastern spiritual traditions, and that Christianity was "finished" and "burned out."

The first person I imposed my new vision on was my best friend, Anne Pennington, a professor of Slavonic studies and a devout Russian Orthodox Christian. Anne listened patiently to my Indian raptures but cut me short when I started to dismiss the whole of Western religious experience. "How can you judge the Christian mystical tradition by what you see in the contemporary church?" she said. "That would be like judging the entire tradition of classical music by the dissonant ravings of the latest so-called composer. When you're settled in and less stubborn, I'm going to send you a book that will change your mind. And perhaps not only your mind...."

The book she sent me was her own worn and annotated copy of *The Way of a Pilgrim* along with photocopies of her favorite quotes on the prayer of the heart from *Philokalia*, the famous anthology of Eastern Orthodox texts on the spiritual life. It was a glowing, golden September, I remember: I took the book and the quotes out into a garden by the river and devoured them there in one sitting, transfixed and humbled by what I found. In India I had encountered for the first time the practice of *japa*—of repeating the name of God in the heart—and now I realized that in the Jesus prayer, "Lord Jesus Christ, have mercy on me," the Eastern Orthodox tradition had made the same simple, all-transforming discovery of the power of the divine name. The ecstasies and revelations of the anonymous narrator of *The Way of a Pilgrim* were no less profound and poignant than those that had so shaken me in Mirabai, Kabir, and Toukaram, the great Hindu and Sufi mystics, the discovery of whom had changed my life. And in the string of quotes from the *Philokalia*—from figures such as Symeon the New Theologian, Isaac the Syrian, and Gregory Palamas (until then totally unknown to me)—I recognized the pure sober note of mystical certainty and rigor that had thrilled me in the Bhagavad Gita and the Upanishads.

The Body of Love

A week later at dinner Anne and I discussed the practice of the Jesus prayer. I asked Anne what it meant to her. She paused a long time and then answered softly, "Everything." Two years later, when she was dying of cancer, still only in her forties, I asked her what was sustaining her faith and courage. "The Jesus prayer," she replied. "It gives me everything I need." After her death, I had a dream of her standing, flooded by divine light, by a statue of the resurrected Christ. She was gazing at me with immense tenderness and some amusement, as if to say, "And now do you at last understand how powerful prayer of the heart can be?" In her right hand, she was holding the copy of *The Way of a Pilgrim* she had lent me.

Although it would be ten more years before I set about practicing the Jesus prayer seriously, I can now say with wonder and gratitude that I am beginning to know what Anne was so anxious to show me. There are many ways you can read this profound and glorious book, which is one of the world's religious masterpieces. Whatever path you find yourself on, you can revel in it as a spiritual adventure story, the account of a man who searches for the meaning of prayer and mystical truth and finds them on a journey peppered with color-ful encounters, visions, and those revealing twists of fate of which any sincere seeker's life is full. If you are a practicing mystic, you can read *The Way of a Pilgrim* as a skillful and wise presentation of the theory and practice of the Jesus prayer, taking to heart its instructions and precise advice, delighting in the many subtle ways it opens up to you the treasures of the Eastern Orthodox tradition. I have known Hindus who have been inspired to return to their own practice by it and Buddhists who have found in its pages deep confirmation of their own experience of meditation. If you are not religious at all, you can enjoy *The Way of a Pilgrim* as a brilliantly sensuous and pungent evocation of mid-nineteenth-century Russia, with its villages and mud roads, snowy wastes and vast virgin forests, and that all-rewarding atmosphere of religious passion that permeates Russian literature from its origins through the novels of Tolstoy and Dostoyevsky, right up to the modern works of Pasternak and Solzhenitsyn. One incorrigibly secular friend of mine, a Russian-born philosopher, once surprised me by saying, "The three greatest books in Russian are *War and Peace, The Idiot,* and *The Way of a Pilgrim.*" When I asked him why he had included the latter, he replied, "Because it breathes the rich leather-and-incense perfume of old Russia with unique force." For myself, now, I find that the deeper and most satisfying way of reading *The Way of a Pilgrim* is as the unfolding of a profound mystical initiation into the ecstasy and truth of what Jesus called "the Kingdom," that state of divine knowledge and love that reveals the world as sacred and all beings as inherently divine that is the true goal of the Christian life.

Many readers who come to *The Way of a Pilgrim* for the first time will find, as I did, that it has a mysteriously initiatory power. The clue to this power, I believe, is that the work itself unfolds in the rhythms of sacred time and providence, with something of the same unpredictable and paradoxical simplicity of the Divine itself. This initiatory intent is stated early on: when the pilgrim meets the man who will become his *starets,* the old priest explains to him why his attempts up to now to discover the meaning of "unceasing prayer" have been unsuccessful: "Until now you have been tested in the cooperation of your will with God's calling and have been granted to understand that neither the wisdom of this world nor mere superficial curiosity can attain to the divine illumination of unceasing interior prayer." And the *starets* adds, making his meaning even more clear, "On the contrary, it is the humble, simple heart that attains to such prayer, through poverty of the spirit and a living experience of it." The entire remainder of the book unveils the radical deepening of the pilgrim's knowledge of poverty of spirit and of the living experience of divine presence that interior prayer opens him to. From the pivotal meeting with the *starets* onward, everything that occurs to the pilgrim occurs in the rhythms of a secret providence that guides him through both exterior events and graded stages of inner self-revelation to an ever more radiant awareness of the Christ-fire burning within him and in the creation, in all its tender glory. It is part of the work's enduring magic that so profound a process should be unfolded in the simplest imaginable prose, with a directness of approach that mirrors the directness of Truth itself. It is this diamantine, Gospel-like simplicity that draws the reader into believing that what is revealed to and in the pilgrim could be revealed to and in himself or herself.

Central to the mystery of intimacy that *The Way of a Pilgrim* creates is the naked, heartfelt intensity of the pilgrim's voice. From his first words we realize that we are in the presence of someone whom life and suffering have stripped to his essential core and seared clean of any desire to impress or convert, someone whose witness, then, to the deepening and miraculous effects of mystical prayer we can wholly believe. As he tells us, quite early on, of his experience of the power of the prayer: "There were days when I covered forty-seven miles or more and I didn't feel the effort of walking; the prayer alone filled my consciousness. When it was bitterly cold, I would pray more fervently and soon I'd feel warm all over. If hunger threatened to overcome me, I would call upon the name of Jesus Christ with renewed vigor, and hunger was forgotten." It is the earthy no-nonsense precision of this testimony that reassures and convinces us, and helps us identify with the pilgrim with real trust. He speaks to us as a humble brother-in-Christ with such naturalness that the amazing truths he comes to share seem to us, in the end, wholly natural and something that an expanded vision of our own nature and of the true nature of God and life could open us to also. It is this naturalness (and the humility that irradiates it) that enable the pilgrim not only to convey to us the depths of his inner experience but also to teach us by example— without in any way imposing this teaching on us—how to work with divine grace. In his ardor, constant receptivity, and exuberant compassion toward all the beings he meets and learns from, the pilgrim becomes a mirror for the best in us, becomes, in a sense, the pilgrim within all of us who longs to find truth and to live a guile-lessly divine human life. As *The Way of a Pilgrim* unfolds, we see the narrator being fashioned by changing events, the hand of grace, and his own rigorous cooperation with providence, into a true teacher, one whom the Christ has brought into his presence and given the radiant authority of his own direct truth. All the different visions and mystical insights of the pilgrim's journey culminate toward the end of the book in his wonderful experience at Tobolsk:

> The prayer of the heart delighted me so much that I thought there could be no one happier than me in the whole world and I could not imagine how there would be any great or deeper contentment even in the Kingdom of Heaven. Not only did I experience all this within myself, but outwardly as well—everything around me appeared wondrous to me and inspired me with love for and gratitude to God. People, trees, plants, and animals—I felt a kinship with them all and discovered how each bore the seal of the Name of Jesus Christ. At times I felt so light it was as if I had no body and were not walking but rather joyously floating through the air. At other times I entered so fully into myself that I saw clearly all my inner organs, and this caused me to marvel at the wisdom that went into creating the human body. Sometimes I knew such joy that I felt like a king. At such consoling moments I wished that God would grant me to die soon, so that I could pour myself out in gratitude at His feet in heaven.

We believe in the pilgrim's awe-inspiring vision not only because of the dazzled and humble way in which he transmits it to us but also because, immediately afterwards, he confesses, "It became apparent to me that my enjoyment of these experiences was tempered or had been regulated by God's will," and goes on to tell us of a period of anxiety and fear that humbles him and deepens his awareness of what a true teacher has to accept and understand:

> Clouds of thoughts descended upon my mind and I remembered the words of the Blessed John of Karpathos who said that often the teacher submits to humiliation and suffers misfortune and temptations for those who will benefit from him spiritually. After

struggling for a while with such thoughts, I began to pray earnestly, and the thoughts were banished entirely. I was encouraged by this and said to myself, "God's will be done! Anything that Jesus Christ may send my way I am ready to endure for my wretchedness and arrogance—for even those to whom I had recently disclosed the secret of entering the heart and of interior prayer had been prepared directly by God's hidden guidance, before I met them."

By implication, we, the readers who have followed the pilgrim so far into mystery and revelation have also been prepared not by him for the truths he is sharing with us, but by God. At the very moment the narrator could have put us in awe of him and of his search, his wisdom enables him to free himself, and us, from anything but wonder at divine wisdom and mercy. With astounding subtlety, then, the pilgrim shows us how he has been guided—and has guided us—by divine grace from mystical ecstasy into holy sobriety and the all-healing recognition of his (and our) own utter dependence on the Divine. In so doing, the pilgrim reminds us that the Divine will only go on revealing itself to one who remains in awe and adoration and ever-deepening surrender to its truth.

It is this awe, adoration, and surrender that the last, wild story the pilgrim tells us shows that he has truly begun to live and know. In it he tells us of how he was staying overnight in the hut of a drunken postmaster, whose cook prepares him a bed. The pilgrim is pretending to sleep when suddenly the entire hut is shaken and the window "in the front corner of the house—the frame, the glass, and all—came showering down with a terrible crash"; a carriage has by mistake crashed into the house. At this the peasant cook "sprang back in terror and jumped into the middle of the room, where she went crashing down on the floor." At first the reader has no idea why he is being told such a bizarre story seemingly unconnected to anything that has gone before. A page later we are given the reason: he tells us that six years later he was passing a women's monastery where he was entertained by the abbess and was moved by the humility of the nun pouring him tea—only to discover that this was the same woman he had encountered in the postmaster's hut—the violent experience several years previously having transformed her into a humble God-seeker. The revelation of the wisdom and mercy of divine providence that this story gives him completes and seals the pilgrim's long initiation and he tells us simply: "Upon this my soul rejoiced and glorified God, who so wisely orders all things for the good." His long journey has brought the pilgrim (and us with him) to the point when at last he is humble (and humbled) enough to see the hand of grace in all the tragedies and disasters of the world, and to surrender completely to a mystery he knows he will and can never understand, but he knows enough to understand it to be a Mystery of Love.

The Way of a Pilgrim ends with the narrator on the threshold of a journey to Jerusalem. In a sense the book ends where language itself ends, on the threshold of the mystery of divine consciousness that the Rhineland mystic John of Ruysbroeck called the "holy unknowing of the Dark in which true lovers lose themselves," and that characterizes the beginnings of Christ-consciousness. We will never know whether or not the pilgrim reached Jerusalem, and in the deepest sense, it does not matter, because we know that he has found the Holy City and the Kingdom within and outside himself, and has helped us to begin to imagine how we also might be led by grace to make the same discovery for ourselves. The silence at the end of *The Way of a Pilgrim* is like the tremendous silences that surround and elevate us at the end of Beethoven's Ninth Symphony or the Bach B Minor Mass. It is a silence that not only rings with the various kinds of music that are consummated in it but seems, momentarily, to call down, to embody and enshrine the divine presence itself. Only the highest art, informed by the deepest spiritual intelligence and love, could lead us to a place where all expression and feeling dissolve in wonder.

I dedicate this foreword to my friend Henry Luce III, in gratitude and love.

Introduction to *Teachings of the Christian Mystics*

There is nothing more important, I believe, for the future of the mystical renaissance that is struggling to be born everywhere in the West—and thus for the future of the planet—than an authentic and unsparing recovery of the full range, power, and glory of the Christian mystical tradition. Without such a recovery, the spiritual life of the West will continue to be a superficial, narcissistic, and sometimes lethal mixture of a watered-down or fanatical pseudo-Christianity, hardly understood "Eastern" metaphysics, and regressive occultism—and the great radical potential of such a renaissance will go unlived and unenacted, with disastrous consequences for every human being and for all of nature.

What is needed is the flaming up on a global scale, of an unstoppable force of Divine-human love wise enough to stay in permanent humble contact with the Divine and brave enough to call for, risk, and implement change at every level and in every arena before time runs out and we destroy ourselves. Such a love has to spring from an awakened mystical consciousness and must be rooted in habits of fervent meditation, adoration of the Divine, and prayer; for only then will it be illuminated enough to act at all times with healing courage, and strong enough to withstand the ordeals and torments that are inevitable. Teilhard de Chardin wrote, "Some day, after we have mastered the winds, the waves, the tides and gravity, ... we shall harness the energies of love. Then, for the second time in the history of the world, man will have discovered fire." Unless humankind discovers this fire and uses it to burn away everything that blocks the changes that must come in order to transform the planet into the mirror of divine beauty it is meant to be, it will die out and take most of nature with it.

At the core of Christ's enterprise is an experience of this fire and the revolutionary passion of charity that blazes from it. This passion, as Christ knew and lived it, cannot rest until it has burned down all the divisions that separate one human heart from another, and so from reality. No authority except that of the Divine is sacred to it; no dogma, however hallowed, that keeps oppression of any kind alive can withstand the onslaught of its flame. All of human experience, personal and political, is arraigned and exposed by it. It demands of everyone who approaches it a loving and humble submission to its fierce, mind- and heart-shattering power and a commitment to enact its laws of radical compassion and hunger for justice in every arena. Its aim is the irradiation of all of life with holy and vibrant energy and truth, so that as many beings as possible can live, here on earth and in the body, in a direct relationship with God, each other, and nature, in what St. Paul unforgettably calls "the glorious liberty of the Children of God."

Many forces, even within the "Christian" world, block the unleashing of this "glorious liberty." Anyone who comes to feel even a small spark of the heat of this fire may look in vain to find any of its truth in the churches that claim to keep it alive. Fundamentalism of any kind is alien to its adoration of freedom and its all-embracing love of all beings and all creation; the narrow judgmental ethics that disfigure all denominations of Christianity represent precisely that separation that Christ himself wanted to end forever. Most Western seekers are refugees from hypocritical, patriarchal, misogynistic, and homophobic versions of Christ's message that are tantamount to perverse, even demonic, betrayals of it. The great mystical treasures of all the Christian traditions have been largely ignored for centuries, even in the monastic institutions that might have kept them alive. With such a grim prospect, it is hardly surprising that many seekers continue to project onto Christ and his teachings only what they learned from suffering the mutilation of both by the churches. The majority of westerners interested in spiritual transformation and aware of its necessity know very little about the Christian mystics; they know more about the Hindu or Sufi or Buddhist mystical traditions than about the one that is the hidden and glorious secret of their own civilization. Many more have read the Bhagavad Gita or Rumi than have read Ruysbroeck or Jacopone da Todi or St. John of the Cross; many more have practiced *vipassana* or *bhakti* yoga than have attempted the spiritual exercises of Ignatius of Loyola or than have prayed the Jesus prayer with Symeon the New Theologian and Nicephorus the Solitary. The result is that the explosive force of Christ's subversion of all forms of authority and all forms of worldly power goes largely unnoticed, and a vast power for fundamental change on every level goes unused.

This is a tragedy because, of all the mystic pioneers of humanity, Christ is in almost every way the most daring and demanding and the most concerned with the brutal facts of this world. His living out of his enlightenment and his realization of his fundamental unity with God has an unique urgency, a poignantly wild passion, and a hunger for justice that make him the hero of love in the human race. Christ came not to found a new religion or to inaugurate a new set of dogmas but to open up a fierce and shattering new path of love in action, a path that seems now, with the hindsight of history, the one that could have saved—and still could save—humanity from its course of suicidal self-destruction.

At the moment when the patriarchy was beginning its long, dark triumph in the form of the Roman Empire, Christ revealed and enacted a way of being completely subversive to all of its beliefs and "truths." To a world obsessed by power, he offered a vision of the radiance of powerlessness and the powerful vulnerability of love; to a culture riddled with authoritarianism, false pomp, and greed he gave a vision of the holiness of inner and outer poverty and a critique of the vanity and horror of all forms of worldly achievement so scalding that most of his own followers have contrived every means imaginable to ignore it. To a society arranged at every level into oppressive hierarchies—sexual, religious, racial, and political—he presented in his own life a vision of a radical and all-embracing egalitarianism designed to end forever those dogmas and institutions that keep women enslaved, the poor starving, and the rich rotting in a prison of selfish luxury. In his own life, he showed what the new life this path would open up to everyone who risked its rigors would be like—how free and tender and brave and charged with healing, ecstatic power. Faithful always to the humble egalitarianism of his understanding of divine love, he refused all the glamour of sagedom, constantly undermining all of the fantasies that others tried to project onto him, and he finally embraced horrible and humiliating suffering on the Cross to break through into that dimension of Resurrection and cosmic life from which he continues to guide, enflame, and inspire all who turn to him.

So demanding and illusionless a path remains a perpetual challenge to anyone who dares to see its truth. This truth in its fullness was almost immediately betrayed by the historical development of Christianity. An egalitarian path that welcomed and celebrated women was turned into a hierarchical and misogynistic church; a vision that criticized all power was conscripted to sustain first imperial and then papal ambitions; a force of love that wanted to end all division and separation became a force of fanaticism and fundamentalism that derided other religions and created one more prison of exclusion. A force of wholeness—Christ was never an ascetic and never denigrated the body or sexuality—became a force of alienation, separating body from soul, man from woman, humanity from nature, and privileging renunciation and celibacy as the surest way to God.

As an integral part of this betrayal, Christ himself was dogmatically separated from the human race he wanted to liberate. He was declared the Son of God, a perfect being whose divinity set him apart from everyone. Christ himself never claimed to be the Son of God; his only claim, significantly, was to be the "Son of Man." It is clear that Christ did not wish to be worshipped as a God; he wanted, in fact, to do something far more necessary and far more subversive—to reveal, by living it, the divine truth of every human identity and so instruct and empower the Christ within each of us and bring each of us into the atmosphere and splendor of the Kingdom of God that is our natural and rightful inheritance. Declaring Christ unique and divine muted the outrageousness of Christ's real adventure and created a subtle chasm between humanity and him that prevented the full, liberating power of his radical discovery of the divine power and truth latent in everyone from reaching and transforming the world. As Jung wrote,

> The demand made by the *Imitatio Christi,* that we should follow this ideal and seek to become like it, ought logically to have the result of developing and exalting the inner man. In actual fact, however, the ideal has been turned by superficial and formalistically minded believers into an external object of worship, and it is precisely this veneration of the object that prevents it from reaching down into the depths of the soul and transforming it into a wholeness in keeping with the ideal. Accordingly, the divine mediator stands outside as an image, while man remains fragmentary and untouched in the deepest part of him.

In the great Christian mystics, however, we can read the words of those who, whatever they may have believed about Christ's unique divinity, did not remain "fragmentary and untouched" in the deepest part of themselves, but staked their lives not merely on following some version of Christ's teaching but on submitting themselves to the same, almost intolerable pressures, vicissitudes, and passions as he had, so as to be "Christed" with him. For them, Christ was more than a teacher or sage or even Divine image; he was the pioneer of a wholly new kind of human being, one who wanted to become one with the fire of love and to be its selfless revolutionary in the dark night of human history. Brave and loving enough—and constantly inspired by divine Grace—these heroic men and women took up Christ's challenge—the challenge, above all, of the Cross—and allowed themselves, like him, to be crucified unto Resurrection, killed unto an eternal life dedicated utterly to love and the service of others. Despite often terrible opposition from the Church of their day—and all forms of scandal and humiliation—they did not dishonor their great brother, and kept the flame of his spiritual truth and of the new being it births alive.

When the Christian mystical tradition is seen in its entirety—and I hope this anthology will do something to enable this—what will, I believe, become most clear is the radically subversive and sobering nature of its humility—a humility that springs directly from the explosive and deranging example of Christ himself. Christ's enlightenment has nothing safe or omnipotent about it; its symbol is not a triumph of effortlessness but one of utter and devastating self-gift: the Cross. Again and again, Christ, in his teachings and by his example, made it clear that the only authentic sign of spiritual wisdom is a progress in the kind of ego-annihilating humility that longs to express itself in the ever-greater and ever-richer service of all beings. There is nothing to comfort the ordinary or subtle spiritual ego in this stark vision, no place for any kind of pride or grandiosity to hide; Christ made this eternally clear when he himself, as one of his final acts among them before his Passion, washed the feet of his disciples. In the Christ path, the richest are those who give the most; the highest are those who lovingly take the lowest place; those who really love God prove it in unstinting service to human beings and the creation, and willingly embrace whatever suffering standing for justice and mercy in a vicious world must bring and whatever ordeal is necessary for their inner purification. Christ himself gave, humbly, everything; those who approach the fire of his love slowly learn the force and demand of his terrible humility.

I believe that seekers of every kind have four essential, exacting, and sobering lessons to learn from the terrible humility of the tradition of Christ, lessons that echo again and again through the pages of this book. The first is that even in the highest and final stages of mystical illumination—even in the "spiritual marriage" of Teresa of Avila or John of Ruysbroeck—a crucial gap still remains between Creator and creature that necessitates a continuing practice of prayer, contemplation, and service; oneness with God in love is possible, but not in nature and being. In the inner lives of even the greatest saints and mystics, there is always still work to be done, for the demand and power of divine love are infinite and endless. Christ himself, though one with God in love, never stopped growing to incarnate more and more of that love. All those who love and follow him submit to the same ruthless laws of continual transformation.

Such a vision permanently humbles all spiritual pride and leads to the second great radical insight of the Christian mystical tradition—that enshrined in Gregory of Nyssa's vision of the doctrine of infinite growth *(epectasis)*. In this vision, entering the force field of the Christ-consciousness opens up the possibility of infinite expansion and change. Consequently, for the Christian mystic, enlightenment is not in any sense a static state of omniscience or oneness with being, as the Eastern religions have tended to represent it—but a continual opening up to and evolution in love. No being, even in the highest angelic hierarchies, can claim to be *wholly* wise or *wholly* transformed; there are always new mountains of gnosis and adoration to climb. Such a vision simultaneously exalts and humbles—exalts because it reveals the law of an evolution without end in every arena and dimension of the universe, humbles because it shows clearly that the prerequisite for such growth is a continual self-donation to an always-higher and always-transcendent power.

Christ and those who followed (and follow) him also teach us a third humbling lesson: that the price for such infinite growth and expansion in love is, as Christ's own terrifying life makes clear, a heroic embrace of the laws of suffering and ordeal. To accept the demands of love is to accept the Cross and the extreme suffering that comes with it. Authentic divine love, St. Francis said, "suffers as a bird sings": there is no way out of such suffering, and it is the peculiar noble greatness of Christ and his lovers that they never wanted a way out. There are no greater teachers of the purpose and alchemical power of suffering in any other mystical literature, because no other group of mystics have faced the necessity of ordeal with such unshrinking precision and so learned how to transmute agony into thanksgiving; or even, in the highest and rarest cases, like Christ himself, fuse them in one continual outpouring of love. The insights of such alchemists of horror are priceless, I believe, at a time when all seekers are called on to transform themselves extremely fast to be of use in a devastated world. To work for a new humanity in a world as violent and corrupt as ours must involve great pain and frightening vulnerability to derision, even persecution, and the temptation to despair: the Christian tradition explores the healing paradoxes of ordeal in a way that can embolden and instruct everyone.

The fourth humbling lesson that Christ and his mystical brothers and sisters teach us is that no mystical training is authentic unless it results in a total commitment to other beings and to the service of justice and compassion in all forms in the creation. There is nothing world-abandoning about greatest of the Christian mystics; they strive to incarnate that electric balance between contemplation of God and action in reality that characterized Christ himself. The tremendous danger that the world is in demands of all of us that we learn to fuse at every level the deepest possible contemplative connection to the Divine with the most precise and responsible possible action in reality so the world can be constantly infused with the creativity and justice of God. We have everything to learn from Christ and the Christian mystics on how most effectively and humbly to do this.

What I hope this anthology will also make clear is that the conventional picture of Christianity as essentially a patriarchal, life-denying, world-despising religion is a travesty—one for which, of course, the churches are largely responsible. The truth is that the authentic Christian tradition, and Christ's teaching itself, is everywhere saturated with the healing and life-affirming truths of the Sacred Feminine, and with its wisdom of sensitivity, tenderness, and honoring of all life, and its respect for the necessity of suffering and vulnerability. Inept translation and patriarchal distortion of what Christ said and did have obscured this truth—and with it a great deal of the transforming and radical power of Christ-consciousness.

The clue to its full recovery, I believe, as I have written in my book *Return of the Mother,* is the full recovery of the mystical role in the birth of Christ-consciousness of Mary the Mother. Until Mary is seen in Her full glory, as the incarnation of the divine Motherhood of God, Christ cannot be seen in his, because he is as much the Son of the Mother, the apostle of the transforming powers and life-rich truths of the Sacred Feminine, as he is the Son of the Father. Christ's experience of the Divine was a complete experience of the Mother aspect of God as well as that of God the Father. It is this completeness that gives his life and teaching such all-embracing authority and such a miraculous fusion of transcendent adoration and immanent concern, of the fiercest clarity and intellectual power with the most acute tenderness for all life.

One of the greatest mysteries of the Christian mystical tradition is how the awareness of Mary's essential role in the transformation of love that Christ came to effect has expanded astonishingly over the centuries. This anthology celebrates this discovery of the power of Divine Motherhood in Mary in all of its crucial stages—from the explosion of interest in and adoration of Her in the fourth and fifth centuries (represented here in two excerpts from the Akathist Hymn of Romanos the Melodist), through the great upsurge of devotion to Her in the Middle Ages (whose pioneer and architect was Bernard of Clairvaux) to the prophetic work in the early eighteenth century of Louis-Marie Grignion de Montfort, whom I consider to be the greatest of all Marian mystics and the one who gives us all the deepest and greatest clues as to the authentic meaning of the Second Coming when he writes:

> It is through the very Holy Virgin that Jesus Christ came into the world to begin with, and it is also through her that he will reign in the world.... Until now, the divine Mary has been unknown, and this is one of the reasons why Jesus Christ is hardly known as he should be. If then—as is certain—the knowledge and reign of Jesus Christ arrive in the world it will be a necessary consequence of the knowledge and reign of the very Holy Virgin, who birthed him into this world the first time and will make him burst out everywhere the second.

De Montfort is announcing a great mystical truth; that the Christ-consciousness, in all its tenderness and radical passion, is born from as complete as possible an adoration of the Sacred Feminine. In the last hundred and fifty years, the Virgin has been appearing all over the world, warning humanity of the danger of living without God and without love and trying to open all beings to the truths of the Heart. She has been, as the mystical Mother of all new beings, preparing the ground for the birth of the Christ in all of us, through wonder, prayer, unconditional love, and unstinting service. At the potential end of history, Mother and Son, then, are returning in a new and revolutionary dance of love and wisdom whose consequences could be—if we allow them to—completely transforming.

The Second Coming will not, I believe, be the return of Christ as a figure: that version perpetuates the old deification of Christ that has kept his force inert in history. The *real* Second Coming will be the birthing of Christ-consciousness in millions of beings who turn, in the Father-Mother, towards the fire of love and take the supreme risk of incarnating divine love in action on earth. This Second Coming could potentially alter the level of consciousness of the whole of humanity and initiate it into that mystical wisdom that it desperately needs if its problems are going to be solved.

May all those who come to this book be inspired to allow themselves to be "birthed" into love and so serve, humbly and with undauntable love, the future of humankind.

"Resurrecting the Authentic Christ: Jesus as Guide to Mystical Love in Action" Interview with Michael Bertrand

Michael Bertrand: Andrew, you were saying that you felt propelled into this work?

Andrew Harvey: We're really trying to resurrect the authentic Christ. I feel it's the most important possible work at the moment, because what is essential is that the heart of the West be transformed. Western civilization must go through a very radical and very complete transformation, because, after all, it's the West that has the overwhelming power at the moment. The fate of the world depends, in a way, upon that power.

I believed once that the Eastern religions by themselves had enough mystical power and great tradition of understanding to be able to transform the West. Now I believe that the Western transformation can come through making available the great mystical practices of the East, but also through a restoration of the authentic Christ to the heart of the West.

This authentic Christ, as I've tried to show in my book [Son of Man: The Mystical Path to Christ], is a mystical revolutionary—an emotional, social, and political revolutionary. The force of the Cosmic Christ is one which arms us on all of these different levels to make us capable of not only being directed to the Divine but of acting with that divine connection in the inferno of reality. This whole vision of mystical action is very important at a moment when we're so much in danger.

I think Jesus and the Christ path are tremendous guides that you need to respect, whatever path you're on. The book I've written isn't just for Christians. It's actually for Buddhists and Hindus and Sufis and shamans as well. It's an attempt to try and bring back the Cosmic Christ into the great mystical dialogue that's taking place, so everyone can hear his challenge, appreciate the depth of his agony, and open to the glory of the possibility that he's enshrining.

MB: In the context of what you're saying, what is the Cosmic Christ and how do we see beyond the church's view? So many of us have rejected Christianity because it seems like they're saying, "This is the only way," so how do we see this Cosmic Christ as something that's inherent in not just this tradition but all traditions and inherent in human beings, too?

AH: I think the Cosmic Christ is the universal force of divine love, the force of active, divine love that streams from the godhead to the creation. It's also the force of divine love that is incarnate in the human being. It's a transcendent and immanent force that is at once one with the divine love that's sustaining the universe at every level and also incarnate in every one of us, whether we're Christian, Buddhist, or whatever we call ourselves, at the very core of our being.

In the Upanishads, God is celebrated as the person, the Purusha, the one who is a person. That person is the Cosmic Christ. The whole of the universe is that person.

MB: What do you mean by a person?

AH: Well, one of the things that you discover in mystical experience is that the universe is alive in its ultimate depths. There's a very astonishing correspondence between the human consciousness and the divine consciousness. The whole that is the universe is both utterly impersonal and utterly and totally personal. The personal aspect could be and is said in many mystical traditions to be a person. In Islam it is said to be a great person. In Hinduism it's said to be the Purusha, and in Christianity it's said to be the Cosmic Christ.

MB: Like the Friend in Sufism?

AH: Yes. The Beloved. Exactly. Everyone who's had a mystical experience has come into contact with what you could call the Cosmic Christ, but a very important way of connecting with the fullness of the Cosmic Christ is, I believe, looking at how the Cosmic Christ expressed his or her nature in the life of Jesus itself. Why this is important is, I believe, because Jesus brought a unique intensity of justice to the world's experience of God.

Other great liberators have helped us to see the nature of desire, to see how we must deal with our emotions, to see the nature of the illusion of the world, but I think Jesus more than any of the great liberators wanted to use this power of awakening to transform the existing conditions of the world, really to create what he calls the Kingdom on earth. This Kingdom is the kingdom of justice, mercy, of radical equality. It's this kingdom, I think, that we need to create on the planet now if it's going to be preserved. We need a mystical awakening that's simultaneously an opening to the highest transcendent godhead and the mystical awakening that makes us aware that we are committed, through that awakening, to act responsibly at every level in society, to change society. We need an awakening, in other words, that's political and active and social and economic as well as purely personal. Jesus is a tremendous guide to the radical inclusiveness of such an awakening.

MB: So, you're not saying it has to be through Christ or through Jesus, as the church is saying?

AH: No, but I'm saying that if you want a mystical activism, a vision of mystical love in action, one tremendous guide to that vision will be Jesus's example. A tremendous guide as to how to enact that vision will be what I call in my book the "Christ path," with its four stages of awakening, elimination, union, and birthing.

The Christian church separated Jesus from human experience by calling him a savior. The Christian mystics, as opposed to the church, experienced the Inner Christ, the Christ within themselves, and [their] union with it and with the force of active love that it enshrines. Their extraordinary testimony to the power of that experience is very valuable for seekers of all kinds, and I think has a lot to teach all seekers—Christians, Buddhists, Hindus. It has a lot to teach in how to make love active within the world and how to go through the various ordeals and strippings and annihilations that will prepare us for that great task of being mystics, awake and alert at the core of realty.

MB: That's a great challenge, because it seems [that] through history there's been relatively few people who have attained anything close to that sort of realization or fulfillment of the human story. At least in the West we think that, as the examples have, certainly in the last few hundred years, been drowned in the general culture.

AH: Yes, but when you look at the Christian mystic tradition, you do find a very extraordinary amount of beings who've been on the journey to Christhood, from the early Desert Fathers, through Gregory of Nyssa, through St. Francis of Assisi and Teresa of Avila. This great force of transfiguration of mind, soul, and body has been continually working to transform beings, despite the lunacy of the churches.

Now, I think, is a marvelous moment, because in my own journey, it was going to the East and going through initiations in the Buddhist, Hindu, and Sufi traditions that opened me up to the mystical truth of reality. Returning to the Christian tradition, I was able to see the mystical core of it and of the path very clearly. So, I think the time is coming now for all of the great religions to be purified by mystic truth and to come into direct dialogue from the core of their mystic revelation.

What I'm trying to do in *Son of Man* is to bring out the mystic urgency and passion, the mystic challenge of the Christ path in all its radical, revolutionary fervor and glory. What I imagine is a dialogue between the Hindu and Buddhist masters and mistresses of emptiness and Sufi lovers of the Beloved and those who've taken the Christ path. From that dialogue will come a new path of love in action, but one tremendous voice has to be heard utterly clearly in that path and that is the voice of Jesus and of the Christ and of the Divine Mother in Her aspect as Mary.

These are the voices I'm trying to resurrect in their fullness, so the dialogue can be as rich and radioactive as possible, as nuclear in intensity and in challenge and dynamic force as possible.

MB: So, you're saying there's a sense of a new concept of what human beings are and can be?

AH: Yes. With a special emphasis on action in the world, because we live at a time in which we probably have about twenty years to make major decisions about every single aspect of world life. If we don't come to these radical decisions about the environment, for example, we as a race simply will not survive and we'll probably drag nature with us in a holocaust of unimaginable proportions. Tremendous suffering lies ahead, and the only response to this tremendous task must be one of love in action.

All the revelations that can help us become clearer about what exactly is the power of divine love in us and how it can be used to transform the Real, any revelation that can help us go deeper into that is priceless. In my opinion the Christ path and the Christ revelation is one of the most fecund, fertile, and exuberant in its vision of a love that transcends all barriers and acts to transform the Real. That's why I think it's so important now and [why] I've tried to bring it out in all of its different facets in my book.

MB: So, in order not to be numbed by the consumer culture that's around us and the great degradation of nature that is so obvious, what I hear you saying is that we have to work with the mystical side of oneself, or the true self, in order to have the energy necessary to do something.

AH: Fundamentally what I think you have to do is awaken what I and the Christian tradition call the Sacred Heart, the life of the heart chakra, the inmost and most passionate life of the divine love that is the core of our being. Awakening and living from the sacred heart is a huge task, because it demands tremendous intensity of being and tremendous focus on the heart and tremendous, endless practice to keep the heart open.

If you do keep the heart open, what you are graced with is this extraordinary energy, divine human energy, which can keep you going in the face of disaster, misery, and catastrophe. It's this divine love energy that all of us need to be empowered within the depths of our lives now. We're going to need it.

It's not just, of course, an energy. It's a gnosis. It's a revelation of the essential relations between ourselves and nature and the world and the cosmos. It illuminates in every moment the necessary ways of action. So, it's energy of love and insight and action, all of those things together. This is what I believe Christ, more than any other teacher, focused on. The Christian mystics are tremendous guides to how to open the sacred heart, how to keep it open despite all the suffering that will come, how to use suffering as a fertile ground for transformation, not to escape or deny it, and how to go forward in vibrant, passionate, active charity in every dimension.

This is the clue to survival. This isn't just something we can debate at this moment. This is something we need like oxygen. The world is drowning in chaos and catastrophe, and the only way to get through is to revivify ourselves at every level by the oxygen of divine love and divine knowledge and to work with them in union and in sacred marriage in the world.

In Jesus's life, you see what it actually means not only to realize the divinity of the heart of one's humanity, but to live it out. Jesus was not content only to realize he was divine at the core of his being. Realizing it made him very conscious of how to act as a divine being in the world, which simply means to act on behalf of everyone who is brokenhearted and destroyed and at a loss and humiliated in the culture, to serve the afflicted and to serve them with tremendous courage at the core of life.

I think this is Jesus's challenge to all of us, whatever path we're on. Do we love enough? Are we prepared to have not merely spiritual experiences and mystical awakenings, but actually to take responsibility for them and to work with their insights in the real, to transform the Real into a clearer and clearer image of that love and justice that we discover to be the truth of God and the truth of ourselves.

This is Jesus's call to the world. He's saying, first of all, open up to the Divine within you. Really open up. Plunge into the divine part, into the core of your being, open up your sacred heart, see the world radiate the fire of the sacred heart, see every being as utterly and totally holy, know nature as holy, know each animal as holy.

Then he's saying you have to take that knowledge into action in the world. You can't simply revel in it and enjoy it. You are responsible for it. You have to enact it, first in your inmost life as a soul, and then in the life of the heart, then in the mind, and then in the life of action within the world, so that you can come into the fullness of your divine humanity, which is to be nothing less than a completely divine, completely human being, working with the Divine in the human to transfigure the human more and more into an image of the Divine.

That is the Christ challenge and the Christ path and that path is very inclusive, all-embracing, demanding, and rigorous—and very scary and very necessary.

MB: It's an awfully large challenge.

AH: In the New Age a lot of people airily talk about being a divine being, but what would it actually mean to be a divine being? I think the Buddha and Krishna and other great masters have shown just how much it actually costs, because to be a divine human being is to live a life of abandoned, selfless service and abandoned, passionate love of all things to its absolute fullest at the core of reality. That is what it means. That is what it costs. That is the only way in which it could mean anything.

Otherwise, we're just playing with words and cheering ourselves up, and that is not going to preserve humanity at this dangerous moment. I think what we have to do now is to take the challenge of the very greatest saints and mystics and really "Christ" ourselves, if you like. Instead of endlessly appealing to their force to save us, we have to do the work that they came to open up to us.

Neither the Christ nor the Buddha said that by turning to them would we be saved. They said, "I have done it. I have lived this life. I am living this life. Now you live it. You too can become Christ or Buddha at the core of your lives."

I think the New Age has to grow up and take that challenge really more seriously and rigorously and passionately than it has begun to yet. We are going to have to have an authentic mystical renaissance instead of a lot of people dancing about and pretending to have mystical experiences, which is what's going on at the moment.

It's a tragic situation in some ways. On the one hand, you have the corporations and the industrial network destroying the planet, and on the other hand, you have a largely fake spiritual renaissance going on, falsely empowering people with half-baked notions of divine identity, instead of bringing people into the full challenge and majesty, glory and power of authentic divine transformation and authentic divine identity.

So, on both sides you are met with different illusions. It's very important now. It's never been more important to have the authentic mystical path out there in its full beauty and full rigor.

The most important thing to do is start practicing seriously. Do you remember the scene from *The Graduate* when Dustin Hoffman is taken aside by the businessman who has one word to say to him, and the word turns out to be "plastics"? Well, the one word I really wish to say to anybody at this moment, in 1999, faced with all we're faced with, is "practice."

We've got to come to a stage where we read fewer and better books and practice more and harder. There's a tremendous difference between reading and feeling and having emotional and spiritual experiences and actually realizing the truth of what the great mystics tell us at the depths of ourselves. That realization can only come through a very intense and very down-home and sober commitment to practice, which is why *Son of Man* ends with twelve sacred practices, drawn from the depths of the Christian tradition or adapted for the Christian tradition from Tibetan Buddhism and Taoism and Hinduism, to enable those who want to get a direct connection with the Cosmic Christ.

It's this direct connection in the heart of life, through sustained intense spiritual practice, that is and always has been available to everybody and is now even more available, through divine grace, to everybody. We all need to claim this as our birthright very, very fiercely and passionately if we're going to have a chance now of being strong, wise, and awake enough to go through.

MB: Could you give an example of what a good practice would be?

AH: It means having a daily period of real meditation, which you hold to—whatever happens—and I suggest a half-hour in the morning and a half-hour in the evening. It means keeping up, throughout the day, a very simple practice of prayer, which can be as simple as saying the name of God in the heart at all available opportunities—be they waiting for a bus, talking on the phone—keeping up a constant attention to the presence of the Divine in the heart through a mantra or saying a sacred word.

It means meditation and prayer, and it also means service. It means treating your whole life and all of the relationships and meetings in your life as opportunities for sacred service, for helping, blessing, succoring, and sustaining real life. I think if you do all three together then, slowly, you will be brought more and more into the fullness of your embodied divine being. That fullness will instruct you as to what to do and will make you stronger in every arena.

What you're being called to, I think, is a life that is both a life of inward prayer and sustenance and external service and action at every level. That's what I would call practice, because what you're doing is practicing the presence, the value, and power of the heart, enacting it and allowing [it]. Your practice becomes a kind of mother to you. Through intense, sustained practice you create a mothering power, and you are mothered by that power into a deeper and deeper fearlessness, passion, and calm.

That helps you sustain a richer and richer life, so you're helping, through practicing intensely, to create a kind of mothering force within your life that will help you go deeper and deeper into service. This is how it must work, I think, for all of us now, whatever path we're on. Christ is a tremendous example of how to live from that power.

MB: You mentioned mothering, which reminds me that you spent a great deal of your intellectual and writing time over the last number of years being part of the wave of bringing the Divine Feminine, or the Mother, back into the societal consciousness.

AH: Yes. I love what Kabir, the great Indian mystic, said, "My father is the formless absolute and my mother is the embodied godhead." We're in the process of destroying the embodied godhead, nature. We're in the process of raping and absolutely annihilating, through our greed and ignorance, the Mother.

It is essential now, the most essential movement of our times, to bring back the Divine Feminine in all its beauty, power, majesty, glory, and fury.

What I discovered when I plunged into the Christian mystical tradition and Christ's own teaching, especially in the Gnostic Gospels, is that the real Jesus and the real force of the Cosmic Christ is as much the child of the Divine Mother as of the Divine Father. What Jesus really was and is in the depths of ourselves is the sacred androgyne, the union of the masculine and feminine in the greatest intensity, and the creation of a being that is at once at home in the Transcendent and utterly at home in the Immanent. It's a new kind of being, which I believe is the future of humanity.

I believe where we're being taken to, if we can survive this transition, is to the creation on this earth of a being who is a sacred androgyne, who does fuse the masculine and feminine, the formless absolute and the embodied godhead, at the greatest level and who lives out of that realization—a completely new kind of divine human life, which would transform all conditions of life on earth.

This is what the book is written as a prayer toward. This is what my work is a prayer for. This is what the work of so many of the major thinkers of our time is heading toward in different ways.

Foreword to *Zohar,* translated and annotated by Daniel C. Matt

Twenty years ago in Jerusalem—momentarily at peace and flowering in a fragrant and golden spring—I made a friend whose wisdom has sweetened my life; I shall call him "Ezekiel," after one of the wild, ecstatic prophets he loved most. He was a wizened, nut-brown, wiry old man in his early eighties, with hair so energetic it seemed to dance in white flames on his head. Although his life had seen every kind of suffering and violence (he had been in a concentration camp and fought in the early days for the establishment of a Jewish state before losing all faith in any kind of nationalism), just to be in his presence was to be intoxicated by his passion for God, his unique amalgam of fervor; dry wit and long, rich quotations in several languages; and a laugh so wild and loud it sounded—his wife used to say—"like one of the trumpets of the seraphim." We met through mutual friends (who were also friends of the great Scholem, master of modern Jewish mystical studies). They had told me, before introducing me, "Now you are ready to meet a real, no-holds-barred kabbalist."

And that is what Ezekiel proved to be. On our very first meeting, after sizing me up and down, asking me point-blank if I knew that the only purpose of life was to know and experience God "like fire in the core of the core of your heart," he grabbed my arm, dragged me into the kitchen, and amidst piles of dishes heaped with salads and whirling, delicious smells of borscht and stew, he launched into a wild and fantastical account of the timeless origins of Kabbalah: secret flashes of light between the Infinite One and the hearts of the angels, Abraham hiding a book in a cave, the four holy letters of the name of God that "contain the entire truth of all knowledge," and a bewildering succession of prophets and holy sages whose names flashed by me so fast I couldn't remember all of them. He ended by taking my shoulders and saying, "If you want to know more, come to my house tomorrow, and we'll take a walk around Jerusalem together and follow the threads of our inspiration from street to street and café to café. You like coffee, don't you?"

In the days that followed—days of holy passion and tenderness that I'll never forget—we strolled together through the winding, narrow lanes of old Jerusalem, talking, falling silent, stopping to eat an apple, an orange, or a piece of the Toblerone chocolate he always carried with him in a trouser pocket; halting at tiny, shabby cafés, where other old men would hail him, clap him on the back, and ply us with cups of coffee. For hour after hour Ezekiel poured out to me a lifetime of distilled knowledge of Kabbalah, pausing, with infinite patience, to explain remarks I did not initially grasp or to unravel, in a dazzling dance of commentary and quotations, new concepts and ideas that he thought I was ready to try to comprehend. His presence, so focused and fiery and vibrant; his learning; his tremendous, poignant simplicity of manner; his gracious, free-hearted hospitality—all fused together to give me a permanent and unforgettable vision not only of the scope of kabbalistic wisdom but of the kind of human being it was intended to engender.

On the third morning we spent together, Ezekiel announced excitedly, "It's another beautiful day; don't let us waste it! Let us go to Safed. You know what Safed means to us kabbalists, don't you? In the sixteenth century, it became the center of kabbalistic learning, the home of such great sages as Moses Cordovero and my favorite of them all—the great Lion, the *Ari*, Isaac Luria."

He almost pushed me into his small, broken-down jeep and, talking all the way, drove me to Safed, where we walked and walked through narrow lanes perfumed by the fragrance of spring blossoms. The goal of our visit, he gradually explained, was to pray together toward the end of the day in the ancient, dazzlingly white, candelabra-filled synagogue of Isaac Luria himself. Just before we entered it, as we stood in the golden, sun-washed courtyard outside, Ezekiel expounded to me Luria's great vision of *tikkun*, the mending of the world through intense soul-work and acts of creative love and justice. "Now," he said, when he had finished, "I think you are ready." I followed him into the pure white radiance of the synagogue. A great, rich peace descended on my whole mind and body. Ezekiel said nothing but gazed at me, smiling with joy. Afterward, we sat silently watching the first stars burst open in the rapidly darkening sky. Ezekiel began to speak, at first haltingly and quietly, then with gathering majestic clarity.

"We are living," he began, "in a time in which the whole future—not only of Israel but of humanity—is at stake. This is why the wisdom of Kabbalah, which was kept hidden for so long, in a closely guarded and protected oral tradition handed down from master to disciple from the time of Moses, is now being written down and given out to anyone sincere and humble enough to try to embody it. Just as the Tibetan mystics kept their wisdom to themselves for almost two thousand years and are now opening its treasures to the world, so we kabbalists understand that the time has come to share what we know. In the pain and struggle of our time, a planetary spiritual civilization is struggling to be born. It will bring together, in a way no one of us can yet imagine, all the highest teachings of all the greatest mystical traditions to give humanity what it needs to meet the terrible challenges it faces, and to prepare it for a wholly new and wonderful flowering that the prophecies of many religions foresee. This flowering is not certain, but it is possible if we want it enough and work for it. Sometimes I think of this new, spiritual, planetary civilization struggling to be born as one vast rose, each of its petals distinct but unified in a larger and radiant order, representing the highest truths of the different traditions. Just imagine, Andrew, what a powerful fragrance it will have! Just to begin to imagine the fragrance of such a rose, the rose for which the whole history of humanity has been a preparation, is to fall silent in wonder and gratitude.

"The glorious tradition of Kabbalah will have a great role to play in the creation and opening of this universal world-rose. The wonderful old man who taught me what little I know used to often say, 'When the world starts to smell the fragrance of the wisdom of the *Ba'al ha-Zohar* (the author of the Zohar), Moses Cordovero, Isaac

Luria, Abraham Abulafia, and the long lineage of Hasidic mystics, even the smallest stones in the dirtiest streets will start to blossom in light!' I think of his certainty often these days, knowing that war will come again. I hope my teacher was right. Would it not be what we need if out of the horror of the twentieth century a new order could arise, like a phoenix, all the more lustrous and magnificent because she has been born from such horror?"

Ezekiel paused, closed his eyes, and seemed to be praying for the inspiration to continue. Then he went on: "There are, I believe, seven interlinked wonders that the tradition of Kabbalah has to offer true seekers everywhere. I think of them as the seven diamonds of a crown of power and revelation that keeps growing and expanding.

"The first wonder that Kabbalah offers is a vision of the Infinite One, *Ein Sof,* as sublime and majestic as anything you can find in the Rig Veda, or the great Mahayana Buddhist evocations of the Void, or the poetry of Rumi. This vision isn't merely grandly poetic; it is in the highest sense a vision that 'reveals' something of the ineffable mystery of how Creation came to be, one that helps us gaze awestruck into the burning core of the volcano of the Infinite One's power, and listen to the mind-shattering words of the *Ba'al ha-Zohar,* describing the 'beginning' of Creation":

> At the head of potency of the King,
> He engraved engravings in luster on high.
> A spark of impenetrable darkness flashed
> within the concealed of the concealed
> From the head of Infinity ...

Ezekiel here paused and wrote out on a piece of paper *Botsina de-Qardinuta*—"a spark of impenetrable darkness"—and then clapped his hands and shouted with joy: "In one brilliant paradox, the *Ba'al ha-Zohar* evokes the Big Bang and goes to the heart of the cosmic dance between matter and antimatter that modern physicists are only now beginning to begin to understand!"

He calmed down and went on. "The second wonder that the

Kabbalah offers is a vision of what I call the Sacred Marriage, the constant fusion of male and female, good and evil, light and dark, through which *Ein Sof* creates and goes on creating the universe. Such a vision of the universe being constantly created and re-created by the opposite powers of the One in a dance of balance is not confined to Jewish mysticism. It is found in ancient Egypt, in the folklore of many tribes, in the Hindu vision of Shiva and Shakti, in the great Taoist unfolding of yin and yang. It is worked out, however, with incomparable precision and richness in the works of the greatest kabbalists. For them the secret of 'participating' in the Creation's endless resources of divine energy lies in an ever more profound knowledge of how the 'marriage' of opposites works on every level of the self, consciousness, and matter. Kabbalists believe that no human being can be completely divine, unless, like the original Adam, he or she fuses within himself or herself masculine power and feminine sensitivity on every level of being and in every activity. As the *Ba'al ha-Zohar* writes, 'The blessed Holy One does not place His abode anywhere male and female are not found together.'

"The third wonder of Kabbalah is the open and flowing system of the ten *sefirot*—the divine archetypes—through which the workings of the cosmic Sacred Marriage can be related to and imagined. The ten different *sefirot* represent the various stages of God's inner life as it unfolds in Creation, the dynamics, if you like, of divine personality. They represent at once a tree of life, and an androgynous, divine body complete with arms, legs, and sexual organs, and the inner spirit-body of the realized human divine androgyne who has, over years of prayer, meditation, and service to others, fused within himself or herself the different 'energies' and 'powers' of God's presence. When you learn to contemplate the *sefirot* both separately in all their many-tiered significance and then together, you begin to have a clearer and clearer sense of how the Infinite One creates everything that exists and of how each moment is another revelation of one or more facets of *Ein Sof*'s splendors. You come to embody that awareness yourself. As a great kabbalist wrote, 'When you cleave to the *sefirot,* the divine Holy Spirit enters into you, into every, every sensation, every movement.'"

Ezekiel paused and took a long sip of red wine, relishing its flavor and rolling it around his mouth.

"The fourth wonder of the crown of Kabbalah—and the clue to the embodiment of divine love and wisdom that I myself love the most, the one through which the other *sefirot* pour their power into this dimension—is *Shekhinah,* "the one who dwells." *Shekhinah* is the name given to God's immanence in the Talmud and Midrash. In Kabbalah, however, *Shekhinah* becomes something even greater and more mysterious—nothing less, in fact, than the feminine side of God, daughter of *Binah. Binah* is one of the most sublime of the *sefirot,* manifesting compassion and understanding, and whom kabbalists call 'the Divine Mother'—mother also of *Tif'eret,* the *sefirah* that breathes harmony and divine beauty. For a kabbalist, the goal of the mystical life is to fuse a living love and knowledge of the feminine Divine in all things—*Shekhinah*—with the deepest inner laws of divine beauty and order represented by *Tif'eret.* This fusion, we believe, makes us vessels and agents of divine power and creativity.

"The *Ba'al ha-Zohar* describes how *Shekhinah,* 'the Queen,' went into exile with Israel itself and how the special task of Israel and all individual Jews is to bring about and participate in the reunion between the Absolute and *Shekhinah,* the 'king' and the 'queen,' the transcendent 'masculine' and immanent 'feminine,' so that the kingdom of God can at last be born on earth. This vision of the reunion of *Shekhinah* with the other *sefirot* and *Ein Sof* is not only essential to the Jews, however. What will happen to the world if we do not all wake up to nature as God's glorious body? How will we revere life and do everything we can to honor and protect it in every way unless we see in all of its manifestations the shining of *Shekhinah,* the radiance of the Mother-Presence of God?

"If all of us—not just mystics and Jews—are not initiated into the truth of the motherhood of God, we will destroy the world.

"The fifth wonder of Kabbalah, I believe, is the fertility,

inventiveness, and creativity of kabbalistic tradition itself. Think of the *Zohar,* the cornerstone of Kabbalah. It is written in a quirky, polyvalent, polyphonic Aramaic; it is at once a commentary on the Torah, in a series of lyrical meditations and visions, and a sort of mystical novel. Its unique form, with its marriage of opposed genres, mirrors the greater marriage that is always taking place in the universe, and is the most exuberant imaginable celebration of all the varieties of sacred imagination that makes us vulnerable to revelation in all of its forms. In the highest and finest kabbalist writing and thought, you will always find this dynamic balance between accepted wisdom and new discovery, reverence for tradition and brilliant embrace of authentic innovation. Moses Cordovero, drawing on the *Zohar,* called kabbalists 'the reapers of the field.' 'The reapers of the field are the companions, masters of this wisdom, because *Malkhut—Shekhinah*—is called "the apple field" and She grows sprouts of secrets and new flowerings of Torah. Those who constantly create new interpretations of Torah are harvesting Her.' To put it in more modern terms: just as physicists tell us, the observer of a subatomic particle transforms reality through the very act of observing; so a true kabbalist is continually reinventing what he or she is 'receiving' through the traditions by continual inspired leaps of sacred imagination. This divine liveliness gives all seekers everywhere a wonderful example of the dance of divine energy in the imagination and of the transforming fecundity birthed from it.

"The sixth wonder of Kabbalah is a secret that transforms your life when you start to understand it. Let me put this secret bluntly: since God is not just static Being but also dynamic Becoming, God needs us as we need God.

"We are not here simply to be 'slaves' to the divine will or to vanish into transcendent union with it; we are here to be transparent vessels of its power and creativity, the healthy and supple limbs, if you like, through which it enacts its dance in the real. Without our conscious, willed, inspired participation, God is incomplete; God needs us to realize God's design in and for the world. We are cocreators, through God's grace, with God itself. What we do and what we choose affects, in fact, not only this world but also the structure of the entire universe. Isaac Luria, expanding on themes already vibrant in the *Zohar*, maintained that when *Ein Sof* contracted to make a 'space' within itself through which it could emanate its primordial light to create the Creation, some of the vessels this light passed into 'shattered,' dropping 'holy sparks' that then became imprisoned in matter. The role of the human being, and especially of the conscious mystic, is to raise these sparks back to origin in two related forms of mending: *tikkun ha-nefesh* (mending of the soul) and *tikkun olam* (mending of the world); in other words, through prayer, contemplation, and acts of holy creativity and justice. When you begin to understand this, a wholly new life stands open!

"We are here to be the 'site' of the Sacred Marriage of heaven and earth, of the primordial light and matter, to be the 'place' where the fusion of all dimensions is effected so that divine passion through us can remake and reshape every arena and institution, every art and science of the world. When all human beings everywhere start to realize both the responsibility and the glorious powers such a relationship to God opens for them, the creation of a new world can begin."

Ezekiel paused and drained the cup of wine in front of him. His eyes wide open and burning with enthusiasm, he ended, "The seventh and crowning wonder of Kabbalah is the participation in the living glory of divine life that those who perform *tikkun* with every aspect of their heart, mind, thought, and being can come to experience. The most wonderful account of this participation is the description in the *Zohar* of the wild and holy death—the wedding celebration—of Rabbi Shim'on. His dying is not merely peaceful: it is a divine rapture in which he is given the supreme privilege of revealing to humanity the secret of the universe. Listen with all your heart and mind and soul to what the dying and illumined rabbi says":

> *All the days I have been alive, I have yearned to see this day.*
> *Now my desire is crowned with success.*
> *This day itself is crowned.*

The Body of Love

Now I want to reveal words in the presence of the blessed Holy One;
all those words adorn my head like a crown....
I have seen that all those sparks flash from the High Spark,
hidden of all hidden.
All are levels of enlightenment.
In the light of each and every level
there is revealed what is revealed.
All those lights are connected:
this light to that light, that light to this light,
one shining into the other,
inseparable, one from the other.

Ezekiel fell silent. Then, leaning forward and softly putting his hands on mine, he said, "The entire universe is a dance of the glory. Pray for me," he said, "that when my death comes—and it won't be long now—some small spark of the glory of Rabbi Shim'on's wedding will illuminate it."

I was too moved to speak. A holy, starlit silence spread its shining around us both.

That holy silence radiates throughout my friend Daniel Matt's matchless translation and commentary of these selections from the *Zohar*. Dive headlong into its light silence and allow its power to transfigure you. Each of the *Zohar*'s words, Ezekiel told me once, has an angel hovering over it, singing, "Illumine! Illumine!" And who is any of us not to dare to be illumined? As one of the greatest of kabbalists, Abraham Abulafia, wrote:

The purpose of birth is learning.
The purpose of learning is to grasp the Divine.
The purpose of apprehending the Divine
is to maintain the endurance of one who apprehends
with the joy of apprehending.

I would like to dedicate this introduction to my heart-sister, Marianne Williamson, as a gift for her birthday, and for the ever-growing truth of her inner and outer work.

Introduction to *Essential Teachings*, by His Holiness The Dalai Lama

With a noble mind, pure and generous, we will spread joy around us, we will feel great peace and we will be able to communicate that to others.

The first words of the Dalai Lama that I read, fourteen years ago, were: "Religion, in all its forms, has at its root endless compassion." I was in Ladakh, living in a small villa in the mountains. A young Tibetan monk was visiting me and had brought me a picture and a book of the man he called Kundoun, "The Presence." The words—simple enough—sent visceral shock through my body. That evening, my friend and I went to meditate in a ruined monastery above the villa. There, on the grass-filled courtyard, was a representation, crude but vivid, of the Buddhist Wheel of Life. In the "hell" section, amidst flames and prowling, savagely unhappy ghosts, stood a tall, thin man surrounded by white light. "That is Avalokiteshvara," my friend said, "the Buddha of compassion. For Buddhists, hell is not final. It is as impermanent a state as all others. There is a way out. *He* embodies the way." *Avalokiteshvara,* he told me, came from the Sanskrit *Avokita,* "to preserve," and *Ishvara,* "lord," or "freedom," and it means "The Lord that protects." A warm summer moon rose and he spoke to me of the Mahayana Buddhist version of the bodhisattva, the enlightened being who, out of love, returned again and again to the world to save all sentient beings. "The bodhisattva," he said, "has taken the most noble vow of all: not to enter nirvana until every creature—even the grass blades in this courtyard—have achieved enlightenment." We both laughed a little nervously, as the grass blades looked particularly bedraggled and irredeemable. When we left, my Tibetan friend went up again to the Wheel of Life. "Here," he exclaimed waving to the ghosts wandering in garish flames, "is the modern world." He paused. "And here," pointing to the tall, thin man now shining in the moonlight, "here is Kundoun." I could not help smiling at the extravagance of his devotion. He caught my smile and said, "You smile now, but one day you will understand."

It has taken me fourteen years to begin to understand, and now that that understanding is dawning in me, I find it being shared by a startling variety of people from all over the world. One of the worst-kept modern secrets, it seems, is that the Dalai Lama is not merely the loved priest-king of the Tibetans, not just the world's most prominent Buddhist leader, but also a guide to the future that everyone, whatever their religion or lack of it, should take seriously. A Greek friend dying of AIDS in Paris told me, "I don't believe in anything but I believe in him," pointing to the one photograph by his bedside, that of the Dalai Lama. "I saw him once on television, and felt that he was sane. I saw that there is no discrepancy between what he says, what he does, and what he is. I saw that although he had suffered everything a man can suffer—the death of those close to him, the destruction of his culture, the genocide of his people—he is not bitter. I do not believe in God but I believe in the power of love. He is that power." Later, at his funeral, his lover turned to me and said, "Do you know what he told me when I asked him before the end how he could be so serene? He pointed to a picture of the Dalai Lama. 'He showed me how,' he said. 'Don't ask me how. But he did.'" I remembered the wall in Ladakh and the tall, thin man moving calmly through hell. I remembered him again in Venice a month later when a German director at the premiere of his film announced, "There is a war going on between inner peace and outer nightmare, between force of mind and spirit and the force of power-for-its-own-sake, between democracy and totalitarianism, between life and death. The wisest fighter in this war—on whose outcome everything depends—is the Dalai Lama." And before an astonished audience he produced copies of his personal selection of the Dalai Lama's philosophy and distributed them to everyone.

What, then, is the Dalai Lama's philosophy? It is Buddhism purified to its simplest human essence, an essence that transcends all barriers, all colors and creeds. It is a philosophy of the most urgent, practical, active altruism, constructed not in a study but lived out at the center of a storm of violence. It is, in the deepest and widest possible sense, a philosophy of peace. The Dalai Lama has understood that there will be no future worth living unless everyone now takes personal responsibility for the pain and misery in the world. He has understood that none of the major, terrible problems that threaten survival of the earth can be solved by merely institutional or political methods. Humankind, to survive, has to undergo a massive and unprecedented change of heart, an ordered and passionate spiritual revolution that changes forever our relation to each other and our relation to nature. It is only from such a revolution that the new vision of the planet so desperately needs can arise—a vision that sees the connections between every thought and every action, the relations between the obsession with the individual self and its hunger for false securities and every kind of exploitation that is ruining the world. As the Dalai Lama says so fiercely in *Essential Teachings,*

> Look around us at this world that we call "civilized" and that for more than 2,000 years has searched to obtain happiness and avoid suffering by false means: trickery, corruption, hate, abuse of power, and exploitation of others. We have searched only for individual and material happiness, opposing people against each other, one race against another, social systems against others. This has led to a time of fear, of suffering, murder, and famine. If in India, Africa, and other countries misery and famine rule, it is not because natural resources are lacking, nor that the means of bringing about lasting well-being are flawed. It is because each person has looked only for his own profit without fear of oppressing others for selfish goals, and this sad and pitiful world is the result. The root of this civilization is rotten, the world suffers, and if it continues in this way, it will suffer more and more.

The only way out of this hell, the Dalai Lama makes clear, is for each of us to take the journey of the bodhisattva into the heart of

The Body of Love

compassion, for every one of us to learn how to enact, in whatever station of life we find ourselves in, that compassion and its forgiveness, clear insight, tolerance, humor, and tireless service to other beings. The only way out of this hell is to learn how to walk in it, as His Holiness does, with the calm passion of enlightened love.

The brilliant clarity and the interconnectedness of the Dalai Lama's analysis of the modern world would have less weight if he had not staked his whole life on its truth and if it had not been forged, as it has been, in the crucible of the forty-year-long nightmare of the destruction of the Tibetans by the Chinese. His talk of forgiveness is the talk of one who has seen his people tortured and murdered in the hundreds of thousands; his belief in tolerance is the belief of one who has witnessed the annihilation of the whole religious world he came from by those who believe that "power comes from the barrel of a gun"; his amazing, humorous clarity is of the kind reached only by those who survived hell, is as earned and weathered as King Lear's, "a condition of complete simplicity," in Eliot's words, "costing not less than everything." When the Dalai Lama speaks, he speaks not just for himself or for his tragic people, but for the humiliated and the noble of the earth, on behalf of the best in us all.

I first met the Dalai Lama in Oslo during the week in 1989 when he received—at long last—the Nobel Prize. I had been thinking about him for years, but it was the first time I was continually in his presence—in processions, at speeches, at press conferences, at dinner. A kind of holy drunkenness—and in Oslo, of all places—reigned at every occasion. The Berlin Wall had just fallen, and that the Dalai Lama should be receiving the Nobel Peace Prize soon afterward seemed an almost hallucinatory hopeful sign that the tide in world affairs might be changing. "Bliss it is in THIS dawn to be alive" an American friend wrote on my hotel door in red chalk, and underneath, "Oslo, December 1989, is the Earthly Paradise." Every room the Dalai Lama walked into he touched, blessed, stroked, teased, enthused as many people as possible, radiating with every moment, every look, every word an unbreakable laughing compassion, whose warmth pervaded everything. Tibetan representations of Avalokiteshvara show the bodhisattva with a thousand outstretch arms; the Dalai Lama seemed to have at least that many, and to be simultaneously present all over Oslo at once. No sooner had you glimpsed him at one end of the room, he would be at the other standing by you, looking deep into your eyes; no sooner had you just left him at a long press conference when he appeared around the corner in the rain, holding hands with two schoolgirls with red boots the color of his robe.

At moments he looked a hundred, a Tibetan Oedipus at Colonus; at others, seven or eight. He had the grace of a woman, the strength of a peasant, the contagious flagrant hilarity of a child, the eyes of a dolphin—sky-candid and serene. His laugh itself seemed superhuman, a burst of spontaneous coloratura that sliced through all pretension, all distance: some wag said, "When the Dalai Lama laughs, it sounds as if all the other thirteen Dalai Lamas are laughing with him." His face changed a hundred times an hour, yet there was always a stillness, a majesty in it that no change affected. I had seen hundreds of photographs of him, but nothing prepared me for the beauty of this slender, fifty-four-year-old man—not a cosmetic beauty at all, but the kind that Ramana Maharshi or Gandhi had—the beauty of a totally good and loving being whose every expression revealed another nuance of truth in action. Watching his face became a meditation as rich as listening to his words; its openness made it seem more intimate to me than that of my oldest friends.

The Dalai Lama's genius for joy inflamed the joy in everyone else; his smile reflected itself in a thousand faces at once. Words of an old Buddhist text kept coming back to me: "By giving away everything, pass beyond sorrow." Here was unmistakably the most strongly and lucidly happy man I had ever seen, giving himself and his wisdom away to anyone who could receive it. Hardly anyone seemed to sleep that crazy, glorious week. Bars and hotel rooms were full of people of all nationalities, talking and joshing until the early hours. I met a distinguished economist on a street corner at three o'clock one morning weeping under his purple umbrella. "Why are you crying?" "I'm not sure. I think I'm going mad. I never, ever *imagined* one could be this *well*."

I met the Dalai Lama alone for forty-five minutes on one day of my stay in Oslo. He sat at the end of a bare, empty, sunlit room in the early morning in a simple red and gold robe, his arms uncovered. He seemed unnervingly still, concentration immensely powerful—hardly a man at all, but a force of laser-like intensity. Then he looked up and laughed, and my awe became laughter too. He put out his left arm and pulled me down gently onto the sofa beside him.

"What would you like the world to know about the Tibetan situation?" I began.

"That Tibet is not, has not ever been, and will never be, legally a part of China. That the Chinese, since 1950, have killed a quarter of the population—about 1.2 million people out of 6 million—and have destroyed almost all of the six thousand monasteries that once existed. I would like the world to know that if the Chinese continue with the population transfer program that they are implementing at the moment, there will soon be many more Chinese in Tibet than Tibetans, and that the destruction of Tibet will be complete."

He paused and added calmly, "There is not much time left."

There was a long, sad silence. I told him that I considered the survival of Tibet as vital to the world's future as the survival of the rainforests of the Amazon. "The forests give the world oxygen; the Tibetans give the world an *inner* oxygen of vision, of holy knowledge—that it needs to continue."

He smiled sadly. "The Tibetans have so much to offer to the world. An understanding of mental calmness, a vision of the infinite potential of the mind. You cannot talk of Tibet without talking of Tibetan Buddhism. This is essentially a collection of techniques for building inner peace through an expansion of consciousness. When has the world needed this more? If Tibet is not freed and the Tibetans are not allowed to practice their culture and religion, this vision will die."

He gazed at his hands. "I want a free Tibet to be a zone of *ahimsa*, of harmlessness, a sanctuary for peace where everyone can feel free to come and be refreshed. A place dedicated to the practice of compassion, of the way of the bodhisattva."

"What is compassion?" I asked him.

"To recognize yourself clearly in every other being and to respect each sentient being's right to happiness."

"Don't the Buddhists believe that the practice of compassion is the key to enlightenment?"

"Yes, because it breaks down all barriers of every kind and, in the end, destroys the notion of the separate self. But this is Buddhist business. Compassion is essential for everyone; it is the key to a happy life. A world without compassion is not a human world."

Then we talked about the dialogue between religion and science that he has advocated, and the way in which Buddhism might be a bridge between the two.

"Some westerners call Buddhism a science of mind," I said. "This is in some ways a helpful description. Buddhism is rational and the Buddha told everyone to test his truths for themselves. Both Buddhists and scientists are trying to know something essential about the universe and know it clearly."

"Buddhism may have a great role to play in being the necessary bridge between religion and science. In many ways Buddhism is like a religion, although it does not believe in a creator god; in many ways, as I have said, it is like science. If science tells me that the world is round, I accept it, though some of the old tests say it is flat. If science can prove beyond any doubt that there is no reincarnation, for example, I will accept that too. One day soon, perhaps more scientists will be open to what Buddhists may have to tell them of the powers of consciousness." "And the survival of Tibet may be vital to this dialogue, because the Tibetans have made the most sustained experiment in history into the nature of the mind."

"Yes."

I then asked him a question that had been haunting me all week.

"You, as the most prominent Buddhist leader, talk always of tolerance, of listening to the truths of other religions. Yet the leaders of the other world religions—of Catholicism and Islam, for instance, and the Hindu fundamentalists—are very far from being tolerant. How can they change?"

He laughed. "Communism is very intolerant, isn't it? Communism hates capitalism. And yet all its hatred cannot destroy it. It is now having to find a way of coexisting with it. Some Christians and some Muslims, and certain Hindus, may sometimes be intolerant. Even if they are, they cannot destroy other religions. The only practical and sensible thing is for all of them to sit down in friendship and discuss everything with respect. Reality is telling us quite clearly that we have to get together to emphasize the unity of our common purpose and exchange our experiences. Exchange with another tradition can only lead to enrichment of your own. What is there to fear?"

"Have you learned anything from Christianity, for example?"

"Oh, so much," he said passionately. "Christianity has a very important and very beautiful sense of service. This service to other beings is essential. Buddhists too often think meditating is enough." He pulled a serious face and started to play with an imaginary rosary in his right hand. "Meditation is not enough. We must help others. Compassion must be active, otherwise it is lazy."

"Can you imagine a world religion ..."

His laugh cut me short. "No world religion. We have enough religions. Enough religions, but not enough real human beings. We need more human beings. Religions should learn from each other, respect each other, but keep their identity. Some people like tomatoes; some people like bread. People should be free to eat what they want and people should be able to choose what religion is most useful to their growth. "Don't let us talk too much of religion. Let us talk of what is human. Love is human. Kindness is human. Everyone needs love and kindness. A dog won't come near you if you're unkind to it. Our world is forgetting what is essential, what is essentially human." His voice rose richly on the word *human*.

After a pause, I asked him if he knew violence within his own personality.

"Of course," he laughed. "Now I cannot watch a bird suffer without pain, but when I was a boy I killed several birds. In the Potala I kept some small, beautiful birds in a cage. Hawks used to come and steal their food. According to my motivation, they had no right to eat those things. So I found a rifle that belonged to the Thirteenth Dalai Lama, transformed myself into a wrathful deity, and shot at one of them, who fell to the ground in great pain. I felt regret, great regret. Once violence is done, there is nothing that can be done to undo it. That afternoon I learned how sad that is."

"Is there a great soul-force in nonviolence, as Gandhi believed, a storing up of karmic power that in the end can change fate?"

"Let us leave karma out of it," he smiled. "My belief in nonviolence is simple realism. It is certainly realism in the Tibetan situation. The Chinese in the past have taken any slight outbreak of violence as an excuse to massacre thousands. But in any case, whatever violence builds up, violence can destroy. Nothing that violence achieves is stable. This is a law. Only a wise, loving, patient intelligence can create anything that lasts; only altruism really helps. This is a law too. My definition of altruism is: be wisely selfish and know that your happiness depends on the happiness of those around you and in the world in general. If society suffers, you will suffer, so love is itself enough to work for the social good.

"You wrote once that you considered Gandhi's nonviolent way 'an introduction of an ancient practice of nonviolence in politics that represents an evolutionary leap for mankind.' Do you believe this still?"

"Yes. Look at what is happening in Eastern Europe. The Berlin Wall is down; so much has altered in Russia, also in a nonviolent way. Mrs. Aquino's change to democracy after the end of the Marcos regime was also largely nonviolent. Nonviolence is the only way for the oppressed people of the earth to move forward into a peace that could be lasting. When I first came to Europe in 1973 and talked like this, people thought 'Ah, well, the Dalai Lama, he is a little strange.'

Now they are beginning to see that perhaps the Dalai Lama was not talking such nonsense after all."

He laughed a long time and then stood up. Our time was about to be over. I stood up and the Dalai Lama held my hand very strongly and tenderly in his left. Slowly, very slowly, and in glowing silence, he walked me to the door. Then, with the deepest, most exquisite gentleness, like that of a mother with a fragile, anxious child, he let slip my hand and said, very softly, "Goodbye."

As I walked away the face of my Tibetan friend returned, with these three lines of a hymn to Avalokiteshvara he had written out for me, fourteen years before, on that evening in Ladakh:

> Who flies unobstructed
> Through skies of limitless love?
> He whose mind is one with Reality....

Back in Paris a few days later I was strolling through La Procure, the largest religious bookstore in St. Sulpice. My mind and heart still full of the Dalai Lama, and I came across the French version of the book that is here translated into English. I bought it and read it over and over and gave copies away to all my friends. It became an indispensable book to me, because in it I hear clearly the unsparing, kind voice of the man I had met in Oslo.

Every time I gave a copy of the book away I used to say, "Here is the clearest guide I know to the mind of the most awake man on the planet." The first part is a series of talks given at Bohd Gaya to his own people on the sublime book of Shantideva, "On the Making of the Mind of the Bodhisattva." Because he is speaking to his own people, the Dalai Lama speaks directly, fiercely, unsentimentally, unedited by "political" consideration, and with a pungent, psychological brilliance and honesty that is always part of his personality, but more on display here than in any other published text of his I know. In a hundred or so magnificent and potent pages he introduces you to what it means to want with your whole being to attain enlightenment on behalf of all sentient beings, and what it *costs* and *means* in terms of aspiration, love, steady forgiveness of one's enemies, and relentless work on wearing down all those negative tendencies that separate all of us from each other.

In the second text, "The Key of Madhyamika," he discusses with precise, intellectual brilliance—and in such a way that the committed reader can actually *glimpse* and *feel* through his presentation of the vision of emptiness something of its soaring freedom—how the greatest mystics of the Mahayana tradition have expressed their knowledge of the nature of reality. So in one small book you have marvelous representations of what the Tibetans call the two interpenetrating aspects of the enlightened mind: its boundless compassion and its "empty" wisdom.

I remember a moment in Oslo when His Holiness was speaking to a small group about the sufferings of Tibet and the modern world in general. For one unforgettable moment, his poise wavered and tears rolled down his cheeks, and he said, "Compassion would be unbearable sometimes without the wisdom of emptiness." I often think of that moment and what he said when I think of the immense labor of transformation that faces the entire human race as it faces apocalypse. On whether we learn how to unite compassion with the "wisdom of emptiness," how both to care enough and to work with enough selfless detachment in the middle of raging and devouring chaos, depends the future. To that future, this book is a wonderful gift, the gift of a wonderful man whose heart and mind are as spacious as the universe, and whose life is that of an authentic and humble hero of truth, who has put into practice, day in and day out, in terrible and tragic conditions, the great prayer of the bodhisattva in Shantideva's *Bodhicharyavatara*:

> Like earth and the great element and also vast as the
>   immensity of space,
> Let me be the living ground of love for innumerable beings.

> I dedicate this introduction and all its meager merits, in love,
> to Leila Hadley Luce, beloved friend and heart-champion
> of the Tibetan cause.

The Body of Love

~~⚬~~

Afterword to *A Journey in Ladakh*—2000 Edition

When I first suggested writing an account of my visit to Ladakh in summer 1979 to my then editor—a brilliant, caustic Englishwoman in her early sixties, who had discovered V. S. Naipaul—she looked at me with ill-disguised amusement, put down her glass of white wine in the restaurant we were lunching in, and drawled, "Darling, forget it. No one on earth is going to be interested in what you have to say abut some unwashed tribe in the Himalayas. As for trying to describe some old Tibetan sage—well, you might just as well put a stone around your neck and jump into the Thames. The English don't give a fig for mysticism; they think it's something for Americans. If you must write a travel book, do it on Italy or Iceland."

I was hurt by what she said, but soon understood that my sincerity was being tested. If I was going to write the book I wanted to, I would have to separate myself from all the games of English society and all the sophisticated prejudices of Western intellectual and literary life. I would, in fact, have to begin to become my real self, and damn the consequences. There was no precedent I knew of for the kind of book I wanted to create—but why should that stop me? I realized that if I really believed in the power of what I had come to know in Ladakh through my relationship with Thuksey Rinpoche, I must also believe that the power to describe it would be given me.

Deciding that I would have to write *A Journey in Ladakh* or permanently stifle something essential in my true nature liberated a wild joy in me. No book I have ever written gave me such clean rapture. All the sights, smells, and sounds of Ladakh seemed to surround me in the poky attic room my Oxford college lent me. Many times as I walked from downtown Oxford, where I was staying, to my college in the early morning I would feel surrounding me a huge, ecstatic Presence. On one early November dawn in particular, which I shall never forget, the whole world seemed drowned in a brilliant,

260

unearthly golden light that gave a divine beauty and splendor even to the puddles at my feet and the worn, sad faces of passers-by. I knew I was being helped and supported by powers not my own, and started to intuit, with greater and greater joy, that my destiny, both as a human being and as an artist, lay in a dedication to the mystical search and to trying to help others discover what was inspiring and transforming my own vision.

Two years after finishing *A Journey in Ladakh*, I returned to the Himalayas and to Hemis monastery, and saw Thuksey Rinpoche for the last time. He was dying from diabetes, visibly sick and frail. I had been scared of seeing him again, frightened that I had "invented" him out of an unconscious need for a "good" father, or that a romantic love of old, vanishing worlds had led me to imbue him with a greater wisdom and power than he in fact possessed.

I need not have worried. His force and inner beauty radiated with an even greater intensity than before, brought into high and poignant relief by the quiet drama of his illness. There weren't many other people in Hemis that summer, just a few anxious monks and a small motley crew of Europeans: an intense, hawk-faced German girl; a scuba diver from Marseilles and his cabaret singer wife; and myself. Knowing that the Rinpoche was dying brought us all extremely close. Every word Thuksey spoke, every look he gave us, every encounter with him had the luster of a final transmission.

What moved me most about the Rinpoche during that last time was that he seemed utterly unconcerned about his increasing frailty. Nothing would stop him teaching, not even the sudden, terrifying bouts of coughing that racked him, nor his inability at times to sit up straight or walk without help. Watching him and being with him I was reminded of the sublime words of Shantideva that describe the inner motivation of a bodhisattva, a being that has pledged himself or herself to the redemption of all beings from suffering: "For all creatures, I would be a lantern for those desiring a lantern, I would be a bed for those desiring a bed, I would be a slave for those desiring a slave."

Again and again, the Rinpoche would interrupt his teaching to impress upon us the necessity of continual spiritual practice. When I told him, for example, that I had written a book about him, he didn't say anything but immediately asked me how far I had progressed with my mantra practice and visualizations. When I told him, he shook his head angrily and said, with a sternness I had never before seen in him, "Writing books is all very well, but spiritual practice is the essential activity of a true seeker. You may write a hundred wonderful books, but what will they matter if you never find out who you are?"

I was, in fact, reassured as well as shaken by his sternness, because it showed me just how authentic his love for me really was. That I had written about him meant nothing to him; what mattered was that I should become wholly earnest in my search for truth. He himself never stopped praying; when he was eating or sitting quietly or waiting for guests his lips would always be moving. It was obvious that in his last days he was keeping himself constantly immersed in the sacred stream of truth. I understood from this one of the most important lessons of the Path: enlightenment is not a "static" state but one of constant inner commitment to, and growth in, love and concentration.

I don't want to give the impression that our last summer together was in any way depressing. Nothing could darken the deep joy that radiated from the Rinpoche. One afternoon, I remember, all of us were waiting for him to return from a doctor's visit. We were standing at the top of a staircase. The car bringing him home drew up; he got out; he looked up at us gazing down anxiously at him, laughed a great leonine laugh, and then proceeded to climb the stairs toward us in great pain but looking at each of us in turn with such naked and tender compassion that we all had tears in our eyes. It was clear that he was far more concerned about our fears for him than he was afraid for himself. My scuba diver friend said to me afterwards, "When he laughed, I felt he was saying to all of us, 'Do not identify me with the dying man you see, I have gone beyond both what you call life and what you call death, I am living a freedom beyond both.'"

Two extraordinary incidents that happened soon after confirmed what my friend had intuited. The first occurred during an elaborate and moving long-life ceremony that was held in the central shrine room of Hemis in Thuksey's honor. At one moment, the Rinpoche had to get down on his knees before his pupil, the young Drukchen Rinpoche. We all watched in anguish as he struggled to kneel. As Thuksey struggled back to his feet, something astonishing happened: he laughed, and a terrific sound like a clap of mountain thunder reverberated round the room. I and two other Europeans present heard the thunder distinctly "speak" the word *Tongpanyid*. *Tongpanyid* is Tibetan for *emptiness*. The entire universe was signaling and celebrating the Rinpoche's liberation from all forms and concepts, from matter and "biography." I can see his beautiful laughing face now as I write, white with strain but suffused with ecstasy and, for that moment, hallucinatorily young looking.

The second incident occurred on my last evening in Hemis. I was sad to be leaving, because I knew that I would never see the Rinpoche again. With my scuba diver friend I climbed a hill behind Hemis and sat silently looking down at the monastery. Suddenly—and both I and my friend heard it—the sound of sacred chanting filled the air around us. That evening I noted in my diary, "I felt as if all the monks who had ever lived and studied at Hemis were singing for the Rinpoche and as if the very rocks we were sitting amongst were also singing for him." Many years later I described this experience to a Tibetan monk I met while cowriting for Sogyal Rinpoche *The Tibetan Book of Living and Dying*. For a long while the monk said nothing, studying my face; then he whispered, "What you heard that night is one of the signs that our texts say signal the dying of an Enlightened One."

The last time I saw Thuksey Rinpoche was not in any way remarkable or emotional. He held my hand briefly, gazed deep into my eyes, and said, "Go on practicing," and then looked down again at the text he was reading. Almost a year later, he died in India, serenely, with little pain. One of the monks who had been with him at the end told me years later, "He died with a half-smile on his face. Everyone knew a Buddha was passing." As he said those words quite matter-of-factly, the full grandeur of the blessing I had received from seeing and knowing so great a man broke upon me and I wept, not from grief, but from joy and gratitude.

Death does not interrupt the inner conversation of two hearts that have met in the light of reality. If anything, it makes that conversation even more subtle and profound. I have many times seen Thuksey Rinpoche in dreams; I feel his protection with me always. When I come to die myself, I know I will have before the eyes of my spirit the image and wordless instruction of the way the Rinpoche met his own dying. What more can any human being give to another than the inspiration he gave and gives me still?

If someone had told me when I finished *A Journey in Ladakh,* almost twenty years ago, that at the end of the millennium Tibet would still be under Chinese domination and more threatened than ever, that Ladakh would be increasingly corrupted by commercialism and menaced by the still angry strife between India and Pakistan over Kashmir, and that the Tibetan spiritual tradition itself would be severely compromised and damaged in the eyes of many seekers by a series of terrible sexual scandals and abuses, I would never have believed him or her; I would have accused him or her of a lack of vision and faith. The tragic facts remain, however. The old Tibet that Thuksey Rinpoche embodied with such natural splendor is now almost totally extinct; the master system he represented with such power has shown itself to be incapable of resisting Western temptation and corruption in all but a handful of lamas. The Dalai Lama himself—marvelous, sweet being though he undoubtedly is—has himself delivered depressingly regressive teachings on sex, made homophobic remarks, and espoused an anticontraception stance in India; the apostle of nonviolence has even saluted India's development of a nuclear bomb! Feminist critiques and modern historical scholarship have revealed the patriarchal bias of much of Tibetan civilization and tradition, and the limitations of their misogyny, elitism, and hierarchies, which restrict access to spiritual truth and power.

There are many sincere and intelligent Western Buddhists who continue to idealize Tibet, the Tibetans, and the Dalai Lama. This serves neither truth nor the cause of a free Tibet. Eventually, the true nature of the many scandals that have shaken the Tibetan world and the foundations of the Tibetan system itself will be exposed, and the disillusion that will follow will be far more dangerous to the Tibetan cause than any "revisionism."

What will never die, however—and of this I am more and more convinced—is the brilliance and importance of the sacred technology—the great treasury of visionary practices and philosophies—that the Tibetan mystical schools developed and preserved. The social and religious systems that formed around these teachings will die; the teachings themselves will go on living and will inspire and shape and awaken seekers of all paths and persuasions.

And in remembering such beings as Thuksey Rinpoche we will keep alive and alight the sign of what such teachings can produce, as a reassurance and a challenge to us all, whatever path we are on.

Nevada, November 1999

Introduction to *The Essential Gay Mystics*

What is a mystic? The most beautiful short definition I have ever heard was given me by an old woman friend in Paris: "A mystic is someone who has a direct and naked perception of godhead, beyond dogma, beyond ideas, beyond any possible formulation in words of any kind." Throughout history, men and women of all sexualities and cultures have had this "direct and naked perception of godhead" and have been transformed by its rapture and challenge. Almost always they have chosen to interpret this perception in terms of the existing religious and cultural symbols of their time; the perception itself, however, remains timeless and essentially beyond all formal expression, born as it is from a wordless conversation between the human God and heart, life and its source, that is more intense and intimate than any other relationship.

In her masterpiece, *Mysticism,* Evelyn Underhill writes, "Mysticism offers us the history, as old as civilization, of a race of adventurers who have carried to its term the process of a deliberate and active return to the divine fount of things. They have surrendered themselves to the life-movement of the universe, hence have lived an intenser life than other beings can even know.... Therefore they witness to all that our latent spiritual consciousness, which shows itself in the 'hunger for the Absolute,' can be made to mean to us if we develop it, and have in this respect an unique importance for the race."

There has never been a more important time for taking completely seriously the evidence and testimony of this "race of adventurers." Without a belief in, and the radical cultivation of, mystical consciousness and the insights into the interconnectedness of all reality in sacred joy and sacred love it alone can bring, we will not be able to develop the necessary awareness to help us solve terrible problems that threaten our lives and the very life of the planet.

In the great chorus of witnesses to the transforming power of direct relationship with the "divine fount of things," a surprisingly large number have been gay. Surprising, because the rhetoric of nearly all the world's major religions would have you believe that spiritual insight and achievement are incompatible with homosexuality. Homophobia has stained all the Semitic religions: Muhammad fulminates against it in the Koran; the Jewish sages who composed the Pentateuch condemn it; the record of Christianity from Paul onward, despite some degree of early tolerance, has been one of overwhelming ignorance, cruelty, and persecution. Nor have Hinduism and Buddhism been exempt from this rejection of a sizable portion of the human race; many Hindu sages, both ancient and modern, have been vociferous in their condemnation of same-sex relations. In his recent *The Way to Freedom,* the Dalai Lama writes, lamentably, that "sexual misconduct ... is a sexual act performed with an unsuitable person ... [for men, this] also includes other males." Nor is the New Age, for all its slogans of universal love and compassion, free of homophobia. Many contemporary "masters" of every stripe are frank about their rejection of homosexuals. I myself have experienced this prejudice in agonizing and humiliating ways, and I have talked to scores of other disillusioned gay seekers from many different churches, religions, and ashrams who have discovered that the definition of universal love mouthed by their guru or priest does not include homosexuals. To those acquainted with the facts of contemporary homophobia in all its forms, and with both the blatant and the subtle ways in which religions of all kinds perpetuate it, there can be little surprise in learning that, according to Amnesty International, homosexuality is punishable by death in over forty countries, in many cases with the full sanction of religious law.

It is as a loving protest against this obscene and tragic state of affairs that I conceived of this anthology of gay mystics. I wanted everyone—most of all my gay brothers and sisters—to be fully aware that whatever the mullahs and gurus and archbishops and pseudoavatars might say, there is no record of the Divine itself in any way excluding homosexuals from the direct contact with its love, which is offered freely and forever to every sentient being.

Delving into the truth of homosexual history, one begins to understand that homophobia is a purely human and relatively recent cultural construct, and it has no basis in divine ordination. In earlier times, up until the Roman era, contemporary cultural historians such as Riane Eisler and Randy Conner make clear in their calmly groundbreaking work, reverence for the Sacred Feminine and the Divine Mother led to a reverence for all forms of life and love. Many shamans were and are homosexual; many of the worshipers of the Goddess under Her various names and in Her various cults all over the world—from the Mediterranean to the Near East to the Celtic parts of northern Europe—openly avowed their homosexuality and were accepted and even specially revered as priests, oracles, healers, and diviners. Homosexuals, far from being rejected, were seen as sacred—people who, by virtue of a mysterious fusion of feminine and masculine traits, participated with particular intensity in the life of the source. The source of Godhead is, after all, both masculine and feminine, and exists in a unity that includes but transcends both. The homosexual was thought to mirror this unity and its enigmatic fertility and power in a special way. The tribe or culture gave to him or her specific duties that were highly important and sacred, acknowledging this intimacy with divine truth and the clairvoyant help it could bring to the whole society. This wise and spacious understanding of what some cultural historians and sociologists have called the third and fourth sexes continues, however fragmentarily, in the Native American traditions in which the berdache, or gay, cross-dressing shaman (known in different tribes by different names), holds an honored, essential place in the life of the tribe.

Many ancient cultures, especially those devoted to celebrating the Mother, recognized and honored the holiness of diversity. The homosexual was seen not as a figure excluded from ordinary cultural life and the embrace of the sacred but as holy as anyone else, and with a special access to sacred understanding by virtue of falling outside the "normal" categories. What we are beginning to learn about the early homosexual priests of Astarte, about the Roman *galli* (gender-variant priests who served and worshiped the Roman mother goddess, Cybele), about the sexual lives of the early shamanic tribes of Neolithic Europe and Siberia, and about the different North American native traditions makes it clear that in past times humanity was far less divided against itself than it is now, and people were able, by worshiping the unity of all life and so the holiness of all that lives, to realize both the value *and* the potential sacred function of the homosexual in society.

The continued resistance to this information in political, academic, and religious circles of all kinds can only mean that allowing for and accepting the holiness of homosexuality and personality would effect a revolutionary change in existing conditions. Allowing the wisdom of the third and fourth sexes to be fully vocal in our culture would dissolve the false, rigid categorization of "male" and "female," and the male-centered, male-dominated, competitive, exploitative, war- and power-obsessed mentality that it keeps alive. The return of the Sacred Feminine that is everywhere trying to occur is, in part, a return of the *uncanny,* of those insights and aspects of ourselves that have been banished from our awareness for too long, repressed or demonized. The Mother is preparing a revolution of consciousness for the whole human race, but this revolution will be possible only when we invite the wisdom of the feminine, with its instinctual understanding of the sacredness of all life and of all true love, back into our hearts and minds in its full radical splendor.

In mystical terms, what is being prepared for humankind—if we are brave enough to embrace the challenge—is our *birth* into a wholly new, unified cosmic consciousness, what many mystics call *divine childhood:* that state of naked and elemental freedom beyond all barriers, dogmas, and conventions, the final reward of long years of prayer, discipline, and ordeal in the crucible of mystical transformation. Many mystics also believe—as I do—that this birth into divine childhood under the direct inner guidance of the Father-Mother is the one remaining hope for humanity. Unless this transformation takes place on a vast, politically and economically radical scale, the race will not survive.

The main mystical traditions also agree that this birth of a new being can only take place through a long, arduous, and increasingly conscious inner marriage of the masculine and feminine within each one of us, male or female. Only such an inner marriage can give birth to the sacred, androgynous, free child of the source that is potential in each of us. Homophobia drastically blocks this revolution of the sacred androgyne by breeding fear, self-hatred, and repression in everyone toward his or her own complex mixture of masculine and feminine traits and prevents the fully conscious and empowering fusion of different energies from taking place. Only the being who can fearlessly embrace all inner facets of his or her self—all the inner

The Body of Love

possibilities and paradoxes—who can see and know all kinds of love as being one with the love that guides and rules all things, can achieve union with the unity of God, and so be born again into the fullness of divine reality.

Such a being is free, under and in God, and this freedom and the radical energy for change to which it gives birth, the all-embracing understanding of relations in the world it engenders, profoundly threatens all forms of patriarchal power, including the power of all the churches and religious leaders and gurus. This, I believe, is the deepest reason why homophobia is still so prevalent. Many, many powers do not want this birth into sacred androgyny to take place, the birth of a self-empowered, free humanity beyond barriers and conventions. Healing the fear of sex and sexual relations threatens absolutely the domination of those whose power depends on sexual fear and rigid distinctions between the sexes.

The best weapon in this war of minds and hearts is accurate information. The testimonies of the homosexual mystics I have collected here speak far louder than any rhetoric could of the extraordinary achievement throughout history of the homosexual mystical genius. It is my hope that this anthology will offer alternative—and divine—images of what gay relationships can be. Plato's testimony to the same-sex beloved as a door to revelation; Sadi's and Attar's knowledge of the same-sex lover as being potentially a *shahid*—a witness to divine beauty; Walt Whitman's and Elsa Gidlow's fearless mystical celebration of holy sexuality as direct initiation into divine being; Edward Carpenter's beautiful argument for homosexuality's essential healing place in the creation of a new worldwide sacred democracy; all of these visions and ideals can inspire the gay seeker to go beyond the limiting and negative self-images this culture propagates—can encourage him or her to see his or her powers of love in their highest perspective. It is also my hope that this anthology will offer to heterosexuals not provocation as to who was or wasn't a same-sex lover but a vision of the noble wisdom that homosexual seeking, both in and beyond relationship, has to offer everyone, and

270

the contribution it has made and continues to make toward healing the heart-wounds of humanity.

In collecting all of these mystical gay voices together—some of these writings are published here for the first time—I have not wanted to limit or overdefine their testimony. As you would expect, gay people have taken many different mystical paths. You will find here austere as well as flamboyant lovers of God. Some are hungry for sacred silence and radiant absence, like Pessoa or Kobo Daishi or Christina Rossetti, while others, like Sappho or Sophia Parnok or Esenin, embrace all the suffering glory of reality. You will find here every aspect of the soul's relationship to its beloved. I have, however, emphasized one particular strand in the gay contribution to mystical understanding, because I believe it to be of fundamental importance for the future: the tantric vision of reality. This is the vision that rejects the old separations between heaven and earth, body and spirit, heart and mind, instead seeing and knowing reality as one constantly explosive dance of divine energy, love, and bliss, interconnected in all of its events and particulars.

You can see traces of this marvelous, liberating vision in Plato, in what remains to us of the works of the Greek poets and dramatists, and especially in Sappho. You can hear strains of its ecstatic music in the praise of beauty in the Persian tradition. But its full truth, challenge, and transforming power enter the human imagination with most complete force in the work of Walt Whitman. He is the pivotal figure of gay mystical history; his work gives total expression to a Mother-vision of humanity, healed within and without and released from all forms of authority and power hunger into a full and normal human divinity. His eloquence and direct gnostic passion make Whitman, I believe, the equal of Dante, a heart-brother of Rumi, and a pioneer more prescient and modern than either.

Whitman's vision—born out of a series of overwhelming mystical experiences in his thirties and out of his own abandonment of sexual fear and shame and consequent discovery of the body's inherent holiness—calls for an end to all patriarchal distinctions between the sacred and the profane. Initiated directly as he was into the source of love, Whitman saw and felt and knew that body, soul, heart, and mind are not separate but one living, divine being; that humanity and nature are interfused at every level in the heart of truth and love; and that the energy of true and deep sexual love is one with that energy that is birthing all the universes. Whitman also saw and felt and knew that allowing such a vast vision to penetrate all levels of one's being brings forth an almost infinite capacity for divine joy and compassionate action. He saw that this joy and its action were the sweetest secrets of every human identity, *and* key to the flowering of a wholly new humanity, released from all fears and confining powers into the democratic plenitude planned from eternity in the mind of God.

As Edward Carpenter, Whitman's brave English disciple, wrote, "We are arriving at one of the most fruitful and important turning-points in the history of the race. The Self is entering into relation with the body. For, that the individual should conceive and know himself, not as a toy and chance-product of his own bodily heredity, but as identified and continuous with the Eternal Self of which his body is a manifestation, is indeed to begin a new life and to enter a hitherto undreamed world of possibilities." Carpenter's whole work makes clear, as Whitman's had done before him, that "entering this undreamed world of possibilities" means making a rubble of all old divisions and certainties, and makes possible an alchemical, tantric transformation at every level of the being; the gates between "soul" and "body," which the patriarchal and homophobic religions keep closed, are flung wide open so the soul's pure fire can penetrate and illuminate and transfigure the body, and the body can taste and live resurrection and freedom in time and on the earth. Neither Whitman nor Carpenter underestimated the cost and difficulty of such a transformation. As Carpenter wrote, "Whilst [this transformation is] the greatest and most wonderful, it is also the most difficult in Man's evolution for him to effect. It may roughly be said that the whole of the civilisation-period in Man's history is the preparation for it."

Introduction to *The Essential Gay Mystics*

We are living in the time of this greatest, most wonderful, most difficult transformation, and as all seekers, gay and straight, try to heal the wounds that patriarchal religions and mystical transmission systems have inflicted on us all in the name of God, the fearless, ecstatic witness of gay visionaries such as Whitman and Carpenter and successors like D. H. Lawrence, Elsa Gidlow, and Audre Lorde will increasingly be seen as crucial. Many modern seekers—and I am one of them—now believe that one of the most important aspects of this difficult transformation will be a return on a global scale to the practice of tantric sexuality. When two beings, of whatever sexes, are in harmony on every level—mental, emotional, spiritual, and physical—and living in tenderness, respect, fidelity, and rigorous honesty with each other, their lovemaking becomes an experience and an invocation of divine passion and divine energy; both are initiated mutually and simultaneously into the dance of the universe in the ground of ordinary life. Slowly, if they persist in meeting the sometimes extreme demands of such a relationship, a transformation of great, intense beauty takes place in all of their senses, faculties, powers, and creative energies. They become two parts of a single, irreducibly powerful and empowered sacred unit, guided by each other and by the Divine that manifests continually in and around them—in dreams and visions, in sacred lights that illumine their lovemaking, in revelations their intimacy continually brings to birth. Whitman knew and lived such tantric relationship, knew its radical power, and knew too how it could be the base of the true, sacred democracy of the Mother—because its very nature frees it from external authority and the need for any outside mediation, because it fuses divine and human things together in an experience of continuing, explosive, sacred joy. It is this radical, tantric path of relationship that the Mother is now opening up to the whole human race as a way of progressing into self-empowerment and as a way of making ordinary life divine and ending the deformations of patriarchal power. A humanity that has been sexually healed and released into full human divinity will not want to destroy nature or exploit the poor. In the new world that this understanding can make possible, gay visionaries will be passionate and informed guides.

Listen to Whitman:

> *O we can wait no longer*
> *We too take ship O soul,*
> *Joyous we too launch out on trackless seas,*
> *Fearless for unknown shores on waves of ecstasy to sail,*
> *Amid the wafting winds (thou pressing me to thee, I thee to me,*
>   *O soul)*
> *Caroling free, singing our song of God.*

Postscript

There is an obvious difficulty one encounters in assembling an anthology such as this: whom can one reasonably "claim" as lovers of their own sex? Social constructionism maintains that terms such as "gay" and "gayness" are imaginary and recent—social constructs. This argument is buttressed by an extremely narrow definition of "gay." As Randy Conner wryly put it in the introduction to his pioneering work *Blossom of Bone: Reclaiming the Connection Between Homoeroticism and the Sacred,* constructionists insist that "gay" basically refers to an individual (often male, traditionally masculine, and middle class) who, living in the West in the late twentieth century, self-consciously *chooses* to identify himself as one who engages in homosexual behavior and participates in a related urban, subcultural lifestyle. As Conner makes clear, such a narrow view entails denying many things: that there was, for example, any cultural or historical interaction at all between gender-variant people in the ancient or pre-modern world.

How can such a claim stand up to the implications of modern cross-cultural research? Moreover, the constructionists' insistence that concepts are dependent on language, and that terms precede ideas, is highly questionable. While defining an activity or way of life might make for a greater degree of self-awareness (and social pride and legal protection), this does not mean that the activity and conscious identity did not occur before in many different settings.

Conner and others have gone a long way toward showing that many of the world's peoples have held that homoerotic inclination and gender variance are traits bestowed before birth by a divine power or powers. As Conner says, "Many peoples have believed gender variance and homoerotic inclination to be essential qualities and not culturally constructed behaviors—whether we like it or not. In spite of various forces of obscuration, awareness of the linking between male gender variance, homoeroticism, and sacred role or function has repeatedly surfaced across cultures and epochs. Those embodying the domain, while dwelling in the shadows, the wings, or the spaces between the text, have not been entirely erased."

A great body of cultural and historical evidence suggests that not only has same-sex desire always existed (and been known to exist), but that in many cultures those who followed its inspiration were seen as connected in particular and luminous ways to the sacred. Such evidence leads us—or should lead us—to expand our vision of what gayness has been and could be. It is this larger human continuity and tradition that I have chosen to celebrate here.

Another difficulty I have had to confront was the dearth of *identifiable* lesbian mystical literature. This does not, of course, indicate lack of lesbian mystics; rather, it shows that they suffered the same fate as so many other women—oppression and silencing. I am convinced that many of the most distinguished women Christian mystics of the thirteenth and fourteenth centuries may well have been wholly or partly lesbian, but there is little evidence to warrant including, as I longed to do, either a Mechthild of Magdeburg or Hildegard of Bingen. I have tried to right this imbalance by beginning with a great lesbian voice, that of Sappho, and ending with four great modern lesbian mystics: Marguerite Yourcenar, Elsa Gidlow, Audre Lorde, and Hildegard Elsberg. Because of space limitations, I have limited this anthology to deceased writers; I might have easily have included contemporary lesbian seekers such as Susan Griffin, Judy Grahn, and

The Body of Love

Dorothy Walters, among many others, whose work I honor and from whom I have learned.

Yet another difficulty I have had to face is the thick silence surrounding the probable homosexuality of many mystics writing within conventional religious structures. How many of the great Christian monks of all Christian denominations must have been homosexual, and how little—even given the efforts of historians such as John Boswell—we will ever know about them. The same silence confronts us in the other major traditions. Fear, embarrassment, and the tendency, especially in the Asiatic traditions, to idealize the Master of either sex as a sexless being beyond desire have obscured, probably forever, the power of many gay voices.

I have chosen to include in this anthology some artists and writers (Oscar Wilde, Jean Cocteau, and Colette, for instance) who would not normally be thought of as mystics. This was partly because I realized—like all explorers of gay history—that many gay people in all cultures, repelled by the homophobia of the existing religions, have diverted their religious passions into art. Also, as a poet and novelist myself, I am aware of how so-called secular art can be everywhere informed by spiritual truth and insight and can be one of the most effective vehicles for its secret propagation. Colette was once described to me by a well-read Japanese Zen abbot as "the greatest Zen writer of the century," and Claudel, in a wild but moving moment of enthusiasm, called Rimbaud "the greatest mystic seer of France, greater than any of the official mystics of the Church." It is also my belief that our current definitions of the word *mystic* are too specialized, elitist, and narrow; everyone is potentially a mystic, given the right training, dedication, and environment. The mystical truth is the truth of every being. When we look at the last two hundred years of the prevailing materialistic culture, we often find the greatest mystical insights in the work of artists of all kinds, rather than in the dreary lucubrations of theologians or the repetitive formulas of those mystics who stick too close to the conventions of their own tradition.

Bringing together *The Essential Gay Mystics* has been one of the richest joys of my life. I can remember myself as a young gay man hungering for images of gayness more noble and inspiring than those I was given by either straight or contemporary gay culture—images that would transcend the stereotypes of tortured aesthete, queen, leather-boy, or promiscuous sexual rebel. Slowly, in the course of long, often bewildering and painful personal seeking, I discovered them both in my own inner consciousness and in the writings of the people whose work I am honored to present here. I feel them now as living and invigorating companions on my journey into entire self-acceptance and fully divine human awareness and compassion. May these marvelous *adventurers* and their wisdom come to live with—and in—you now.

Foreword to *The Book of Mirdad,* by Mikhail Naimy

There are, in essence, two kinds of mysticism: a mysticism that teaches the way to transcendence and union with the light alone, and an "evolutionary mysticism," which honors the union with the Transcendent but stresses the birth of the Divine in matter that can take place as its transforming grace. History has shown us that the first kind of mysticism can coexist effortlessly with hierarchy, inequality, and injustice, because in its vision, the world is seen and known either as inevitably flawed or as an illusion, with the only refuge possible being a transcendent freedom from it.

In the second kind of mysticism, we are all challenged to go on a difficult and mysterious path of constant transformation of our entire being and action, so as to embody the Divine more and more completely, and to be agents of an evolutionary will that longs to transfigure all conditions of life on earth. This second, "evolutionary," kind of mysticism has always been a scandal to the orthodoxies of the first kind, and while its tremendous secret (that humanity is an unfinished adventure, with all kinds of evolutionary transformations possible through its innate divine nature) has always been experienced by a few mystics in all traditions—by kabbalists in Judaism, certain secret schools of Hindu tantrism, the Jesus of the Gospel of Thomas, and the Christian Orthodox mystics who underwent *theosis,* or "transfiguration"—its great liberating truths are still too little known.

That this should be so is especially tragic in a time like ours, when humanity is going through an unprecedented evolutionary crisis, on the outcome of which its survival depends—a crisis that can be successfully negotiated only if its true meaning is understood and if its devastating demand for a complete transformation of human nature and action on a massive scale is faced without flinching. Our evolutionary crisis is both a necessary death of all our collective fantasies of human uniqueness and our right to dominate and destroy nature, and also, simultaneously, a birth of a wholly new way of being and doing everything, far more humble and also far more powerful than anything we have yet lived or imagined, because it is aligned with divine will. The clue to knowing and understanding this lies in the pioneering testimony of the great evolutionary mystics who refused the consolations of purely transcendental mysticism and dared to plunge into the turbulent, unfolding mystery of the divine birth in matter, with history as its wild midwife.

It is in the twentieth century that evolutionary mysticism began to find its truest and most potent voice, as if in divinely inspired response to the growing barbarism and destructiveness of human action. Sri Aurobindo, Teilhard de Chardin, and Father Bede Griffiths all proclaimed, in different terms but with one voice, that an unprecedented crisis was opening up an unprecedented opportunity, and that the growing "dark night" of our species—obvious in war, genocide, and environmental matricide—heralded potentially not extinction but transfiguration: a transfiguration by divine grace of the very terms of human nature. Each of these brave and wise pioneers knew that such a transfiguration was not inevitable (it would have to be earned through a concentrated intensity of devotion, passion, faith, discipline, and sacredly inspired action) but was possible, because each of them was living its divinizing mystery in the core of their hearts, souls, minds, and bodies.

Mikhail Naimy was one of the most gifted and eloquent of these evolutionary pioneers, and *The Book of Mirdad* is one of the masterpieces of evolutionary mysticism, inspired as it is by a radical and all-comprehensive vision both of the Divine and of a potentially divinized humanity. Naimy writes, "As a living branch of a living vine, when buried in the ground, strikes root and ultimately becomes an independent grape-bearing vine like its mother with which it remains connected, so shall Man, the living branch of the Vine Divine, when buried in the soil of its divinity, become a God, remaining permanently one with God."

Do not be deterred by the fustian and sometimes outdated esoteric "scaffolding" of *The Book of Mirdad*. Its vision of humanity capable of overcoming all self-limitation and cocreating a new world out of the smoking ashes of the old is essential for our time.

There are six characteristics that mark authentic evolutionary mysticism:

- a celebration of the Divine as both fully transcendent and fully immanent;
- a glorying in the essential divinity of humanity;
- a profound knowledge of reality as an alchemical cauldron of opposites in which death can prepare birth, evil a wiser good, and catastrophe a new vision of order;
- an unflinching look at the inner shadow of humanity—its cowardice, greed, delusion, and hubris—and at the destructive shadow of the outer institutions it has created from its addictions;
- an awareness of the sacred androgyny of the new human born from a fusion of matter and spirit, masculine and feminine; and

- a rugged understanding that for an evolutionary leap to be possible, all consolations and comforts will have to be risked in an adventure, the end of which cannot be foreseen.

Careful readers of *The Book of Mirdad* will find all of these themes intricately woven in the text, with an authority and lived passion of conviction that makes page after page brilliant with the dawn of a new creation. Naimy was at once an ecstatic visionary, a fierce psychological realist, a political radical, and a passionate opponent of any dogma, religious or scientific, that keeps humanity imprisoned in a limited vision of itself and so doomed to repeat itself until its own hidden self-pessimism explodes in a crisis of extinction. In Naimy's work, Nietzsche, Marx, and the exalted knowledge of a Rumi or Meister Eckhart are fused in a unique and stunning challenge to all conventional understanding and in eloquence all his own.

It is one of the greatest strengths of Naimy's vision that he fully understood how terrifying the transition to the new humanity must necessarily be. As he writes: "To tear men free of their nets, their very flesh must needs be torn; their very bones must be crushed. And men themselves shall do the tearing and the crushing. When the lids are lifted—as surely they shall be—and when the pots give out whatever they contain—as surely they shall do—where would men hide their shame and wither would they flee? In that day the living shall have envy of the dead and the dead shall curse the living." As we, at the end of the first decade of the twenty-first century, experience the perfect storm of a series of interlinked crises—environmental, cultural, economic, political—and begin to understand what horrors may be in store for us, these words of Naimy's have a chilling ring, and we ignore their agonized, prophetic warning at our peril.

The apocalyptic prophet in Naimy, however, was balanced by the ecstatic visionary of a new creation. While he does not flinch from the dangers and price of evolutionary transformation, he also unhesitatingly proclaims its radiant possibility and the laws of discipline, radical compassion in action, and humble devotion that would engender it. It is clear to many of us that the "dark night of the species" ahead will be excruciating and extremely dangerous; knowing that, however, need not destroy our strength or diminish a hope that is founded in unshakable faith, for, as Naimy writes, "No fraction of Himself did God endow you with—for He is unfractionable; but with His Godhood entire, indivisible, unspeakable did He endow you all. What greater heritage can you aspire to have? And who, or what, can hinder you except your own timidity and blindness?"

It is this "timidity and blindness" that are humanity's greatest blocks to rising up to meet the challenge of our crisis. Naimy is clear that all those who risk the evolutionary adventure will have to endure sometimes atrocious difficulty. He writes "The pride-ridden and intoxicated world shall heap up injuries upon your heads and shall unleash on you the bloodthirsty hounds of its tattered laws, its putrid creeds and moldy honors. It shall proclaim you enemies of order and agents of chaos and doom." Naimy also knew, however, that to those who risk embodying the Divine, tremendous powers both of endurance and of unconditional compassion are given. As he writes, "Let not your hearts be faint. But like the sea be broad and deep, and give a blessing unto him that gives you but a curse. And like the earth be generous and calm, and turn impurities of men's hearts into pure health and beauty. And like the air be supple and free. The sword that will wound you will finally tarnish and rust. The arm that would harm you will finally weary and halt. And Understanding shall carry the day."

It is with the hope grounded in this understanding that *The Book of Mirdad* can guide us and inspire us. And it is with this mystical and prophetic hope that we all now need to inflame ourselves, to set about the difficult inner work that must infuse with its wisdom all our outer actions for us to be able to save ourselves and our world. Read *The Book of Mirdad* and prepare yourself for the storms and victories ahead.

—❦—

"Radical Mystic Andrew Harvey"
Interview with Felicia M. Tomasko, RN

The first time I saw Andrew Harvey speak, during one of Shiva Rea's teacher trainings, he delivered his appeal for listeners—for all of us—to engage in activism from a grounded place of sacred passion with such fire that I thought he would combust right in front of our eyes. He has been kindling and stoking the fire of sacred mysticism for his entire life, an ongoing study in the integration of a love of the Divine with our everyday lives. He is a translator and interpreter of the mystic, passionate writings and life of the Sufi poet Rumi.

Many people know Harvey through his numerous books, which include *Sun at Midnight: A Memoir of the Dark Night, Teachings of the Christian Mystics, Teachings of Rumi, A Journey in Ladakh,* and *The Divine Feminine,* and he coauthored *The Tibetan Book of Living and Dying.* Born in India, he was educated in England, attended Oxford, and returned to India on the journey of his lifelong spiritual quest that has transcended dogma to culminate in a synthesis of tradition and action. Harvey sees spirituality and mysticism along with a call to action and activation as the solution for the current crisis we are facing in the world today. To these ends, he is currently working on a book on Sacred Activism and developing a curriculum and institute for Sacred Activism.

Felicia M. Tomasko: People describe you as a mystic. How would you define what a mystic is and the role of a mystic in the modern world?

Andrew Harvey: A mystic is someone who has a direct connection with the Divine, beyond dogma, beyond religion, beyond concept. I believe everybody is a closet mystic, because when you wake up to your own inner divinity, you wake up to the inner divinity of everybody and of every sentient being. So I know that within every human being there is a spark of the divine consciousness and this is the universal testimony of all the mystical traditions.

The Upanishads say the Atman, the individual soul, is Brahman, the eternal spirit, so the individual soul is one with the eternal consciousness. In Christianity, the soul is referred to as a *favilla dei,* which is the "spark of God." And when I was working with a group of Tibetans on the book I cowrote with them, *The Tibetan Book of Living and Dying,* we used to chant—in between trying to get minutiae of Tibetan philosophy right—"My Buddha nature is as good as the Buddha's Buddha nature."

This testimony that at the core of everyone lies the divine consciousness waiting to be experienced is crucial for the future. We've created an increasingly violent, desolate, meaningless, desperate world out of our mistaken belief that we are separate beings. This terrible belief—that is profoundly untrue—is the root of growing devastation that we see everywhere. The healing of this devastation can only come from two linked things: our universal mystical awakening of the innate divinity of human consciousness, and a wholly new kind of sacred action born from that consciousness.

FMT: How did this lack of consciousness begin?

AH: For divine consciousness to incarnate itself, it had to lose itself. The individual being who was created to lose itself in divine consciousness was also shrouded by the ego, or what we call the "false self" in Sufism. In Sufism it is said that we are separated from our deep self by 72,000 veils of illusion. In order to incarnate, the Divine travels through those 72,000 veils, which are, of course, different aspects of itself. In order to experience our innate divinity, we have to go on a tremendous journey through those veils, which we can do through grace and deep spiritual work.

This game of hide-and-seek with itself seems to be at the core of the Divine's plan for the universe. And it's a very dangerous—and exciting—plan. Because if we do not wake up to this innate divinity, we will destroy what the Divine has seeded in us for the transformation of ourselves and our world.

FMT: It's gambling with the highest stakes. The Divine is betting everything.

AH: Yes, the Divine is betting everything out of supreme love. Supreme love creates all of the world, yet it cannot command beings to love it back; it wants to be loved for its own sake.

In creating and inseminating the human race with divine consciousness, the Divine took an enormous risk of being abandoned, rejected, forgotten, and humiliated. History has shown that humanity has, to a large extent, abandoned, rejected, and humiliated the Divine.

This abandonment and rejection of the Divine does not exhaust divine love nor the operations of divine grace. Let us look at the parable of the prodigal son. The prodigal son abandons his world and his generous father, to go off in a fit of independent pique and destroys his life, or comes close, in an orgy of selfish greed and addiction. In the despair that follows, he remembers his father and goes back. The reunion with the father after the depths of shattering is more intense, illumined, tender, and humble. I see the whole of humanity going through this story right now.

There will be those that will die in the pit of addiction. There will be those who see that a desacralized world and life are utterly doomed; they will then undertake the journey back to origin, back to the Divine, and be inflamed by passion to act in very wise ways to save the planet.

FMT: What about people who feel the Divine has forsaken and betrayed them?

AH: That is a complete illusion. The Divine cannot forsake anyone, because the Divine is living as a spark within everyone. When you wake up and see the divine light, you see that the whole universe is radiating from that light. All matter is frozen light and all beings, good and evil, are pillowcases stuffed with light.

The idea of being abandoned by God is just that: it is an idea, a concept born out of a very incomplete knowledge of the Divine. It can only be healed by radical knowledge of gnosis, of mystical illumination. When you take the path to that illumination, you realize that it is not God who is abandoning you. By retreating into your ego, into your self-concern, into the agendas of your illusory fantasies about life, you are abandoning God.

God is always here. God is always available. God is always extending infinite love. Rumi says this with characteristic brilliance:

> The wine of divine Grace is limitless.
> All limits come only from the fault of the cup.
> White light stretches from horizon to horizon.
> How much it fills your room depends on the windows.
> Grant a great dignity my friend, to the cup of your life.
> Eternal life has designed it to hold eternal wine.

Rumi is making clear what all the mystics of all the traditions discover: divine grace is always flowing. And as Ramakrishna said, "The winds of grace may be always flowing, but we forget to hoist our sails."

FMT: Since the stakes are so high, the Divine is asking for its heart to be broken.

AH: I think the heart of the Divine has been broken again and again since the beginning of time. To undertake the adventure of incarnation is to invite radical and terrifying heartbreak. Anyone who comes into contact with the Mother side of God has come into contact with what Jewish, Christian, and Sufi mystics call the heartbreak of God at our forgetfulness of the Divine, our maltreatment of the sacred, our brutality towards each other—at our insane cruelty.

The Body of Love

FMT: How can someone open the door to their closet mystic?

AH: There are three essential ways to open the door to the closet mystic:

A discipline of meditation, which enables you to experience the divine sun of consciousness behind the passing clouds of thought.

A discipline of prayer, which enables you to experience the rapture of being able to commune with the force that your deepest self is in touch with.

And a discipline of service in which you express what you learn from meditation and prayer in real work of love in the world.

Those three disciplines, of meditation, prayer, and service, done with great humility and faith, are invitations for divine grace to take away "the me." Over time, the innate divine nature is revealed; when it is revealed, everything is changed and a wholly divine nature of consciousness, power, generosity, and passion are installed in the human being.

FMT: How do we get ourselves out of the massive heartbreak and violence in the world today?

AH: The first thing we need to do is to be extremely real, radical, and honest about where we are. My great mentor, Father Bede Griffiths, told me at the end of his great life, that he'd come to believe that there were three possible scenarios for the future. This was in 1993, and he was talking about the next twenty years.

Either we will wake up very fast and change everything, recognizing the horror of what we've created, and bring about a heaven on earth, which is extremely unlikely. Or we will continue to be hopelessly addicted to a dissociated vision of the world, and in all the attendant greed of power and in this addiction, we will destroy everything. He felt that this was more likely, but still unlikely, given the presence of divine mercy. The third possibility, and this is what he believed would happen, is that humanity would pass through a great and tremendous death that would mirror the initiatory deaths in the mystical systems that prepare not the end but the transfiguration of the human being.

This initiatory death is known in all of the mystical systems: the shamanic systems, in Mahayana and Hindu tantra; it's known as annihilation in Sufism, and it's known as the dark night of the soul in Christianity. This initiatory death is actually a burning down of the false self of the ego's identifications, separations, fantasies, illusions, and agendas. It is a devastating process, which demands enormous courage.

At the end of this process the phoenix of divine consciousness rises purely and splendidly from the ashes of the burned and incinerated false self. What seems like horror and death and cruelty and madness and destruction reveals itself by the supreme paradox of ruthless mercy to be radical healing and radical liberation.

I believe this is happening: we are passing through an initiatory death on a major scale. Just as the mystic has to pass through the dark night to become humanized, so the human race has been brought, both by its mistakes and also by the hidden logic of its own evolutionary passion, to a moment when it will have to transform or die out. Where, in the words of Teilhard de Chardin, it will have to choose between suicide or adoration.

You can see this choice in two ways. You can see it in a frightened, scared, extremely depressed way, or you can see it in a joyful, impassioned, and thrilled way, knowing that the fact that this choice has appeared in history means that this tremendous crisis is also a tremendous opportunity.

The first thing to see is that we're going through not just a scientific or technological or political or even psychological crisis. In its essence, it is a mystical crisis. The crisis stems, on the one hand, from our abandonment of the sacred and, on the other hand, it stems from the necessity of an evolutionary process that is taking us and will take us through an initiatory crucifixion into an extraordinary resurrection as divine being. Once you have seen that, something in you is humbled and inspired.

Once you have allowed that steady inspiration to take over your whole being, you need to do two things: you need to plunge deep into sacred practice, spiritual practice, mystical practice; and you need to start doing something that reflects the urgency of your compassion.

FMT: This is where service comes into play?

AH: Service is the only possible response to a world in chaos—that is falling apart in every way.

FMT: In the face of so much difficulty and destruction how can one person's efforts begin to make a dent?

AH: The truth is that any action, done from a profoundly open and compassionate heart, has an effect, through divine grace, far greater than anyone can ever imagine. For example, you might find yourself in a queue in Safeway, and because you really want to extend compassion and you feel full of love, you spend time with the person serving you. You don't know that this person has decided to commit suicide in the evening, because his or her life has reached an impasse. Your few words of ordinary courtesy change his or her decision. You never know that, but what you've actually done by just chatting with a smile could very well be saving a life. The world is full of examples like that.

FMT: Many people feel hopeless.

AH: One of the ways the ego keeps us in its thrall is by massively depressing us. As long as you are trapped in the ego and the false self, however intelligently, this crisis is going to look hopeless, dark and dense and terrifying. That is the real reason why without a profound mystical revolution, without a real mystical awakening, this crisis is going to drive us into madness and despair.

Once you step out of the confines of the prison of the false self and the ego, with all of its false hopes and false illusions and false

288

agendas, you stand in the eternal light of divine love and the flow of divine grace. When you are that eternal light and flow you know there is always the possibility of giving love and exercising compassion that can subtly shift the situation.

If you stay in the false self and the ego, all that you will see in the world around us at the moment is a nightmare exploding. If you step out of that vision into the vision of the eternal heart, what you will see is that this extreme and terrifying process is a stage in an evolutionary unfolding of God's divine plan for human transformation. That won't reduce absolutely your fear, and you will continue to cry and tremble and sometimes want to die. But, what it will give you, over time, is a calm and fervor, and a supply of deathless energy that will enable you to go on going on with joy.

FMT: This idea of going on with joy is needed by people doing activist work. I see so many people who are trying to make change in the world but really are doing it from this place of anger.

AH: The mystics and activists are probably the two most sensitive groups of people. But I think that both mystics as we know them and activists as we know them are not at this moment as helpful as they may be, and that's putting it gently.

Many mystics I meet are addicts of transcendence. They believe that only the light is real; the world is ultimately just an illusion; and human relationships and the body and all forms of politics are somehow dirty and fallen. This view, which is backed up by a great many of the patriarchal mystical traditions, is an absolute catastrophe for the world at the moment. It means that those beings who are in partial contact with the Absolute are not letting that contact inform real, wise, tender, compassionate, helpful action in the real world. They're using that contact as a kind of heroin to sign off from the real world. They're making the mystical ecstasy and bliss and peace the final drug instead of the support for compassionate, just, transformative action.

Activists are motivated by tremendous righteous passion for justice; I think that's at the noble core of everything that they do. The problem with many activists I have met, and I say this with great humility, because I admire them, is that many are still in an unhealed, divided, angry consciousness, which condemns others. This perpetuates, through that divided consciousness, some of the very problems that are destroying the world.

Just as mystics are addicted to being, activists are addicted to doing. The mystics do not always act with enough generosity out of the depths of their wisdom. The activists do not always ask themselves the three crucial questions that a truly mystical sacred activist should ask:

> What is your prime intention in doing this action?
> How does this action express your unconditional love for
>   all beings?
> And what is the goal of this action in the evolutionary
>   unfolding of humanity?

Activists are addressing the major problems of this upheaval from an impassioned but limited consciousness. This limits their response and the power of their actions. Only those actions blessed by the Divine, infused by divine compassion, inspired by divine wisdom, only those actions can really transform a situation as dark as this.

The beauty of Sacred Activism is that it brings together what is best in both the mystic and the activist: the mystic's fiery passion for God, and the activist's fiery passion for justice. What is born from the fusion of those two great, ennobling fires is a third fire that is love and wisdom in action.

When that fusion takes place in a person and that third fire is born, the addiction of the mystic to being is healed by the activist's passion for action.

The activist's passion for doing is healed by the mystic's bliss, peace, and understanding of the eternal protection for being.

Interview with Felicia M. Tomasko, RN

FMT: You need them both.

AH: Yes. And in the birth of this third fire is the great hope.

FMT: The great hope uniting the best of both of these ways of being in world.

AH: Yes; it is realizing that they need to fuse together to be effective. The divine truth behind the mystic's passion has created the major religions, built Chartres and the pyramids and burns in the work of both Beethoven and Rumi. The passion for justice is the divine truth at the heart of activism, because justice is one of the holiest names of God.

If you bring these partial enactments of the divine truths of both positions together, you have the birth of a nuclear fire of passionate compassion in wise, lucid action. This is the force that could transform everything. The fusion of the two fires, the mystic's passion for God and the activist's passion for justice can transform the horror and darkness of this situation and take the whole of humanity into the next evolutionary stage in which human consciousness and divine consciousness will work in cocreative and glorious ways to transform the earth and create justice and harmony.

FMT: What is the role of righteous indignation?

AH: I think that's one of the most important questions you could ask. What I feel at the moment is this: the patriarchal mystical systems have demonized anger, because they are terrified of the potentially deranging force that it can unleash. But they're also terrified of the ways in which outrage can lead to a fundamental readjustment of society. At this core, the demonization of anger is a refusal of the transformational powers of the dark feminine, since true holy outrage can unleash in a way that restores balance and transforms society. If you aren't angry at how the environment is being destroyed and how we're being governed by corrupt gangsters, how the corporations have no controls on their greed-inspired action, if you aren't angry at the fact that billions of people are living on less than $1 a day, you aren't human. If your anger masters you and drives you into hatred, you aren't human either. What is needed is what the tantric feminine mystical traditions give us, and which Jesus exemplifies: a way of using the energy of outrage, transmuting it by dedicating it to the Divine for purification into fierce, compassionate energy that sustains constant action.

Chapter Four

The Light of Love—Honoring
the Divine Within

Introduction

In this chapter, "The Light of Love," I celebrate what I consider to be the key to the next evolutionary stage of humanity—the Direct Path, unmediated by traditional churches, religions, priests, or gurus—the path of naked, radical, authentic, moment-by-moment, direct connection in the heart, mind, soul, and body with the Divine in both its transcendent peace and immanent, embodied passion.

As many of the greatest spiritual pioneers have known (most notably Jesus and the Prophet Muhammad), in order for a liberated and embodied Divine humanity to be born, humankind must claim and live in a direct connection with the Divine, honoring its laws and celebrating its presence in every aspect of our being and in the whole of life. The religious and guru systems, as we have known them, belong to a stage of evolution that has all too clearly revealed its disastrous, dissociated bias, its addiction to transcendence and elitist authoritarianism. What is needed, as Matthew Fox and Caroline Myss make clear in their pungent interviews, is for all of us to make the radical leap of claiming our Divine identity, plunging into the sacred disciplines necessary to unveil, sustain, and expand it, so that we may live it out with radical peace and prophetic passion in the heart of the world.

The authentic Direct Path unites the disciplines that enable us to enter into our transcendent origin, as well as to revel in and honor our sacred immanence. As we move through the growing chaos and horror, this path will help us find the sacred peace and passion energy that is needed in order to birth new visions and enduring structures. What are urgently required at this time are authentic, sacred disciplines of the body—disciplines that not only honor the body as the temple of the soul, but that open it on a vibratory cellular level to the evolutionary love force and love fire of the transcendent Father-Mother.

For over five years, I worked with a great and wise yoga teacher, Karuna Erickson, to birth what we have called "Heart Yoga"—a yoga that fuses together traditional asana sequences with evolutionary, mystical light-practices of great power taken from various traditions. We worked quietly, doggedly, and mostly in secret, with a dedicated and adventurous group of students. Our book, *Heart Yoga,* came out in 2011. To our great joy, it was celebrated by both leading spiritual and yoga teachers. It is Karuna and my deepest prayer that the book will help the worldwide yoga community connect far more consciously with the sacred origins and potentially transformative, sacred power of yoga. We also believe it can provide all those who take up the challenge of birthing a new divine humanity with a source of calm and passionate, vibrant energy—the energy of the Father-Mother that can keep us both peaceful and dynamic in whatever circumstances we encounter, as well as, over time, helping us experience with awed intimacy the birth of the divine light in the core of our body and its cells.

Karuna and I have taught Heart Yoga now both in the Institute of Sacred Activisms yearly initiation programs and across the United States and Europe. We continue to be amazed and humbled both by the response from our pupils, many of whom are activists who are burned out by the suffering of the world and their impassioned reaction to it, and by our own growing experience of its power of radiant embodiment. As Karuna said to me recently "I always knew our bodies were meant to be glowing lamps of Divine love. Now, at last, I am beginning to live this knowledge—beyond words or concepts—directly and with growing amazement."

Andrew Harvey

Introduction to *The Direct Path*

As I look back at the journey that gave rise to the vision of *The Direct Path*, I can see that the inspiration for my book began in an exchange with a remarkable, realized being—the Dalai Lama.

In 1989, I was commissioned by an American magazine to interview the Dalai Lama in Oslo during the time he was to be awarded the Nobel Peace Prize. I had had the honor of meeting and working with him several times before and had been profoundly moved by his electric tenderness of being; to have the opportunity to sit with him for two hours in a bare Norwegian hotel room, asking him anything I wanted to and on such an extraordinary occasion, was a blessing whose radiation continues to illumine my life. At the end of our long interview—which ranged over a vast array of topics, from the Dalai Lama's childhood to the power of nonviolent protest to the state of the environment—I plucked up my courage and asked His Holiness point-blank "What is the meaning of life?" He threw back his head, roared with laughter, and then grew immensely concentrated, and, pointing at me, said slowly "The meaning of life is to embody the Transcendent." I felt my whole being fill with a flame of calm bliss and could not speak. His Holiness, with motherly tenderness, reached for my hand and walked with me shoulder to shoulder, to the door of the hotel room. As I walked away down the long, beige-carpeted corridor, I turned and saw that he was still standing where he had left me, smiling from ear to ear, with his right hand raised in blessing.

What continues to astonish me about His Holiness reply to my question is how all-comprehensive it was and how it transcended any specific tradition, even his own. He was pointing me to the central mystery at the core of all mystical traditions, the mystery of what Matthew Fox has called "Original Blessing": that we are all gifted by divine grace with a spark of divine consciousness and that the purpose of life is to realize that gift and embody its truth in an increasingly illumined mind, heart, and body and in the actions of justice and compassion that flow from such an integral realization. And in the luminous grace and sweetness of his own being and courtesy toward me, the Dalai Lama was showing me—not as a "Mahayana Buddhist" but as a simple, divine human being—what "embodying the transcendent" looked, felt, and acted like.

It was this encounter that helped me survive the shattering of my faith in the guru system that followed on my break with Mother Meera in 1994. As I describe in *The Direct Path,* the shattering I endured proved to be a savage grace in three related ways: it exploded me free from the "golden shadow" of my own deepest realization of the Mother that I had projected onto Meera; it baptized me into the reality of a direct and unmediated relationship with the Divine beyond all religious, mystical traditions and guru systems; and it focused fiercely the meaning of what His Holiness had told me about "embodying the Transcendent" by revealing to me how such an embodiment would not only transform the individual but could also lead to a wholesale economic, social, cultural, and political transformation of all the terms of earth life—nothing less, in fact, than a birth of the Divine in the human. The agony and revelation of what I lived in a long and brutal dark night opened me to the essential truth of our time—that we are all now in the cauldron of a vast, evolutionary crisis, a "dark night of the species," that is also the birth canal of a new humanity, empowered by the radical connection of the direct path to act on every level and in every realm of our world to transform chaos into order, terrible danger and division into unity and peace with all sentient beings and the creation itself. It is this vision that has inspired all my work during the decade since *The Direct Path* and that has flowered in the beginning of a global movement of what I have called "Sacred Activism," activated by my recent book, *The Hope: A Guide to Sacred Activism.*

During the experience of my personal dark night, I came to understand three interlinked truths of the birth that is now struggling to take place as our communal dark night continues to erupt in ever-fiercer intensity. The first is that this birth of an embodied divine human is being made possible by a return on a massive scale of the full glory of the Divine Feminine to human consciousness. The Mother has, of course, always been here, but for several thousand years we have been divorced from Her all-healing revelation of the sacredness of all life and the interpenetration and intercommunion of all aspects of reality. At the very time when we need Her ecstasy and wisdom the most, the largest and widest possible vision of the divine Motherhood of God is being awakened in us to inspire us and infuse us with both the sacred knowledge and the compassionately passionate energy to act on behalf of life in every arena of the world to save the world and ourselves.

The second truth I came to understand—and this is something I learned from the variety of my own mystical education that has embraced many different paths—is that this return of the Divine Feminine has made available now to all human beings the deepest treasures and revelations of all the mystical traditions. The last thirty years have seen an outpouring to humanity, unprecedented in our history, of all the major revelations of all of the traditions—available to anyone who wants to approach them in a smorgasbord of ways, from books to CDs to documentaries to long articles and teaching videos on the web. What this potentially means is that any human being, if he or she wants to, can approach the mystery of "embodying the transcendent" from any path that suits his or her mental disposition and cultural temperament, beyond the control of any dogma or religious or guru system. This amounts to a revolution in terms of human empowerment and liberation, and heralds, I believe, the birth on a worldwide scale of the kind of universal mysticism that I have espoused in *The Direct Path* and in all my subsequent work.

The third truth I understood, and which made clear to me and crystallized the meaning of my own journey of mystical awakening, was that the mercy of the Motherhood of God has made available to us, at our moment of greatest crisis, not only the revelations of the various traditions and systems of awakening, but also, even more importantly, their "sacred technology." What are now open to all of us are both the maps that the different traditions offer us of the journey to awakening and the wonderful and potent practices from all the different systems that can now work together to help us birth the Divine in ourselves and in the world.

In *The Direct Path* all these three truths dance together in what I intended to be both an exalted and down-home practical handbook for the birth. The book begins with a short account of my own journey to the revelation of the direct connection, which opens onto a vision of the stages to "embodying the Transcendent" that is drawn both from my own experience and from my knowledge of the mystical systems I have been initiated into. *The Direct Path* then continues with a description of what I consider to be the eighteen essential practices drawn from a variety of traditions that can, I believe, most empower us on the journey to birth a new level of evolution. The book proceeds with what is perhaps its most radical and valuable contribution—a celebration of the possibilities inherent in the divinization of the body combined with a selection of practices that will enable you to start working toward and experiencing this most liberating of mysteries. No complete embodiment of the Transcendent can be possible without a progressive divinization both of the body itself and of its desires; in this section "Embodiment and Integration" I make as clear as I can the terms, difficulties, and empowerments of such a divinization process. The last, short chapter "A Passion to Serve" focuses everything that has been said and learned on the essential task before us all—to put the truths of our inherent divine identity into wise, radical action on all levels to insure the survival of the human race and protect the menaced creation.

In the decade since I wrote *The Direct Path,* our communal dark night has become both brutal in its destructiveness and more obvious to millions of human beings all over the world, who are being roughly awoken to the necessity of meeting its challenge with a profound, inner transformation that expresses itself in urgent and sacredly inspired action. In our world crisis, where everything is at stake, everything now depends on whether you and I will embrace the grace that the Motherhood of God is opening up to us and come into the full vigor, calm, passion, and active compassion of our divine humanity. As I wrote at the end of *The Direct Path,* "The goal of *The Direct Path* is the divinization of our existence—social, sexual, economic, and political—into living, dynamic harmony with the will and love of the Divine. This demands of all who take it that they place their whole being into service of the Divine's unique plan for a unified, integrated, self-empowered humanity and that they work selflessly, inspired by divine wisdom and divine love, to release in the heart and endangered world the truths of divine equality, justice, and compassion for all beings."

"The Unfolding of a Prophet"
Interview with Matthew Fox

It is a great honor for me to be asked to participate in the Festschrift for a man I greatly admire and love—Matthew Fox. As a spiritual writer and prophet, Matthew was a model and inspiration for me long before I met him, and now that I have come to know him, he has become a friend of my heart.

Almost eighteen years ago, I picked up a copy of *The Coming of the Cosmic Christ* in a bookstore in New York. Very few books have had such a galvanizing effect upon me, although at the time I was profoundly occupied with Eastern metaphysics. What Matthew Fox gave through that book, I now realize, was the first wholly convincing vision of the Christ that I had encountered. When I came to write *Son of Man,* my old copy of *The Coming of the Cosmic Christ* kept me constant company. I realized I could not have begun to create my own vision of the Christian revelation without Matthew's help.

About three years ago, I bought Matthew's great and luminous masterpiece on Eckhart, *Breakthrough,* in Paris, where I then lived. I read the book perhaps ten times during a solitary Paris winter. It thrilled me by its brilliance and depth and commitment to social compassion. When I began to lecture on Rumi, Matthew's commentaries on Eckhart gave me inner permission to bring the whole of my social and political concerns to bear on his mystical legacy. Matthew's willingness to expose the full range of his prophetic concerns (as well as the precision of his scholarship) served as a powerful example.

When I helped make a film on Bede Griffiths in 1993, I had a conversation with Bede about the modern church. Again and again, he brought up Matthew's name, citing him as "the new prophet of Christianity." Bede's enormous joy at Matthew's work heartened me and confirmed what I had felt and made me anxious to meet Matthew in person.

We did meet, briefly, in 1994, over a lunch in San Francisco. From the first, I think, we felt relaxed and spiritually exuberant in each other's company. Six years later we were together again, teaching Rumi and Eckhart for a whole week at UCS [University of Creation Spirituality]. For me, teaching with Matthew was a highlight of my spiritual and intellectual life. There was a rare, glowing harmony between us, and our different styles enhanced and complemented each other.

Dear Matthew, thank you for all your brilliant, provocative, passionate work. Thank you for the warmth and generosity of your friendship. Thank you for your heroic example of dedication, stamina, unwavering focus on the social and political issues that should engage *all* spiritual writers—but alas so rarely do. May your sixtieth birthday be a celebration of all you have been and given, and all you are, for those who love you, as I do, and who are grateful, as I am, for all you have made possible.

Andrew Harvey: I'd really like to plunge in and ask you about the road of the prophet and I'd like to ask you to look back on your life and tell us about the stages you see in the maturation of your own prophetic stance and voice. How do you see the emergence of the prophetic voice inside you? How do you see the situations and historical circumstances that shaped it? And where do you see it taking you now?

Matthew Fox: Well, I think coming of age in the 1960s was certainly a conscious unfolding of the prophetic strand of my faith and life. And, of course, it was gradual. Being in the seminary, we were somewhat protected from this stuff. We didn't get the daily news. We didn't read newspapers that much. But certainly things came about; I had some amazing encounters around civil rights, the Vietnam War, and that all came to a head for me in the mid-1960s. And it was my passion to relate mystical experience with the prophetic call of our culture. Then, too, living in Paris in 1968 when the students brought down the government—which was happening archetypically all over the world, certainly in America. When I was in Germany, we were marching in an antiwar parade in Münster and the question was which group to join—everyone had their banners. So I ended up joining the Maoists— they looked the most interesting, all wearing red.

The Dominicans—that was probably powerful too. The young Dominicans who gathered in Paris—which, of course, had an interesting history of protests—to protest the order in the church and the war and all these other things. That was powerful for me—especially interacting with a lot of these Marxist Dominicans. One fellow from Spain became a good friend of mine; he was studying political theology with Johannes Metz and that was the real critique: the Marxist critique of culture, and I found that very important. Then, of course, hanging out with Marie-Dominique Chenu and just realizing his life's work as a Dominican priest and as a grandfather of liberation theology.

It was just in the air. It was in the air in America; it was in the air in France and in Germany at the time. I drank it in.

Everyone thought I was doing this odd thing, because I wasn't just drinking in the Marxism, I was also working on spirituality. Marxists thought I was crazy when I was working with spirituality; and when I was working with spiritual types, they thought I was crazy working with Marxist types—so I didn't fit any place. And then when I said I was doing my doctorate on *Time* magazine, then everyone knew I was crazy. But in a way that brought it together, because it's all about culture—spirit and culture.

And for me personally, the radicalization was from working at *Time* magazine, because I realized how toxic the messages were that came into our living room every week, my whole high school year, in the name of *Time* magazine. I was reading this regularly, my whole family was, and there is a whole ideology behind it—Henry Luce's ideology of *America first* and *capitalism first*, and wrapped up in religious language. So, intellectually my most radical experience actually was working on *Time* magazine, getting into its bloodstream and finding out what the real ideology was that was running the American economic and media system. And to realize how powerful the media is. The president of the University of Chicago said that *Time-Life* has had more influence on all culture by far than all the university systems put together. I realized I was in the belly of the beast. Of course, when you look at it historically, Henry Luce had a lot to do with the war in Vietnam, because he sat down with Joe Kennedy when Jack was elected. They were together and they made a pact that Henry Luce would be easy with Kennedy around his domestic civil rights program, *if* Kennedy was strong about anticommunism in Southeast Asia. I remember Luce had a special investment around Southeast Asia, because he grew up in China.

So all those connections were part of my growing up, politically and prophetically.

Then, too, returning to the United States was important. Being in a house with young Dominicans loving what I would say, and the older ones being totally freaked out. Realizing this was not just a Dominican problem, that the Vietnam War had split the generations all over America, split families. I couldn't talk about the war with my father because I knew where he stood and I felt very passionate about it.

Another factor was moving to Barat College, a women's college, and having four years there. That made me a feminist. Hearing women's stories got me involved. I could contribute to that liberation movement.

There was just one thing after another in the 1960s and 1970s.

The environmental movement came along, and the gay and lesbian movement, and it was clear to me very early that I couldn't forsake either end of that spectrum. I often tell a story about my last night in Europe. It really was metaphorical for me. I stayed up all night arguing with this brilliant Dutch philosopher who had just produced a doctoral thesis on Marxism and Christianity—everyone was saying that it was the best work done on Marxism in ten years. I argued with him about what was missing in Marx—the aesthetic and the mystical. And unlike German people you usually argue with, he actually ended the night by saying that I had taught him something. That had never been my experience with German intellectuals, but he listened. At the end of the night he said, "Yes, there's definitely something missing and you're on to something." I literally flew out of Europe that morning, so it was really a very powerful moment.

All these influences were strong—plus reading the liberation theologians. For example, the way they connected love to justice showed that the split between love and justice was Hellenistic and Greek; it was not Jewish and biblical. The very word for love and justice, *hesed,* is really the same in a Jewish consciousness. Reading liberation theologians was important to me. I always felt—and this came out in my book on liberating gifts *[Creation Spirituality]*—that too many northerners were romanticizing South American liberation. If you talk about northern liberation, it has to be done very differently, because we've got a whole different history and sociological structure.

AH: I'd like now to concentrate on the mystical path, on the mystical evolution of the soul of a prophet, because I feel that one of the things that you need in developing the prophetic voice (and correct me if you don't agree), is internal models of what prophets are, how they act, how they speak, how they protest, how they make this tremendous fusion between a mystical vision of the kingdom and a savage and accurate critique of the actual power structures. From my meditation on your work, I see your prophetic self having been fundamentally shaped by five people. Obviously by a "re-visioning" of Jesus that permeates the *Cosmic Christ;* by Eckhart; by Hildegard of Bingen; by Aquinas and by your own meeting of your own spiritual double that comes to you as you grow in the mystical journey. There is a very extraordinary meeting with the secret image in yourself that emerges out of this connection with all of these different forces.

Now if you don't want to address just the last one, and you may not want to, would you address the other four? It seems to me that what you've done in your work is re-visioned the whole Jesus enterprise by making explicit in it both the intensity of the mystical endeavor and the furious, practical application of that mystical endeavor to nothing less than a transfiguration of the whole society. How did this re-visioning of Jesus, how did your meeting internally with Hildegard, how did your passion for Aquinas and Eckhart help you form this prophetic soul and prophetic voice? This has really been your tremendous contribution, not only to Christian subjects, but to Western mysticism and Western mystical practice, because you have been the one voice—the *one voice* in this wilderness of chatter—that has connected the divine law with human transformation and justice.

MF: You left out Chenu. You see, the bridge between the two, the mystic and the prophetic is art and imagination. This was happening in the 1960s too, with folk singers like Bob Dylan and Peter Paul & Mary. The antiwar movement took to song. I felt that, and I experienced it: these singers could move thousands. The first thing I did when I got back in America was to start writing poetry and music. Brendan Doyle, as a musician, and I wrote the lyrics, and we would go around and do what we called concert commentaries on college campuses. It was the arts, and in the arts you can't escape, because it opens the heart and gets us out of the head.

AH: That's one of the ways Rumi is activating now. Rumi is working as this great can opener on the heart to expose people to the glory of creation and therefore initiate them into the pain of what's been done to creation.

MF: Which presumes the heart is pretty "tinny." *[Laughs]* We'll not debate *that!*

So, in a way, I came later to Hildegard and to Eckhart as well. First of all, in my *Musical, Mystical Bear* book *[On Becoming a Musical, Mystical Bear: Spirituality American Style],* where I go into "what is prayer" and try to deconstruct prayer, I say it is not about saying prayers, it is not about talking to God. Prayer is a radical response to life. One direction of "prayer as radical response" is mysticism, which is our "yes" to life and the joy of celebrating it. The other element is the prophetic, our "no" to that which interferes with life. I relate that to the Trinity: the yes, the no, the life.

So, writing that book was very formative for me. I've never disowned it—I've never wandered that far from what I said there. And I remember the experience I had writing it, how exciting it was for me to be able to bring the prophet and mystic together, because, as I said earlier, people didn't understand the connection. They either understood one side or the other side—so few were putting them together. When you put them together, all kinds of electricity happens.

AH: It's the equivalent of nuclear fusion.

MF: *[Laughs]* It's like that. And that's why I call it the Trinity: It gives birth to spirit, which is life. The Creator represents creation, the "yes." The liberator, the Son, if you will, represents the prophet, the "no." And when you put them together, you have an explosion that is spirit, which is life.

The response to the book was amazing! The book started selling, and I got all these invitations to ordinary places like parishes and talked to "ordinary" people—not clergy and theologians—and they began to get it. So you see, before I got to Eckhart and Hildegard, I did that *Bear* book, then the *Whee! We Wee [All the Way*

Home] book and then *Compassion [A Spirituality Named Compassion and the Healing of the Global Village, Humpty Dumpty, and Us]*, and that's what got me into Eckhart. The key word was *compassion*. That's what was missing from Christian theology for fifteen hundred years, the word *compassion*. I went looking for sources, theological sources, and looked and looked, and found so little. There was so much about contemplation—a word that never dropped from Jesus's lips once, because it's not a Hebrew word. It's a Greek word. But then finally I realized that where it comes together is with compassion.

Then I met Eckhart, who has incredible exegeses of "be you compassionate" and "be creative in your compassion"—all this wonderful stuff! So, Eckhart came first, although Aquinas was always with me, as was Chenu. I knew that Aquinas was a fighter. I knew that he represented a deconstructing of the whole feudal political and economic system, and that he dared to get his ideas from Islam and from pagan scientists like Aristotle. I knew that story very deeply, in my bones I think. But Eckhart led me to Hildegard and then back to Aquinas.

AH: What was the aspect of Hildegard's vision that shaped your soul? What was it that thrilled you most in it? What was it that gave you great *"aha's"*?

MF: The capacity to soar—musically, mystically, and imaginatively—and her groundedness in healing and the arts. There is a person who chose the arts as her medium too for waking people, for healing, and not only music but also painting and healing arts. The fact that she was a woman meant a lot to me, because at that time I was very embroiled in women's issues, and to realize that here is treasure that had laid buried, practically, for seven hundred years in the West, because she was a woman and she was literally mocked. But even when my book came out, *Illuminations [of Hildegard of Bingen]*, the *National Catholic Reporter*, [which] considered itself liberal, said something to the effect that she was obviously crazy. Oh yes! Shocking!

AH: When I read your work on Hildegard, what I discover you being thrilled by is Hildegard's vision of cocreation with the Divine. Hildegard has an astonishing, un-passive view of the human role in creation—and not just creativity—but the mystical awakening as a direct awakening of primordial power, which is then to be directed toward the transfiguration of all the conditions of the world, and culture and society and economics and politics. That is a vastly demanding, vastly empowering vision and it's also one that really does challenge all of the other forms of mysticism. It challenges the transcendental form, it challenges all escapist, creationist, passive forms of mysticism. And it challenges all mystics to become vessels of a very difficult transfiguration.

MF: It is interesting that you talk about this, because this is what we talked about in our Eckhart class this morning. We talked about the *Via Negativa,* about how it empties you. Eckhart has a great passage where he says that we don't just become a place where God can work, but rather God becomes a place where we work, where we co-work. And then he says the soul's name is compassion itself, we become instruments of Divine compassion, we get carved out for that purpose. So it's interesting that you see this in Hildegard. It's wonderful! You're right. There is such an opening of the soul with Hildegard, where so much is pouring through—and it is all about cultural awakening.

AH: She's clearly living as a transfigured being herself. She knows that these divine energies can transform everything. They're giving her the music, the poetry, the wisdom to rule her nuns; they're giving her the savvy to deal with all the crazy churchmen; and they're giving her a constant vision of the divine world as it could be. And all of that is happening as irradiation of the central sun of illumination. And she knows that this new future is possible to humanity because she is the new future. And I think you have that in Eckhart, in Hildegard, and in what you did in the early work of Aquinas. You brought together that sense in Aquinas of what this mystical power on earth is and what, unleashed, it could actually do. From that came this tremendous vision that you have of the four paths ending in the *Via Transformativa*. That's been your great contribution—the vision of the whole mystical path that culminates in a passionate and continual birthing of sacred works.

MF: That's where the mystical and the prophetic come together—in these four paths. Again, my first articulation of that was on encountering Eckhart. He brought it out of me because, although they're not explicit in him, they're absolutely implicit.

AH: Let's be honest. You've had direct initiations by both Eckhart and Hildegard. I think you have been chosen to do this work in this time. I think you've been put through the horrible fires necessary to do this work in this time. Eckhart met you by the sea and gave you illumination; when you were doing your work on Hildegard, you told me the angels were flapping in your room. Doesn't this seem to suggest that these people chose you to have these difficult, irradiating branches, and that this was the work and the line that you're carrying on?

MF: Also Aquinas. When I was doing the Aquinas book, and missiles were being fired between Rome and Chicago and Oakland, I felt this big presence behind me, looking over my shoulder while I was working.

AH: I love the Aquinas book in many ways over most of everything you've done (apart from the Eckhart book), because it's such an extraordinary reversal of all that the church teaches about Aquinas. In a way they could say about your work on Eckhart and Hildegard that you were taking fringe mystical figures and re-visioning them in your own image, but what could they do when you exegete the texts

Interview with Matthew Fox

of Aquinas and reveal that he has another whole enterprise.

MF: Do you want to hear an example? *[Laughs]* The president of the Aquinas Institute, a Dominican university in St. Louis, said to another Dominican, "Oh that awful book by Matthew Fox! Who does he think he is, interviewing Aquinas?" And the other Dominican said, "Well, have you read the book?" And he answered, "I would *never* read a book by Matthew Fox on Aquinas!" And this is the *president* of the Aquinas Institute! He's not only not read the book, he's denounced it without reading it! Which is very intuitive, when you think about it. *[Laughs]*

AH: But you see, what I think that you've done is position the whole mystical transformation in a marvelous way, because you selected the two transfigured visionaries, Eckhart and Hildegard. Then you brought in the central figure and showed that his whole vision is a sacramental vision, a vision of the transformed creation, and *man* is the agent of transformative change within that transformation of creation. And that is thrilling, because it means they can no longer hide in a passive, pacifist, transcendental, essentially mind-boggling, conservative vision of what the actual force of Jesus, the Cosmic Christ, is meant to be doing in this culture.

MF: Right! They are not soldiers in the traditionalist army any more. For those who have dared to really get into it, you're right. I really appreciate the fact that you understand that.

AH: This is the genius of your work. Amongst the many things that you've done, this is the core, I think, for me. This is the core bomb that will continue going off.

But I want to lead you from this vision into the Cosmic Christ. How do you now, at this moment, at sixty years of age, see the position and the role of Jesus as re-visioned by the modern historians and as experienced by the great lineage of the Christian mystics? How do

311

you see his role, as a figure, as a teacher, in this transformation that we're trying to live through? Because some people would say that in your work, you've gone away from Jesus. But I don't see that at all. I see you as having explored the prophetic lineage of Jesus and having brought it back in a sort of massive symphonic way and focused it momentarily through the Cosmic Christ in that book. But now I want to know how you see him. Has any change happened in your vision of him? Do you see him as even more central than before? Are you trying to detach from him, and see all the different teachers as part of the Cosmic Christ? Or is there something unique about Jesus's focus on justice that still haunts and inspires you?

MF: Absolutely! I call myself a Christian because I think Jesus did tremendous things in focusing the very essence of the Jewish ethical, prophetic, and wisdom traditions. And I've always understood Jesus as a mystic. I'm glad now that the historical scholars caught up with this in the wisdom tradition, because I always felt there was a mystic there and not just a prophet. And yet, a lot of Christian theologians stay away from the word *mystic*—as do a lot of Jewish theologians—because the word *mystic* has often been so peculiar. Especially with the modern era, which associates it with *aestheticism,* a word invented in aesthetic theology in the seventeenth century.

So, my understanding of Jesus has simplified, and I have great respect for what the historical Jesus scholars have done, although I have to confess, at first I did not. I felt they were asking overly textual questions about what was really an experience. And I felt it was such a modern thing to do—getting at what are the real words of the text, what are not. I just felt it was reaching the trees and forgetting the forest. But now I respect what they've done. They've really helped to slim down what we know about the historical Jesus and therefore to separate him from Paul, which is important, and from the Cosmic Christ, and from the community's projections and response to the amazing event that was Jesus—who came at obviously the right time to effect a profound change in human consciousness. When it comes to Jesus I like to quote Gandhi's saying: "I learned to say 'no' from the West." It is that prophetic tradition that Jesus imbibed that makes him different from other mystics. He got himself killed at thirty, and Buddha died naturally at eighty-four. There's a difference there, a difference in the story. Jesus was this Jewish rebel prophet.

AH: He got himself killed because he confronted the political and social realities of his time. He got himself killed because he dared to fuse the prophetic and the mystic, and he got himself killed because, in the course of doing that, he realized that there was a wholly new power that would come into human history if the prophetic and the mystic were fused. And that path threatened all the elites, all the hierarchies, all the power games of all institutions. And that's one reason why it has never been allowed in, because if it were allowed in, it would be a conflagration in which all forms of power would perish.

MF: Yes, and to put it very literally, he was "a-head" of his time. That's why the church, the Piscean Age, has not really been able to deal with the impact of his presence and his message and even what traditions call "the coming of the spirit." The coming of the Cosmic Christ that he unleashed in his way (though I say that Buddha and others have unleashed it in their way too), his special fusion of the mystical and the prophetic has nibbled away at human culture for at least two thousand years. I think the prophets did it before him, so it's been nibbling throughout the Jewish tradition. So, I think our species has come to such a point today—we're in such dire straits—that it's time that energy not just nibble away but begin to really assert itself as an authentic path for humanity to take. I think nothing moves humanity like necessity. Because of the dire straits we're in, humanity is more open now, two thousand years later, to the essence of Jesus's message than it has been for the last two thousand years.

I would hope at some point that the churches will allow themselves to get out what Jesus's message really is. I certainly don't think that the church in any exclusive way will; some grassroots Catholic churches might. The base community movement of Latin America was right on in its time, and it's now been destroyed, but something else might emerge. I don't want to restrict it to in or outside of the church, though. I like what Teilhard de Chardin says about the church—it is not a box, you're not in or outside; it's about *ecclesiogenesis:* What are we giving birth to? What kind of church, what kind of communities are we giving birth to? Community is very important in this, and we have to think in terms of prophetic communities, prophetic movements, not just prophetic principles.

AH: And education, the prophetic crucible.

MF: Absolutely!

AH: This is what I'd like to talk to next, your prophetic work. The first thing I want to ask you about is something you and I have discussed: how annoying it is to be classed as New Age writers and New Age prophets and mystics when so much of the New Age is repulsive to both of us. What I'd like you to do is to define what in this New Age movement you find positive, helpful, nourishing, creative. And what you feel in the New Age movement is conspiring, in some ways, with the coma that we're in and enabling people to believe they've had divine experiences when they've just had a few illuminations—actually deadening their prophetic sense of injustice rather than encouraging them.

MF: First of all, when I think of New Age, I think of the spectrum, and there is a healthy, and half-healthy, and a sick end, not unlike Christianity or any other human gathering. So, at the healthiest end, I would give New Age credit for, first of all, caring about mysticism and about science and about bringing science and mysticism together. Second, for caring about the body—the whole massage movement. However, you can go too far. I remember when a friend visited our school in Chicago after a trip to California and he said, "Do you know that there are people in California whose eyes are falling out from too much massage?" *[Laughs]* The whole point about bringing body back is obviously very important for healthy spiritual countenance, and some of that we have to get.

The New Age deserves a little credit also for its sense of eschatology, of a future, a sense that we can change our consciousness, that we can break out of boxes.

On the shadow side, for many New Agers it is all about the light and not about the darkness, meaning the personal shadow and the collective shadow (which is about injustice). I sometimes call the New Age "fundamentalism for the rich," because it's saying, "We're saved and you aren't, because we can afford $2,000 a day with Shirley MacLaine and you can't." Then they go away in the BMWs—high until the next shot. That bothers me a lot.

The other thing is the lack of appreciation about tradition. Even though the New Age claims to imbibe science, it's actually antievolutionary, because evolution teaches us that we inherit our ancestral genetic code, our genes. Not just our physical genes but our cultural genes. So you don't start religion over; Jesus didn't start religion over. Buddha didn't start religion over. Buddha got into Hinduism and tweaked what was useful. So this whole idea that we cut off the past is wrong. Ninety-nine percent of New Agers I've met have been wounded by their religion, whether Judaism or Catholicism or what have you, and they've slammed the door on it. But that's not ultimately the way to deal with the tradition. You have to open the door and separate out what was good and be grateful for that, and let the other go. You can't just shut the door on something as powerful as your inherited religious tradition.

AH: And, without the traditional mystical system, the New Age vision of the transformation lacks rigor, lacks a sense of stages and stations of change, and lacks any mystical or spiritual discipline. And that means that the actual birth cannot take place, because the birth can only take place through rigor and discipline and commitment and knowledge.

MF: That's right. Otherwise it becomes a shopping spree. And also, it can be anti-intellectual; it's all about right brain activity. Of course, a lot of this is a pendulum thing. Many of these people have been so starved spiritually that when they find there is such as thing as a mystical life and they actually have a soul they can feel at times, they go whole hog. That's kind of normal in human practice, but it's not healthy, because the fact is [that the] left and right brains have to line up on this.

There is an intellectual component, and that's why we have a university at this point in time: so we can study these things and deal with both brains and not just the right brain. The right brain by itself is at least as dangerous as the left brain by itself. Lurching from one malaise to the other is not the solution.

AH: Well, what I see happening in your life is that you've had the initiations that formed the prophetic voice and the prophetic soul in you. You've formed the vision in these great sets of works that really root that vision in the *Via Transformativa*. And now, as you say, you're paying for it by trying to embody it, by trying to bring it down, by trying to grow down into this dimension, this world, this crisis, this culture, this coma, this possibility. And, at the core of this embodiment of your prophetic vision is your vision of education and of this place and of the University of Creation Spirituality. Can you describe the different ways in which this form of education acts as a crucible to prophetic endeavor?

MF: I remember when we were being expelled from Holy Names College. It occurred to me that we had options. I thought, "Gee, I could just write and teach where I wanted to and never have to deal with administration again and all that! Wouldn't that be sweet!" Then I said to myself, "But this faculty we've got here is very special and we shouldn't allow them to disperse." And then I encountered a young man who asked me a very important question, "Does Creation Spirituality have a strategy for social transformation?" That clarified what I had to do. I answered, "Yes. Reinvent work, reinvent worship, reinvent ritual." And that's what this school is about. You can't reinvent one without the other two. It's a trinity, isn't it, because what is education if not training for work and for living? If you're going to reinvent work, you've got to reinvent the place where we train workers—everything from seminaries to medical schools. You've got to back up and go to the university when you do that. So, what we try to do here is reinvent all three.

Now something else has come our way; there's a fourth thing. In class this morning, one of the students told a story. She said that if you become a UCC minister, you're interviewed by all these theologians and lay people. And when one candidate was interviewed, they asked her: "Do you believe in the Trinity?" And her answer was, "Why stop at three?" They just stood there and never said a word.

The fourth thing here is the recovery of the indigenous mind. And the more I think about it, the more natural it seems to what we're about, because the medieval mystics are the indigenous mind of the West: Celtic and premodern and cosmological—and so much in common with other traditions. I feel a kind of groundswell of energy behind that fourth dimension of what we're doing here. And that's reinventing work, education, and ritual because indigenous mind does it all very differently. Many indigenous peoples don't even have words for work in their own language. I remember Jose Hobday saying the Seneca have one word and it means "play." You play at home and you play on the job. They don't have words for religion either. It's one word and it means "life," and it's all sacred. Did I answer the question?

AH: I think you have, because I asked you how was this a crucible for the prophetic transformation. I think what you're saying (and correct me if I'm wrong), is that by reinventing work, by reinventing creativity, and by bringing in unifying insights and the unifying insights of the indigenous mind, you're helping people to recreate their primordial source. Source themselves from that source and act in their lives and in the world with the joy and passion and bliss and peace and fecundity of that.

I'd like to ask you another question. A word that you've always mentioned as being key to your vision is *infiltration*. Could you describe a little bit more what you mean by *infiltration*?

MF: To take a transformed consciousness—one that includes spirituality and a spiritual practice and the new cosmology—into our work worlds, into all of our professions and institutions and relationships. I see that as infiltration. The modern approach to social change was to beat down the door until your team won. Infiltration is more postmodern and more subtle. It's about growing alternative shoots within these spaces that are full of dying plants right now.

AH: Inspire hearts and minds to open so that they can reinvent dead technologies, dead sciences, dead institutions.

MF: That's right. I think that from the beginning at our institute in Chicago, we've talked about training the mystic and the prophet in our school. That's been the goal from the start, developing a pedagogy that makes it possible. It was clear to me, even back then, that our current models of education—including seminaries—do not turn out mystics and prophets. And I think there's a pedagogical reason for that as well; a philosophy of education as well as other reasons. It's the form that makes all the difference.

That's something I'm really keen on now—the form. Something Francis Bacon said woke me up to it: "What previous generations called *form* we will call *law*." That's the freezing of form into law, which is what eighteenth-century science did, disempowering the rest of us from taking responsibility for birthing form. We don't even think in terms of form in the West. We think when a school system is in trouble it's about electing a new superintendent or paying the teachers more money. What if the form is wrong? If the form is wrong, good people will lose their energy. The same is true about worship. It's not about whether there are good priests, ministers, and rabbis; it's whether the form is wrong. If the form is wrong, even good priests, ministers, and rabbis are going to get bored and are going to lose their energy.

So that's what we've done here, both with education and with worship. Here's another point: if the form is right, you will attract powerful beings. They will feel at home there. And I think it's not so much the quantity of what we do as the quality of people we're attracting. Not just in the school but in our Techno Masses. The artists are showing up, and diversity. Pagans and Buddhists, Natives, Jewish people, and Christians come—because they feel at home in the form and therefore they can pray—which is what it's about.

AH: And gays and lesbians and blacks and Hispanics who find no place in the traditional structures can reexperience the benediction of the Mass in a new form.

MF: Yes, absolutely—and their own empowerment.

AH: What's so positive about the Techno Cosmic Mass, also, is that you're really using modern technology. Instead of taking a Luddite approach and smashing it all, you are using its potential for profound initiation. Imagine if we had a mystically inspired cinema! Imagine if we had a mystically inspired popular music! Imagine if we had great visionaries working in rap! Imagine if we had great mystical photographers! We would have all of these amazing technologies being used to transform people's minds, imparting a transformative vision. That's what your Techno Cosmic Mass is opening on to. It's allowing that influx of sacred creativity to come in, using all of these tremendous possibilities, but for a sacred purpose.

I felt when I participated in your Techno Cosmic Mass in Kentucky that this larger possibility is now here. It's quite clear that we can save the planet if we want to; we have the technology, we have the skills, we have the sciences, we have the infrastructure, we have the internet, we have the whole thing in place. What will determine whether we will or not is whether we really decide—out of love—to become inspired enough to change. And that's where the Techno Cosmic Mass can both image the way in which technology could be used for the sacred, and also provide the mystical transformation—or at least could point to the possibility of the mystical transformation. So, to use the technology out of love and not for power: that's the key to the whole transformation, isn't it?

MF: Yes, and it's part of a tradition. The fact that we're deconstructing a tradition, we're not making this up off the top of our heads, makes it doubly political: because we are critiquing those who are still within the tradition and we are critiquing the world that thinks it's beyond tradition. But it's not critiquing by confrontation; we critique by the beauty of the experience. Ultimately it's the beauty that's going to change the hearts and raise the soul of the community.

AH: One of my favorite quotes from your book is: "The world is saved by Beauty." And the greatest critique, like the critique of Rumi or the critique of Jesus, is ultimately a critique of a higher, richer, infinitely more gorgeous, infinitely more beautiful vision which can't help but intoxicate, can't help but seduce it into growth. That is really the aim of education and teaching, isn't it: to provide the lucid intoxication, the sober drunkenness that brings together the mind and heart.

MF: That's right, in a paradoxical way. The next revolution is a revolution in aesthetics. That's why it's very important that the Techno Mass not be co-opted by the entertainment industry or those people who are cheapening the aesthetic experience by buying and selling it. It has to be a giveaway. Ritual is empowering because it is participatory, not because some great geniuses are putting it on for us. That's where it becomes a real community activity. The word *liturgy* means "the work of the people" and that's what I want to see happen. And it is happening. Young people are committing themselves to this because they feel the power of it with great passion. This next generation has to catch the fire of this and then make the commitment—and it is a commitment—to really see it through, see it happen and see its potential for changing consciousness quickly. Clearly ritual is a quicker way to do education than education is— and it's more fun! You can reach the "masses," if you will, with ritual.

One of my favorite thinkers is Otto Rank. He says there are three modalities of healing: one is one-on-one, which is what doctors and therapists usually do. The second is groups, which is what artists do. And the third is what the religious prophet does, which is to heal the masses. He's saying, you know, that healing has to take place at all levels, but to be able to mix the artist and the religious prophetic tradition is doubly powerful, because you're dealing both with groups and with mass movements. The potential there is so great! Especially with organized religion so flat on its back, it's not as if there's a lot of competition out there for healthy aesthetic renaissance.

AH: Did you ever go to a rock concert of a great performer, say, like Tina Turner? You are participating in a hidden Mass, a disguised Mass. So why not have all of those energies be consciously directed to a real Mass that works with that same passion and devotion and intensity? That's very difficult to achieve. You have to constantly work at the balance, the extraordinary balance between true sacredness and hokeyness. True use of technology and obsessive use of technology. You have to constantly hone spiritually the perception that will enable the two to marry, to fuse really, in a new birth, and that's a tremendous challenge.

MF: Yesterday I talked with Tadhi about this Techno Mass we're preparing, which will be held on the Queen Mary, and she was saying, "My group says it shouldn't be a Mass." We go back and forth about this. It always comes up. They say, "The Mass is Catholic." I say,

"No. Leonard Bernstein wrote a Mass, and he's Jewish. Bach wrote a Mass, and he's Lutheran." It's something bigger than just Catholic. And *Mass* is the name for what it is. I have nothing against rituals, but a Mass is a Mass. It's more powerful.

AH: The roots are there too. If they take the Mass out of that, that's a pretty unrooted ritual that could degenerate into "New Age." That's not what you created, Matt.

MF: Actually we're doing both. We did a ritual at a conference on reinventing medicine two months ago in Los Angeles. There were three days on reinventing medicine and then we did a ritual on the sacredness of the body, and it was so powerful! There was an effect. It got them thinking. It moved them into the sacred dimension.

There was another conference this summer in San Francisco on the sacredness of animals, sponsored by the Association Against Cruelty to Animals, that had a similar effect. There were three days of talks, then I gave a forty-five-minute talk on the sacredness of animals in the world's traditions, and then we did a ritual. We had pictures of animals coming toward us, talking, and dancing in their context— and had people speak the language of their totem animals. At both conferences, they said the ritual brought everything together and blew their souls apart!

AH: So, you've found a form that can be used in all kinds of different situations release the sacred energies and do the work. I would like to ask as a final question: If the angel Gabriel came to you and said, "God is very pleased with what you've done, Matt, and will ensure that your work and your vision continue in exactly the way that you want," how would you describe that to the angel? What would you really like to leave; what would you like to be said about the work that you've done; what would you like people to do with it; what is the real essential spirit that you would like to see continue? What is the most precious aspect of your work that you would like to see developed and elaborated upon by other thinkers and other artists and other creators?

MF: I liked your phrase, "lucid inebriation." Whatever it is, it has to be paradoxical; it has to be playfully serious and mystically prophetic and youthfully wise and intellectually grounded and spiritually sensual. This is one reason we chose to be in downtown Oakland. Whatever it is, it has to infiltrate the culture, it has to include, it has to celebrate diversity, not just talk about it, but to honor that which we all have in common—which is creation and spirit and the yearning of the human heart for justice and celebration. So, I would like the model of education here to begin to permeate our high schools and grade schools and our colleges and our professional schools and our seminaries. I just think we should get more conscious about the models and forms in which we are doing education. That's really the problem. I believe that the prison industrial complex explosion is, in fact, the convex of the concave surface of failed education. Because education is boring, many young people are not being touched in their powers in a positive way, so they end up in crime, drugs, or violence. I see what we're doing as prison prevention. To honor the indigenous mind of the African American, of the Native American, Celtic European can be prevention of a lot of addictive habits ranging from alcohol to shopping. Therefore what we're doing could actually deconstruct our culture at the economic level and the political level as well as the spiritual. And I don't know why that couldn't happen. People need to see that it would be a good use of our energies to create forms for education and for worship and infiltrate our professions in ways that make more sense and make life easier for everybody—simpler, more joyful.

AH: At this moment in your life are you an optimist or a pessimist?

MF: [Laughs] I say that the very despair of our age gives me hope, because I think that often our species has to break *down* before it breaks *through*. It has to bottom out, basically. That's part of the spiritual journey. I think we're very close to bottoming out. It's like this electrical crisis that's going on in San Diego now: will this finally get us thinking about solar energy instead of building more nuclear energy places to pump electricity into San Diego and lower the prices. Why don't we just finally think about moving to the next step, which is solar energy in all its forms? We have to come to a crisis like this before we wake up. So most of my hopes come from the serious peril in which we find ourselves. I do believe that humanity changes when it has to. And we have to. But I always say any hope is conditional. If we're willing to make changes—beginning with personal change but also institutional, cultural changes—then there's hope. But if we aren't willing to make these changes then we definitely are not a sustainable species. We're not sustainable on our present path, there's no question about that.

AH: I think continually these days about what St. Paul said about love. That it endures all things, believes all things, and hopes all things. The more I live in this time, the more powerful those words become, because at a certain moment you have to make a very radical decision between in any way contributing to the despair or living as a flame of the possibility. From that living of the flame, from that orientation of the whole being toward the Divine, comes the divine hope—which is inexhaustible, because it is rooted in the divine consciousness and divine being. That, to me, is what you're doing in this institution. You're giving people that form of divine hope—you're empowering them with that divine hope so that even in this chaos, in this potential apocalypse, they can go on inventing, go on dreaming, go on feeling for the new possibilities. I think that comes from your own choice of that divine hope, because you could so easily succumb to an apocalyptic despair, since you saw it so clearly, from very early on. It's informed your work and yet—what's astonishing about your whole achievement is your relentless, ruthless reinvention of all kinds of possibilities on every level, as if you're constantly offering new food to the starving. I really honor you for that, because it's such an inspiration to all of us, the way in which you refuse to give in to one of the temptations of the prophet, which is to call down terror and horror upon their houses. You've really lived out what is the highest and the most difficult role of the prophet, which is to keep hoping in the ultimate face of despair, keep hoping with the divine hope and really out of that hope, inventing all kinds of new possibilities and offering them and trying to embody them at their fullest so that they can become real.

MF: There's a line that's meant a lot to me—by T. S. Eliot. I put it up front in my *Magical, Mystical Bear* book. I found it at just the last second as the book was going to press; it just popped into my world. It says, "Perhaps it is not too late. Dance, dance. We must borrow every form and shape. Dance, dance, like a dancing bear." That's really what you're talking about, you know: how close are we to apocalypse? The answer has to do with dance and finding shape and forms. The dancing bear had already come to me in a dream. That's why I gave the *Bear* book its name. It is the ancient archetype of the Christ on this soil, because the oldest form of worship in North America has to do with the bear. This book was [subtitled] *Spirituality American Style,* so it was coming out of my culture. I was really writing about the Native American heritage. But I didn't know that; it was all unconscious. It's interesting that you used the word *dance.* But you're talking about "perhaps it's not too late." It's the "perhaps" that I like. It's so realistic. It may be too late. I felt that in 1970 or 1971; I felt apocalypse. Looking back on it, what it really was, was the end of the modern era and the beginning of the postmodern era. That's what we're wrestling with.

AH: When trees at the end of autumn are about to die they fling out the most beautiful fire, and somebody once said you can see that most beautiful fire as the end and the prelude to death, or you can see it as the fire that reappears as the green of spring. I think that's what we're all doing and have come to know what this time is. We're dancing with our full colors and it may be the end, but if it's not going to be the end, it will be the dance that carries us over into the new beginning. So either way, the choice is to dance. To celebrate the whole thing before it blows up or to end the dance, explode with the new energies that can begin the new beginning.

"The Compelling Power of Teresa of Avila" Interview with Caroline Myss about *Entering the Castle*

All Caroline Myss's work is characterized by a forensic clarity and pioneering courage and brilliance. In her superb new book, *Entering the Castle,* Caroline enters new territory—that of the divinization of the human through mystic devotion, passion, rigor, and illumination. Her guide to this most demanding and complex of territories is the great Catholic mystic, Teresa of Avila; Caroline does a near-miraculous job of helping the modern reader imagine and enter the seven mansions of Teresa's "Interior Castle" of the soul. In Caroline's hands perhaps the greatest of all Christian mystical classics is reinvented and reimagined for contemporary seekers of all kinds and paths. Caroline and I sat together on a luminous day in January 2007, in her dining room in Oak Park, Illinois, and, as the winter sun danced around us, embarked on the wild, rich, exploratory conversation that follows. I pray that all of you who read this will share the holy joy that flowed between us.

Please read our interview slowly and with your deepest attention. May it bring you what Teresa of Avila called "the inspiration of the loving soul." May it take you into your own "interior castle" and invite you to become "mystics without monasteries" and "sacred activists," beings who fuse sacred wisdom and passion, with clear wise radical action, in an endangered world. In St. Teresa's words:

> *The Divine has no body on earth but yours,*
> *no hands but yours,*

no feet but yours,
Yours are the eyes through which the Divine compassion is
to look out to the world
Yours are the feet with which he is to go about doing good;
Yours are the hands with which he is to bless men now.

Andrew Harvey: Why at this moment in your great career did you choose to write a book about a sixteenth-century nun and her map of the mystical path?

Caroline Myss: When I was writing *Invisible Acts of Power,* I was absolutely broken wide open. I took a look at the nature of service and why people were drawn to be of service after surviving a crisis. Somehow, a "resurrection force," like a primal light from the soul, gets ignited in people who undergo a life-transforming crisis, such as loss or disease. This light is the underlying grace that activates personal transformations and specifically the transformations that I noticed included a fundamental need to be of service. These people no longer wanted to take from life; they wanted to give to life. That fascinated me. Something had shifted their interior compass. A passion was awakened in them that gave them a new appetite for life that was made up of an entirely new interior alchemy that was lying dormant before, combining gratitude for their own survival, an appreciation for the simple things of life, and a genuine awareness that the meaning and purpose they were searching for in life was to be found in improving the lives of others. So, I did a mailing on my website and I asked people, "What does the concept of service mean to you?" and "Who have you served?" and "Who served you?"

As a result of that inquiry, I received over 1,200 responses within ten days. I did not expect that the responses of these people would have the soul-opening effect on me that they did, but I have to say that these responses broke my heart wide open. To this day, I'm not sure that I can communicate exactly how or why the stories of those wonderful people had that effect on me. Maybe it's because I read all

1,200 in such a short period of time, although I don't think so. I think it's because I had the realization for the first time of how profoundly powerful the force of love, generosity, compassion, kindness, and the nonjudging heart truly is. These letters were filled with accounts of people who literally decided to not commit suicide or pulled themselves out of the despair and broken-spirited crisis of being homeless because one human being smiled at them with respect or held a door open for them. That single act was enough to breathe life back into the soul of another human being. I was stunned by how little it took on the part of one human being to do so much for another.

The more I read these stories, the more I thought, "Do human beings have any idea what power they have at all?" I thought, "They don't go anywhere near this power because they can't see it." And I thought, "What is it they can't see? Why isn't that power even seen?" And then I realized that that is the soul, and we don't see that power because it is so profoundly humble, it's such a sweetly humble light.

I decided that these stories had to be shared, which is why I wrote *Invisible Acts of Power.* In gathering all these stories of how a human being resurrects another human being through such simple means, I turned to sacred literature, thinking that I would weave the teachings of all great sacred traditions in between these wonderful accounts, as they were living, breathing proof of the miracles of grace that the great saints and mystics and the greatest holy beings like Jesus and Buddha said occurred when human actions were blended with the power of divine grace. But as I was saturating myself in the sacred literature again, just thinking I was on an academic mission to find the right pieces of sacred literature to put into my book, I thought, "Uh-oh, I've put myself on a retreat." My spiritual instincts were awakened immediately with that realization as I knew I had, in the language of Teresa of Avila, crossed over the drawbridge and entered into my Castle, only at the time, I had no idea what that meant in terms of the profound depth of the journey that had just begun. I sat in my office one day and thought, "This peace I'm feeling, this rich, delicious peace. Where am I?" I realized I'd crossed something and I'd gone into a deep, deep retreat space, and I felt, for the first time in my life, that I had become soft in the sacred. I can't say it any other way.

AH: Melted into the sacred?

CM: Melted, yes, I guess that would be a better way to say it. I had melted into God. I began to merge into the meaning of divine language instead of the definition of it. The light from the language of the Divine felt, but only for the briefest second, as if it was coming right through me. I felt a mystical fire enter into my entire body. Shortly after that, I had a grand mal seizure. And when I came to, I realized that I had drifted into a space of hell, I knew that my wiring—my interior wiring—was different. I knew that. I also knew my interior life was different. A passageway had opened up within me that I could sense vibrationally, energetically, spiritually. I could feel it through silence, through prayer. The seizure had blown open the door to my Castle.

AH: I would love you to talk about the timeless relationship with Teresa that began after the grand mal seizure. This is an extraordinary story, Caroline, and you must share it.

CM: You know you cannot return to your base of power from which you feel safe once you've had a mystical crisis, and it is a crisis. And, what I mean by that is I have an Institute [the CMED Institute] and I was teaching a class and I very much wanted to teach my course on how intuition inevitably evolves to the mystical bridge. And I was going about it, mind you, as a scholar. It's all I knew, but I approached this subject with great reverence, because I deeply believe in what I teach. And, so there I was, prepared to teach how we naturally progress from creatures of instinct to a yearning for self-awareness to a desire for consciousness guidance to a passion for a mystical connection. I intended to show on this day the archetypal evolution of the soul through all the great traditions. I was actually going to begin with St. John of the Cross, but I grabbed *The Interior Castle* by Teresa of Avila accidentally and didn't feel like looking through my stack of books to find *The Dark Night of the Soul*. And I thought, "What difference does it make anyway?"

Earlier that day, someone in the audience had asked about my personal spiritual history and my spiritual life, which I had always kept private. And perhaps opening up to this wonderful group of individuals created the atmosphere for my encounter with Teresa of Avila, I really can't say for sure. But that morning, after I shared my history with this group more openly than I have ever discussed with any group of people, I returned to the class after break prepared to plunge right into a lecture. No more personal stuff. Suddenly, instantly, I felt something near me, someone near me. And I paused for a moment, as I could feel something in my field and that something had an exquisite field of grace. I thought, "Who's with me?" and then I heard, "Follow me, daughter." And I knew it was Teresa. I knew it was her.

AH: I want to suggest something and that is that one of the things that you discover on this journey into the soul is that you are capable of having the most passionate and powerful and exquisitely empowering relationships with divine human beings from another epoch. Rumi wrote in one of his poems that the relationships between the divine beings of the past and the divine human beings who are trying and struggling to realize themselves are part of the mystery of the godhead and one of the most exquisite of those mysteries.

I myself have had a very profound soul friendship with Rumi, who is more vivid and more alive to me than any other person in my life, and with Jesus. And what I've discovered in my relationship with Rumi and Jesus is that there are definite aspects of my own all too human nature that are fulfilled divinely in their nature, and in a way that constantly works to transform me. I want to suggest to you that there are three aspects of the person I know as you that are close to the personality, divine and human, of Teresa.

The first is that Teresa is both sublime and extremely practical, and your nature has that wonderful marriage of great elevation and very keen, sometimes fierce, down-home truthfulness.

The second element that I think links you and her is your extraordinary gift for honest self-revelation. Both Teresa and you are people who are faithful and rigorous to the truth of your own experience and very naked about the realities of that experience, what it costs, what it demands, what it means, what it entails.

The third aspect that I think links you is that you both have a genius for synthesis and clarifying very complex information into luminous and simple diagrams. What I'm suggesting, Caroline, is that Teresa knew who she was choosing and she chose you because of these resonances between your nature and hers, so that her divine nature could communicate its essence to yours, because yours was— in such remarkable ways—so prepared to mirror hers.

The other thing that I think is essential in this extraordinary relationship that you've had with Teresa is that your very extensive Catholic education, including your graduate work in theology, prepared you from the earliest part of your life for this mystical experience.

I would like you to talk about what you feel you derived from that education, and how you feel it has influenced you and sustained you in this mystical partnership that you've had with Teresa.

CM: First, I would like to clarify in great detail exactly what my very delicate and subtle relationship with Teresa was like during the writing of *Entering the Castle,* lest I give the wrong impression. Working with Teresa did not involve episodes of her grabbing my hand and writing through me, as if she or some other secondary spirit had possessed me. It was none of that kind of nonsense. Working with her also did not involve hearing her every day as in that very extraordinary first encounter. Rather, it was subtle, what she would call intellectual revelation, and that's her name for it—as described in the sixth mansion of her great classic, *The Interior Castle*.

I experienced a dialogue of intellectual revelation, and it required that I, myself, become a vessel, which required a great deal of preparation. I had to attain a certain state of tranquility, a certain height of interior clarity. This required prayer and silence, which I had to maintain as much as possible within me as well as within my home. My office space became a sanctuary that began to feel like an embodiment of the sacred. This was the only way I could attain the altitude necessary to perceive, or receive, perceptions that I knew were not mine. The way that I would explain that is that any parent who knows his or her child recognizes when the thinking of someone else has influenced that child. The parent then asks the child, "Who have you been talking to?" A parent knows how that child thinks, and the parameters of that child's perceptual systems, so he or she recognizes immediately when his or her child has been exposed to a new way of thinking.

And in that same way, you know the way you think and you know the parameters of your thinking, and when you have been given an idea or infused with a perception that is outside your realm of thought. Then you observe how that single perception reorders an entire cluster of thoughts and perceptions that are familiar to you or that are in the formative stages within your sensory system. That is, they are perceptions that you have sensed, but not yet given language or structure to, yet these perceptions incarnate into clear form almost instantly as the result of being given one core truth. Teresa's guidance was one truth at a time and each one ordered an entire chapter in the book, for example.

AH: You could only really receive her divine instruction and be receptive to the images of perceptions of her divine instruction if you become like a mirror, cleansed of all your false self-impressions.

CM: Exactly. I had to know where I stopped and where she began.

Interview with Caroline Myss

AH: So, your job was to stay in that state of radiant nothingness so that the everything could flash messages on to the screen of your mirror mind, mirror heart. That's the truest meaning of humility, isn't it? To stay in that silent receptivity, that silent, grounded, divinely tender, divinely prayerful receptivity so that into that ground the Divine can pour its truth and its brilliance.

CM: First, Andrew, let me say that no one can describe the experience I had more exquisitely than you. Just the phrase "radiant nothingness" is something I would never have thought to say. On a more grounded level, I had to maintain my inner tranquility, to the best of my ability, given the daily struggles with my own life. But the effort is so worth the rewards. I think it is appropriate to ask about the relevance of the teachings of this Carmelite nun from the sixteenth century in today's society whose great work was a treatise on mystical illumination through prayer. At first glance, the ordinary mind would be inclined perhaps to dismiss her work as too Catholic or just for Catholics or just for nuns or monastics. But nothing could be further from the truth. We are living in a world gone mad, but not just mad in terms of war and chaos. There is a madness in this world that is the result of living too fast, forcing yourself to function without time to reflect upon the cause and effect of your choices and the quality of your relationships and the consequences of your actions. People live so scheduled, so pressured, so bound up in this nonsensical adoration of doing things faster and faster and faster among other superficial values that this adoration of speed has transferred to what they expect from their spiritual life, if you want to call what they have a spiritual life at all. A yoga class and a vegetarian diet is not a spiritual life, nor is therapy and learning about self-empowerment and how to get what you want in three easy lessons. What on earth does that have to do with the soul?

Small comments are great indicators of what people really believe, as opposed to what they say they believe; and the following example, which is among the most common that I hear, positions the matter of

333

faith as the last empowered option that people turn to. When a crisis occurs and everything "humanly possible" has been done to rectify or treat the problem or illness, people will always say, "All we can do now is pray." Prayer is seen as a last option, or the tactic one turns to when the really effective things that they were counting on have failed. The statement is really a symbolic admission that says prayer is the caboose on the train of life for people, and not the engine. If people truly understood the power of prayer and the power of grace, they would pray as their first step in every thing that they did and not as a last resort, because everything else on the human level failed. But that is not how most people truly and authentically relate to the power of prayer. It is not a real power for them, at least it is not as real as a power they can touch.

It's more than appropriate at this critical stage in our spiritual, social, and political climate, that the work of Teresa of Avila be reintroduced into the mainstream of our culture. People need to discover the profound power of their soul. We need to discover the power that the mystics uncovered when they fell in love with God. We need to discover that more than needing to be healed, that we have the capacity to heal others, and that our deepest calling in life is to move beyond needing to have more and more and more. We need to step beyond ourselves and discover what it means to be of service, beyond the experience of taking care of others in such a way that it leads to self-exhaustion, resentment, and burnout. That's not spiritual service; that's self-pity and working from the motivation of the ego. The soul doesn't exhaust from serving others, regardless of the arena, but one has to learn how to merge service with wisdom, self-reflection, and the management of grace.

As odd as this may strike the reader upon first glance, the fact is that the call to be a "mystic out of a monastery" and to serve humanity through acts of the soul is now falling upon the shoulders of the ordinary human being. Mystics have long been associated with being recluses, running away to monasteries in order to keep their own company. But they were wild, strong, stubborn, powerful, and rebellious personalities who led rebellions and wrote great books and turned their worlds upside down. They became the healers of their day and the educators and the ones who withdrew into prayer in order to receive Divine revelation about what the society should do next in times of great change. The last thing Teresa of Avila or Francis of Assisi or John of the Cross or Eastern mystics such as Rumi or Rabindranath Tagore were, [were] recluses. They were profound and powerful leaders of eras of transformation, not unlike the times we face right now.

What they knew is what many people are now discovering in their own way: the more the outside world spins out of control, the more your interior world must assume full control. Acquiring material goods will not help you to make sense of the massive changes occurring in this world, and you have to be blind to think that America or the rest of the world is headed toward peace. We are headed toward more and more chaotic change and we must rise to face that change with courage and not denial. That is why I feel compelled to lead people across the drawbridge and into their inner Castle. Each person is born with a passion to connect with the sacred. We have a yearning for that. We have an absolute passion to be brought to our knees before the Divine, to witness a miracle, to see the waters part, to see the blind recover their eyesight, to see people healed from incurable diseases. We long to see the presence of God among us in these ways, which is why people make pilgrimages to sacred spots or even go on nature outings and swoon over a sunset. They will reach to anything to be near God, or as close to a version of God as they will allow themselves to go near. Teresa's teachings are perfect for this time. They are perfect for the modern sojourner. I know because I have worked with people for twenty-five years and I have come to the conclusion that this search for highest potential that drives the contemporary spiritual seeker is really a search for the drawbridge into the Castle. It's really a search to find a way not to be afraid of your own life, or to hear guidance that tells you to help a homeless person. It's tragic to live in fear of your own life. Tragic.

AH: Let's get back to the influence that your Catholic background had on you. I think it's crucial.

CM: Well, I'm no devotee of the Vatican, so let's just say there's a difference between religion and the soul path. And the religion, any religion, is an expression of the politics of God, so all religions have that in common; therein lies the politics of God, so whether you're dealing with Judaism or Islam or Catholicism, all of them are a manifestation of the power of God reduced to tribalism and tribal masks and tribal myths. But Catholic mysticism absolutely intrigues me, the tradition of the saints, the tradition of the mystical experience, the tradition of being passionately drawn to the soul's journey. I believe I would be a mystic no matter what tradition I had been born in, because that is the nature of my soul. I happen to have been born a Catholic, which is the most mystical tradition of the Christians. So the ground rules were set for me to walk this path within the Christian tradition.

So I have this tradition in my bones that says, "Heaven walks next to you." Not above you, within and next to. It breathes with you. The Madonna is not some imaginative force, she's not some goddess—I can't use that word very comfortably, actually, as it's not natural to me. But she is very much a Divine Mother and she appears when this earth is in trouble. And you know what, she does, like her famous apparitions at Lourdes, Fatima, and now Medjugorje. Her messages are consistent in all apparitions, messages calling for prayers—conversion not to Catholicism, by the way, but to prayer and to peace. In return, places of profound miracles are left behind, such as the healing water of Lourdes. In none of her apparitions has she urged people to convert to Catholicism. She urges conversion to acts of love, prayer, and compassion, so that all of humanity can cease its unnecessary suffering.

Now, the concept of what mysticism is, is very much a mystery. It is a deep and profoundly conscious mystery that beckons one to tamper with the very structure of his or her cosmic compass. A person who says: "I don't think I want heaven to be way up above me. Rather, I think I want it next to me, indeed, I want heaven to exist within me. What would happen, for example, if I shifted the location of my idea of God and decided that the Divine did not exist in some sort of cosmic distance above or beyond the celestial bodies of light. What if I lowered that equation and breathed the Divine next to me and within me, surrounding myself with the presence and power of God. That shift in compass would mean the end of all boundaries between this physical world and a Divine world as the two would merge into one."

Our five senses want immediate gratification. We want to see the cause and effect of our actions right now, and it's very hard to compete with the speed at which our five senses want a cause and effect. Like money, we want to see a cause and effect on the interest of our investments immediately. It's very difficult to compete with that reality. So, when you say to someone that prayer is far more powerful than any force in the physical world, I realize that to the five-sensory-driven individual that remains incomprehensible. People often ask, "Well, which prayers work?" They treat prayers as magical spells.

AH: I think that is true. I think you were saved from what I call "the marzipan mysticism of our time" by being schooled in this clean, clear, fierce, rigorous school of Catholic mysticism. There are five aspects of this schooling that have actually been penetrating your work from the beginning, and that are now coming to fruition in *Entering the Castle*.

The first thing that you got, I believe, from this amazing education that you had was what you describe as the feeling that heaven is walking in you and beside you—a profound sense of the sacred and of the cosmos as sacred, which is the essence of the great Catholic mystics from Eckhart to St. Francis to Teresa herself.

The second thing I believe that you have derived from the Catholic mystical tradition is a profound sense that the core of the relationship between the soul and the Beloved is a great passion—a great, holy, divine passion. You have this in your personal life, in the way you teach and in the way you speak about Teresa, but it's one of the things that has deeply intoxicated you when you speak about Teresa, you speak about her with a great, holy passion of the soul, and it's this holy passion of the Christian mystics, for Jesus or for the Madonna, that has actually ignited the great stream of Christian mysticism, and it's something that you share and transmit.

The third thing that I believe you derive from your Catholic schooling is a very deep discipline of devotion. All of the great mystics of the Catholic tradition speak again and again in different ways of the necessity for a daily, down-home practice of deep contemplative devotion as a profound means of uncovering the inner life of the soul. And, one of the things I love deeply about your book is your constant emphasis on the unending need for this sacred discipline.

The fourth thing that I believe that you have inherited from this tradition is one of its greatest contributions to world mysticism—an absolutely no-nonsense psychological realism. And one of the great strengths of the book that you've created is how again and again you help people see how their fears, fantasies, and illusions are blocking them.

Finally you have inherited, I believe from the Catholic mystical tradition, a deep belief in sanctity. You deeply believe in the divinization of the human through the disciplines of mystical rigor. You truly believe that through these exercises, through this discipline, through this devotion, through following this rigorous road map of the soul that all of the Catholic mystics have—and Teresa, of course, is the supreme teacher of it—that the human being can go to a completely new level of self-empowerment, radiance, humility, and unconditional compassionate action in this world. This is a very powerful transmission that's come through to you from your tradition.

What is going to make this book so helpful is that you have separated the essential jewels of the tradition from the dogma and the authoritarian aspects of the tradition, which are clearly destructive. Now, these jewels—of a profound sense of cosmic sacredness, of a deep sense of holy passion, of an absolute commitment to true discipline, of a profound psychological realism that is absolutely unsentimental, and of a vision of the potential sanctification of the human can now, through Teresa and your work together, be given to any seeker on any path of any religion to be used in the core of modern life.

I am so moved by the way in which you have been able to universalize and rescue these truths from all of the excretions of the tradition, which you nevertheless celebrate with such profound humility and gratitude.

What you're looking at in our world is an overwhelming, even demonic triumph of the false self in all the different aspects of human endeavor. This is why your enterprise in this book is so important. Through Teresa's grace and with her help, you are bringing back an authentic mysticism that is deeply rigorous, that shines a divine, clear, fierce light on all illusions, all agendas, all fantasies, and helps people enter the truth and the peace and the real self-empowerment of the soul.

What is especially exciting to me about what you're saying is your insistence that the demands of this time have ended the privileged vision of the mystic as a person who withdraws into a monastery or an ashram. I agree deeply with you that our time of vast and challenging change is inviting all of us to become what you call "mystics without monasteries," and to act from the deepest spiritual wisdom in all the arenas of our burning world.

Am I characterizing your thought?

CM: Yes, absolutely. And within that context of transformation that you described, again the question needs to be posed, "Why would someone want to enter his or her Castle?" I bring this up again because the fact is this journey is one of great power. No one makes this journey and continues to live an ordinary life. The Castle is the deep metaphor for the soul. Why would someone want to enter the journey of illumination? What's in it for them? When a mystic speaks about how painful the journey into the soul could be, for example, what are they talking about? And that is an appropriate question, among the many we could bring up, because, as I have discovered in my work, most people are terrified of an intimate experience with God. They fear that they will lose their worldly goods and suffer illness, loss, and poverty—an image that we can thank Catholic history for fostering.

But what I explain to people again and again is that a mystic's pain is not ordinary pain, not at all. It's the pain of seeing clearly, a pain that comes from waking up and seeing that life could be other than the way it is. It's the pain of recognizing that humanity does not have to struggle the way it's struggling, or to see clearly that there is a cost to seeing truth and living within a culture of deception.

AH: T. S. Eliot puts it beautifully when he says that the choice is between fire or fire. The fire of being destroyed by a culture of negation, irony, desolation, cynicism, and a total addiction to lies; or the fire that is the divine fire that purifies and that can sometimes feel like agony and death.

CM: Rightly so. A person should say, "What do I want this for?" And it's like what you face when you motivate people in Sacred Activism. "Why do I want to become active with the sacred? Why? When in fact I could indulge myself and continue to indulge myself. What do I care about the next generation I'm not going to be here?"

AH: The chaos and deceit that is occurring all around us today can be so overwhelming as to lead to complete denial, like in ancient Rome, where they turned to a culture of bread and circuses.

The thing that does motivate people, I've discovered—and this I believe is what all mystics discover—is that the radiance and power and joy and ecstasy and deep health of the heart that come to those who undertake the mystical journey intoxicates them with a real promise that their life can be a transfigured life.

CM: What ultimately I have hope in, as I talk to people about this mystical renaissance that we are in the midst of right now, is that people are being called, just like they were in the old days of the classic mystics who were called into monasteries. The difference is these individuals are not meant to be recluses, but mystics without monasteries. They are being called to fall in love with God in an impassioned way, wherever they are, and they are given a ferocious appetite to discover that power of prayer, to discover that force to hold a door open and watch that simple act of respect give a man back his will to live. Nothing is more profound than to awaken your power to channel grace at a distance and know that the grace that flows through you is a source of healing. That they can access what the mystics did, that they can become a vessel of transformation through the power of their soul, which is what the journey of illumination within one's Castle is all about. That's when a person discovers for the first time what the real meaning is of knowing he or she was truly born for a higher purpose. That higher purpose has to do with a Divine calling and not an earthly occupation. Therein lies the seduction of God.

AH: I believe that this book represents your own transformation as well as a transmission from Teresa to your heart. I believe that you've been taken into the profound and fiery crucible of a mystical transformation. I believe too that the process of the writing of the book and getting all the different mansions of the soul clear for other people has also been a tremendous process of self-reflection and self-transformation for you.

And I wonder on this morning, as we sit with the winter sun streaming through into your dining room—where are you in your journey now? Where has this sublime and harrowing journey with Teresa taken you?

CM: Where I once felt that I didn't have any active spiritual life, I feel completely alive spiritually. I feel alive, whereas before I felt like an outsider, looking in. That's the best way I could put it.

> *May God let you taste*
> *the incredible joy of complete union.*
> *Nothing the world can give us*
> *Not possessions, not riches, not delights or honors, not great*
> *   feasts or festivals*
> *Can match the happiness of a single moment*
> *Spent by a soul totally united to God.*

Teresa of Avila

Articles from the Huffington Post by Andrew Harvey and Karuna Erickson

Yoga: The Quiet Revolution

All across the world, in response to the stress of our growing world crisis, millions of people are turning to yoga as a way of discovering the peace that can be experienced within the body, heart, and mind. This peace has been described in all the mystical traditions as the primordial gift of the source.

For yoga to be truly transformative, it needs to return to its ancient roots in a universal mystical vision that celebrates the body as the creation and temple of divine consciousness. The danger of a great deal of the modern teaching of yoga is that it either glosses over or ignores this essential teaching in favor of a seductive emphasis on optimal health and physical appearance. While these are, of course, radiant by-products of yoga, they were never intended as its exclusive goal.

Thankfully, there is now a gathering movement within the yoga community to take the instruction and practice of yoga beyond these limited goals. It is to illumine and crystallize this movement that we have written *Heart Yoga,* which both returns yoga to its ancient roots in the Hindu tradition, and marries it, in very simple and potent ways, to the evolutionary mysticism of other mystical traditions.

The body is an exquisite crystallization of spiritual and psychic forces. This view is corroborated by the latest discoveries of modern physics, which reveal that matter is light-energy. When the body is consciously experienced as concentrated light-energy, it can be profoundly affected, and a wholly new level of dynamic healing and transformation is accessible.

This is not a truth known only to great yogis; it is actually something that many people have already experienced. Remember those moments when you have felt great bliss, ecstasy, or sudden rushes of energy through your body. These may have come to you while deeply connecting with a loved one, listening to great music, being outside in the majesty of nature, in the tender joy after lovemaking, or when you felt at one with all creation. All these are moments when the essential light-energy of the body and your essential nature as crystallized consciousness are revealed to you. These direct experiences allow you to open to the mystery of the subtle anatomy of the body.

The aim of heart-centered yoga is not only to make the body healthier and more supple. This yoga also creates an open and spacious foundation to receive the direct transforming energies of the divine light consciousness. Eventually every cell can enter into lucid, joyful, and constantly regenerative communion with its origin. We are here to embody spirit.

Our prayer for our work, *Heart Yoga,* is threefold. First, we hope that it will inspire all those who have already tasted the benefits of yoga for promoting health and well-being. May these beings be encouraged to go much deeper into the direct relationship in and through their body with the divine consciousness that resides in every cell, and that is concentrated, as all the mystical traditions tell us, in the heart-center. Second, we intend that our vision inspires those seekers who have been discouraged by a purely physical vision of yoga to dive into its authentic healing waters, and to experience the vast spaciousness and all-embracing perspective of yoga. Third, we pray that *Heart Yoga* will be a wonderful gift to all those who are activists on the front line working peacefully to preserve our world. Through the great stress and demands on their energies, may it keep their hearts, minds, bodies, and souls illumined and compassionate. Through a simple yoga practice connected with the ancient wisdom of mystical tradition, people will find the strength, courage, and inspiration so necessary to sustain them through our difficult times.

Heart Yoga: A Response to Today's Stress

All the authentic mystical traditions tell us that the cosmos is a sacred marriage of seeming opposites, such as spirit and body; light and matter; good and evil; masculine and feminine; the transcendent aspect of the Divine and its immanent embodiment. They also tell us that the purpose of being born a human being is to become conscious in the illumined mind, awakened heart and soul, and increasingly peaceful and vibrant body of this sacred marriage, so as to be flooded with its peace, bliss, and power. With this energy, we are able to access and act with unconditional compassion and wisdom.

One of the reasons why we wrote *Heart Yoga* is to express our conviction that it is this vision of the sacred marriage that can rescue humanity from its tragic paralysis in the face of world devastation. Experiencing this union of apparent dualities can heal us from the split that is aiding and abetting this devastation—our dissociation from the body, from the creation, and from the experience of divine love as our true essence.

Yoga can be a powerful healer of this dissociation because of its popularity, fundamental simplicity, and availability to people of all ages and body types. When remarried to its ancient mystical roots and to the vision of divine consciousness that is enshrined in all mystical traditions, yoga provides a wonderfully direct and potent crucible for the experience of the sacred marriage of spirit and body, and for the subtle transformation of the whole being that it unfolds.

To that end, we have constructed our book, *Heart Yoga,* as an initiatory journey into the vision of the sacred marriage that anyone with devotion, faith, and the willingness to explore their inner experience can pursue. They will feel the heartfelt embrace of all aspects of this earthly life that the sacred marriage inspires.

This vision that we present is not at all esoteric or complicated, but is, in fact, extremely clear and practical. Since the universe is a sacred marriage in its essential reality, there is within every human being a latent consciousness aware of this liberating truth that is waiting to be awakened joyfully to its ecstatic and empowering reality.

Heart Yoga is designed to help us all remember what somewhere we all already know; that we are a sacred marriage of spirit and matter, masculine and feminine, light and dark, mind and heart, body and soul. The more we experience, remember, and practice this, the more our ordinary life, in even its most mundane circumstance, reveals itself as a constant unfolding of grace and fountain of subtle miracle. This realization brings a cessation of stress, increasing release from anxiety, a profound desire to celebrate life, and a deepening gratitude for all that is and all that lives.

Invigorated, refreshed, and restored by this great joy that slowly awakens in us, we can meet difficulties with our full powers intact, and endure disappointments, defeats, and ordeals with growing grace. Since it now appears that the human race is going into the storm of a crisis that will determine either its extinction or its survival, a simple daily discipline that connects us with the basic truth of the universe and the energy it releases in the core of our being is crucial.

It is in dedication to helping the human race live, thrive, and work for peace and justice from the core of this joy, that we offer Heart Yoga. Heart Yoga is one of the universally available essential ways of bringing order out of chaos, light out of darkness, grace out of turmoil, peace out of torment, and focused clarity out of the maelstrom of bewildering change in our world today.

A Response to Today's Challenges:
Sacred Activism and Heart Yoga

It seems like every day we're faced with more disturbing news about what is happening in the world. In these stressful and challenging times, our personal lives can also feel overwhelming. It can be difficult to see how to respond skillfully, and how to act effectively without becoming exhausted and burned out. Many of us are longing to find more peace and balance in our lives, and to feel more strength and courage to continue to work for healing, social justice, and environmental balance in the world.

In the business of daily life, we can find it difficult to remain connected to a source of inspiration that will sustain us and help us remember the essential joy of life. A daily spiritual practice that unites body, mind, and heart can keep us inspired by the joy that is the essence of our being, so that we are able to serve others joyfully. As it is written in an ancient yogic text: "From joy all beings have come, by joy they all live, and unto joy they all return."

In these chaotic times, the union of grounded passion and peace in the body and heart that everyone needs to keep strong, creative, and inspired by love can be awakened by a spiritual practice such as yoga. A heart-centered approach to yoga, like Heart Yoga, unites an awakening into the luminous body with a meditative peace of mind. From this sacred marriage of body and mind, the heart is naturally filled with the holy desire to see all beings safe, protected, and happy.

We all are now called to respond with compassion and wisdom to meet the challenges of our world, fuelled by sacred energy to act to preserve our planet. This energy, burning in every cell of our hearts, minds, souls, and bodies, will give us the courage and vision to heal and transform the earth. The Buddha, in his Fire Sermon, spoke of a humanity burning tragically in the fires of anger, ignorance, greed, and delusion. Heart Yoga engenders a fire that meets these fires and transmutes them. This transmutation contains the key to the future of humanity, and is the alchemy that can birth the Divine in the human.

All authentic mystical traditions proclaim with one strong voice:

the aim of spiritual awakening is not merely to realize one's own divine identity, but to serve all beings with compassion and a commitment to justice. The enlightened life is one that balances ecstatic inwardness with dedicated action, profound inner surrender with unceasing service to others.

A great Indian saint, Anandamayi Ma, once said, "Just as God is both utterly peaceful and utterly dynamic, so the being who realizes God is at once sunk in a calm that nothing can disturb and active with a love that nothing can defeat. It is so simple." She added, "through sacred practice you breathe in divine inspiration, divine strength, divine peace, and divine passion. Then you breathe them out in acts of wise compassion. This is the real life to which all of us are called."

To connect to this natural desire of your heart to love and serve, begin by sitting quietly and noticing how you are feeling. By listening to your body and mind, you can choose whether you need a heating, awakening practice or a cooling, restorative practice to support you to remember and experience this connection.

When you sense that you need grounding or extra vitality, or if you're feeling distracted, unfocused, or not present, an active, heating practice can help you return to the strength of your body and restore your energy, intention, and clarity. Strengthening yoga postures develop courage and stamina for the practical healing, creative, and transformative service you do in the world.

When you're busy and not attending to the messages of your body, heart, and mind, it's easy to feel overwhelmed, ineffectual, stressed, or burned out. You can reconnect directly with your own source of inspiration with a relaxing, restorative yoga practice, bringing you to the place where the desire to serve others naturally arises.

Those who come to know and trust in the sacred heart and act from its passion of compassion are Sacred Activists. Sacred Activists unite peace, strength, and courage with the holy desire of the heart to see justice established everywhere. They work passionately to see the poor housed and fed, the environment cherished and protected, and all sentient beings revered as Divine, and so, in turn, experience the joy of service.

With bodies infused with the inspiration of the Transcendent, and with mystical awareness grounded in the present moment, those of us who are responding to the call to serve the creation of a new humanity will be able to devote ourselves to service wholeheartedly, without growing exhausted. Through our ever-deepening experience of the power of spiritual practice, we will find the strength and wisdom to serve all beings and to live in deep peace and joy.

Through living and serving in this way, we become the new humanity we are longing for. We both embody the light and serve the light's compassionate desire to illuminate and awaken all beings.

The practice of yoga, when united with a precise and luminous mystical consciousness, offers an unshakeable foundation for the great work ahead. This is the great work we have been destined for since the beginning: the birthing of a humble, generous, tender-hearted, illumined divine humanity on earth. Through our own direct experience, we realize the ultimate purpose of embodying the light, which is to be a light for ourselves and others and to serve all beings with a full and glowing heart.

"Andrew's Story" from *Heart Yoga*

At the age of thirty-seven, after an awakening that revealed to me that all things are created and born from light, I had a startling encounter with the Dalai Lama. *Elle* magazine sent me to interview him in Oslo in 1989, during the time he was to receive the Nobel Peace Prize. At the end of two marvelous hours, I plucked up the courage, as I was saying goodbye, to ask him, "What is the meaning of life?" I shall never forget his roar of laughter at my question and how he suddenly fell silent. He stared deep into my eyes and said, in a loud voice that seemed to come from his belly, "The meaning of life is to embody the Transcendent." My whole being shook as he spoke. It was as if an electrical current passed up and down my body. I felt my body bursting with a strange new power that shocked me by its intensity.

In the weeks and months that followed, I found myself returning again and again to that moment of parting and to the Dalai Lama's answer. Nothing could have surprised me more, I realized. If His Holiness had said, "The meaning of life is to enter the Transcendent," or even "become one with it," I would not have been so strangely and marvelously disturbed. What he had said, however, was that it was necessary to embody the Transcendent. My own experience, up to that moment, had been of the overwhelming power, glory, and bliss of the divine light. Now I was being gently challenged to go beyond that awareness and somehow to bring the light down into my skin and bones and action. I was being asked to embody it and become, as I now clearly saw that His Holiness had become, its humble, living, breathing, grounded, utterly real, and utterly authentic instrument. As I started to take in, in ever deeper ways, what His Holiness had said to me, I also began to uncover both the depths of what I came to call my addiction to transcendence, and the psychological, biographical, sexual, and spiritual reasons for it.

I came to understand that my longings to vanish into the light, to drop my body altogether, to go beyond human relationship into what I imagined to be a far more ecstatic and transforming relationship with the One were, in fact, symptoms of a kind of dangerous, subtle illness. This illness, I recognized, had five main roots:

1. My early abandonment by my mother, who sent me away to boarding school at age six;

2. The brutal rigor of my English education, with its disdain for physical weakness or vulnerability;

3. My early plumpness and lack of athleticism, which led me to feel excluded from the camaraderie of sports;

4. An introjected and largely unconscious self-loathing that came from my awareness of my homosexuality;

5. My uncritical acceptance of the Judeo-Christian denigration of the body in favor of the soul and spirit, which I had
   found echoed also in the mystical traditions of Buddhism,
   traditional Hinduism, and Islam.

What the Dalai Lama awoke in me, then, was an increasingly precise critique of this addiction to transcendence, which I now noticed
was shared by nearly all the seekers I met.

Many of them were also possessed by the kind of subtly devastating split between body and soul that I had diagnosed in myself. I
began to read Sri Aurobindo and Walt Whitman to try to heal this
split, and pursued what I thought was a healthy sexual life to try
to heal my self-rejection as a homosexual. These were, however,
frustrating endeavors. Most of my friends were atheistic, and the
majority of my lovers were either still subtly tortured by self-hatred
or cheerful sensualists without a spiritual life. I could find no help,
either, from the Indian master I was devoted to, for she obsessively
stressed celibacy or heterosexual marriage as the path to God.

Then, in 1993, I met the great spiritual being who was to change
forever my vision of the mystical path and the role of the body in it,
Father Bede Griffiths. I met him when he was eighty-six years old,
in the ashram he had created in south India, Shantivanam. I felt an
overwhelming love for Bede. I felt, too, in his presence—in some
way I could not understand but knew was real—that he was a living
embodiment of the Christ. His heart was immense, his mind grand
and supernaturally lucid, but what was most moving about him was
the way his whole being, including his body, seemed to radiate the
light of the humble majesty of his realization. I saw him one morning
walking alone in the distance by the river Cauvrey, and for a moment
it was as if he were a walking flame, a human fire angel.

I had come to meet him as part of a film crew that was shooting
a documentary of his life. I had been asked to interview him. On the
last day of filming, Bede took us all to a small, dilapidated hut outside
his ashram, in the middle of gently swaying, golden fields of corn.

"Andrew's Story" from *Heart Yoga*

There, lying back on an old cot in his orange robes, supremely tender and relaxed, he spoke to me of the stroke three years before that had shattered his patriarchal dualism of body and spirit, and baptized him in a wholly new nondual relationship with reality. He said, "What I realized after the stroke is that the body, too, must be transformed. The body, too, must be possessed and taken over and divinized in all its centers and desires by the spirit. This is an immense, deep, slow, rich work, and since my stroke it has been going on all the time. I feel that at every moment spirit and body are marrying within me more and more intensely. The spirit is constantly coming down, first through the center at the tip of my head—which the Indians call the *Sahasrara*—then through the heart-center to every other center. It has entered by the sex region also. I am rediscovering the whole sexual dimension of life, at eighty-five. A wholly new power of love has flooded me because of this. I find I love all beings more fully and tenderly, because my love is now in the body as well as the heart and spirit. Both Mother and Father, the Immanent and the Transcendent, are, through grace, integrating themselves within me. They are having their marriage within me and this inner marriage is birthing a wholly new being. The process isn't completely realized, and sometimes it is very bewildering, but when I get bewildered, I enter into silence and I allow the confusion to settle. Order comes out of chaos again and again. Increasingly, I find myself one with all things and beings; able to participate in the infinite beauty and bliss of the One appearing everywhere as the Many."

Every word and gesture of that miraculous morning imprinted itself on my being, and I knew that I was being given the most accurate, candid, and exquisite teaching on how, without grandiosity or inflation, to embody the Transcendent. After he had finished, I cried with gratitude. At last I had heard the whole truth from someone whom I loved with the whole of myself, and in a way that I could receive without any resistance and with all of myself on fire.

After filming ended, I returned to Paris, where I was living. I heard then that Father Bede had had a series of strokes and was dying. I couldn't bear not see him again, so returned to India to spend two weeks with him as he battled, in extreme suffering, to stay alive. One night, as I sat by his bedside holding his hand, stricken by grief at how much he was going through and at the thought of losing my heart's beloved so soon after having found him, he sat up suddenly, naked in bed. With his eyes streaming tears of bliss he said loudly, as if receiving dictation from another world, "Serve the growing Christ. Serve the growing Christ. Serve the growing Christ," again and again. Grace opened my mind and heart to hear the full glory of what he was transmitting. I knew that shattering pain and love was birthing Bede into direct prophetic consciousness. I knew that what he meant was that an apocalyptic time is the birth canal of a new kind of human being, the divine human, and that the time had come to give everything to serve its birth in humanity.

Bede, as a Christian monk, had used the word "Christ," but I knew he meant something far beyond any religious vocabulary. I knew, too, that "serving the growing Christ" would mean serving the growth of the divine human within myself, dedicating myself to birth divine love and divine knowledge, not just in my heart, mind, and soul, but also in the cells of my body, as Bede himself had done. If I did not strive with all my being to serve my own growing Christ, how could I serve its birth in humanity?

After two weeks I had to return to France. Only a month later, I met the man, Eryk Hanut, with whom I was to spend the next twelve years. Bede had spoken frankly to me of how the spirit had entered his sex region. He had, in another conversation, given me what I knew to be a precise and succinct teaching on tantra. With his hands in mine he had said, "Repressing sexuality does not work. It leads to bizarre and perverse behavior, as I have seen in many priests, monks, and ascetics. Indulging sexuality does not work either; it leads to a kind of physical and psychic exhaustion. The only solution is to consecrate sexuality, to offer it wholly to the Divine, and to experience it as a form of Holy Communion."

In my marriage with Eryk, I was able to live at last this Holy

Communion and to experience, in astounding depth and radiance, the all-healing and all-transforming power of tantra. Since my body was blessed by the love of another, I was able at last to begin to bless it myself, and in fearless abandon to accept sexual rapture as a facet of the diamond of the divine *ananda* ("bliss"). Many times, as Eryk and I were making love, our bedroom would fill with divine light. I would see his hands, face, and body radiate green or golden light that is described in tantric texts as the lights of the embodied sacred heart. From this holy experience I derived increasing strength, confidence, passion, and an abiding sense of the truth of ecstasy as the ultimate sign of the divine Presence, and as the ultimate identity of the body itself.

During this time, I began to teach all over the world and especially in America. The message I was inspired to share was one that fused a tremendous sense of urgency about the world and its difficulties with a growing sense that the deep meaning of the death we are going through is that it is a necessary condition for the birth of a new kind of human being, one who humbly but passionately embodies the Transcendent.

For all the grace that had been given me, and for all my deepening experience of tantra, I was still in many ways, disembodied and overidentified, although unconsciously, with the Transcendent. In 2000, when I was forty-eight, I had the great good fortune to have, as a pupil in my Rumi class, Karuna Erickson. She had the courage to point out to me that while I was able to transmit sacred passion in my words and teaching, I was not embodying it completely. She perceived that I was in danger of burnout, because I was not balancing passion with the radiant calm and fortifying peace that an illumined body could give me. I trusted her immediately, because I knew her assessment was accurate, and did not come from any desire to denigrate what I was offering, but only to help me offer it from a more mature and integrated self, one that truly married transcendence and immanence and did not merely talk about it, however eloquently.

So began my adventure into yoga. I do not think I could have had a gentler and wiser guide than Karuna. Her compassion for my body has finally helped me to have compassion for it also. Her exquisitely profound understanding of the ancient tradition of yoga and its grounding in a living experience of the self has increasingly helped me to bring down the Divine light into my skin, bones, cells, and feet.

What I have been able to offer Karuna, and I hope through her to the yoga community, is the marriage between physical yoga and the yogas of mystical ecstasy, visualization, meditation, and passionate energy that I have been working on for more than twenty years. Because Karuna and I so deeply trusted each other, we found that our experience and knowledge could fuse and merge effortlessly—in essence they came from the same source. Karuna had over many years experienced the source through her body. My search had led me through an increasing experience of it through my heart and mind. In our mutual love and work, grace could merge heart, mind, and body, and Heart Yoga, the yoga of celebration, was born, the Divine Child of the sacred marriage.

In the last seven years I have come to know, beyond any doubt, the following things as a result of Heart Yoga.

1. The clue to the birth of the divine human lies not only in the awakening of heart, mind, and soul to the light, but in bringing down the light into the body and awakening the cells to the light in the body.

2. The most powerful path to this that I know is in the marriage of yoga and mysticism that Karuna and I have pioneered. The full impact of the marriage broke upon me gradually as Karuna and I dived headlong into the ancient mystical traditions of yoga and experimented with marrying yoga postures with mystical imagery and visualizations that worked directly with the transcendent light. Over time, I found that my whole being was being subtly opened to bliss energy, as if every cell were being kissed tenderly awake by the combination of the peace of yoga with the intense illumination of the light.

3. As my vision of Sacred Activism has grown, I have had to transmit it in sometimes very difficult circumstances. My marriage collapsed, I lost all my money, but I had to keep on working incessantly under great psychological duress. Without the practices we share in this book, my being would have buckled under the demands. With the help of these practices, however, I was able not merely to survive but to refine my vision, to calm and ground it, and to find the inner and outer strength, peace and passion to embody it more and more authentically. The adventure into the marriage of yoga and mysticism turned into a necessity that I increasingly understood could inspire and ground others in our tremendously difficult times, as it had for me.

4. What became clear in the last years is that the great work of preserving the world, the work of Sacred Activism, cannot be done except by hearts awakened to love, minds instructed by wisdom, souls alive to their transcendent origin, and bodies increasingly supple to divine joy, divine energy, and the union of passion and peace that the marriage of yoga and mysticism makes possible. The world is not going to be saved by the guilty or desperate or the merely agonized. A new world can only be created by beings who know how to renew themselves constantly in the fires of the sacred heart and its radiation as bliss energy in the awakened body.

5. It is also becoming clear to me from my own daily and deep experience that the yoga we're sharing here is changing not only my body, which is becoming far subtler and far stronger, it is also deepening immeasurably my capacity to love all beings, to appreciate, savor, and adore the magic of divine beauty, and to go on, in hope and faith, pouring out my energies and vision to do what I can to help the world. In other words, I know there is a divine birth taking place in and through the Great Death that is everywhere destroying the old agendas and illusions, because through the grace

of Heart Yoga and despite my own resistances, habits, and failings, I am living this birth.

May all those who come to this book also be blessed by the Mother-Father, and learn through their grace how to marry the Immanent and Transcendent within themselves. May they be born peaceful and passionate, lucid and juicy, tender and exuberant, and completely committed in heart, mind, body, and soul to serving the creation of a new world from the ashes of the old.

> From joy all beings have come, by joy they all live, and unto joy they all return.
>
> —Upanishads

"The Sacred Activism of Heart Yoga"
Interview with Michael Bertrand

Michael Bertrand: Andrew, it's great to talk with you once again. You've been working with two books: a new one coming out called *Heart Yoga*, and, of course, the one on Sacred Activism, *The Hope*. So, you've been very busy and trying, I guess, to find some tools for us all to help ourselves face up to what's going on in the world as it is.

Andrew Harvey: Well, the two books are deeply interconnected. With *The Hope: A Guide to Sacred Activism*, I really try to lay out in as clear a way as I can what I believe to be the Great Birth happening through the Great Death that we're enduring. I believe we are living through periods of the dark night of the species, and just as the mystics know the dark night prepares a whole new level of divine consciousness, so as we progress through this shattering, this searing and terrible process of disintegration that we're living through, what I deeply believe is that a new human race will be born from it, and that this new human race will be one that embodies divine peace, divine passion, divine love in sacred action on every level of the world.

This is the meaning of the words *sacred activism,* and that is profoundly the marriage of the two most noble fires in the human heart and soul—the fire of the mystic's passion for God and the fire of the activist's passion for justice. When these two fires come together they birth a third fire, which is the sacred evolutionary fire of the sacred marriage, the fire of love and wisdom in action.

It is this third fire that is the heart fire of Sacred Activism and also of the new ancient yoga that Karuna and I have created. Heart Yoga is the marriage of traditional yoga with sacred mystical practices that enable the light energy of the Divine to be born in the body. In *The Hope* I say it's really essential now for everyone who wants to be a midwife of the birth to have four essential kinds of practice in the core of their life: *cool practices* that calm and unite you with the peace of divine being; *hot practices* that ignite you with the passion of divine becoming; a *prayer practice* that can always align you with the Beloved; and—most importantly of all I think for our time—*body practices* that enable the divine light to descend into the body to empower, illumine, and wake up its essential light energies to birth the Divine in matter.

This fourth practice is I think the clue for us, because what's trying to be born is a divine humanity that embodies radical compassion in action. Because of my profound belief that this embodied divine consciousness is trying to be born in us I've been working over five years in secret with a great yogini—Karuna Erickson—to marry traditional yoga with the light practices of the mystical traditions that can help all yoga practitioners everywhere take their practice to the next level, so they can use a renewed, restored, renovated, and reinvigorated yoga as the crucible for the birth of the Divine in matter at this moment when everything is telling us that unless we birth the Divine in matter in our hearts, minds, and bodies, we will simply not be strong or illumined enough to do the great work of birth.

If we do, then we can become a conscious instrument of the birthing energies of the Mother-Father and participate in the most glorious and massive transformation that the human race has ever gone through, to take an evolutionary leap into our future destiny, which I believe is nothing less than to be cocreators with the Divine of a new world.

MB: Well, that's quite a prescription for what we need.

AH: It's very clear now that we cannot solve the problems with our shadow [that are] exploding everywhere from the patriarchal consciousness addicted to power and transcendence.

We now need interconnection with the deepest vision of the mystical traditions, which is the one of the sacred marriage of heaven and earth, heart and mind, soul and body, prayer and action, and [we need] to let this tremendous vision that's at the heart of all the serious and noble mystical traditions infuse us with its sacred passion, peace, and power.

If we can do this, and we can, because there are hundreds of thousands of people who realize it and are practicing this at this moment, then we can birth a new humanity. The yoga that Karuna and I have created—one that has behind it all the major spiritual teachers (Deepak Chopra, Marianne Williamson, Caroline Myss), and all of the major yoga teachers (Shiva Ray, Seane Corn, Rodney Yee, Judith Lassiter)—is, I believe, one of the most important tools of this birth. There are fifty million people now practicing yoga and if they can come to the vision that we have presented in this book of this marriage through using yoga in this renewed way—presented as a crucible of the divine birth in matter—then the possibilities are limitless.

I am also working on a book with Gabrielle Roth to fuse her extraordinary vision of the Five Rhythms that govern the cosmos and the coming of the Divine with the five stages of Rumi's ascent to divine love. This is going to be my way of opening up the sacred dance community with Gabrielle to helping make sacred dance as well as yoga a crucible for the divine birth. This will be the next book—it will make a trilogy that I hope helps people in both the most exalted and most practical ways to start becoming midwives of this birth in the core of our burning reality.

MB: In order for humanity to not go down the drain and take the rest of creation with it, we need to have some sense of the purpose of being here with all the other sentient beings on this planet. We have to transcend this ego-based world that seems to want to force us back into being nothing but consumers and people who don't have their hearts opened enough, and [we have to] have the strength to work with and from the heart.

AH: Well, unless we do take the enormous menace of our potential extinction as a challenge to go through a radical, divine transformation that embodies us as servants of divine love in the world, we will die out. There is absolutely no doubt in my mind that none of the problems we are facing can be solved in any way from our existing ego consciousness and our existing addiction to power and holy crazed celebration of materialism, consumerism, and a debased vision of science.

If we persist in this addiction to control that governs our actions, we will die out and take out a large part of nature with us, leaving nothing but a devastated, smoking, burning world as a memory of our presence on the earth. This would be an appalling tragedy, but, most of all, would be an appalling waste of an extreme crisis. When extreme crisis hits [people] on the authentic mystical path, they know that it's sent to them by the Beloved as an immense challenge to go deeper and deeper into the core of divine love and divine consciousness.

This extreme crisis that we've manifested through our lust for power and domination of nature, I believe, is an evolutionary crisis that we were destined to pass through and that is, when understood from the deepest mystical levels, not something to be afraid of or disturbed by, nor something to be embittered [about] or driven into paralysis, despair, and cynicism by, but something to embrace, so to surrender more deeply to the Divine and take up the challenge of the great traditions of the sacred marriage to start embodying that on earth.

If we can see the crisis in that way, an enormous hope is born in us. That is why I called the book on Sacred Activism *The Hope*. This hope is nothing less than knowing this crisis is a dark night of the species destined to compel us to take a great evolutionary leap forward. When you've seen and known that, when you've understood and "innerstood" it, when you've connected the enormous global crisis with the truths of the great mystical traditions that are compelling us to die to the agenda of the ego into the radiance of divine love, then you know this crisis is not the prelude to the end of humanity but actually the birth canal of a new humanity.

So I am urging all mystics and spiritual people and activists who are pursuing justice everywhere to realize what this spiritual crisis really is and to start doing the serious, beautiful, frightening, grueling, but marvelous work of calling upon the Divine to awaken their minds to illumination, their hearts to sacred rapture, and their bodies to divine strength, so that in this unified force field of the sacred marriage we can be born into our divine identity and start working with divine help and divine wisdom to transform our apocalyptic nightmare into a new kind of grace.

MB: What is your meaning when you say the word *Divine?*

AH: Well, I have to speak as a mystic, and what I mean by it is that everyone is born with an original blessing of divine consciousness. All the mystical traditions proclaim this with one voice, and when you wake up, you realize your innate consciousness is radically nondual with the light consciousness that is creating and engendering all the world. The entire universe is created out of a pulsing, dynamic light, love, bliss, knowledge, consciousness—*Sat-chit-ananda*—and everything that exists is a crystallization of this light consciousness in matter. The "Father" has been described in the great Hindu traditions as a transcendent light and the "Mother" as the shining of that light that is embodied in every single sentient creature, every rock and tree and leaf. The entire universe is a divine manifestation and human beings are the peculiarly privileged locus of that because they have been given, as a primordial blessing from the Divine, a divine consciousness that is everyone's duty on this earth to realize and embody.

I was fortunate enough to interview the Dalai Lama on the day he won the Nobel Peace Prize in Oslo. At the end of the interview I found the guts to ask him, eyeball to eyeball, "What is the meaning of life?" He roared with laughter, flung his head back, and then became extremely focused and serious and said, "The meaning of life is to embody the Transcendent."

The Divine is everywhere, it is in everything, and it can be uncovered through a long and arduous journey at the core of every human being. It's the duty now, I believe, of every human being to go through whatever they need to go through to realize the truth of this divine consciousness being the fundamental essence of reality and of their being. When they do have that all-transforming experience, they will then be driven to embody the laws of love, compassion, and justice of that consciousness in everything that they are, that they think, and that they do.

MB: So your books are trying to point us in that direction, and we're not talking abut someone going to sit in the Himalayas and studying Tibetan Buddhism for twenty-five years.

AH: No, we don't have time for that. But what I and a lot of other mystics have become conscious of is that in the horror of our nightmare there is also present a torrential divine grace, a divine life that is descending on us to give us the power, if we want to awaken, at a quite extraordinary level of truth and intensity.

Everything is speeding up in our world, including the ability to awaken. So anyone who turns up now and asks the Beloved to be transformed and chooses any of the really authentic paths to that transformation will be given a massive, massive influx of grace. The Divine wants the transformation—wants the birth of the Divine in matter—and is allowing this crisis to ferment because it knows it is the potentially evolutionary gate into a new humanity. It is time for everybody to wake up to this and do the work and to risk the transformation and start becoming, in their own way, with their own resources and passions and from their own religious positions, sacred activist people who are willing to put love, justice, and compassion into action.

MB: One of the things that you say in *Heart Yoga* is that it's essential to dedicate our practice.

AH: Yes. One of the things I learned from Sogyal Rinpoche and from the Dalai Lama and the Tibetan masters whom I worked with when I cowrote the book *The Tibetan Book of Living and Dying* is the great truth that the Mahayana represents, which is that before you begin and when you end your practice you dedicate all the merits of it to the liberation of all sentient beings from fear and pain and ignorance.

This takes you out of the ego and any self-absorption and gives you the real truth of sacred practice and the sacred mystical journey, which is you're not doing it for yourself alone or taking the journey for yourself alone. You're practicing for the whole of humanity and taking the journey for the whole of humanity.

The greatest mystical practice I know is a Tibetan one—*Tonglen*—in which you learn how to take on the pain of the world and address the pain of the world before the glory, passion, peace, and compassion of your own essential divine nature—your Buddha or Christ nature.

Recently I had an absolutely unforgettable experience of the power of this practice. I was in South Africa and I was dying. I had an exploded gall bladder and I knew I was within hours of actually leaving my body. But in that experience I was extremely calm, through God's grace, and I found myself doing *Tonglen* and dedicating the enormous suffering that I was in to healing the suffering of the planet. The experience of that, when you are in extreme circumstances, is very ennobling and gives tremendous hope, because even in that extremity, when you know you could be dying, through the merit of dedicating your practice you also know your pain can be dedicated to helping and relieving the pain of humanity. It is a very powerful practice, the most powerful.

We put this at the core of *Heart Yoga* because we want our book to be not a book that imposes any more the kind of narcissism and self-absorption that characterizes so much of the New Age exploration of mysticism and a great deal of the contemporary practice of yoga. We are serious about Heart Yoga being a principle for divine humanity and we are serious about the necessity of dedicating practice in this way so as to help people out of the pit of their self-absorption and narcissism, [and] into realizing just how powerful practice can be as a way of radiating compassionate love energy to the entire world and to all sentient beings.

MB: Right. So as you—and, of course, all sorts of contemporary teachers—have said many times, the whole point is to get out of the tyranny of the ego consciousness, to let it go and surrender.

AH: Yes, I think yoga is a wonderful way of learning how to surrender. The body is essentially crystallized light-energy. I think we know this from all the mystical traditions, and we now know it from modern physics. And anyone who starts to awaken begins to experience this in the most radiant way. If you practice yoga knowing that your body is crystallized light-energy and bring into your practice the kinds of mystical light practices that we have given in this book, then your surrender is to the essential light consciousness of the universe, the essential divine consciousness that is animating and living in and creating all things, and through the practice of yoga you can realize that surrender leads to ecstatic joy.

The Light of Love

In our book we have really devoted ourselves to the five transcendent joys of the sacred marriage and these are the joys that will come to you when you surrender in practice to the essential light-energy of your body and to the light-energy that is trying to empower you at deeper and deeper levels.

MB: Can you quickly outline those five, or is that the whole book?

AH: The whole book is really the unraveling and flowering of these five transcendent joys that we imagine as the five rays of sacred marriage consciousness from the sun. I think if you really want to explore the depth of what we're trying to say, I think you would need to engage with the whole of the book, because it took us five years to create this yoga, and a long time to write the book in exactly the way that we wanted to get it out.

But the five transcendent joys are:

1. The Joy of Transcendence—which is the joy of connecting with your innate light consciousness that is transcendent and generative at every level. You cannot come into the fullness of the *ananda* without experiencing the *ananda* in its purest form as transcendent light, the light consciousness that is creating everything—and yoga can be an amazing tool for realizing the light foundation of all things.

2. The Joy of Creation—When you awaken to your innate light nature you also see it subtly blazing in every stone, in every flea, in every animal, and in every sentient being, and you come to realize, beyond thought, in an overwhelming joy that the whole of the cosmos is a manifestation of the transcendent light. You realize then that everything you love in the creation is a love of the transcendent light that engenders it.

3. The Joy of Love for All Things—which arises out of the first two joys. Once you've realized your own nature as

364

being one with the transcendent light and the transcendent light as engendering all things, and you've realized that the creation is a manifestation of that light, a great compassion and joy of love is born for all beings—because you know through your awakening that all beings are utterly holy, utterly sacred, utterly precious and loved by love itself with an infinite love that you come in connection with and can be the instrument of, and that gives you a huge compassionate rapture.

4. The Joy of Tantra—which I think is one of the greatest gifts of the Sacred Feminine in our time. I believe the return of the Divine Feminine in our time is opening the whole human race to the possibility of a complete reimagining of sexuality and human relationship. When we experience our nature, creation, and all sentient beings as divine then body hatred, shame, and self-loathing evaporate. We come to understand that our human relationships, our relationships with animals and our deep, consecrated sexual relationships with those we love and respect can become the birthing ground of a holy, new level of impassioned sacred energy. I believe one of the great gifts of the Divine Mother to us is this liberated tantric energy, which is the source not only of a tremendous joy but of a tremendous energy that can become the fuel for Sacred Activism.

5. The Joy of Service—All of the mystical traditions tell us with one voice that the supreme discovery in the mystical path is that you do not have a hope in heaven of being truly lastingly happy until you truly discover [that] the deepest aspect of the nature of the Divine is its lavish, unconditional service of all the beings that it creates out of itself. Through service—which we call Sacred Activism, the joy of putting compassion and love into action in every part of your life—you discover and live the joy of God.

The Light of Love

So when, through the practice of Heart Yoga, you unite the joy of transcendence with the joy of creation, with the joy of love for all sentient beings, with the joy of a tantric, rapturous connection with all living beings in new and vibrant sacred relationship, and with the joy of putting all of those joys into sacred action, then you can over time become the divine human, a being living a divine human life on earth consciously and humbly and with great gratitude and commitment.

MB: Presumably in this situation we're in, this is about the only way we're going to get through this—if enough of us live these truths in a real way.

AH: There is no other way now. I think the depths of the crisis as an evolutionary crisis is compelling us to see that this is our only way through. You can put it like that and it sounds rather grim, but why not put it [in this way], that here at last are the conditions for a massive transformation of humanity. A crisis we cannot escape, united with a coming in of a tremendous vision of divine embodiment that will help us not only to transcend the crisis but to use it as a way of birthing a wholly new kind of humanity, which can create with the Divine a wholly new way of being and doing everything.

When you look at the crisis from the position of the ego all you can see is horror, terror, madness, and the potential extinction of the human race and nature, and all you can feel is terror, despair, and doubt. But when you look at it from the calm and lucid, passionate self, you can see this crisis is actually a huge, terrible grace that is summoning all of us to finally become serious and transformed enough to be cocreators with God.

MB: Your passion and commitment are so appreciated. I know you've gone through many hard times yourself to come to these places that you can live them and share them with us, and we're very grateful to you for this.

AH: I've learned to bless the hardest times. It is our deaths that lead to our resurrections and our agonies that lead to our deepest joys, and it is our strippings and burnings that enable us to at last become humble enough to incarnate the Divine. So I know from the very harsh and sometimes very frightening and terrifying journey that I've been on that there is a great hope for those who see the pain, suffering, madness, and unbelievable bewilderment that can happen as gateways into a wholly new way of being and doing everything. I have lived this. It has lived me. And what I'm saying is not said theoretically. I know that for all my flaws and faults and failures and mistakes—and perhaps partly through them—that the Divine is living in me in a way that it could not be had I not gone though the ordeals that I've had. Each of the ordeals is precious and sacred to me.

Rumi wrote: "The grapes of my body can only become wine after the winemaker tramples me." The whole human race is now going through that sacred trampling, and those of us who know the secret of the dark night through grace can say to everyone to allow that trampling to press out your own most sacred wine of divine love and compassion, and the passion to put it into sacred action.

MB: I find that the greatest enemy to this in my life is a comfortable complacency that we in the rich West sometimes have.

AH: That comfortable complacency is doomed. The whole world is about to be shaken by a crisis that will make it impossible for anyone, even cocooned and privileged, not to be burned to their roots by what is happening. Only those, I think, who have truly surrendered to the Beloved will be awake to this alchemy that the Beloved is asking of us. That is why these great truths of death and resurrection, of the dark night and the new level of embodied power that come from it, now need to be given to everyone, because everyone is going to need them.

The Light of Love

MB: And everyone needs to have not just a vision of what a true human being is but, as you're offering in your book on Heart Yoga, they need to have experience of it

AH: Everybody who really is awake to what's happening needs to realize there is one duty before everyone who is awakening, and that is to become, as soon as possible, a midwife of the birth that is taking place through this death. Everyone can do it. My work, and that of all those who are really serving this birth on the earth now, is about giving people the practical tools to do this. If I can begin to do it with all my failings, there is nobody who can't do it if they're sincere. The Beloved is waiting for millions of sincere seekers to be brave enough to go through this transformation.

MB: The Beloved. That's a word we can almost become immune to. What is it? This is something that we experience through practice and surrender presumably.

AH: I don't think we just experience it through practice. I think everyone has had an experience of the Beloved, even if they don't call it by that name. Every time you make love to someone you truly love, and experience the union with them in rapture, that is a taste of the holiness and love of the Beloved. Every time you look at a flower and are dazzled by its beauty, that is the Beloved's beauty you are looking at. Every time music awakens you to ecstatic joy, that is a taste of the joy of the Beloved. So the Beloved is everything and everywhere and at the core of every experience. Every time you suffer deeply and your suffering takes you to a new level of compassion, you are beginning to taste the unconditional compassion of the Beloved.

So I believe that everybody's had dreams in which the Beloved has taken them to new levels of love. I believe everyone's had experiences that have awoken them in the core of their lives to the deep joy, peace, and rapture that underlie everything, and now I think it is everybody's responsibility to awaken to the source of that and start adoring, longing and hungering for the Beloved, going through whatever they need to, to more and more embody it.

MB: It's the embodiment that will give people the energy to move through what is ahead of us and what is already happening now in many places.

AH: Yes, without the embodiment—nothing. Without bringing the realization of the embodiment into the cells of the body—nothing. Without realizing that we are not invited simply to speculate about the Beloved in the mind and not just to experience it in the deepest raptures of the heart but actually to embody the transcendence, as the Dalai Lama said, in a living experience of the presence of God within every cell of our body and in an actual coring out of that experience in sacred action—nothing. Without this the world will die out—and with it all human beings will be transformed.

MB: In Vancouver we're currently having an early spring, and there's cherry blossoms everywhere on all the streets. It's the most amazing expression of the beauty and unselfish, giving nature of the universe.

AH: Yes. And we have to give that love back, to embody it and put it into action. It isn't hard to grasp. It's hard to do, but it's not impossible. All of the great mystics have shown us the way, and we have on the earth people who are doing it so splendidly.

Look at His Holiness The Dalai Lama, who continues to radiate absolute cheerfulness, joy, and compassion, even from the heart of a long genocide. Look at Jane Goodall, who, with all she knows about the horrific way we are treating animals, nevertheless never loses hope, and whenever she speaks, radiates the confidence that we can overcome our addictions and start living in peace with the animal race. Look at Nelson Mandela, who came out of twenty-seven years of imprisonment not with words of blame or anger but with a whole program of reconciliation that gave South Africa a decade of grace, a decade of breathing, in which it could begin its reconstruction after years and years of horror.

We have on our earth now people who are embodying the transcendence in the most noble way, and there are thousands and thousands of so-called ordinary people who are doing this. I've met many of them—one of the great beauties of the work I do is to be able to meet them. I've met young women who are working with widows in India; young men who've been seized by the love of the Christ and are working with the homeless; middle-aged ladies who suddenly wake up to the horror of the world and start corralling all their friends to help schoolchildren in Africa. The army of the lovers is very great and now it needs to come together. That's why I've written my books, *The Hope: A Guide to Sacred Activism* and *Heart Yoga,* because I know that in the world as it is now are millions of beings who only wait for a clear vision with practical instructions and a way of organizing themselves to be able to put into practice a global revolution of love in action.

MB: Thank you, so much, for doing this, and for embodying this energy yourself and laying out what you see as some simple paths for us to work with to be who we can be, and to let the earth and its human population come into where it needs to be.

AH: Thank you too, Michael, for all the work you do.

Chapter Five

The Shadow of Love—The Dark Side of Guru Worship and the Essential Nature of Spiritual Discernment

Introduction

Jesus's injunction to us to "be wise as serpents and innocent as doves" is one of the most important and demanding pieces of advice for any seeker, especially for one trying to be a midwife of the birth of the embodied divine humanity. Authentic and radical discernment—the wisdom of the serpent—especially in regard to the danger of the pursuit of power at any level and in any realm, is in spectacularly short supply in our inane "New Age." As guru scandals continue to explode and the appalling child-molestation scandal continues to unveil the corrupt authoritarianism of the Catholic Church, an increasing number of seekers are coming to understand the danger of following patriarchal visions of authority and the necessity of owning up to their own roles of keeping them alive.

Our entire degraded culture is organized around an interlocking series of celebrity systems. The guru system, as it has evolved in the East and the West, plays all too neatly into this destructive shadow play. In order to deconstruct the power of these greedy, disempowering systems and to release the passionate sacred energy they are vampirizing for their own purposes, we need to take a stark look at our obsession with power. We must examine our lust for celebrity along with our delight in magical thinking and pseudo-visionary experiences rather than in the grueling and humbling rigor of the real mystical life. Of all the many dark shadows we need to own in ourselves, one of the most dangerous is what I call the "Golden Shadow"—our avidity to project our own sacred, innate essence and passionate nobility onto others. We do this in order to avoid the work involved with integrating our own sacred power so that we can develop the self-abandon and fearlessness that is necessary for enacting those qualities in the world.

The birth of an embodied Divine humanity can only take place through the death of the old systems of patriarchal hierarchy, elitism, and control in every realm. The authentic evolutionary path is founded in radical humility and absolute surrender to the infinite glory and power of the Divine. It is this path that will give us the radical wisdom, peace, and passion we need to reconstruct the almost destroyed world. Those who take it sincerely discover there is no such thing as static and final enlightenment. There is an enlightenment field, but it can only be entered into through a burning down of the false self, with all its addiction to power, celebrity status, and control.

Anyone who, through their own struggles and Divine grace, is taken into this field will discover three extremely humbling truths. First, that evolution never ends, since the process is one of infinite expansion. Second, that there is always, at every stage, difficult shadow work to be done. Third, that the conditions for authentic progress lie in a paradoxical knowledge both of one's innate divinity and of the subtle treacheries of one's imagination and subtle ego.

I once asked my beloved mentor, Father Bede Griffiths, the great evolutionary pioneer, what real holiness was. He replied, "Real holiness is to know just how much your ego and shadow are blocking you at every moment. No one should ever claim 'enlightenment' or 'perfection.' These are fantasies of the subtle ego and not the reality of the path of Divinization."

On this path, whatever horizon you reach, you discover another horizon to be attained. Whatever peak you climb, you see another higher mountain range stretching ahead. The only way to assure that you continue to evolve is for your heart to blaze with humble adoration, for your mind to be continually open to new and larger revelations, and for you to remain on your knees in reverence.

Andrew Harvey

—⁓✧⁓—

"On Divine Responsibility" Interview from *The Return of the Mother*, adapted from an Interview with Rose Solari in *Common Boundary*

When I rang the doorbell of the apartment where Andrew Harvey was staying in Washington, DC, I felt more than a little intimidated. An Englishman born in India and educated at Oxford, Harvey became, at 21, the youngest fellow in the history of All Souls College. Success as a poet, novelist, scholar, and teacher came early; so, however, did discontent with the intellectual atmosphere he lived in—what he refers to as "the concentration camp of reason." His subsequent spiritual quest led him back to India and resulted in two of his best-known books: *A Journey in Ladakh* (1991), an account of his studies with Tibetan Buddhist master Thuksey Rinpoche, and *Hidden Journey: A Spiritual Awakening* (1991), which tells of his relationship with the Indian woman known as Mother Meera, who followers claim is an avatar, or a divine presence on earth.

In the last ten years, Harvey has become known for his role as Mother Meera's spokesperson, spreading her ideas in the West. Even his most recent books, published early this year—*Dialogues with a Modern Mystic,* a question-and-answer book on spiritual and social issues coauthored with *Common Boundary* contributing editor Mark Matousek; and *The Way of Passion: A Celebration of Rumi,* in which he translates and comments on the poems of the thirteenth-century mystic and poet Jalal-ud-Din Rumi—reflect his relationship with Mother Meera. She is quoted in the former volume, and the latter is dedicated to her and Shams-i-Tabriz, Rumi's teacher. Perhaps because Mother Meera herself rarely speaks—the centerpiece of her practice is *darshan,* or "divine transmission," a ritual in which devotees kneel before her and look directly into her eyes for guidance or enlightenment—Harvey's name had become, in spiritual circles, inextricably linked with hers. But shortly before his meeting with *Common Boundary,* he broke with

Mother Meera and with the spiritual system that he had practiced and written about for the last fifteen years. Harvey, who once believed that the wisest and safest path involved commitment to one teacher and one tradition, now advocates a wholly different approach: the direct relationship of each individual to the Divine.

In this interview, Harvey gives some of the reasons for his split with his former teacher. The strongest and the most controversial of these has to do with what Harvey describes as her homophobia. Harvey himself is openly gay and he recently married Eryk Hanut, a French photographer. Harvey says, in fact, that it was his entrance into a committed, public relationship with Hanut that precipitated the end of his link to his former teacher.

When asked about Harvey's allegations, Mother Meera, reached at her home in Thalheim, Germany, said through a translator that she is "not opposed to homosexuality." She referred further inquiry to James Thornton, a devotee of hers and executive director of Positive Futures, an organization formed to combine environmentalism with spirituality. According to Thornton, "Mother [Meera] fully accepts and appreciates homosexuality as a normal and good way of being human.... Why else would she ask me, a gay man, to speak for her on this issue?" He added, "People with AIDS have come to her by the dozens and received nothing but her blessing."

Yet Harvey's experience seems to be not an isolated one. Early this year, Carol Ricotta, a lesbian follower of Mother Meera's, called the teacher to ask for a blessing on Ricotta's relationship with her lover. "She answered that she didn't want to bless such a union because she disapproved of my way of life," says Ricotta, who lives in Belgium. "I was told that I should give up the girl I live with, get married, and have children." Ricotta, who had been a follower of Mother Meera's for a couple of years and had made a pilgrimage to Thalheim for *darshan,* was shocked and hurt. "I used to call her Mother," Ricotta says, "but I don't call her that anymore."

Despite the controversy surrounding his break with Mother Meera, Harvey seems barely to have broken stride—teaching, promoting his new books, and speaking whenever possible of the benefits of walking a guru-free spiritual path. Any fear one may have of being overwhelmed by his intellect is dissolved almost immediately by his warmth; although fiercely articulate, he is also accessible, and the depth and confidence of his Oxford education are softened by his poet's heart. Harvey seems to have been able to reinvent his life—not once but twice—by trusting his instincts.

The evening following this interview, he spoke at the Smithsonian Institution in Washington, DC, on "The Goddess Experienced," a lecture in which he explored aspects of the Divine Mother from various religious traditions. He combined readings from his own books and from Ramakrishna and Rumi with descriptions of what he sees as possible if we combine the wisdom of pre-Christian, matriarchal cultures with the intellectual advances of the patriarchy to create a "third stage," a divine marriage of masculine and feminine. Although his message entails a drastic redefinition of the connection between spirituality and politics—which he sees as essential, given environmental crises that threaten to destroy all species—perhaps the most radical aspect of Harvey's message is also the simplest: only the transforming power of love can make the salvation of the human race possible.

Rose Solari: You've written so much and spoken so eloquently about your relationships with your spiritual teachers. In many of your books you talk about the necessity of having an advisor or teacher. Why do you feel that having a teacher is so essential?

Andrew Harvey: Actually, I've changed my opinion since I wrote those books. I think that I have greatly exaggerated, and that most traditions have greatly exaggerated, the necessity of a spiritual teacher. I now believe that what we need is a direct relationship with the Divine, a direct empowerment by the Divine, a direct going to the Divine Mother for the love, peace, bliss, and energy to transform oneself. So I'm very much looking now for ways—simple ways—to make that possible. This is what I'm trying to transmit at the moment.

RS: What led to that change?

AH: I left my teacher. I have left Mother Meera, separated completely from her. I no longer believe that she's an avatar.

I have realized that many of the gurus who claim, for example, to represent the Sacred Feminine are in fact just Jehovahs in drag. They are reproducing the old patriarchal hierarchies, the old patriarchal lies, the old patriarchal ways of dominating, ruling, and accruing personal power and fortune. The revolution of the Sacred Feminine—which is what I've devoted my entire life to—can now, I believe, happen only if we get rid of the old guru model, if we empower ourselves, if we establish a direct relationship with the Divine Mother Herself, who is willing to initiate us directly. This new way of getting in contact with the Divine Mother is, I'm convinced, the way that the great spiritual transformation will happen.

RS: How does one directly contact the Divine and transform oneself without a mediator?

AH: It's very simple. It's so simple that it's shattering. The way to do it—the way it's been done in all major religious systems—is by three things. First, by direct prayer—sincere, loving, passionate, fervent prayer—and the simpler the better. If you can say the name of God in the heart, then God will come to you in whatever form you address God. Ramakrishna said this again and again. He said, "Don't go through masters or through me. Go directly." The Divine Mother wants to initiate you directly.

The second is through simple forms of meditation—at least half an hour in the morning and half an hour at night of silent, tender meditation, which opens the heart and allows the Divine to come in. This has immense transforming powers.

The third thing is service. We must serve, honor, and respect every living being—every flower, every fern, and every leaf—as a divine event. Through service—respect for everyone and everything that comes to you—you train the mind and heart to learn their divinity and the divinity of all things.

These three things together—prayer, meditation, and service—will take you right into the heart of a direct relationship with God. That is the secret that religions and gurus have tried to appropriate for themselves. They all say, of course, that they are trying to empower us, but in fact, if you look at the ways in which their authoritarian systems work, they're not trying to empower us; they're trying to manipulate us.

RS: Can you give me an example?

AH: The Sacred Feminine is unconditional love, and yet many of the women gurus who represent the Sacred Feminine are, in practice, homophobic. I separated from Meera because she wished to break up my relationship with my lover, Eryk; she said that I had the choice of either being celibate or getting married to a woman and, when I got married, writing a book about how the force of the Divine Mother transformed me into a heterosexual. She then set about censoring my new work, *Dialogues with a Modern Mystic,* removing all homosexual references; forbade me to sell the video of my life the BBC had made, which contained one fleeting reference to my sexuality; and told me to withdraw an interview on gay spirituality I had given Mark Thompson for his book *Gay Soul.*

I went through a period of tremendous suffering and confusion, thinking that all this might be a divine teaching of some kind. But after deep self-questioning, and considering the appalling details of what unfolded from every angle, I realized it wasn't a divine teaching of any kind. It was pure prejudice—a conservative, cruel, and dangerous prejudice—and I was certainly not going to follow it because it would have meant the end of everything that I believe in, and Eryk's and my complete spiritual destruction.

The Shadow of Love

RS: Yet Mother Meera must have known about your sexuality.

AH: She seemed to have been accepting of it initially. But what had happened was that I'd become famous, I'd become her spokesperson, and she didn't want to have a homosexual spokesperson. Besides, in meeting Eryk, I had met real love, and so was no longer alone, melancholy, fixated on her, and always manipulable. To keep me where she needed me, she had to try to destroy any life not centered on her.

RS: How do you think it was possible for you to have believed in her to begin with?

AH: I have begun, in these last months, to unravel my relationship with her. I think that gurus aren't the only ones to blame for the ways in which we've put them into positions of power. We are also to blame, because we're looking to reproduce the glory of our imagined childhood, we're looking to have magical solutions to our lives, we're looking to have a totally divine being to love in a totally simple way, and all of this is hooey and illusion—and narcissism, too.

Gurus really may believe that they're doing God's work, which, of course, makes them near crazy and very dangerous. They really may believe that they are divine, and so therefore that they can do anything and manipulate people's lives in whatever way they want. But we are also to blame for letting them believe that and for feeding them the kind of undiscriminating adoration that enables them to go on believing that and doing what they want without any check of any kind.

I discovered that there were three components to my obsession with Meera. First, there was my desire for a perfect parental relationship. Often our guru represents the parent we had the worst relationship with, and I had a difficult relationship with my mother. Meera reproduced in a higher dimension that ancient childhood relationship, and I fell for it again.

The second thing was that Meera represented India for me. I was born in India and was forced to leave that country when I was nine to come to school in England. A long period of unhappiness followed. Meera was, for me, India—India in its essence, India in its sweetness. Also, I'd hated my family's imperial engagement there and felt very guilty about it as a child. So by serving a largely unlettered, "simple" Indian woman, I was both half-consciously expiating the karmic sins of my family and having a final and exquisite revenge on my family.

The third thing, which also comes out of my relationship with my mother, is that I had always been fascinated by powerful female stars. And in a sense, Meera is the Garbo of the spiritual Hollywood. She is the one who is rarely seen, the mysterious one who never speaks, and I fell in love with this ultimate kind of control. I fell in love with the ultimate star.

I see, too, that all of this hooked into a profound need, in my own nature, to be a messenger. I had to reintegrate myself after a shattering childhood and after seeing through the illusion of worldly success. I needed to find a stunning role, and the most stunning role you can find is to be the angel messenger of an avatar. So my unconscious, narcissistic desire was fueled and fed by her. Her need to have someone be that and my need to be that coincided exactly.

RS: It must have been devastating when it ended.

AH: It's been a huge and shattering disappointment for me, a savagely heartbreaking experience, especially since Meera has compounded her initial cruelty by lying about what happened, so as to attempt to discredit Eryk and myself. This has put us both in great spiritual and physical danger. But the experience has also been liberating because it has made me define what the Sacred Feminine is. It has made me come to understand that trying to attain liberation by worshipping a so-called divine being, which is essentially a system of projection, doesn't work. It gives you certain experiences and even certain visions, and I've had those experiences and those visions. But to liberate yourself, you have to enter into a relationship with your own divinity without any master, without any intermediary.

The patriarchy can well afford 150 divine mothers who keep alive the old lies of the patriarchy. That's exactly what the patriarchy would want, wouldn't it—imitation divine mothers keeping alive the old lies and, in the name of the Divine Mother, selling the lies of the patriarchy. That's what I've come to understand is mostly going on, and it's a very frightening system. It's much too dangerous and much too late to be with these people, because what's at stake is a reevaluation of the entire mystical relationship with the Sacred Feminine, and there could be no more important thing at the moment.

RS: Why at this moment?

AH: Well, I see this as the age of Kali. Kali is trampling every illusion—political, emotional, sexual—every construct, every concept, including all the religious, mystical, and spiritual ones. They're all going, because they're all inefficient. They haven't worked; they haven't got us into a direct relationship with ourselves and with nature. If they had, we wouldn't be destroying nature.

What we're all living through is massive disappointment after disappointment. Kali is doing this because She wishes to shatter us free of our enslavements. She wishes to bring us into a final adult relationship with the Divine, to hear us say, "You and I, Mother, are one. I'm your directly empowered, sacred, heavenly child. Give me what I need."

What is trying to get born is a human race free of the old slaveries to systems; even the mystical systems have to go because those are the last illusions, the last cinemas of *samsara*. They will have to go, because there's a completely new, radical relationship being formed. It is already being formed in the mind of the Divine Mother, and the human race is being brought up to that, is being shattered to that outrageous possibility. If we can get to that direct relationship with

Her, then She can directly initiate us and give us the divine energy that we will need for this great transformation.

We've go to learn both how to stand alone and how to work together humbly in unhierarchical, democratic ways. We've got to learn how to respect ourselves and each other, and not just to choose three or four people, three or four avatars onto whom we project all our needs and divinity. I've got to learn to see the divinity in you, and you've got to learn to see the divinity in me, nakedly and directly, and then we have to live and act from that reality. That's the real relationship—that's the relationship that will provide the sacred energy of transformation.

RS: It sounds like a real celebration, too, of the fact that we're embodied creatures.

AH: That's the whole thing—the sacralization of the body, the real honoring of the body. I've had all the out-of-body experiences that an accomplished escapee can have. I've seen flashing lights of every kind. But what I'm really just beginning to have is the in-body experience— the experience of the integration of the light with every moment of ordinary life—including the radiance and holiness of sexuality, the sacredness of sexuality.

The Sacred Feminine is the experience of life as the normal flow of unbroken miracle. That experience contains, embraces, celebrates, ennobles sexuality. It's lethal and obscene to keep alive the old patriarchal fears about sexuality. What is needed is for the body to be blessed. Why? Because we're in it. Why would we be here if we weren't meant to love and celebrate our bodies, and to ennoble and irradiate the joys of the body with the wisdom of the soul, and to find out that sexuality can be the physical grammar of the lovemaking of the soul? That's what we're here to find out.

RS: And our traditional religions have failed to lead us to that?

AH: The patriarchal religions separate the body from the spirit. In doing so, they keep alive all the old sexual prejudices. But when you finally learn how to love and celebrate your body and your sexuality, it's then that the full miracle of life becomes obvious to you.

It is then, too, that you understand that nature is also your body. That is a crucial understanding for the human race now, because we are destroying nature. Why are we destroying nature? Because all the religions have taught us that our bodies are fallen and irrelevant and a block to spiritual progress. Therefore, nature is by implication fallen, irrelevant, and a block to spiritual progress.

What we need now, and what the Divine Mother is offering us, is a vision of the holy splendor of the body-spirit and of nature. That is the complete, the full, the glorious revelation, and it's the only revelation that can heal these appalling thousands-and-thousands-of-years-long wounds—sexual wounds, emotional wounds—all of which have come from our separation from our bodies and from nature and their natural sanctity.

We have perhaps twenty years in which to save the environment. How are we going to save the environment unless we realize where we are?

RS: Where are we?

AH: We are in a sacred dance of light and love. That's where we are. Our bodies are doing that sacred dance. Nature is ablaze in that sacred dance. And if we're thinking all the time about getting out of our bodies, how will we ever turn to bless nature?

RS: So there is no division between our souls and our bodies, or between ourselves and nature?

AH: There is absolutely, at no moment, ever any division.

RS: Because you're also a poet and a fiction writer, how do you connect the path of being an artist with your spiritual path?

AH: I think being a poet has been the prime energy of my mystical search. It has also been a drawback, because I think my own passion for poetry was probably what led me into announcing Meera as an avatar. My desire to see her in the most extreme and gorgeous terms was probably what enabled me to purvey that illusion, which I'm deeply sorry for, because I think it has misled a great many people and done real harm.

The danger of being a poet is what Plato says it is—that a poet lets the longing run away with reality. If I'd been less of a poet and more of a scientist, I would have realized that it was my energy of adoration that was creating this illusion, and not her power. I would have realized also that she could be someone with many powers and not be anywhere near enlightenment.

So I'm very aware now of the dangers of being a poet, of the dangers of that visionary, ecstatic view of the world, because I mustn't allow that ever again to interfere with the sobriety of real judgment. I hope that after this shattering experience, I will have a greater sense of the responsibility that belongs to a mystic.

RS: How do you define the word *mystic?*

AH: A mystic is someone who has a naked, direct relationship with the divine presence, direct cognition of the godhead. I used to believe that there were very few real mystics; I now believe that everyone is a closet mystic. Everyone has deep glimpses of the Divine in dreams, in lovemaking, in exalted moments of friendship, in moments of aesthetic ecstasy, looking at a great painting or listening to music. We're not taught to recognize these as glimpses of the godhead by this culture, and so we forget them or half-ashamedly hoard away their memory and don't acknowledge, don't share them.

RS: So every one of us has glimpses of the Divine?

The Shadow of Love

AH: All the great teachers have been trying to tell us that each of us is Divine. What we have done with all the great teachers who have told us this is the worst possible thing: we've made them into the founders of religions. Christ said this, and we killed his message by building Christianity around it. The Buddha gave us this vision, and what did we do? We created Buddhism around it. So that the outrageousness and the splendor and the radicalism of the message would be covered over and contained and tamed by the edifice of religion, by the disciplines of religion.

We can't afford that taming of the outrageousness of the truth anymore, because we need—each one of us on the earth needs—to face up to our divine responsibility. To say that everybody is a mystic puts a tremendous responsibility on everyone to live up to the honor and beauty of that relationship with God. It puts a tremendous responsibility on everyone to transform the ground of their ordinary living into a divine ground. People much prefer to feel that there are only three or four accomplished mystics, or that if you want a mystical experience you have to go through this guru or that church, because it actually takes off the pressure.

What we need to do is to put on the pressure. I think the Divine Mother is saying, "Get rid of all of these illusions, get rid of these religions and these gurus. Own up to what you are. Face it directly, own it directly, suffer it directly, claim it directly, be it directly, alone and together, and save the planet."

I think we had this relationship once with the world, and I think we can see it in the ancient matriarchal traditions, the first stage of our existence. Then there was the second stage, the patriarchal stage—with the growth of the hero myth, the growth of dissociative, righteous forms of thought. Now we're entering the third stage, which is not a return to the matriarchy. That isn't possible. Patriarchy taught us some very important things. What we're entering now is the era of the sacred marriage, the union of the masculine and feminine in our psyches, in ourselves, in nature, in the world—the era in which a direct relation with the Divine will result in direct

386

action in every arena of life, the era of engaged and passionate enlightenment.

RS: I was wondering how you might see us taking that union into the political arena. I was intrigued by the conclusion of *Dialogues with a Modern Mystic,* where you make a call to readers to go out into the street and reform the world.

AH: First of all, what has to be done is to reimagine what the Sacred Feminine is. It embraces life. It longs passionately to preserve life and to make *this world* the mirror of the justice and love of the Mother, and therefore to transform political conditions: to transform the conditions of the poor; to transform the media, which is just an avalanche of trash pouring into our minds; to take on the burden of altering all the industrial relationships between the nations; to take on the burden of using technology to clear away pollution; to pull down the whole worldwide concentration camp of reason and fear and guilt we live in, and establish justice, harmony, and balance—not merely intellectually or spiritually but actually, in terms of the conditions in which we live, in terms of the conditions of the environment.

What I see happening in the next fifteen years is that there will be terrible ecological disasters, and the facts of our devastation of nature will become more and more obvious and more painful. At that moment, it's very important there be in place spiritual friends who can say to the world, "We have all got to get onto the streets now." People protested against the war in Vietnam in the 1960s, and amazing things were done, because of the power of their civil disobe-dience. What is needed is for everyone who cares for the future of the world to take to the streets in a massive, worldwide civil-disobedience movement. People must join together and come out—onto the streets in Washington, the streets of every capital city all over the world, and say no to pollution, no to the proliferation of nuclear arms, no to the destruction of the earth.

The situation cannot go on in the way that it is going on. We are being given a message: transform or die out. None of the governments are taking this seriously. We have to take it seriously.

RS: So you envision a spiritual revolution that leads directly into social activism?

AH: There is no spiritual revolution worth the name at this moment. There isn't a revolution that is passionately concerned with poverty, with justice, with the end of the destruction of the environment. Without that, what is happening is not a spiritual revolution. It's a masturbation of the soul.

Meanwhile, the politicians are in a dream of their own power. The gurus are in a dream of their own power. The majority of spiritual seekers are really looking for a little bit of aspirin rather than enlightenment, because the last thing they want is to be enlightened and therefore to be in a state of love in action toward the world. So we're in a terribly dangerous position in which the narcissism of the people in power and our own narcissistic desire for security in a terrifying world coincide and collude.

I'm not leaving myself out of any of this criticism. I feel implicated in this escapism because I've been one of the purveyors of it. What was lacking from *Hidden Journey*, lamentably, was the sense of the political dimension of action. So I'm not saying I've been awake; I've been asleep. But 99 percent of the other Western seekers on the planet have also been asleep, because I know many of them, and I tell you, I've heard their snores.

RS: It sounds as though the changes you've gone through in the past year have been liberating. Has your marriage been part of that process?

AH: Marriage—the contact with a real human being and with real human love—has absolutely transformed my life. I'd been so battered as a child and so disappointed in love in my twenties and thirties that

I thought that the only relationship with any hope was the kind of exotic, intense, subtly sadomasochistic relationship I had with Meera.

But there's noting more redemptive than a real relationship with another human being. There is nothing more difficult and more spiritually transforming, because you're really compelled to take responsibility for every breath, every action, and what you do profoundly influences the other person's life. So you have a very direct teaching in responsibility. And also you have a very direct teaching in unconditional love, because if there is true love, it is unconditional.

I've been blessed with somebody who really does love me unconditionally and who is the most honest person I know. To be with someone who is not playing any games is a tremendous spiritual education. Eryk has taught me more than anyone I've known simply by being completely himself and by forcing me to be completely myself.

What is revealed through deep love of another being, and the responsibility of that love, is the inherent sacredness of everything in life. In a real relationship, you see how everything, at every moment, is at stake. And that is exactly what life is like: at every moment, everything is at stake. So you're initiated into the sacred intensity of life in its most normal aspect.

"Teachers and Seekers" Interview from *Return of the Mother,* adapted from an Interview with Catherine Ingram in *Yoga Journal*

Catherine Ingram: You have said that when you were pretending to be mad everyone thought you were wonderful, but now you've truly gone mad, they consider you dangerous. Why is that?

Andrew Harvey: Because the real madness is the embrace of one's own and everyone else's complete freedom and equality before God. When you are doing that, you are doing what Christ and the Buddha and all the real mystics have done. Think how the whole human race has conspired, while adoring them, to eliminate their message.

I think we are now facing an entirely new era of enlightenment, an era of passionate enlightenment, in which enlightenment will not be seen in the old way as detachment, as an escape, as a way of fading out from existence, as a way of being separate in poised peace, but will combine the ancient and original knowledge of the ground of Being with a very radical commitment to life at every point—emotional, physical, political—to save the planet and transform the quality of life on it. And we don't need any gurus for this. I've come to believe that most of the masters and gurus are actually the patriarchy's most brilliant way of keeping these always-revolutionary truths of divine identity and equality under wraps. The last thing the patriarchal societies have ever wanted was for women or homosexuals or the untouchables or the poor to get hold of these truths, because then all power elites would crumble. And, unfortunately, the guru systems have nearly always been indirect servants of power.

CI: Do you think there are any redeeming elements to those systems? After all, many of us have benefited from them, whether we are still involved in a relationship with a master or not.

AH: Whatever successes they have had, and they've had real successes, they've also conspired with that infantilism and that incessant desire for authority that has kept the human race trapped and unempowered. If you take that along with the fundamental body-denying schizophrenia and imbalance toward transcendence of the patriarchal notion of enlightenment, which all these people are serving, whether they are male or female (and it has been so disappointing to see that so many women gurus turn out to be Jehovahs in drag), you realize that they are not revolutionizing the system, not radically undermining its folly by bringing in a new sacred perspective from the feminine, which would say "Let's admit that we have bodies, let's find the divinity in the body, let's consecrate sexuality, let's adore nature and preserve it."

In fact, to preserve their power as so-called divine beings, they just repeat all the shadow fears and sexual taboos of the patriarchal tradition, with its decadent rhetoric of the world as illusory. They pretend that they don't have a body, because the body is going to give the continual lie to their claim to divinity in the patriarchal way of understanding they claim. Then, because the followers, to preserve their fantasy, believe the guru has transcended all physical needs, they cannot face the shadow side of the all-too-human guru, and the guru himself or herself is discouraged from facing that shadow side as well. And this results in, as we know, disaster after disaster.

CI: Yes, in recent months we've seen a new eruption of scandals involving Asian teachers and abuse of sex, money, and power. It is becoming clear that there are areas of psychological development and relational experimentation that were missed by many of the Asian masters, either because these areas of development were not fostered in their cultures or were thought to be transcended in the master. Do you think it would be possible for us to, just as we go to a therapist for psychological needs, go to gurus or masters for spiritual understanding and not expect them to be psychologically developed?

AH: I'm beginning to doubt even that. I wonder what use is this transcendent knowledge that they claim to have if, in fact, it results in manipulation. Let's face it, what's going on is much more than people sleeping around and misusing funds or whatever. It is abuse of a very profound kind. It is child abuse. It is abuse of someone in their most defenseless position, because no one is more defenseless than a devotee rapt in adoration before a master. So what kind of wisdom could they possibly have if they are first indulging in that kind of abuse and then denying it in sometimes criminal ways? We really do have to face the full extent of their failure, and that is very painful, because we then have to face our illusions about them and the ways in which we colluded with them in our hope for magical solutions and transformations on the cheap.

The Shadow of Love

CI: Yet people are having extraordinary experiences in the presence of masters, experiences of bliss, openings, visions. What accounts for these experiences?

AH: I am going to say something that might shock you, but it is my belief that 90 percent of the so-called masters in the modern world are not enlightened at all, but are, in fact, occult magicians. The occult magician will use his or her occult powers to ensnare the devotee in a posture of adoration by feeding them visionary experiences, which may seem to open things up for the devotee but actually keeps one dependent on the guru. It's a kind of drug pushing, as dangerous on the spiritual level as cocaine or heroin is on the physical. Because people don't know the difference between the Divine and the occult, nor how accurately the occult can mimic the Divine, nor how easily occult powers can be cultivated by the unscrupulous and ambitious, they take these powers and experiences to be unmistakable signs of divine presence and go on worshipping as divine these people who have, in fact, shown that they are neither good, nor kind, nor humble, nor generous.

They cannot truly help anyone, because they are not free themselves. They are not free, because they have chosen power, not love. They are the heads of occult power corporations, trapped at the highest level in the very system of greed and illusion they claim to see through and transcend. It is time to look at the guru system in terms of an all-comprehensive critique of power. The search for any kind of power kills the sources and centers of love and so blocks all access to real enlightenment.

CI: And wanting power over anyone is only possible if there is a belief in separation, which is the antithesis of what most of these people espouse.

AH: Oh yes, the cleverer gurus are always saying, "You are divine." They ape the highest truths while running fascist organizations that thrive on intimidation, lies, secret core elites, and the rewriting of history to suit whatever they want to be told about themselves.

CI: Aside from occult powers, what about the simple projection that occurs on the part of the devotee? I can't help but think of girls fainting in front of the Beatles.

AH: Well, the whole society is run on a star system; the entire media is dedicated to creating star systems; and the guru system, as it has developed in the West, plays neatly into this. We must now look at our fascination with power, our own hunger for power, our delight in the satisfactions of visionary excitement rather than in the rigor of the real mystical life. We must do a major self-psychoanalysis with regard to this.

CI: What do you think it is in our psyche that so makes people want to project their divinity onto another?

AH: I think the fundamental rationale behind this projection is terror. I think people are mortally frightened of naked contact with the Divine, of claiming their fullness, of being totally authentic and responsible for every waking and sleeping moment of their lives. Projecting their divinity onto someone else, who is all too willing to accept that projection, is a secretly convenient way of getting out of the appalling responsibility of becoming divine and acting as a divine human being in the world, which means an endless disruption of one's life and the perpetual scrutiny of one's motives. This kind of surrender is always exposing you and dissolving whatever certainty you have in order to draw you deeper and deeper into its passion and its love. But this is a terrifying prospect, and people will go to masters and gurus and pay them anything, give them anything, even their children, if they will live out the burden of our own unlived sanctity. So we then find ourselves the prey of people who are, in many cases, much less divine than their ardent devotees.

I think there is another aspect, which is also in keeping with the star system, and that is that, if you are projecting adoration onto someone, you yourself start to shine with the reflected luster of that projection, so you experience a covert self-adoration. You are now decorated with a little aura of sanctity that you didn't have to earn. This is corrupt, because if you were really to own those qualities that you are projecting, you would have to be responsible for them.

Coming close to truth demands rigorous goals of service and real charity. To be hooked on the experiences that adoration brings, without enacting and incarnating that adoration in service and charity, is fundamentally not to be adoring God but to be adoring one's own spiritual ego. There is so much suffering, and there is so much help each of us could give. It is shocking to me how little the so-called New Age is doing to help out, and how little the gurus talk of environmental or social transformation, or political justice, or any kind of service. The only service most of them talk about is service to themselves!

CI: There are some notable exceptions, in my opinion, such as His Holiness The Dalai Lama; my own teacher, Poonjaji; and others. After all, it is the existence of real gold that makes selling the counterfeit possible.

AH: Though there are exceptions, despite the system, I think the guru system, as it is now, is flawed at its core. Anyone in that system is going to run extreme dangers, whether they are the guru or the devotee. I think the next five years will see a massive shattering of the idols. What is now a light summer rain of scandal is going to become a blizzard. The guru system in its current state of dangerous corruption will be revealed.

CI: The sadness in that vision is that many people may then turn away from dharma, from the love and the mystery, and just abandon themselves to *samsara*, chasing their desires and resisting their fears in a dog-eat-dog world.

AH: Yes, our current orgy of credulity may be succeeded by an even more dangerous orgy of nihilism and cynicism, an orgy that the culture at large is longing to throw anyway. And that's why it is so important that a group of us who have been through the fire of disappointment in the guru system and the fire of facing our own collusions, follies, and lusts to project should try now to model a radical, practical, and humbly direct relationship with the Divine. I am extremely disappointed with those Western adepts who are adopting the Eastern models of masters, who are playing the stars of the spiritual world and parading a sub-Hollywood glamour. This is the opposite of what is needed now and a profound failure of spiritual intelligence. For, adopting any of these old dying forms is to keep their blocking effect alive. That's why it is important to go through the pain of this critique, so that a group of us will be able to say, "I find my relationship with the Divine to be enough; I don't need any intermediaries; I'm serving and I'm making mistakes, but I'm living my own life in this direct relationship, and you can too. The suffering that you are going through in facing the death of the guru illusion is real suffering, but get over it, learn what you have to learn, and come and join us as equals in this celebration."

CI: But in a way, that puts one in the role of teacher, if even to say, "I know what you're going through; I've been through it." Do you think there is any place for spiritual mentors or guides?

AH: Of course, it would be absurd to say that we weren't to revere anyone, weren't to respect the spiritual achievements of anyone, that we weren't to sometimes go to others for advice, or that we weren't for particular purposes to have spiritual guides and friends and teachers.

CI: What would be the criteria for a healthy relationship with a spiritual guide?

AH: What I have understood, after years of meditating on this, comes out of a very positive relationship that I had with a great Christian saint, Bede Griffiths, at the end of his life. I realized that Bede had got the relationship of spiritual friend exactly and perfectly right, because he was in a clear and humble relationship to God. So in thinking about what it was in this relationship with Bede that was so inspiring, I came up with the following. A real spiritual guide never, ever, tells you what to do. Ramana Maharshi said, "He who instructs an ardent seeker to do this or that is not a true master. The seeker is already afflicted by his activities and seeks peace, rest, and quiet." A guide may suggest, may try and draw out something they know to be there already, but they will never interfere with the karmic course of your life. They will be a source of support, encouragement, radiance, tenderness, and generosity, but never of control.

The second point—and this is crucial—is that a real spiritual friend would never claim complete enlightenment. A great guide might want to witness supreme spiritual and mystical experiences that they had had, but if those were true experiences, they would have created in that person a fundamental awe and humility before the Divine, which would make him or her scrupulously aware of precisely those things in himself or herself that had not yet been transformed. Everyone who enters the enlightened field realizes that enlightenment is endless transformation. It is not static. Gregory of Nyssa calls this *epectasis,* "endless opening." Rumi speaks of trans-formation being a glory that goes on from light to light.

So anyone who is in the enlightenment field is, by definition, aware of all the mountain peaks of gnosis that they haven't climbed, all the love that they haven't grown when faced with this massive, vast, insanely powerful and beautiful presence. What a real spiritual friend is trying to do is to send you wild with love of *That.* Real spiritual friends are trying, as Rumi is in his poetry, to communicate to you a fatal attraction not for them, but for *That.* A real friend knows that when you are nakedly in contact with the Divine Mother in every moment, in every rose, in every face, in every breath of wind, it is so much more vast, ecstatic, and transforming if there is no name or form between you.

CI: So if one calls oneself free in referring to perhaps a lack of identification with one's personal story, this is not by your definition the end game.

AH: I think one should be very suspicious of anything anyone says. I think it's more important to see what they do, how they act. Is their freedom transformed into passionate daily service of other beings, into radical humility before the universe, into a visionary tenderness?

I think that the true spiritual guide admits that he or she is still in process, that they are always aware of their own shadow and of the limitations of their upbringing, their cultural conditioning, their particular religious views. The true spiritual guide never claims to be unified with the Divine. The human being can merge with God, but can never become God.

CI: Let's be clear about this. From another point of view we are totally infused with God, drenched in the Divine.

AH: We are drenched in God, we can participate in the glory of God's working, we can have experiences that show the oneness of our consciousness and the divine consciousness but, paradoxically, we can only have those if we are also aware of what we could call our lack, what the Christians call *hamartia,* "missing the mark," the part in us that is not yet divinized. Knowing this is precisely what keeps you receptive, humble, and loving enough for innate divinity to come through. Real mystical growth arises from a never-ending dialectic between humility and grace.

I have come to believe, too, that real spiritual guides welcome disagreement and doubt. They are actually delighted when you disagree or have doubt, for two reasons. One is because those who are really awake know that they can learn from anyone, and the other is that doubt is part of the necessary finding out of the secret hiding places of the false self. Someone who is truly realized would have no need to cling to any role or position, so why would they mind being doubted? If they're not interested in power, in money, in control over others, in having an organization, then why not say, "Doubt on! Let's see whether truth is to be found or not in these doubts."

CI: What you're describing is a relationship of true equality. It bears little resemblance to what mostly passes as a relationship with a master, where doubt is the greatest taboo, and belief in the master's omniscience is a requirement.

AH: Indeed. What you feel in the presence of a true spiritual friend is equality, the real equality of soul. That is the priceless gift of somebody who is in that state of humility. It is like a rose opening and sending its fragrance. It isn't involving you in any game, you don't have to believe that it is enlightened. You can just enjoy its perfume.

CI: We're speaking about a new era of spiritual possibilities. In this tantric, naked, direct relationship with the Divine, "How then shall we live?"

AH: I said at the beginning that I believe we are entering an era of passionate enlightenment. Another way of looking at this era would be to see it as the era of the sacred marriage, the marriage between masculine and feminine, action and prayer, politics and mysticism. We are entering an era in which all of the old distinctions between sacred and profane will be rubbled to inaugurate a new human divine freedom.

For me, one of the main forms of this new human divine freedom is the tantric marriage, a consecrated relationship in which two people devote heart, body, mind, and soul to each other and to God. My own relationship with Eryk has absolutely transformed my spiritual and mystical vision of the world. Through it and through divine grace I have discovered that when deep, passionate, pure love is the architect of the emotional, sexual, mental experience, then what takes place is the alchemical fusion of the entire self. In this alchemical transformation, the heat of love, of consecrated passion, is the Shakti, the divine fire that ensouls the body and embodies the soul, and so heals and melts together all division between inner and outer, holy and unholy, heaven and earth.

I have begun to taste that liberation of all the senses into their bliss essence and to know that natural immersion in sacred unity that comes from adoring another human being and being adored by that person in this way. And I have come to realize that there is no separation between human and divine love, because all real love is divine. Keeping a true vision of this great tantric work, however, is hard. Most Eastern and Western philosophical systems have done a tremendous disservice to our vision of sexuality, and we therefore have to steer a reverent and refined balance between denial and shame on the one hand and pornographic license on the other. To create the alchemical vessel in which tantric transformation can take place, both beings have to be dedicated to using their experience of mutual love and abandon as a way of entering more deeply into the divine beauty and glow of the universe. They both have always to be preserving the heart space of the other by offering total fidelity—and I mean real fidelity—without which the infinite trust that has to be born for merging to take place cannot be engendered. If these laws are observed, ordinary miracles are possible. This kind of sacred marriage, I am certain, will become more and more the site of the tantric encounter.

CI: What about a tantric relationship with the Divine for people who do not have partners?

AH: Oh, there are ways other than the relationship with the true soul consort, I think. There is also the deep spiritual friendship in which two or more souls really honor and respect each other in the divine beauty of their spiritual growth, and cherish and protect that with every resource available. It's clear that when two or more are gathered together in that spirit, as Christ himself said, "I am present." What I have been discovering in the workshops I have been facilitating is that when thirty or forty people are gathered together with open hearts and sincere passion in the name of the Divine Mother, then not only is astonishing wisdom shared by all, but there are moments in which everyone recognizes a fusion taking place, and everyone realizes that the Mother is speaking through each voice, moving in each hand, laughing in each face, crying in each tear. And that is a tantric experience.

CI: What about service?

AH: It can never be said enough that there can be no complete awakening without service. Service is tantric, because it slowly dissolves boundaries between ourselves and others and invites us into the all-healing compassion of the Mother. The highest service is to consider all beings as divine beings and to honor that divinity in them, to see life as a sacred experience from beginning to end. The Mother is offering us union with Her, if only we can open ourselves to the essential bliss nature and to live it at every moment, whether putting a flower in a vase, cooking a meal for a friend, listening to someone's pain over the telephone, or giving money and time to a valuable cause.

CI: Yes, and it means living with a broken heart, because in our adoration we develop the eyes and tenderness of a mother ourselves, and we are then open to the sorrow existing all around us.

AH: And that sorrow is going to become greater and greater. There is no way out now. We are brought by the catastrophic destruction of the planet to the terrifying moment when we will have to accept the terms of a great alchemical transformation or die out. To save the planet and ourselves we have no choice but to finally enter our bodies, enter time, enter the world, and to love them with the naked, undefended passion for equality, justice, and creativity of the Mother.

CI: It is exactly this engaged love that will give us the strength that is needed to endure, the strength of the mother who lifts a car off of her child.

AH: Yes, love brings everything—the courage, the intensity, the peace, the hope. Love brings the capacity to suffer and to go on suffering in the dark with only the Mother's light for a guide. Love brings the depths and passion and illumined wisdom necessary to take on this immense burden. This catastrophe that we face is inviting us into the reign of love.

We haven't been sitting here criticizing the master system because we want to tear something down. We haven't been trying to define what a real spiritual friendship is and what a real tantric relationship is simply because we are dissatisfied. We're doing this because we see an immense evolutionary vista opening up of freedom and love for the human race, when each one of us accepts the gifts and the burdens of the Divine Mother and realizes our fundamental direct intimacy with Her and so with all beings. Imagine if there were no hierarchical divisions—political, spiritual, sexual, racial.

Imagine that we understood each of us to be on a unique path, each of us a unique flower of the Mother, budding in Her wild ramshackle garden as to its own laws. Imagine the divinization of life—humble and ordinary life—that the rubbling of all ancient divisions could bring. This vision we are trying to describe does not want to destroy anything, only to strip away the scaffolding that is stopping the light from burning through to the human heart, so that human life can at last be experienced completely as what it is, a continual flow of divinely given, ordinary miracles, the sublime theater of the Mother's love.

CI: Many people throughout time have imagined glorious possibilities for life on this earth. Do you feel that our imaginings have any chance of catching on?

AH: This work of massive exposure to love and of ending the old structures is not something we can afford to turn down; it's not a luxury or something we can just discuss in coffee houses. It's not an opinion; it's an imperative. We must all leave our small prisons of the past and go into this unknown mystery. We would go mad at that moment, which is exactly what we need to do, because if we started to go beautifully and completely mad with love for Her, we would become infused with Her grace, Her confidence, Her wisdom, and Her power, and nothing could enslave us and nothing could stop us. So let us remember Pythagoras's words, "Take courage, the human race is divine." All of us who know that now have the responsibility to live it totally and passionately, without any barrier. In this lies our hope.

Foreword to *The Other Side of Eden: Life with John Steinbeck,* by John Steinbeck IV and Nancy Steinbeck

I am honored to write a foreword to this lacerating, profound, and exquisitely written book. *The Other Side of Eden* has harrowed and elated me, shattered my heart, and made me laugh raucously out loud. In John and Nancy Steinbeck's sophisticated and naked company, few extremes of human emotion go unexplored, often with a brutal brilliance that is as purifying as it is terrifying. This is one of the most original memoirs of the twentieth century. Anyone who finds the courage to read it as it deserves to be read—slowly, rigorously, bringing to it the whole of their feeling and intelligence—will find themselves changed.

All great memoirs are a clutch of different books marvelously conjured into one. *The Other Side of Eden* is no exception. It is at once an exorcism of family wounds and secrets, an exposé of the projections of religious seekers and of the baroque and lethal world of New Age cults and gurus. This poignant unfolding of a great love affair between two wounded, difficult, but dogged lovers is also the account of a journey into awakening through the massacre of illusion after illusion, to the awakening that lies on the other side of Eden. Few books risk, or achieve, so much under such blisteringly candid authority. Reading it is as much a rite of passage as a literary experience.

First, the exorcism. Many readers will undoubtedly be attracted to the most "sensational" aspects of the book—John Steinbeck IV's terrible alcohol- and drug-ravaged struggle with the shadow of his famous father. Anyone hungering for cheap dirt or the easy satisfaction of the destruction of a celebrity idol will go away disappointed. The younger Steinbeck shirks nothing of his father's violence, inner desolation, addictions, occasionally pathetic and outrageous phoniness, and is honest about the lifelong, life-sabotaging wounds these caused him. He is far too intelligent, however, not to know and celebrate also how generous and tender his father could sometimes be. John is also far too wise not to understand that the very terror of his father's legacy was itself a kind of appalling grace—one that would nearly kill him again and again, yes, but which would also constantly goad and harass him, against great odds, to discover his essential self and the supreme values of spiritual clarity and unconditional love. Those who admire the elder Steinbeck's writing, as I do, will find nothing here that sours their admiration. If anything their respect for both the work and the man will only grow sadder and more mature as they acknowledge the struggles both had to endure. Dreadful though his father's legacy partly was, the younger Steinbeck did not allow it to annihilate him. He fought it, and himself, with agonizing courage to finish his life at peace with those he loved, with his past, and with the world. His father left two or three real masterpieces as signs of his truth. The younger John's masterpiece was the scale, reach, and passion of his life, a life that could only be written by a combination of Thurber, Dostoevsky, and Milarepa. The marvelous writing he achieved in this memoir is also in itself a victory, all the more rare because of the atmosphere of forgiveness and awareness that bathes it with a final, and healing, light.

This light of rare, bald awareness also bathes Nancy and John Steinbeck's exposé of their disillusion with Tibetan Buddhism and its guru system. Searching for a spiritual truth that could spring them free of their inherited agonies, and also for a "good parent," they both became in the 1970s, like so many other seekers, enamored of the "crazy wisdom" teacher, Trungpa Rinpoche. As Nancy Steinbeck writes, "A magnetic aura surrounded Rinpoche.... Infamously wild, in his mid-thirties, wearing Savile Row suits, he smoked Raleighs, drank whiskey, ate red meat, and sampled the entire panoply of hippie pharmaceuticals." Initially intoxicated by Trungpa's extravagance and brilliance, the Steinbecks came gradually to see how abusively and absurdly, dangerously grandiose he could be. They began to understand how sick with denial of his alcoholism and sexual cruelty the community that surrounded him was. This shocked them both into awakening from "the guru dream." Inspired by their own struggle with abuse and codependency, they were compelled to speak out, especially when Trungpa's successor, Tom Rich, ran the risk of spreading AIDS with a complete lack of conscience and with the corrupt connivance of his "henchmen." Just as the Steinbecks had both lived through the exposure of their own family myths, they now lived together through the equally anguishing process (one that I know too well) of recovering from the delusion of projecting their own power onto a so-called enlightened master, and from the savage, intricate cruelties of a community rotten with denial. Their account of this devastating time is one of the triumphs of their book. Both admit they learned a great deal from Trungpa and praise his sometimes astounding acumen. It is this fairness that makes all the more unarguable their analysis of his hypocrisies and ruthlessness, along with those of his community. All those who continue, despite a mountain of damning evidence, to believe that Trungpa and his obscene Regent were "enlightened masters" and who, in the name of "crazy wisdom" continue to threaten and deride their critics, need to suffer and read *The Other Side of Eden*. So, in fact, do all serious seekers, especially those still in the thrall of the various contemporary manifestations of the guru system. The New Age at large is still horribly vulnerable to the fantasies of brilliant maniacs and the all-explaining, all-absolving circular rhetoric of a guru system that is now, to any unbiased eye, wholly discredited. The Steinbecks make clear that the alternative to the worship of false gods is not despair; it is freedom and self-responsibility, the dissolving of a brilliant illusion into a far more empowering, if less glamorous, truth.

The most moving of all the different facets of *The Other Side of Eden* is that it is a great love story, all the more greater and challenging because it shows how the jewel of unconditional love is only revealed when all the fantasies about love are incinerated. In the course of their extreme and extraordinary marriage, the Steinbecks explored and exploded all love's ravishing but lesser myths. In the end, they were left not with disillusion, but with a mystery, the mystery of a love that transcends all known categories to exist simply in the boundless and eternal. As Nancy Steinbeck writes, "I rode astride the razor's edge with John and although we placed our bets on victory, the odds were on insanity or death, or both. As a result, I learned about unconditional love. There is a bond so profound that it can surpass the ravages of child abuse, a garbage pail of addictions, and finally even death." The road to such a love cannot be smooth or dragon-free. Because it gives everything, it costs everything. One of the permanent contributions this book makes to the exploration of the nature of love lies in its blistering honesty about the price of authentic commitment and about the continual leaping-off into darkness and mystery beyond all dictates of sense or even, sometimes, self-preservation. At stake in the alchemy of such a love is nothing less than the forging of the whole human and divine self of both partners. The final, amazing grace of the Steinbecks' marriage reveals that this, in fact, took place. Their long, often tormented struggle yielded the golden peace that passes understanding and the divinity of human passion lived out to its end in acceptance.

The Shadow of Love

If *The Other Side of Eden* were simply an exorcism, exposé, and account of a transfiguring marriage, it would still be a most haunting and remarkable book. It is, however, something more than the sum of its parts. After many readings and rereadings, I have come to experience it as an account of the cost and joy of real awakening in a modern world largely controlled by competing lethal myths.

Those who want true and unshakable self-knowledge have to be prepared to sacrifice every inner and outer comfort, every consoling fantasy or dogma, every subtle hiding place, everything that prevents them from taking full, stark, scary responsibility for themselves and their actions in and under the Divine. There is no other way to full human dignity and no other way to the radical self-empowerment beyond the betrayal of dogma, religion, and system of any kind. The human race now needs to reach for this degree of honesty if it is going to meet, embrace, and survive the challenges of our time.

All systems, religious or political, have clearly failed us. We stand, naked and afraid, before doors that are opening into the apocalypse of nature and the massive degradation of the entire human race and creation. If we go on letting the lies or half-truths of the past haunt and mold us, we will die out. If we risk the terrible and dangerous journey into naked truth beyond illusion, we have a chance of discovering what John and Nancy Steinbeck both discovered at the exhausting but exalted end of this book—an unshakable belief in the sacred power of true love to overcome and transform extreme disaster. The Steinbecks' eventual ferocious spiritual strength allowed them to witness truth and justice in all circumstances against all possible opposing powers. From this marriage of what Jesus called the "innocence of the dove" and the "wisdom of the serpent" outrageous possibilities of freedom and creativity can still—even at this late hour—be born.

The questions that this wonderful book leaves us all with are these: Are we willing to pay the price for this marriage of unillusioned hope and illusionless wisdom to be born in us? Will we risk, as John and Nancy have done, the stark and glorious alchemy of honesty and embrace the spiritual Darwinism of the survival of the most candid? Are we ready to travel through the incineration of every false truth to arrive in the Real, empowered with its hilarity and mystery? One of the most moving legacies of this book is that for all its exploration of horror, agony, betrayal, tragedy, corruption, and sheer, brutal psychic suffering, it leaves us with the conviction that the truth is worth everything it costs because it sets us free. Free to love and weep and laugh and rejoice, free to witness, with steely and beady eyes, the rigors of justice. Free to become as Nancy and John Steinbeck became, electric nuisances to all myth-breaking systems—personal, political, and religious—that in any way diminish or imprison the secret of our splendor.

Foreword to *Hidden Journey*—2011 Edition

When I was beginning to write *Hidden Journey*, I had an extraordinary and life-transforming conversation with my great friend and Rumi translator, Eva de Vitray-Meyerovitch in Paris. I described to her what I wanted to write and what had happened to me in my mystical initiation into the Divine Feminine, and she listened, attentive and beady eyed. When I finished she said, with the bluntness and panache with which she said everything, "The Sufis say there are essentially two journeys on the real path. The first journey is the hidden journey to God, the journey to an awakening to divine light consciousness. This journey is finite and ends with an awakening experience in which you know that the divine light that is appearing in and as everything is also your essential self. The second journey then begins. This journey is infinite and keeps on expanding in all lives and all realms."

Then Eva paused. "There are three things you will have to respect in your writing, or you will fail and just add to the many delusional tracts out there. First, you will have to be as naked and transparent as you are able about the facts and twists of your own biography and nature that have shaped your ego. Second, you will need to be as precise as possible about how the journey unfolded for you, noting exactly and precisely the progression of experiences that led to your awakening as the divine self. Third, you will need to find a language at once poetic and realistic to describe each of these experiences, without false exaltation or poeticizing, so that people through you can begin to have some taste of their own inner radiance and its miraculous possibilities."

Then she laughed, hoarsely but not unkindly. "You are going to need luck," she said. "Writing what you want to write will be the hardest thing you have ever done. Pray constantly to be inspired. The reward for going through whatever you need to go through to complete this task will be that the entire experience of your first journey will become a permanent inner possession. A hidden diamond at the core of your being that time and your own failings will not be able to destroy."

Eva's voice haunted me during the difficult years of writing *Hidden Journey* in Paris, America, and India. The first draft was hundreds of pages longer; in one last, brutal revision I honed it down to the book that exists now. The hardest aspect of writing *Hidden Journey* was that I had no modern models that I could refer to; I had to invent its reality as I went along, attempting to be as faithful as possible to the authentic experience of what I had been given to transmit. This took a courage that frequently deserted me and had to be reclaimed again and again through meditation, prayer, and an ever-deepening surrender. By the time I had finished the book, I was myself different, as Eva had predicted; the truth of what I had first lived and then struggled to describe had, through the Mother's grace, crystallized in me permanently.

What I understand now in my late fifties is that everyone takes the first journey, the hidden journey, in the unique terms of his or her own karma, personality, need, and destiny. I took the journey with Mother Meera, someone I believed then to be a divine incarnation. Through this projection, which was rooted in the complexity of my own childhood and spiritual destiny, the first journey was able to be completed. I was born in India and saturated early in India's vision of the motherhood of God; I had a difficult relationship with my own mother and needed to find an idealized "divine mother" to be able to survive the wounds of my childhood and to believe in the Divine Feminine; a passionate and sublime nonsexual love, such as the one I lived with Meera, was the kind of devotion that could help me soar free of my terrors of commitment. Although I now see the experiences I recount in *Hidden Journey* from a very different perspective, I understand that, given who I was and what I needed, I couldn't have lived the extraordinary experience it represents in any other way.

I see what I recount here very differently because of what happened soon after the book was published. In Thalheim, December 1993 Mother Meera told me to leave the man I was in love with and whom I would later marry, become heterosexual, and marry a woman. I was bewildered and devastated, left Thalheim and began the soul-shattering process of dissociating in public both from Meera and the guru system. I was compelled to tell the truth about what happened, a truth that Meera was compelled to deny and in a way that plunged my and my future husband's life into prolonged horror and chaos. I have described this in detail in my sequel to *Hidden Journey, Sun at Midnight: A Memoir of the Dark Night.* Out of the long agony of the dark night that I describe in *Sun at Midnight* was born a wholly new vision of the mystical path of the Mother and of its potential to help transform the world and existing structures of power, a vision that has culminated in my trying to create and inspire a global movement of Sacred Activism and in my book *The Hope: A Guide to Sacred Activism.*

It took me more than two decades to begin to be able to see what I had learned from Meera clearly, and during that time I refused to allow *Hidden Journey* to be reprinted. But now I have come to a time when I feel at peace with my past with Meera and feel able to see her and what I lived with her from a perspective beyond suffering or recrimination, and as part of a journey that continues to unfold through the grace of the Divine Mother.

The transformative turning point came for me on a pilgrimage to Israel in 2000. I found myself in the meadow at Tabgha near the Sea of Galilee, where Jesus is said to have given the Sermon on the Mount; a divine peace settled in my soul and I knelt in the sunlit grass and blessed and forgave Meera for everything that happened between us, and forgave my own ignorance and prayed with great joy for both of our transformations and liberations. Since that grace-filled afternoon, I have come to see three things more and more clearly: the fact that our sacred relationship ended tragically does not destroy the truth of the fifteen years of beauty and transforming ecstasy I write of in *Hidden Journey*; that Meera's later behavior does not wipe out the holy truth of the wise, tolerant, illumined love she poured into my life for so many years; that both of us were and would continue to be fallible, evolving beings on our paths to freedom. After that experience in Tabgha I understood, too, that whatever strange and mysterious contract her and my soul had made was now dissolved and that the rest of both of our journeys would be our responsibilities alone.

So here, Dear Reader, is *Hidden Journey,* as an account of a journey to divine light consciousness in all of its drama and enchantment, as a record of a transforming, sacred love affair of the soul, and as an offering of inspiration to all of you who do me the honor of reading this. May this book illumine and encourage you on your hidden journey to the discovery of your essential self, and then on the journey that follows of enacting that discovery in sacred service to the world.

Chapter Six

The Suffering of Love—The Spiritual Path of the Broken Open Heart

Introduction

The greatest mystics of humanity are alchemists of agony, unafraid of the extreme suffering that evolutionary transformation demands, because they know it is essential for authentic growth and as a purificatory preparation for the great joy that can only install itself in you as your fundamental reality when all the blocks to it have been dissolved. As Rumi wrote:

Love comes with a knife
Not with some shy question
Not with fears for its reputation.
Love is a mad woman, roaming the mountains
Tearing off her clothes, drinking poison
And then quietly choosing annihilation.
You have been skirting the ocean's edge
Hoisting up your robes to keep them dry
You must dive deeper, a thousand times deeper.

In preparation for the birth of the Divine, the entire human race is now going through a global dark night, which will result in a new humanity that has been humbled and chastened by tragedy, so that it may open completely to the mystery of divine grace. This dark night cannot be bargained with, explained away, leapt over or mitigated. It is the destined crucifixion of a communal human ego, now clearly revealed to be suicidal and matricidal, dangerous to itself and to the whole of creation. No one and nothing will stop Kali dancing Her terrible dance of destruction and re-creation. There will be no resurrection of an embodied divine humanity without a systematic, perfectly organized, brutally complete crucifixion of everything in us that keeps us addicted to the systems of illusion that are now rapidly destroying everything.

413

Facing and accepting this is itself a death of the false self that wants transformation on the cheap and Evolution Lite. There will be no return of a Star Wars Jesus, no sudden lifting of the whole earth into a new vibration, no squadron of rainbow lightships sent to ferry us to another planet. All these are childish fantasies. Authentic evolution, both on a physical and mystical level, is a bloody, ferocious affair. The butterfly has to struggle fiercely in the cocoon in order to develop the strength needed to cut through its shroud and fly free.

If we continue to choose the false consumerist spirituality that is being offered in the contemporary corporate bazaar, and to believe we can make authentic spiritual progress without surrendering to the logic of an inner and outer dark night, the human race will die out, because the coming catastrophes will drive it mad and in its madness, it will ensure its own self-destruction. As an old Shaivite yogi told me years ago in Benares, "When Kali starts to dance, you either dance with Her in adoration and surrender, or go mad and die." If a significant portion of the human race can awaken to the real rhythms, costs, and demands of divine transformation, and create, through sacred practice, a container strong enough to accept and survive them, then unimaginable miracles are possible.

There are two linked aspects of the dark night that those mystics who have entered into the divinizing field know and can guide us into. The first is passive and demands total surrender to the necessary brutal alchemy of the Divine—the surrender that can only be sustained by abandoned faith, incessant sacred practice and an increasingly passionate love of the Beloved as circumstances become more extreme. This is the way of the lover, known in all authentic mystical systems. It begins where reason and any desire for comfort, security, and ordinary survival end. To carry it through to its transfiguring goal, you have to be, as Rumi said, "strong, wild, and fearless as a lion."

The second linked aspect of the dark night process is active. As horror, chaos, and agony do their ordained work of burning down in you every hiding place of addiction and illusion, you have to find the courage to awaken, without mask or illusion, to the agony of the burning world. Then you will discover in yourself the compassion for all sentient beings trapped in this worldwide fire. In and through your own heartbreak, you have to open to the heartbreak of the planet, be shattered finally open by it and set about with grounded peace and focused passion to put all your inner and outer resources into radical action. The way of the lover then opens into the way of the sacred warrior—the one who has been burned so completely that no fires can terrify him or her—the one who has been brave enough to suffer the heartbreak of the Mother side of God and so is rewarded by the Mother with divine peace, divine compassion, divine wisdom, divine purpose, and the astute, skillful means needed to enact their laws in the exploding nightmare of reality.

Marry the opposites of unconditional, passionate surrender to the inner and outer disintegration process of the false self with an active, passionate, fearless commitment to do everything you can with your own unique gifts and resources for the world, and you will be given all the divine energy, power, and love that you need to become a midwife of the birth. Then, whatever happens, you will be living a humble, authentically divine life.

Andrew Harvey

Foreword to *Day Breaks Over Dharamsala,* by Janet Thomas

I am honored to write the foreword to *Day Breaks Over Dharamsala* by Janet Thomas for three reasons: I have known Janet for four of the many years she has been working on the book and have been an intimate and awed witness to her unflinching, heroic struggle with the material she presents. I was born in the sacred world of India and the lessons of my childhood's exposure to India's mystical cauldron of chaos and the wonder born from it have infused everything I have done and written. I find in Janet's marvelous descriptions of India and in her stunned and transformational reactions to it the richest kind of confirmation. The third reason I am honored to be writing in praise of *Day Breaks Over Dharamsala* is that it is a masterpiece on many levels—as travel writing; as a passionate and wise account of inner revelation; as an account, at once restrained and searing, of a great healing from the kind of extreme and prolonged abuse that most of us would have been annihilated by. *Day Breaks Over Dharamsala* is the rarest kind of book, an accessible, utterly human and wonderfully unsparing and intelligent description of the hardest task that faces a human being—that of transmuting, through surrender and great longing, horror into grace, soul-stealing brutality into universal, active, joyful compassion, and unbearable trauma into a burning, sacred passion for all life and all beings.

For all of us who are coming to know that our times are plunging the world into its final ordeal in which human destiny will be decided, Janet Thomas's telling of the story of one woman's wrestling of illumination from the deepest and darkest despair will give us all the kind of hope we need. This hope does not thrive on denial but on the knowledge of the secret resurrection—the power of dogged faith and the divine blessing it draws down. This hope, rooted as it is in the growing experience of a love beyond reason and a mercy beyond judgment, cannot be withered by any cruelty, destroyed or downhearted by any defeat, or diverted by any ferocious assault or misery from flowering in a passion of compassionate action on behalf of all sentient beings. Grounded in and empowered by such rugged hope that springs in full strength from the heart of divine reality, *Day Breaks Over Dharamsala* shows us that there is no atrocity we cannot forgive, no depth of abuse we cannot heal from, and no grueling inner and outer work we need be afraid of and cannot bring, with the ever-present help from grace, to a consummation both more dazzling and effective than anything we could imagine as prisoners of self-love and despair.

As you will discover, Janet's evolution into such hope began in horror. Her childhood was sacrificed on the obscene altar of a satanic cult in which both her parents were active and enthusiastic participants. Janet was used in child pornography and farmed out as a child prostitute. She experienced electric shocks, drugs, acute and terrifying sensory deprivation, and was repeatedly experimented upon for medical and mind-control purposes by the very people she would normally have turned to for love and tenderness. Surviving this meant dissociating from the pain, the abuse, the defilement, the shame, the hatred, and the nihilism it bred—and dissociating in such a way that burdened her with an isolating multiple personality "disorder," profound self-loathing, and a deep terror of life.

In a recent letter to me, Janet wrote: "We are living in an age of abuse and a culture of denial. Evil exists. And nothing is more evil than the destruction of the fundamental innocence of a child. When deviant thought systems attempt to shape minds into obedience and hearts into shame and defilement, a great rage arises. This is a rage that can play itself out through insanity, through nihilistic cynicism, through sociopathic behavior, through unending hatreds, addictions and despairs, and through barren isolation. It can also play itself out through love. And love is a hard taskmaster. It demands that we love back."

Not without extreme difficulty—and with many detours, dead ends, and collapses—Janet made the life-saving decision to "love back" and put her whole being, in fear and trembling, into the hard taskmaster, love. One of the greatest and most helpful strengths of this book is that it shows that such a healing journey demands of the one brave enough to undertake it every ounce of courage, every capacity for persistence, every ability to endure often harrowing insight, every form of difficult surrender to the rigors of an alchemy that remains both ferocious and mysterious in its operations. Janet's extraordinary and, I believe, archetypal journey weaves through twenty years of psychotherapy; battering and bruising failed love affairs; poverty and ungrateful work; battles for social and political causes; a healing in island quiet surrounded by whales, wild turkeys, and hummingbirds; and a system of multiple selves, each competing for recognition, attention, and respect, and threatening at times to tear Janet finally apart.

What has saved Janet—and, for once, "saved" is not too rhetorical and theatrical a word—is that, through all the ordeals her childhood inflicted on her and bequeathed to her, she never completely lost her faith in a capacity for infinite transformation, a faith that crystallizes in this book around the down-home but diamond radiance of His Holiness The Dalai Lama. Janet never surrendered the longing that lives in her like a wild, crackling fire to be whole, to be her true self, to love life despite its crucifixions, to believe in the reality of the creation of a world order rooted in justice and compassion, to come at last into the blessing of what she calls "the greatest miracle of all, the miracle of the holy ordinary." It is the ordinary that knows that making a rich cup of tea, eating pizza with a loved friend, seeing a dog asleep in the sun are revelations of what Gerard Manley Hopkins called "the dearest freshness that lives deep down things."

Perhaps only those who have exhausted in their inmost selves the various fires of hell on earth can see as brilliantly clearly as Janet comes in *Day Breaks Over Dharamsala* to do, the "dearest freshness" of the "heaven" that also lies shining all around us in all the subtle details of ordinary pleasure, delight, and communion with others and with nature that we are all too often blind to, or too rushed to savor, or too addicted to victimhood or grandiosity to be grateful for. Rumi wrote: "True lovers use their shattered selves and heartbreak as a torch to burn away the darkness and light up the whole creation." No reader who is lucky enough to come to this book will doubt that she has become, in Rumi's high sense, "a true lover," someone who has been resurrected from a death far worse than any physical extinction and found the courage and fierce compassion to see and take on not only the system of cold evil that nearly destroyed her but also all those systems of mind and corporate control that are now threatening the survival of our world. The journey *Day Breaks Over Dharamsala* unravels and enshrines has not left Janet merely "healed," it has forged her into a gentle but fearless warrior for a whole host of causes—environmental, political, sexual, social—that she holds dear at heart. It has made her a convinced and authentic sacred activist, someone who has fused within herself a profound love of the sacred with a resolute determination to stand up for the poor, abused, and voiceless whenever and wherever justice and compassion demand it.

None of us in a time like ours are going to escape the ferocious alchemy of the "hard taskmaster, love." Few of us, of course, will have personal journeys as extreme as Janet's, but all of us are going to be shaken to our roots by the onrushing collapse of civilization as we know it and by the ever more destructive eruption of a perfect storm of interlinked crises that will compel us either to change the way we think about and do everything, or die out. Millions are now awakening to this truth, its terror, and the possibility of an amazing, unprecedented, difficult rebirth. Janet's great book and the archetypal journey it so movingly depicts will shine out like a great torch of hope for all of us who know that nothing less than an unconditional surrender to divine love and grace can possibly transform us enough to rise to the challenge we face, not with denial or paralysis or despair, but with the great, heartbroken bliss of compassion and the unstoppable energy of divinely inspired and empowered action.

Day Breaks Over Dharamsala is a book of the highest seriousness of purpose, but it is also a delight. It is a book not just for survivors of abuse and for all travelers and spiritual seekers; *Day Breaks Over Dharamsala* is written with such nakedness and such grit and wit and jeweled panache that it is also a book for dog lovers, people passionate about pizza, gourmets of eccentricity, bookworms hungry for arcane information about British churches in the Himalayas, and all battered survivors everywhere of postmodern cynicism, corporate nihilism, consumerist fantasy, and religious fundamentalism, for anyone, in fact, who, in Janet Thomas's words, "wants to know I have been alive before I die."

Janet has cooked up a literary Babette's Feast with enough

pungent, spicy, and enticing dishes to delight any palate. To have done so with such a shrewd and exuberant generosity of soul and such directness of heart is the greatest proof of the depth of Janet's healing and the most blatant sign that Janet has learned well from her soul mentor, the Dalai Lama, how to open her arms to everyone in the telling of her story and how to enchant them to rediscover—or discover for the first time—the holy enchantment of an ordinary illumined life. I once asked His Holiness at the end of an interview I had with him, "Why are we here?" He flung back his head and roared with laughter at the bald naïveté of my question. But he knew I was asking him seriously, and so, when he had finished laughing, he said, very calmly and quietly, "We are here to embody the Transcendent."

Day Breaks Over Dharamsala "embodies the Transcendent" in the journey it incarnates with such wisdom and in so lithe, dancing, elegant a prose, it helps us start to sing our own songs of redemption and begin living and acting from their radical wisdom.

Andrew Harvey
September 1, 2009
Oak Park

Interview with Janet Thomas

Andrew Harvey: *Day Breaks Over Dharamsala* is a very personal book about a very personal struggle. How do you see it in relationship to the greater collective struggle we are in to survive?

Janet Thomas: What, exactly, does it mean to survive? To me it's all about survival of spirit. Until I could name myself spiritually, I meant nothing. Until everything and everyone can be named spiritually, it means nothing. Naming ourselves spiritually means we suddenly have everything we need; there is no need to exploit, nothing to be greedy about, nothing worth competing for. It's all about divine love—within and without. I was raised inside profane hatred; getting to love, of self and other, has been a momentous personal challenge. We are living in a world fueled by hatred and greed—most of it organized politically and corporately. Getting to love, of self, neighbor, and global community, is a momentous collective challenge. Yet it is waiting for us—simple, unadorned adoration is our birthright. We are born into perfection and then, as a society, we go about defiling ourselves and the perfection of the planet, in order to do what? To prove we are here by associating ourselves with that which we can destroy? Why not associate with that which cannot be destroyed? When we do this we enter the ecstatic where all there is, is joy, and a cellular celebration of this miraculous timeless moment in which we live. It is love that inspires and compels survival in its most profound and encompassing manifestation—of people, planet, and every sentient being. Every day it is a struggle for me to know this. But every day it is true.

AH: The legacy of abuse is often more abuse. We see it playing out in every level of society. How is this cycle broken? How does healing happen?

JT: The struggle and suffering of survivors of childhood abuse begins to lose its power over us when it becomes conscious. Then we spend our lives healing from the trauma and learning from the healing. Our collective challenge on this planet is to become conscious of the suffering—really conscious, on-our-knees conscious, broken-open heart conscious, despairingly conscious, no-looking-back conscious, kick-ass conscious—of what is happening to our sacred home, our sacred children, and our sacred brothers and sisters everywhere. You write and talk about this sacred heartbreak nonstop. But our "have-a-nice-day" culture has seeped so destructively into a "buy-a-better-day" mind-set, that real grief and heartbreak are perceived as uncool, inappropriate, tawdry, and suspect. Survivors of childhood trauma know about the spiritual intervention that comes with helpless, wailing heartbreak. They know how Love works, as it comes out of the hidden places and washes our souls and spirits clean and sparkling, like a new day. And it's always a new day—there's the miracle. We are riding on miracles with every breath. Heartbreaking miracles are unfolding with every hummingbird flight, every leap of a whale, every emerging crocus. When we wake up to the depth of our loss, we wake up to the ecstatic gift of being alive. And there's the great and holy paradox. When we become kin with our own individual struggle, we are able to feel kinship with the struggles of others, and this collective consciousness begins to ask why and how did it get this bad. And when we start asking these questions collectively, we find the courage to know the answers and to stop the exploitation and injustice in which we have been unconsciously participating. It's all about waking up to it all.

AH: It's all about waking up into the heart of knowing. The awakened mind can see only within the framework of its own understanding. Opening the heart has its own mind—a heart-mind without borders.

JT: Yes. I first started writing *Day Breaks Over Dharamsala* in 1990; back then its title was *The Minds of Recovery*. I was a few years into therapy and thought I had something to say about healing and the possibility of healing. But I was fooled by my thoughts. And this is the biggest lesson: what I think always fools me. The first three hundred pages I wrote were brilliant with personal betrayal, inner devastation, unassailable anguish, and a great ferocity of thought. There was nothing redeeming going on. There was no recognition of divinity, no spiritual longing, no love. It was a display of intellectual understanding that had no inner truth. It was therapeutic to write it, but it was not redemptive. Something in me must have known this, because those hundreds of pages refused to become a book. Shifting from reductive mind consciousness to expansive heart consciousness had to happen before I could write *Day Breaks*.

Interview with Janet Thomas

AH: And how did that happen?

JT: I went to India. Almost accidentally. And it turned out that what I'd really done was return home to Mother India. From the moment I arrived in Delhi, in late November 2004, and for the next six weeks, I was suspended in such surprise, spirituality, and synchronicity that I never took a normal breath. I slept with my eyes, mind, and heart open. There was no other way to survive India. And when I got back to my other home I was plunged into deep, under-the-covers depression. And I couldn't figure out why. The answer came, like all real answers, out of the blue and of its own accord. In India I hadn't been lonely. And it was only when I realized this that I realized how lonely I'd been all my life. My next question was: why wasn't I lonely in India? The answer was because I met all my selves, all my fragmented parts, all my joy and suffering everywhere and all at once in India. No part of me was left out. And when I came back, most of me felt left out. India was an epiphany of acceptance. And suddenly I knew I could write my story riding on the beautiful, broken, and always healing bones of Mother India. I started the book over and spent the next few years writing my way back. That's when *The Minds of Recovery* became *Day Breaks Over Dharamsala*.

AH: And what about the *Battle in Seattle?* Where do these two books find common ground?

JT. In rage. Inner, undifferentiated, appalled, and appalling rage drove both those books. Any exploitation of power—within home, playground, or global politics—presents me with an exploding heart of rage. Transforming this into compassion is an ongoing wrestling match; it wrestles with me and I wrestle with it. The only thing I can do is write it out. Both books were written after the fact. After the unique epiphanies that marked themselves as truth. *Day Breaks* was written out of rage at the loss of innocence that comes with childhood abuse. *Battle in Seattle* was written out of rage at a mainstream media that refused to see the truth and beauty on the streets of WTO Seattle. And in doing so, the media perpetrated the corporate lies and perversions that we are only now beginning to reckon with through the Occupy Movement—more than twelve years later, I might add.

AH: You went to India "almost accidentally." How did you end up on the streets of WTO Seattle?

JT: Actually, I was inspired to go to the 1999 WTO demonstrations by a talk that David Korten gave at St. Mark's Cathedral a few weeks before the event. He spoke at a Forum on Global Economic Justice, and I was drawn by the fact that this was being held at the cathedral. It implied something about spirit and justice; and just as I had been drawn into the antinuclear movement by Japanese Buddhist monks back in the 1970s, it was a compelling calling card. St. Mark's Cathedral is huge, and it was packed with my generation of fifty-somethings. I sensed that we all knew something was wrong, that we were actually part of something that was wrong, and we wanted to know what it was. Korten connected the dots between our blissfully ignorant lifestyles and the environmental and economic suffering of others around the world. Bingo. It was before the internet became such a tool of communication. All we had was each other. And when Korten charged us with showing up to support global economic justice on the streets of Seattle, I suspect most of us did. What we weren't prepared for, I also suspect, were the thousands of others, the hundreds of organizations, and the breadth and depth of the participants from all over the world who showed up to share their lives. I walked into Memorial Stadium, where representatives from labor unions from around the world were gathered, and it was like walking into a sea of love. Some guy handed me a sack lunch and a plastic raincoat and said, "Glad to see you." I was dumbstruck. My heart wept tears of recognition that I didn't recognize. For me, it was the beginning of a day of rapture. I felt finally at home. The human yearning for freedom, for fairness, for communal connection brought

424

me to my knees. It was simple human recognition of us all as human beings struggling in a world we neither created nor recognized. We wanted our world back. In some way it was as though we were seeing and recognizing each other as the immanence of love. All day I was awash in love. As I walked the few miles to downtown with thousands of other workers from around the world, I was buoyed by a great sensation of belonging to a thriving, loving tribe of my own kind. The Japanese rice workers who couldn't speak English but who could sing, the Spanish-speaking farmers with their beaming smiles, Tibetans with big grins and big signs, Canadian airline pilots, nurses and educators from around the world, and music—every possible kind of music. The rage came when I got back to the office and found everyone in a state of panic about my safety. The media was doing its despicable job of arousing fear and loathing and then perpetrating fear and loathing. I became a one-woman shout-out for the love of it all. Someone said, "You should write a book about it." So I did. And as I researched, I found out why the world was in Seattle that week, and why it mattered. And if the media had done the same, we might have been part of a global transformation a decade earlier. And it might not have cost so many beloved lives.

AH: The tragedy is hard to bear, but it is bearable. And therein is found its beauty and its truth. This is the greatest lesson.

JT: Yes. And your work, throughout all these years, has exemplified this for us all. Plowing through the heartbreak and despair and humiliation brings us face-to-face with our divinity. Who knew? When I think of His Holiness The Dalai Lama and his ability to radiate compassion in the face of annihilating tragedy, I am awed and incredulous. Yet this is the template of our times. We live in a dark age, an age of abuse and a culture of denial. We are abusing our children, our elders, our communities, our histories, our earth, and all that we hold sacred on earth. Within this maelstrom of annihilation we are called to rise up in love and compassion. What a calling! What a magnificent challenge! What a triumph of the Divine! Anyone working through the lifelong aftereffects of child abuse knows this wrestling match all too intimately. It is the shape of life. Those who survive to adulthood, who survive to love and be loved, are our unspoken warriors of divine light. I believe this with my whole heart. They have won the greatest battle within and their living legacy is Truth. The Truth, no matter how dire and defiling, has set them free. Knowing rage is part of this Truth. And so is entering the deeper heart of shattering compassion and realization. Those in my living history who do this—His Holiness The Dalai Lama, Nelson Mandela, Martin Luther King Jr., Aung San Suu Kyi, Gandhi, and the millions, perhaps billions, of survivors of war, famine, and abuse who rise in compassion every day—are brilliant guiding lights in this dark age of greed and corruption. They are hearing and seeing beyond its howling death throes. They are the Light.

Prologue to *Sun at Midnight: A Memoir of the Dark Night*

When I came to live the long death of the Dark Night that destroyed and transfigured my life—and that I know now as its most profound blessing—three conversations with three spiritual friends of different religions and worlds kept returning to me. Their clarities circled my spirit like majestic tigers, protecting against despair, reminding, sometimes wrathfully, and with a certain scorn, of what it was to be brave enough to embrace and endure. Long before I could understand the value of the gift they were giving me, these three friends distilled for me the wisdom I would need when my killing came.

In the first conversation, I am a fierce, unhappy, intellectual twenty-eight-year-old, still uneasy with all things "mystical," stalking in old jeans and cheap army boots around Jerusalem. My guide to the mysteries of the Old City is "Isaiah," a plump, bald, late-middle-aged Israeli poet and mystic who looks, as he himself says often, "like a semi-enlightened sunburnt frog" and who has, over two days, become a friend. I love his sardonic wit, his baroque flights of phrase, his kabbalistic learning, the way his eyebrows twitch asymmetrically when he gets excited, which he does often. Today he is wearing bright red sneakers and a short-sleeved Hawaiian shirt with great orange suns on it. Our talk is light, fact-stocked, and airy until we find ourselves in the early afternoon on the Mount of Olives, and stand, suddenly silent, in the stubbly ochre olive grove where Christ wandered on the night before His crucifixion.

"Even on a cloudless afternoon like this," Isaiah whispered, "this place is so sad. It is as if you can still hear Him weeping for all of us, for what must happen."

He stretched out his arm and pointed to the bricked-up golden gate in the wall of the Old City opposite us.

"Some Jews believe that the Messiah will come through that gate." He started to laugh. "Don't hold your breath. And suppose *He*'s a *She*? Wouldn't that drive all the old boys in black out of their curlered heads?"

It was then that I noticed the faded black numbers on the bare arm sticking out of his Hawaiian shirt. I gasped; the afternoon before we had walked in silent anguish together through the Holocaust Museum. Isaiah had said nothing then. Now, he turned slowly and stared at me, into me, steadily, as if weighing my soul.

Then he began to talk in a low, even voice I had not heard from him.

"Yes, I was in Auschwitz. As a child. From nine to thirteen. I don't know how or why I survived, but I do know what I learned."

I waited.

He opened his mouth, then stopped, and shrugged his shoulders.

"Words are hopeless. I want to say something so big, but I only have small words to say it with. That is why I speak of these things so rarely and to so few people. Perhaps the old Jewish prophets were right; some things are too terrible and too holy to be spoken of."

The afternoon darkened slightly. He paused, as if to gather strength, and went on: "I am not going to dishonor the horrors we all lived through in that hell by going over them. You know many of them, and you have the heart to imagine more, although nothing you can imagine can come close.

"But it is not of these things that I wish to speak to you. I want to tell you what I discovered in hell. It may shock you.

"In Auschwitz, I discovered that there was one thing I was even more terrified of than death. When you live in an atmosphere of terror, you realize that all the fears you shrink from in 'normal' circumstances are relatively minor and that there is one terror that everyone has which is overwhelming, and that hardly anyone ever talks about, because very few have gone through enough to find it out."

"And what is this terror?" I asked, a little afraid by now.

"The terror of Love, of Love's embrace of all things, all beings, and all events. Everyone pretends they want to know and experience Love, but to know and experience Love is to die to all your private fantasies and agendas, all your visions of 'right' and 'wrong'; even 'good' and 'evil.' Everyone who comes to that death is dragged to it kicking and cursing and screaming and weeping tears of blood, just as Jesus was in this garden."

He breathed deeply as if to steady himself.

"I was twelve years old. It was mid-winter. I was in despair. My mother, father, and sister had all starved to death. I knew by then that the chances of surviving or of being saved were very slim. There was a guard who was particularly sadistic who used to beat me with his leather strap until I bled.

"I was only twelve. What did I know about anything, about God? All I knew was that I had to decide, once and for all, whether the horror I saw around me was the ultimate reality or whether the joy and tenderness I could still feel stirring inside me was the truth. I knew that they couldn't *both* be the truth; if the horror of the camp was the reality about human nature and life, then what was stirring in my heart was some kind of mad joke. If what was stirring in my heart was real, then it was the horror that was the mad joke.

"I thought about this for months. 'Thought' is too polite a word,

I *bled* about this, I wept over it, I wrestled with it as Jacob must have wrestled with the angel, for my life. I had to know, or I would drown in the darkness. For the first time, I started to pray. My prayer, which I began to repeat at every moment, was only four words: 'Show me the truth.' Nothing came. Not a single insight, not a single vision, no dream with any comforting angel. Nothing at all.

"But I went on praying, more and more desperately, and then early one winter morning I heard a quiet voice say to me, 'You must decide.' What did it mean? For a week, I wrestled with this. What could the voice mean? How could I, a child, decide the truth of the universe? Was this the devil laughing at me? Was I God in disguise? The maddest thoughts swirled round my brain.

"Slowly, I began to understand. I understood that I was always free to decide whether the world I was being shown was the real one or whether the world I felt in my heart was the truth. When I really thought about it, the second choice seemed even more frightening than the first. What if Love was the real choice? Would I have to love the guard who had beaten me? Would I have to forgive the apparatus that had killed my parents and hundred of thousands of others? Would I even have to forgive in some mysterious way God Himself for having allowed these horrors to take place?

"I lived through indescribable torment, much worse, even, than what I had suffered in the camp at the hands of the guards. A twelve-year-old soul, let me tell you, has abysses some of the angels would be scared of.

"Then, one morning, I awoke and knew quite simply what I had to do. I had to choose what was at the bottom of my heart, the fire I felt there when I thought of my mother, or our cat at home, or the flowers and vegetables in our kitchen garden. So I went out into the camp yard, covered with snow, with a gray, lowering, hopeless sky overhead and, closing my eyes, I screamed with my whole being silently, 'I choose Love! I choose Love! I choose Love!'

"And then it happened. When I opened my eyes, a sun not of this world had come out and was blazing in glory all around me;

the snow along the barbed wire glittered like diamonds, and the air was sweet and hard like the skin of a cold apple against my cheek. The guard I hated at that moment came out of another building, smoking a cigarette. He didn't see me, but I saw him and—this was the miracle—I felt no fear at all, and no hatred, only a burning pity that scalded my eyes with tears. I did not feel vulnerable as I had feared; the *Thing* in me that was crying was stronger than anything or anyone I had ever encountered. It or He felt like a calm column of fire that nothing could put out.

"Somehow I survived for another year until release came. Whenever I could, I would gaze at the way the ordinary light changed on the ground, along the wires, on the roofs of the huts and the crematoria. I knew now Whose light it was a reflection of. The fire in my chest did not leave. It has never left. I have tried to live and breathe and act from it and from its laws."

The sun was setting in a riot of rich red light in the sky, setting the gold dome of the Temple Mount alight. Isaiah took both my hands in both of his.

"I doubt if we will meet again. You are leaving tomorrow, and I am in the last stages of cancer. I am not afraid. The Glory is here always. I see it with open eyes, every day; I am not unique; there are thousands of us, maybe millions, all over the world, of all kinds, classes, sexes, and religions. The Glory gave me life and It is giving me now my death; but through another death long ago It gave me a Life beyond all dying. And it is into that Life that I am going.

"You have a long journey ahead of you. I have a feeling it will be a difficult and wonderful one. Remember always three things—forgive me for being so 'rabbinical,' and in such a shirt and wearing such sneakers—but write these down in that black notebook of yours. (And you don't have to worry about your ideas being stolen, not even the seraphim could read *your* writing.)

"Pain can be terrible beyond any human description, but it is transient; Bliss is eternal.

"Evil is real, but only in its dimension that includes this world; the Glory shines forever here and everywhere in a way evil cannot stain or defeat.

"Horror has its day, or year, or decade, or century; the Sun of Love has never, and will never, set.

"And here's a fourth: *whatever* you have to go through to come to know this beyond any shadow of a doubt is worth it.

"And now I am going to buy you a dinner of the best shish kebabs in Jerusalem in a little place off the Via Dolorosa."

"I thought you only ate kosher food!"

"Are you mad? Arab cooking is wonderful. One way to start making peace with your neighbor is to eat his food. Don't they teach you anything in that university of yours?

Paris, 1992. I am forty, living in a gussied-up maid's flat in the seventh arrondissement, working in the mornings on English re-creations of the Persian mystic Rumi, and, in the afternoons, on a book of conversations about him with Eva de Vitray-Meyerovitch, Europe's leading Rumi translator and scholar; she had become a friend.

Ten years before I had found Eva's French translations of a thousand of Rumi's Odes in a second-hand bookstore in Saint Germain. I still remember sitting by the Seine reading them, shattered and astonished, my chest thumping. When I met her in 1991, at lunch in the country with mutual friends, I warmed to her—immediately. She was in her early eighties, tiny, plump, moon-faced, with slanting melancholic eyes, a feisty, sometimes savage, wit, and an old-world way of talking in perfect soaring sentences, rich with her learning in Arabic, Persian, Latin, Greek, and all the major European languages. She moved me with her paradoxical mixture of French grande dame hauteur and girlishness, of extreme, even contemptuous, authority and vulnerability of heart that often brought a catch into her voice, especially when she was talking about the one she called "our Master."

The Suffering of Love

The day after we met, Eva rang me. I heard her precise voice pouring down the phone, "It was marvelous yesterday! Our Master has brought us together! We are two pearls on the same string, you and I! With you I don't have to edit myself! I'm too old to edit myself! We have the same culture! I saw from the fire in your eyes that our Master is for you as he is for me, the Light of my life, my journey, my soul! I have decided we must do a book together! We must do it soon, because I am about to die! Let's start today!"

In fact, we started the next afternoon. Every afternoon after lunch, for five months, I would race across Saint Germain and the Luxembourg Gardens to the fifth-floor, poky, dingy flat where Eva lived, which always smelled of old books and vegetable soup, and which had the kind of antiquated kitchen straight out of 1930s French film that makes you fear for your hostess's life every time she gets up to make a cup of tea. There Eva and I would sit on her sagging gray-brown sofa, strewn with yellowing manuscripts, with a microphone between us, and talk and talk; sometimes she would tell stories of her first researches into Rumi, when no one had ever heard of him; sometimes she would recite one of Rumi's Odes in Persian, and translate it word for word and pour out for hours all her love and learning and inner knowledge of what she called "the Path of Fire," the Path of Love.

She was always precise, scholarly, obsessed with dates and textual accuracy; sometimes, though, another Eva would surface, the Eva who, although she would never claim to be a mystic, had had what she called, somewhat dramatically, her "hours of lightning" and longed more than anything to come into the Divine awareness of the being she had worked on and lived with for so many years. "So you think He will be waiting for me when I die?" she would ask often, not expecting an answer. After a while we both realized that we would never be able to finish a book; we went on recording, but, as Eva said, "Something more important and wonderful than a book is happening between us." She was handing me, naturally and with an aristocratic abandon, the jewels of a lifetime's search; I was giving her the ardor and inquiry of my own journey and love of Rumi.

One particular afternoon I shall always remember as the most profound hour of our friendship. I was late for our daily appointment; it had been raining. Eva met me at the door, her hair unraveled from its usual tight gray bun, tears racing down her face. This was so unlike her usual, slightly sardonic self that I was momentarily speechless. Staring wild-eyed at me, she broke into sobs; I took her hands and steered her gently onto her sofa in her living room.

"Eva, what on earth is wrong?" I asked, sitting down close to her.

"Don't you know? It's November 29th."

My mind went blank.

She became impatient and started to shout. "November 29th, 1244, is the day Shams is supposed to have met Rumi, the day when Rumi met his Beloved and his killer, the day when he met the one who would bring him death and resurrection."

I had never heard her speak in such a way. The sobs grew louder. Her sobs grew so violent I was scared she'd choke herself.

"Shouldn't we be celebrating?" I suggested, trying to calm her down. "Shouldn't we dance and sing? The mystical love story of Rumi and Shams has lit up the whole world."

"I'm not crying for us, you idiot." She was almost shrieking. "I'm crying for him. I'm crying for Rumi! I'm crying for how much he had to suffer! Don't you see, don't you understand? Everything we have been given by our Master—all the glory of his Odes, his *Mathnawi*, his table talk, of the life he lived as an enlightened being for thirty years—all of this comes to us perfumed by a terrible death, an agony and grief that would have killed you or I. I have Christian friends who on Good Friday weep for what Jesus had to suffer to leave us all that He left; well, today is the day I always remember the sacrifice that our Master made."

It was both more than a little absurd and extremely moving— seeing, behind the facade of her fifty years of scholarship, the wild, personal, protective love she still had for Rumi.

"I know that one day I will understand. Perhaps he will tell me himself when I see him, and it won't be long now. But why did Shams and their love have to be so fierce and terrible? Why did Shams have to meet so much jealousy from Rumi's disciples? Why did Shams have to be murdered after only three years of their being together, and almost certainly by Rumi's oldest son? And why did Rumi then have to go mad with grief, to be wrecked and ruined, before there could erupt from him the burning fountain of Glory that is his work? Why is God so terrifying? Why must there always be Gethsemane and the Cross before there can be Resurrection! I'm eighty-one. I've seen two world wars, Dachau, Hiroshima, Pol Pot, and now Nature burning to death. What does all this horror mean? What will it birth? There are days when all I want to do is beat against these walls and howl with rage. Don't try and give me any answers. I know all the answers. Just sit with me."

An early Beatles song, "She loves you, yeah, yeah, yeah," floated up from the student flat below and we both laughed. Eva, quieter now, wiping her eyes, turned to me and began:

"I want to tell you about the afternoon I first arrived in the city where Rumi spent most of his life—Konya, in southern Turkey. It was twenty-five years ago, and Konya was a quiet, ancient, civilized place: wandering around it you could almost believe you might meet Shams or Rumi or at least glimpse them, sitting by candlelight in an upstairs window, deep in love. All that has gone now, of course, like almost everything else sacred and beautiful.

"That afternoon, I arrived about four, went immediately to my hotel, left my bags, and asked directions to go immediately to visit Rumi's tomb. I had wanted to kneel and pray to him there for fifteen years. As I walked toward the museum where it is, down the main street of Konya, I seemed to enter a dream state. Street noises reached me, yes, but as if from a distance; the air seemed to be shining. I thought to myself, 'Watch out! What will they say back at the university if you return a little weird in the head!' As I approached the tomb, the whole sky seemed to split open in the cries of the muezzin for afternoon prayers; everything in me and around me rang with that wild sound. Blessing after blessing seemed to be raining down on me from the ringing sky and something in my chest opened and I felt a pain like a spear going through my heart.

"I found my way to the tomb. You have never been, I know, but you have seen pictures, no? It is large, fifteen or twenty feet long, indescribably magnificent; that evening it was hung with gold brocade, emblazoned with verses from the Koran, and ringed by hundreds of lamps that made the gold brocade melt and swim before my eyes. I stood by the tomb, and the strangest thing happened. I started to laugh wildly. Thank God there was no one else around. I laughed so hard I doubled up."

"What on earth made you laugh like that?"

"Here I was coming to pray to our Master at his tomb as if he was dead, and yet …" Eva paused, groping for words, "and yet, as I stood there, I felt that the tomb was a volcano erupting again and again, covering me with the boiling lava of a Fire and a Presence that had never died, never been born, and would never die. I wanted to laugh and shout and dance.

"I went back to the hotel still in ecstasy and couldn't eat dinner and retired early. I prayed to Mevlana, and then opened my copy of the Odes at these lines:

> My heart is a vast tablet of light;
> An ocean of agony drowned it again and again.
> It has become a warrior, after being martyred a hundred times;
> I venerate each one of the waves of this ocean;
> I'm at once the feast and the disemboweled victim.

"The pain in my chest that had started with the cries of the muezzin now became almost intolerable. I cannot explain what happened next and I have never before talked about it to anyone. Paris isn't exactly made for mystic confessions, is it?"

She paused for a moment, looking frightened.

I squeezed her hand. "Please go on, Eva."

She stood up and started to pace around the room.

"What happened after I read the lines I told you was that I

entered into the pain of Rumi's heart. That is the only way I can say it. Suddenly, I was made to feel without any mask as much as I could stand of the agony that he had endured after Shams died. I had been given the Glory first, I see now, so I would be strong enough to stand this. It was greater than anything I had ever felt or imagined feeling. I have suffered in my life. My life has been hard. But what I felt on that night and throughout the night was a kind of pain I didn't know existed. I know now what Teresa of Avila means when she writes in *The Interior Castle* that 'there is a spiritual pain so great that when it possesses you, you would not mind if your body was cut to pieces.'

"Even as I was wriggling on my bed like a stabbed animal, I knew that I was being given a gift; I was tasting just a tiny fraction of what my Beloved had to go through to be changed into the being he became, the volcano of Divine Love whose blessing had poured eternal gold over me in the afternoon. I had spent years translating his Odes; now the Divine was giving me a glimpse of the furnace the Odes had been forged in.

"I wish I could tell you that the experience transfigured me and that I spent the rest of those two first weeks in Konya walking around in bliss, having conversations with the risen Rumi in my head. That is not true. In fact, what I experienced that night made me frightened and furious, more furious than I knew I could be. As dawn came, I found myself screaming at God (thank God, the room had thick walls and heavy Turkish carpets.). Words, filthy words, poured out of my mouth; I didn't know I could curse like that. I hated God for torturing Rumi so. How could Love really be Love and ask and demand so much, so horribly?

"I was so angry I stayed in my room for two days, eating very little. There were many times I feared I would lose my mind. At last I had the presence of spirit to start to pray; I have never prayed like I did then. I begged to be helped to understand why Rumi's annihilation had been necessary, why annihilation itself is necessary on the Path of Fire. The Sufis call this stage *fana*, you know. Al-Hallaj wrote, 'Take away the me so only You remain.' *Fana* is when the 'me' is utterly unraveled, burned down to its roots, so the 'You' of God can take over the whole being and use all the operations of the ego and senses as its expressions. Oh, I know the theory, you see! You should hear the lectures I give on *fana* in Ibn Arabi and Al-Hallaj and Lahiji! They are miracles of precision and textual corroboration! You can have read all the texts, Andrew, and know the theory, but when you begin to taste the awfulness of the reality, all of your learning becomes dust and ashes in a whirlwind.

"I prayed to be helped to understand. No peace came. I prayed for twelve days, in my room, at Rumi's tomb. Nothing. Each day I understood less. I couldn't even read our Master; the letters would swim before me and become meaningless. Then, on the last full afternoon of my visit, I met someone who helped me more than anyone has helped me in my life, who gave me, gently, a few simple keys to help me understand the necessity of annihilation. I still wrestle with that necessity, as you saw when you came in, but I think that I know the truth, even if I cannot wholly accept it. One part of me accepts it; the other, you know now, still screams in the night."

Eva went to the window, opened it, breathed in deeply the freezing rain-wet air. Turning, she said, "Never forget what I am about to tell you. If you come to *fana* and enter the dark hurricane, it will help you. It will not save you—only you and the Divine Grace can do that—but it will help you on those many, many days when nothing will make sense and your whole being will be a cry.

"I had gone, worn out and miserable, to say goodbye to Rumi at his tomb. I was still desperate, too—how would I return to Paris after what I had experienced? I was in pieces, like a pot thrown against a wall. I talked to our Master then as I had never talked to him inwardly before. I was direct and abrupt. I remember, I said, 'You have plunged me into this chaos; it's your fault; you have to do something about it now.'

"I came out into the late afternoon air and sat down by one of the fountains in the museum's courtyard. I noticed an ancient, wizened old Turkish gentleman sitting by my side with a face like a big-eared elf. He was dapper, with brilliant black shoes, a pin-striped suit with a red tie, and smelled heavily of rosewater cologne. Normally I wouldn't have spoken to him. For no reason I can think of, I turned to him and started to tell him everything that had happened to me. It all tumbled out, just as I have told it to you. At the end I looked at him and asked him, 'Are you a Sufi?'

"He replied, gazing at me directly, 'One day I hope and pray I may be.'

"I noticed for the first time how beautiful his deep, rich brown eyes were. He took my hand and began to talk quietly and gently as if to his own daughter. This is what he told me: 'To accept that Divine Love will ask us in the end to die into it—that is, for everyone, even the greatest of saints, the hardest of all things on the path. Even Jesus in Gethsemane begged, "Take this cup from me." Even Jesus, Who had seen God, heard God, healed with the power of God, been seen transfigured by His disciples on Mount Thabor. Even Jesus wept tears of blood at what had to be. So you should not be surprised at your rage or your fear. They are natural. They are inevitable. They are part of the process.

"'Divine Love begins by seducing you, by kissing you on the inside of your heart. That is how it hooks you. Then it feeds you with ecstasy and vision and revelation, drawing you deeper and deeper into a devouring longing to be one with it. When your longing is great enough and you are surrendered enough to it, Love changes into a Black Lion and tears you limb from limb. Then when you have been scattered to the four quarters of the universe and not a scrap of "you" remains and darkness reigns, the Lion turns golden and roars and "you" are reassembled, resurrected, and your whole being shines with the Glory of the Lion's own Light, the light of the Sun.

"'All this is natural and logical in the dimension of Divine Nature and Divine Logic. You cannot begin to understand it through human reason or through the intellect or even through contemplation; you can only begin to understand it through Love. Love itself will teach you what you need. But to be able to learn at all, you will have to have made yourself open through many years of prayer, meditation, and service of all living things and beings.'

"He smiled and pointed to a rosebush near us with one full luscious red rose on it.

"'The whole meaning of the planting of that bush in the first place was to obtain that open, fragrant rose shedding its perfume in all directions. The whole meaning of the Creation is to birth beings like Rumi and Jesus, the full, open, Divine human roses, who inebriate us all with the fragrance of Divine passion. Isn't it written in the Koran, "I was a hidden treasure and I wanted to be known; that is why I created the world." Those who know the "hidden treasure" of their innate divinity are those who have opened completely in the Sun of Divine Love. To birth that opening is the secret meaning of the Creation, its goal, its justification.

"'Look at that fragrant rose, open so abandonedly, giving itself with such purity and truth to us! Just imagine what has to happen before that bush can produce that rose! First, a clipping must be taken from a healthy original rosebush and planted in good earth; then, it must endure living underground and pushing its way upward in the dark; after that, when it finds the sun it has been dreaming of and longing for, it has to protect itself against predators, grow thorns and struggle to create a solid stem; and after that, it has to fling out from its secret sun-kissed depths such energy and passion that from that stem branches start to grow, branches on which the roses it dreams of making begin, slowly, to appear as bigger and bigger buds. All this takes a long time, constant effort, focused passion, season in, season out. Everything has to follow natural order and logic; you cannot go from a clipping to a branch thick with buds directly. All the different stages have to be honored one by one.

"'Imagine now that you and I had been sitting here a week ago. What would we have seen where that full rose now is? We would have seen a big, juicy, still-enclosed bud. What has to happen before the bud can become a rose?'

"I was at last beginning to understand. 'The Sun has to break it open.'

"'Yes,' he whispered. 'The Sun has to train its fire on it and break it open so everything that has been carefully, over many stages, enfolded within the bud can now be unfolded for everyone and so that the perfume that bud is keeping secretly hidden within itself can be given now to everyone who wants it.'

"His rapt calm voice had spread a carpet of peace over my mind. 'You see, my child,' he continued, 'God, as the Sun and the gardener, knows what He is doing and what must be done. Before Rumi met Shams he had already, through prayer and study and inner aspiration, grown a solid stem; falling in love with Shams drove him to fling out branches; the ecstasies and agonies and revelations that loving Shams brought him grew the buds along those branches, buds juicy with knowledge and hidden Divine fragrance. Then the moment came when all of those buds had to be broken open otherwise all the long alchemy of the growth of the Rose of Glory would have been wasted. Shams was killed; what had been "Rumi" was destroyed by grief. A being both "Shams" and "Rumi" and neither was born. Now, at last, all the buds could break open. The entire world is still reeling in their perfume.

"'Yes, this is a terrible alchemy. But it is natural in Divine Nature; the shattering of the bud is the condition of the flaring open of the rose. How can the secret dream of the rosebush and the gardener who planted it be realized if that does not happen?'

"We sat silently and then, still in pain, I said harshly, 'What you have told me is fascinating, but there is something too pretty about it all.'

"My wizened, shining-eyed elf laughed out loud. 'Pretty? Have you asked a bud how it feels when it is shattered open? But I know what you mean. Let me try again. All that I can offer you anyway is analogies, images. I think I know how much what I am stammering to convey to you means to you. I think I know that it is a matter—how shall we put it—of life and death.'

"'Yes it is.' I had not admitted that to myself and my nakedness shocked me.

"'You already know enough,' my new friend went on, 'to know that *fana,* or annihilation, the Dark Night, is the ultimate mystery in this life. Mevlana has taken you to the time when you can start to see the Black Lion prowling in the distance and hear perhaps some of his growls in the night. That is already a blessing. Most people die without even suspecting that there is such a thing as a dying in life that makes you eternal.'

"'Have you been through this dying?'

"'Yes,' he laughed gaily like a child. 'Yes, thank Allah. And I am only a baby in the new life. Eighty-five years old and a baby. It's silly, but it's true. Blame Rumi! It is all his fault! … And now, I'm going to try once again and share with you what Rumi has taught me, and this time I will ask your forgiveness in advance, now that I know how hard you are to enchant.

"'Another way of coming to contemplate the mystery of annihilation is to see it as the pangs of a great childbirth. I will explain this slowly.'

"He took my hands in his and patted them tenderly.

"'Ten years ago, when my time came to be killed by the Lion, I, too, came every day to pray at this tomb and I was just as lost, angry, and desperate as you. If you are not lost, angry, and desperate the Death cannot happen. But there is always protection—you will find this out, perhaps you are finding this out already—and there is always direct guidance for anyone who asks for it. This I know as I know the name of the man who made these black shoes for me. Perhaps the greatest paradox of all the paradoxes that dance around *fana* is that while you imagine you are at your furthest from God, you are actually so close that you are blinded by His Glory and think it night. Stare into the sun, after all, and your eyes will in the end see only dark; they cannot stand too much Light. What the Darkness really is, is the dawning of a Light too immense for your yet-untransformed senses to register.

441

The Suffering of Love

"'But it isn't metaphysical paradoxes that I want to share with you; I want to tell you of what happened to me ten years ago, after I had been praying to Rumi for guidance for a long time. My wife sent me out to buy some bread at about five o'clock one evening. I took the long way round to the bakers, stopping off here at the tomb. I came out, and when I walked out of the front door I saw a young woman lying on the pavement and screaming horrible screams that tore the air and made my blood curdle. I immediately imagined the worst: she must have been raped or stabbed. I ran to her, held her up, and started to look for some telltale wound or bruise. She was too far gone to understand anything I was saying to her, and her screams got worse and I got more desperate. Suddenly, I noticed that she had spread her legs, and then all of a sudden it struck me: she is screaming because she is giving birth! She wasn't dying at all, she was having a baby! I ran and found an old woman who knew how to deliver children, and the child, a healthy boy, was saved. The woman had been shopping when labor pangs started and had made her way in a hallucination of pain to the entrance of Rumi's tomb, thinking that there she would be safe and find help.

"'The screams of the self being torn apart in annihilation, the screams that you hear in Rumi's poetry as Shams rends his false self limb from limb, the screams of Rumi's madness—all these are not the howls of death but of birth. And Rumi must somewhere have known that; he must have known that what was killing him was also helping him to give birth to the New One in him, the Divine Child.

"'Remember what he said in his table talk: "This body is like Mary. Everyone of us has a Jesus within him, waiting to be born. If pain appears to be our midwife, our Divine Child will be born. If not, our inner Jesus will return to the Origin by the same secret way He came, and we will be deprived of His mystic joy and splendor."

"'Annihilation, then, is the dark birth canal the inner Jesus has to pass completely through to be born in the Sun. If you can hold to that knowledge and have faith in its reality, through everything, then the Rose of Glory will be opened in you.'"

442

Eva finished, stood up, and poured us two stiff brandies. We sat in silence a long time. Then she asked me, "Where do you think you are on the Path?"

I tried to answer her as precisely as I could. "I have been through many minor deaths. Each of the stages of the Path, after all, demands a death that is a metamorphosis. What I wrote about in my book *Hidden Journey* was the passage through the first purification on the journey—what the Christian mystics call, I think, 'the Night of the Senses'; when the senses one by one are transformed so that the Divine Light can come up in consciousness and start to use them for its own purposes. This Light has come up; I see it normally; with it has come energy, vision, a totally different level of longing for God. It is strange that we are having this conversation today, because last week I read for the first time the Ode of Rumi that begins:

> *You've endured many terrible griefs!*
> *But you're still under a veil*
> *Because Dying to yourself*
> *Is the fundamental principle!*
> *And you haven't adhered to it*
> *Your suffering cannot end*
> *Before this death is complete*
> *You cannot reach the roof*
> *Before climbing up the whole ladder.*

"These lines pierced me like so many swords and I saw just how far I still have to travel."

"And did you pray for *fana?*"

"No," I said. "I didn't dare."

Eva laughed drily. "I don't blame you. I have been too proud, too rational, even with everything I have been given, to risk 'completing my death.'"

She got up unsteadily, went into her bedroom, and came back with an open red rose. We stood together and drank in its rich, heady perfume.

"You know what the Turkish Sufis like to say? 'Isn't God amazing?' Remember today and this rose and the old Turkish man when your time comes. I have a feeling it will. Something in you has fallen in love beyond reason with the Beloved and 'something' will drag you beyond yourself in the end."

She stroked my cheek for the first and last time.

"There are two questions I have," I asked unsteadily. "How do you know when your Divine Child has been born?"

"I asked the old man that. He said, 'You know when you no longer hate or fear anyone or anything, and when your deepest desire is to serve all beings with everything you have forever.' Your second question?"

"What was the old man's name?"

"I thought you might ask me that. I asked him, too, when the time came for us to part. I asked him also for his address so we could stay in touch. He looked amused. 'My dear,' he said, 'we have been talking beyond names and addresses. I have nothing else to give you than what I have given you. Seeing each other again would only ruin the perfection of this meeting.' Then he turned abruptly and walked, surprisingly fast, off into the night of Konya. Sometimes I have thought—no, this is too crazy."

"Say it." We were both smiling now.

"That it might have been.... No, I am *not* going to say it. I have already said a great deal too much."

In many ways, the third conversation, whose gift of wisdom was to guide and steady me, was the most significant; in it I learned of the Dark Night from someone who had lived it consciously, as the most decisive part of the long and passionate search for God. Only two weeks after my talk with Eva, I found myself sitting with the man whom I came to think of as my deepest spiritual friend and father-in-God—Father Bede Griffiths, an eighty-six-year-old Benedictine monk and mystic.

An Australian film director had rung me in Paris and asked me to go at short notice to southern India to interview Father Bede in his ashram for a television documentary about his life. I said yes at once, dropping whatever else I had to do: I knew and admired Bede's books; I had heard him speak the year before at the Camaldolese monastery in Big Sur, and he had made an indelible impression on me by his gaunt, white-haired, austerely radiant presence and by the reverent but no-nonsense precision with which he spoke of the mystical life. And now here I was—sitting with Bede alone in his small, bare hut after our first day's interviews—with the sounds of the tropical south Indian night whirring and clicking around us, and its perfume of wind and moist grass scenting the air.

Bede lay back in his orange robe on his bed, gazed piercingly but tenderly at me. There was an almost full moon, and thick, silver light poured through the open door.

"I am happy you have come," he said softly. "I feel we are already friends and that you understand what I have lived. I feel we have come together now for a purpose. I do not have much time left. I feel well, but I *am* eighty-six, after all." A bright, almost mischievous smile lit up his face. "I feel only eleven or twelve, of course, but I know that is an illusion."

Bede had the authority, even grandeur, of a sage, but also the sweet artlessness of a child. As I gazed at him, I drank in the grace of being with him, here, in India, in the place he had lived and prayed for almost forty years.

"What are you reading these days?" he asked.

It was such a deliciously "English" question that I chuckled. Bede had, after all, like me, been educated at Oxford, at Magdalen College. Englishness was another force that drew us together.

"I'm reading St. John of the Cross's *The Dark Night of the Soul*," I replied and explained to him how absorbed I had recently become by the subject. I told him, in detail, about my conversation with Eva, about the old Turk and his remarks.

When I finished, Bede sat up straight, leaned forward, cupped his face in his hands, and remained silent for a long time, as if listening to something behind my words.

Then he began to speak, in his clear, serenely precise, and cadenced voice. "*The Dark Night of the Soul* is the supreme mystery of the Path and the true passage into Christ-consciousness. Jesus lived, you see, the entire Path out for us, both externally and internally. All of those who wish to follow Him will have to go through what He did—Gethsemane and the Cross and the Descent into Hell and the Resurrection. What I am telling you is not new. All the great lovers of Christ have known this. St. Francis knew this; Teresa of Avila knew this; and St. John of the Cross, of course, knew it with a wonderful precision. To come into the freedom and deathless joy of the Christ-consciousness you have, as St. John makes clear, to go through two deaths, in fact, two 'nights': the first Night is that of the senses, which enables you to ascend from ordinary 'psychic' consciousness into what modern transpersonal philosophers call 'subtle conscious-ness'—the consciousness open to Divine knowledge and inspiration. When I read *Hidden Journey* I realized that you had lived through this first Night; that is what your book is describing.

"What happens in this first Night of the senses is, as you know, that each of the senses is purified one by one so that they can all become instruments of Divine awareness and Divine Love and no longer the servants of the false self. But—and this is what St. John of the Cross makes clear—the old false self still survives in a subtle form. Amazing experiences now happen to it, all kinds of visions and illuminations, but it still remains as the 'witness' of these experiences and as their 'focus.' In other words, you still think you are Andrew, although you know by now that you are one in your depths with the Divine Light and the Divine consciousness.

"The logic of the transformation into the Christ demands that another and far more drastic death now takes place—the death of this false belief in personality itself and this focus, however subtle, on the still-'existent' false self. This is the Death of the Dark Night of the Soul. St. John of the Cross says that while the first Night cuts off various branches of the tree, the second pulls the whole thing up by the roots, systematically, and with terrible precision.

"What the Dark Night of the Soul makes possible, in fact, is the transition from 'subtle' consciousness, where the false self is still a subtle focus, to 'causal' consciousness, where the Cosmic Christ is known and felt as the 'cause' or 'experiencer' of all things and events. This is the stage which opens onto the Resurrection and Resurrection-consciousness; it is this awareness that St. Francis lived in at the end of his life and Teresa of Avila describes in the seventh mansion of the *Interior Castle* and that St. John of the Cross celebrates in *The Living Flame of Love,* and it is this consciousness that all of us who love the Christ must aspire to realize here on earth while we are in the body. Jesus had to abandon and leave behind everything He thought He knew or believed in, even His understanding of who God was—even His most precious mystical awakenings—in order for Him to discover and become the One beyond all form and name and understanding, and so do we. Just as He did, we have to undergo the crucifixion of everything we believe we are and know, before we can come into the radiance of the Resurrection. This is the essential mystical process that Christ came to live out, embrace, and reveal to all of us, and it is because the churches have lost its secrets that they are mostly now so narrow and soulless, and largely impotent to birth the living Christ-consciousness."

He paused and began again, more softly this time, his voice hushed as if by the grandeur of what it was recounting. "I don't just want to talk theoretically to you, Andrew. Please listen with your heart because I have the feeling you will one day come to need what I say. I shall pray for that, in fact."

I shivered slightly at his words and waited, watching his hands folded in his lap.

"Something absolutely new has been taking place within me these last three years, through the grace of God," he began. "In my early eighties, I have made more profound inner progress than during the whole of my life. I hardly recognize myself as the person I was before.

"On January 25, 1990, I was sitting meditating on the veranda of this hut as I usually do at six o'clock; suddenly, with no warning, a tremendous force came and hit me on the head. It seemed like a kind of sledgehammer. Everything went fuzzy. Then this force dragged me out of my chair. It was coming from the left and pulling me out of my chair. It was terrifying. I don't know how, but I managed to crawl on top of the bed. One of the monks came and found me about an hour afterward.

"For the next week, they tell me, I didn't say a word. I don't know what happened during that week. I was immersed in a vast darkness. Slowly, very slowly, I started to come round.

"Then on February 25, exactly a month later, I had another death experience. I had about five or six altogether in those first two months, but this was the most significant. I woke up at about two o'clock at night and felt that my time had come to die and that Christ was coming for me. I began to pray to the Virgin and the angels and waited for death. Nothing happened. Then after an hour or two, one of the monks came in and massaged me, and I started to get back to normal.

"I had a little breakfast but was still feeling restless, not knowing at all what was happening. Then quite suddenly, I seemed to hear a voice inside me. Its message was totally unexpected, but very clear, 'Surrender to the Mother.' Somehow I *did* surrender to Her. Quite suddenly, I was overwhelmed completely by an experience of extreme love. Waves of blazing love flowed over me and into me. Judy, my great friend, was watching and so were other friends. I called out to Judy, 'I'm being overwhelmed by love.'

"It was the most extraordinary experience of my life. Looking back now, I can see that it was a breakthrough to the feminine. It had to be violent; I had to be hit, as it were, and then immersed in fear, bewilderment, and darkness, because I had been so masculine and patriarchal and so continually left brained. I loved India from the moment I arrived here in 1955, loved the sensuousness of the people, their animal grace, the way in which in the villages every hill and river and field is sacred; I had recognized with my mind how in India the feminine is adored as sacred, and I had been moved by this, but it has never truly permeated me, never really transmuted the depths of my being. Now India and the Mother had decided to intervene; the right brain—the feminine, the earth power, the glory of Creation—came and hit me.

"It is a very strange thing, Andrew, but when I thought of surrendering to the Mother I naturally, of course, thought of Mary—I often say the Hail Mary—but it was Mary as the Black Madonna that came into my mind. For me the Black Madonna is the Mother of the earth as well as heaven, of the body as well as the soul, the Mother of the subconscious, the hidden, of all those powers that the 'masculine' mind represses, the Mother of the sacred darkness. In Her the Western Christian vision of the Divine Mother and the Eastern one merge and meet; you can think of Her as both Mary and Kali, both preserver and destroyer. From that time on, I have turned to Her again and again: invoking Her strength and grace, I find, makes the 'birth' go so much faster and more cleanly. None of this knowledge was accessible to me before the strokes. She has changed me."

His face seemed almost to shine in the darkness.

"How exactly?" I asked.

Bede smiled at my boldness. "It is hard to put these things into words, Andrew, but I know you really want to know, and so I'll try." He turned and gazed directly into my eyes. "After the stroke, I could no longer think in the old way; my left brain and the whole rational system was knocked down. At first I panicked. It was as if everything I had relied on all my life was being taken away. There were many, many moments of terror in which I felt I had been abandoned. St. John of the Cross speaks of this. All those who go into the Dark Night to have their entire being broken down, dissolved, and remade necessarily feel this way. Then, very slowly, I realized that nothing had been destroyed. It was just that the stroke had opened up—like a can opener—my right brain, the intuitive in me. What I was now living was a far deeper and richer experience of reality than I had ever had; it was an experience of what in India is called *advaita,* 'nonduality.' The divisions between things started to melt away, and everything was flowing naturally into everything else. My left brain was still there, but now it was the servant of this amazing experience, its interpreter, and not the force that prevented it happening.

"During the days after the experience of the stroke I felt extremely close to the death of Christ. I realized in the core of myself that what happened to Him on the Cross was that through intense psychological and physical suffering He came to the point where He, too, had to lose everything He had ever understood of God. Facing the darkness of death, He had to abandon His mind. Then He entered into the darkness beyond the mind, that is the darkness of Love.

"One of the greatest of all the Christian mystics, St. Gregory of Nyssa, said that beyond the purgative and illuminative way, which is the way of Light, there is the unitive way, the way he said 'of love in the darkness.' Jesus went through the darkness into total Love. He became total Love because He surrendered everything. His whole body and His whole soul. Both were swept up and taken completely and together into the fire of the Spirit. This is the real meaning of Resurrection."

"So," I said haltingly, "the body as well as the soul is transformed. Both are transformed together in the sacred marriage in the darkness."

Bede clapped his hands. "Yes, this is so important. John of the Cross understands everything there is to understand about the psychological and spiritual torment and radical adjustment of the Dark Night; he knows every nuance of fear and abandonment. What he doesn't understand and so few people do, because of the almost complete ignorance of the feminine not only in the Christian traditions but also in the others, is that, in this fire of the sacred darkness, the body is also transformed, the body is also, in a sense, broken down and remade.

"It is as if there are two related Dark Nights—one of the soul, and one of the body. Both soul and body have to be refashioned in the sacred marriage if we are to come into the dimension of Resurrection and know ourselves in every way nondual, both with the Creation and the Transcendent, just as in the ancient Mother mysteries, and just as the Christ did, after the Crucifixion and the Descent into Hell.

"All my life, I imagined that Awakening would come from freedom from the body. This is, after all, the patriarchal way, and I have been celibate. What I realized after the stroke is that the body, too, must be transformed. The body, too, must be possessed and taken over and divinized in all its centers and desires by the spirit. This is an immense, deep, slow, rich work, and since my stroke it has been going on all the time. I feel that at every moment spirit and body are marrying within me more and more intensely. Before the stroke, I lived largely from the head; then after the stroke, I got into the heart. But now the Force of the Mother is going from the heart-center down to all the others. The spirit is constantly coming down, first through the center at the top of my head—which the Indians call the *Sahasrara*—then through the heart-center to every other center. It has entered my sex region also. I am rediscovering the whole sexual dimension of life at eighty-six, imagine that! A wholly new power of Love has entered my life because of this; I find I love all beings more fully and tenderly because my love is now *in the body* as well as the heart and spirit.

"Although I pray continually to the Mother, the Black Madonna, and know that in this luminous darkness I have been taken into, She is gradually taking over, I also know that it is not the Mother alone. Both 'Mother' and 'Father,' the Transcendent and the Immanent, are integrating themselves within me. They are having their marriage within me, and this inner marriage is slowly birthing a wholly new being."

"The Divine Child."

"Yes," he smiled. "It is strange to be becoming a child in your middle eighties, but the Divine can do anything, after all! And God knows the process isn't completely realized. Sometimes it is very bewildering. There are always forces opposed to the marriage taking place that try to interfere with it, but they don't win, and the integration continues. And when I get bewildered and confused, I enter into the silence and the emptiness and I allow the confusion to settle. The order comes out of the chaos again and again. I have all the time to try and *not* control what is happening. I have been so used to controlling myself. But if I do succeed, everything stops."

His humble and guileless precision brought tears to my eyes. Trying to control my voice, I said, "And what are you seeing as this marriage deepens in you?"

"Let me tell you first what I am *not* seeing. I do not see all things and beings as being *One Thing,* undifferentiated. Each thing and each being seem, and are, unique and holy, far more unique and holy than I ever understood before. The universe in this state does not disappear into a kind of radiant Whole. And yet while each thing is differentiated, they are also, obviously and profoundly, related, contained, in fact, in a deeper unity and always part of it. Let me give you an analogy. Mozart, apparently, could conceive a whole symphony in one note. In such a symphony, the notes are not confused; every single note and every sophisticated shift of harmony is there, separately, but still all contained in one moment. This is how I am coming to see the world—everything separate but present together in each moment. In Christian mystical terms you might say I am coming to see and know the truth of the universe as the body of the Cosmic Christ and of myself as a living cell of that body, part of all things, yet not lost in them, but completely 'myself.' We are all one in God and one in each other, but the miracle of this relationship is that we are not dissolved in it; we are found in—or born into—our total being 'as persons within the Person,' as St. Augustine said, or, if you like, as different-shaped flames of the One Fire.

"The great mistake some Indian thinkers—both Hindu and Buddhist—have made is to see this state or union as one in which the Creation and all beings are recognized as dreams or illusions. This is not true. I cannot say it strongly enough: in this state, every being and thing is recognized as sacred. Every bird and slug was holy to

St. Francis. That is why, when you come to this awareness, you wish to devote your entire life to serving and honoring and protecting not only human beings but all of the Creation. Why it is so important that as many people as possible now come to know something of the holiness of this inner marriage is that, through it, they will be inspired to do and give everything to start saving the environment."

"Because they will know who they are and what the world is at last?"

"Yes," said Bede. "You know that you and everyone else is the Child of the Father-Mother and that the Creation is the Dancing Ground of the Glory. Or, to put it in the terms of the Christian mystical tradition, you know the whole universe as the 'display' of the Trinity. Everything flows out eternally from the Father, the Godhead beyond name and form, the Ground of Being, in the Son, the Word of the Father, the Creation and all its forms, and returns in the Spirit. The Father is pouring Himself out eternally in the Son, and Father and Son return to one another, unite with one another eternally, in the embrace of the Holy Spirit. We are enfolded forever in that eternal Love, and we have come here to experience that eternal Love in all of its facets, in our transfigured bodies as well as our illumined souls."

"To be born twice, in fact."

"Yes," Bede said. "And in the second birth we are born as sons and daughters of the Living God."

We sat a long time in silence.

Then he said, "Your generation will be able to go further than mine did. The world's mystical teachings are available to you; you haven't inherited so hysterical a split between mind and body as we did. You will be able to bless your sexuality more completely."

Then he said, "I am going to pray that the Holy Spirit comes to you."

I smiled. For the first and last time, Bede was stern with me. "Do not smile. I mean what I said. And, believe me, when the Spirit descends, it changes everything."

Again, something in his voice made me tremble slightly. I got up to go, and took his hands.

Looking deep into my eyes, Bede said, "One last thing.... Remember that to participate in the birth of the Child what you most need is a direct relationship with the Divine. Many of the gurus now are not enlightened beings but black magicians, occult masters manipulating millions of seekers; what Jesus calls 'wolves in sheep's clothing.' All the serious mystical systems know of the existence of these occult powers, but modern seekers are naïve and uninformed and so vulnerable to them. These 'masters' are not actually helping the Great Birth but working against it, aborting it. I have never had a guru; the power of the Living Christ and the Black Madonna is enough. I am not saying anything for or against your guru, Mother Meera. But remember my words when your time comes."

I turned at the door to smile back at him, but his head was bowed in prayer.

Introduction to *Navigating the Coming Chaos: A Handbook for Inner Transition,* by Carolyn Baker

It is becoming increasingly clear to many of us that our culture is utterly inadequate to the enormous world crisis that is now erupting on all sides, and so is, unavoidably, doomed to an agonizing collapse on an unprecedented scale. This clarity is, of course, brutally hard-won and extremely hard to sustain, since it involves accepting that we are all entering together a whirlwind of ferocious ordeal at a time when the human race is profoundly unprepared and in a state of paralysis and deep denial.

Without this clarity infusing and informing both our inner work and our outer engagement with the world, we are, however, doubly lost, since it is only by knowing where we are and what faces us that we can begin to do what is necessary—undertake a massive inner transformation to be strong and calm and passionate and focused enough not only to endure what is now inevitable but to guide others through it, and midwife, in the middle of a seismic death of all previous human agendas, the birth of an embodied Divine humanity that is also being offered us by Divine grace.

Carolyn Baker, in her great book *Sacred Demise: Walking the Spiritual Path of Industrial Civilization's Collapse,* challenges us all to face the coming collapse of civilization unshrinkingly; in it, she lays down, with inescapable precision, exactly why our current mindsets, addictions, and economic and political policies are doomed, and what we all must start to feel and to do to respond to such a devastating situation.

Sacred Demise is one of the most essential books of our troubled time, and perhaps its most important gift to us is the tone in which it is written, a tone that shirks none of the difficulty and suffering ahead for all of us, but which remains steady, joyful, and resonant with the kind of profoundly grounded, wise, and down-home instruction that can help us prepare ourselves both inwardly and outwardly for what is to come.

Carolyn Baker's equally important and essential new book, *Navigating the Coming Chaos: A Handbook for Inner Transition,* begins where *Sacred Demise* ends, and should be read, carefully and slowly, alongside its predecessor. In it everyone who has woken up to where we are will find the kind of guidance we now need—one that does not play down either the severity of our crisis or its potentially atrocious consequences, but which still provides us with a comprehensive set of inner and outer tools, skills, and practices with which to meet it in such a way that its ferocity can help us birth a new world and a new kind of humbly empowered divine human being. In the deepest sense, *Navigating the Coming Chaos* is a handbook for midwifing the birth that is struggling to be embodied through the Great Death that is erupting, and like any authentic handbook of sacred midwifery, it is at once stringently unsentimental in its facing of the gritty and grueling process of birth, and loving and joyful in its depiction of what could be possible.

There are other wise books coming out that address with great intelligence the practical aspects of the transition we are going through, and focus on the new kinds of community building, organic agriculture, survival skills, and revivified local culture that we are going to need to start building now, with great focus and fervor, to have a chance of surviving the future. What these books, for all their usefulness, have not begun adequately to explore—and perhaps don't want to explore—is the vast and frightening emotional trauma that the transition ahead will inflict, a trauma that can only be healed by attention as radically directed to inner, spiritual grounding and preparation as to outer actions. Carolyn Baker's *Navigating the Coming Chaos* fills this gap with rich wisdom; in it she lays before us a brilliant and vivid smorgasbord of tools and practices by which we can prepare to be strong, empowered, and joyful enough not only to endure the great shattering ahead but to use it to birth ourselves into a new dimension of spiritual depth expressed in wise action and so help birth, amidst and through, the burning chaos of the Death, a new way of being and doing everything.

Perhaps the richest aspect of Carolyn's book is her unflinching exploration of what she calls, inspired by the great psychologist Miriam Greenspan, "the alchemy of the dark emotions." The vast trauma that the transition into a new world is inflicting and will continue to inflict will inevitably bring up all our shadow emotions—rage, fear, grief, and potentially annihilating despair. Patiently and precisely, Carolyn Baker takes us through the demanding process by which the very emotions we are all terrified of can become, through surrendering them to compassionate consciousness, our deepest guides to a new form of being and action. Only someone who continues, at personal cost, to surrender to the mystery of this alchemy could have given us such profound and helpful instruction; this is not the work of a person who knows all the answers and poses as a New Age guru of the birth but something far more valuable—the clear message from the cutting edge of our evolutionary process given to us by a being who dares to be its humble pioneer, surrendered to a mystery she knows she cannot fully predict or control or even completely understand.

In being such a messenger and giving us such a message, Carolyn Baker makes us aware that evolutionary process itself is something that we cocreate at each moment and which is therefore a great adventure, demanding of us that we stay at all moments as responsible, clear, inspired, and humble as possible.

The other aspect of Carolyn Baker's book that I want to salute is its note of dry-eyed but insistent optimism. For everything that Carolyn knows about our situation and our current dangerous inadequacy of response to it, she is far from being in despair, either about us or about the potential result of the alchemical process we are burning in. She is herself someone who has risen phoenix-like from the smoking ashes of many previous selves and psychic and conceptual deaths, and knows from her own experience how the deepest crises birth the most astounding and transformative possibilities. *Navigating the Coming Chaos* ends then, not in gloom and dire finger-pointing, not in stoic resignation, but in an unabashed celebration of the kind of world it is still in our power to imagine and will and create if we have the courage to face where we are and to plunge into the inner and outer work that we are challenged to. All of my work in Sacred Activism is dedicated to this celebration of what could be possible, and I recognize in Carolyn someone who has dared to see both the face of our communal crucifixion and that of our potential beauty and glory in and under the Divine.

All I can do in closing is thank my dear friend for having lived, worked, suffered, and rejoiced enough to write such a book, and urge everyone who wants to be useful in our time to read it.

"Transition and Transformation: The Joy of Preparation"
A Conversation with Carolyn Baker

Andrew Harvey: I'm Andrew Harvey, and I'm here with Carolyn

Baker, my great friend, in Boulder. We've just had the most amazing two days together, teaching together for the first time. And we've been teaching about, I think, the most essential aspect of our time— the absolute necessity of accepting that this is an apocalyptic situation and deriving the greatest kind of joy and hope from that acceptance. This is a paradox, of course, and what we're going to be doing now is to explore this paradox.

Before we do so, I would just like to say something about your work, Carolyn, and why it's so important and why I love it so much. After I'd written *The Hope: A Guide to Sacred Activism,* Carolyn sent me her book, *Sacred Demise: Walking the Spiritual Path of Industrial Civilization's Collapse.* Usually I don't read the books I'm sent because, quite honestly, most of the books I'm sent are just the same-old, same-old, regurgitated for financial gain, and I'm so sick of reading books about how we can become happy in seven easy stages or how we can become unbelievably successful by manifestation. All of this seems just the chatter and prattle of the ego. But when I read the title, *Sacred Demise,* I read it, and I was amazed by it, because it is by far the clearest, the most lucid, the most down-home guide to the essential theme of our time, which is that we are going through a massive death, which is the potential crucible for a massive birth. And I felt such resonance with your work, resonance with the deepest themes that you explore in that book. And then we became friends, and then I had the honor of writing the foreword to your next book, *Navigating the Coming Chaos: A Handbook for Inner Transition.*

I'd like to begin by talking to you about what we were talking about in the car after the workshop—about how it is essential to redeem the word *apocalypse* from the fundamentalists, because the word *apocalypse* turns in two directions from its Greek origin. And those two directions exemplify the paradox of disaster and opportunity that is at the core of our work.

So what does *apocalypse* mean?

Carolyn Baker: Well, I'm really glad you asked, because when you started with your remarks, you were using the word *apocalyptic* in them, and I was hoping I'd get a chance to comment. Actually, in its literal meaning from the Greek, it simply means "the unveiling." Now, what fundamentalist Christian religion has done is to define it as the end of the world, the rapture, the final judgment, and so on. It's very interesting because a few years ago, I was talking about the collapse of industrial civilization with a friend, and my friend said, "Oh this sounds very apocalyptic," as if I shouldn't be saying these things, or as if no sane person talks about apocalypse. And I explained that it really just means "the unveiling." Now if you think about the things that are getting unveiled ...

AH: Well, let's look at that word *unveiling*. So what's being unveiled are two different things. What is being unveiled?

CB: Well, we're in a situation in which every institution on earth is collapsing, but in the process of that, a number of things are being unveiled. Let's look at the financial crisis of 2008. None of the major players in this crisis have even gone to court, let alone spent any time in jail. Right this moment as we're recording this video, the Penn State University scandal is raging, with jaw-dropping sexual abuse being unveiled. The emperor has no clothes. We're now seeing with the Occupy Wall Street movement the extent to which political candidates and congress are bought off.

The other night I saw an interview with Jack Abramoff, who was a very corrupt lobbyist during the Bush presidency. In the interview he was admitting that he committed terribly illegal acts, but he served time in jail and has now seen the error or his ways and has changed. He used to brag that he had at least one hundred members of congress in his pocket. Abramoff is yet another person in the whole corrupt political system who is being unveiled.

AH: Everything of the patriarchal system, of the military industrial complex is being unveiled as the corrupt conspiracy of addiction to power that it is. The Catholic Church is being unveiled by the horrific scandal of child abuse. The capitalist corporate system is being steadily revealed as the death machine it is—like Exxon and Enron and the tobacco companies withholding information about health. We've had the whole thing. Everything is being shown to be hollow. We now have to be really dumb and really out of it not to know that the corporations are controlling the politicians, and that the media is in the control of the corporations, which determine what news gets out, and that between that unholy trinity, what they have created is a death machine that is ravaging and destroying the entire planet. We have two billion people living on less than a dollar a day; we have 95 percent of the seas polluted; we have the Brazilian government allowing the Amazon rainforest to be logged and burned down—allowing the lungs of the world to disappear. All of this is now exploding open. And that is the first meaning of unveiling, but what this situation is really saying to the whole of humanity is: "You have bought a mess of pottage; you have bought a set of very dangerous illusions; you've given your soul, heart, body, and mind to these shattering, dangerous, exploitative illusions. And now these illusions are being stripped naked before you so that you could see exactly what the consequence of following these illusions will be— which will be the annihilation of the human race and the extinction of a great deal of nature. And everybody is now facing the truth of what we've become addicted to, and that it's a system of cold evil and destruction.

CB: Well, unfortunately, not everyone is facing it. Everyone is surrounded by the reality of it, but your work and my work is about supporting people in facing it. Unless there's a certain amount of support, emotionally and spiritually, people *can't* face it.

AH: Right. I certainly get that, but first, let's look at the other meaning of *unveiling,* because what's also being unveiled is a set of amazing possibilities of creativity that this disaster is opening up. What's being unveiled is what Paul Hawken describes in his magnificent book as "Blessed Unrest." This means millions and millions of different kinds of people are rising up and saying a vast "no" to this terrible system and a great "yes" to the possibility of a wholly new way of doing everything. What's being unveiled is an Occupy Movement that is really a movement of the most extraordinary diversity of people who are coming together and saying, "We cannot and will not support any of this madness any longer. It's got to change, it's got to shift, because we cannot live under this anymore."

What's being unveiled on a higher and perhaps more mystical level is that this death of illusion is potentially the birth of a wholly new kind of humanity that is capable of being transformed enough to cocreate with God a wholly new world.

CB: Well, this is what I say in my work as well; [it] is that we are standing on a threshold, and we have the opportunity to step across that threshold to become a new species—or not.

AH: Everything is in the balance. Everything is lying before us. For those people who are conscious at this time, we have a choice—a choice to go on as we are, and that can only end in the extinction of the human race and the extinction of a great deal of nature. Or to look at the other aspect of this unveiling, to look at the astounding possibilities that are being born—the magic of what is being born—and choose that with our whole being and to start acting out of sacred hope, sacred passion, sacred joy to create a new world. So both are now possible, and everything depends on the level of inner maturity and desperation and sacred passion that a human being brings to this challenge.

CB: Well, I want to say two things about that. First, you're talking about opportunity, and I always sign my copies of *Sacred Demise* that people buy with, "Demise brings opportunity." And you know, you and I both get accused from time to time by folks of being doomers and gloomers. We're told that we're so depressing and so on. And the truth is—what I'm finding in my coaching practice and in my work with people in general is that they are telling me things like, "I've come so alive since I've learned about all these things and since I'm preparing for the future and since I'm making contact with other people who are preparing. I feel so alive." And I've got to tell you, Andrew, it's incredibly—and I'm sure you know—invigorating, and there's such a vibrance when I'm with these people and I'm doing this work. How could we ever get depressed?

AH: Oh I'm not depressed. I've never been more joyful or happy in my life, because I've surrendered to the truth of this process. I've surrendered to the truth of a death/rebirth process. I've surrendered to what I understand to be the divine will for this transformation. I do not believe this culture has a hope in hell of continuing as it is or a hope in heaven. I don't think it will, I don't think it should. This civilization is unsustainable and is going to disintegrate by its own hubris, its own madness, its own exploitation. Do I shrink at the suffering it's going to entail? Of course I do. But do I believe that this is necessary? Yes. Do I believe that it's going to provide a human race with a wholly new set of inner understandings, creativity, passion, compassion? Yes. Does that fill me with joy? Yes. Do I really believe that the divine love is behind all this and will see us through? Yes. Do I think it's going to be incredibly hard, difficult, menacing, painful? Yes, I accept it. What I'm interested in doing is being someone who will help the human race go through the most terrifying and amazing evolutionary shift in its history by giving to it a vision of Sacred Activism which I profoundly believe is the birthing force of the new world.

And what you are doing is showing people that this collapse is inevitable, that the only way of releasing hopeful, creative, vibrant, passionate energy is to accept it and to start preparing for it and to start creating the "inner bunker," as you call it, that will enable us not only to get through it, but to get through it with great creativity, great joy, great coming together—and great capacity to endure unbelievable suffering. All of these things are hard, but they are possible. You know it, and I know it. And the reason why we know it is because we have both been through very, very great suffering, very deep, dark nights, and have learned two things: in that great suffering we are accompanied by the great spirit, by the mystery; and through that great suffering, a clearing of the false self is made so as to enable the birth of a wholly new level of consciousness, which is a consciousness of love and action. And this is why you're hopeful and why I'm hopeful, and this is why our work is actually a work of releasing those energies of creativity that are only kept depressed and paralyzed by denial. Denial is our enemy; apathy is our enemy, but accepting the truth of this appalling and amazing process is our deepest friend.

CB: And I wanted to say, because you were mentioning the word *maturity* to talk about how we have to be prepared for this emotionally and spiritually, so I want to talk about what you and I have been talking about all weekend with folks in our workshop, which is the whole notion of initiation. In this culture we don't hear that word very often, except maybe in reference to fraternity hazings. But in indigenous cultures, it's a common word, and it's a process in which young people are taken usually out into nature where they need to experience some ordeal. The purpose of that is not because the culture is sadistic, but in order to take them to the edge of a near-death experience so that the young people will find out what's really inside of them and in the process, really be remade. There's never any guarantee that they will survive it, sometimes they don't, but that's the risk the culture feels is necessary to take.

AH: And to get people real and humble enough to cooperate with the dance of life, instead of believing that they can impose their own will upon the dance of life, which is far beyond their powers to control.

CB: Absolutely. And then the young person is more integrated into the culture, they become more involved in the culture and the village, and they mature into elderhood. And I really want to emphasize that notion of elderhood, because an elder is a steward of the culture. They are there to support the younger people and to support everybody in the community in living according to the indigenous traditions and in harmony with the earth. And so I like to say that we are going through a *planetary initiation,* and it's for the purpose of our maturing emotionally and spiritually; it's for the purpose of ending this notion of separation. And it is for the purpose of our becoming elders and stewards of the earth and of the culture. Whatever sacred, harmonious, life-supporting, loving, truthful, beautiful—that will come out of the collapse of industrial civilization, we must be there to steward, support, and give more life to. We cannot do that unless we begin preparing now, emotionally and spiritually, to be such an elder.

AH: And if you think of the Indian goddess, Kali, She's presented in the most terrifying, ferocious shape, but actually, if you go behind the image, She's gold. So the disaster that we're living through is terrifying, but it's terrifying in order to liberate us from the sicknesses we don't even know we have—an addiction to power and domination, an addiction to separation, all of which seem to be offering us an amazing life, but actually are imprisoning us in a lethal, suicidal, matricidal, communal ego, and what this process is, is a process of liberation. A liberation through destruction, a creation through annihilation. A rebirth through death. A resurrection through crucifixion.

And this is the essential process of the entire universe. This is the real process of evolution. So an elder's role is to hold that paradox with serenity, with joy, knowing that that process mirrors the universal process, mirrors the evolutionary process, and ends not in an extinction but in a beginning of a wholly new kind of reality.

CB: And what I want to say, and what you and I have both been saying all weekend, is that *anybody* who is waking up to this

A Conversation with Carolyn Baker

reality—who is reading about it, watching documentaries, talking about it, getting involved in preparation—any of those folks, no matter how old they are, are truly becoming elders of this process, this ability to hold this collapse.

AH: I've been so amazed by the people I've met in Occupy Vancouver and other Occupy movements. It's not the older people who are now making a difference, it's the twenty-three- and twenty-four-year-olds, who know perfectly well that this system is doomed. And yet, they are not in despair, but feel that this is an amazing opportunity to start inventing a world based on compassion, on justice, and on a new version of leadership, and based on true stewardship of the earth. And these people are also potentially our elders, aren't they?

CB: Well, absolutely, and I always say that elderhood has nothing to do with age. It has to do with wisdom. And I often say that we all know people in their 80s and 90s who aren't very wise and may actually be foolish, and they're looking back on their lives with great regret, and by the same token, we know many young people who are absolutely wise beyond their years. We stand in awe of them, like the young people involved in the Occupy movement.

AH: I was awed and moved to my core and cried and cried, because here I was seeing the Divine speaking through these ragged young men and women who just know that this is the time to birth a new world.

CB: Absolutely.

AH: Let's talk about what denial in this situation creates. Because when you talk about us being accused of doom and gloom, it is so boring, because what we both want to say is, "Welcome to the joy that is released when you accept the situation. You're talking about us as if we were apocalyptic doom merchants when, in fact, what we're trying to do is to initiate you as elders into the joy that comes from surrendering to the divine evolutionary process. That is the only real joy, and that can transform everything.

CB: I would like people to google an article that I wrote for the website Collapse Network (www.collapsenet.com) in 2010 called "The Joy of Preparation." I write a regular column there twice a month called "Collapsing Consciously." One of the things I stress in the article is the tremendous joy of people coming together and looking at this together. It's similar to the experience of watching a movie with someone else rather than just watching it by yourself. When you watch the move alone, you have one kind of experience, but when you watch it with someone else, you have a different experience.

But back to denial. Denial is deadening.

AH: Deadening and constricting and paralyzing and keeps people slaves of the very death machine that is destroying everything. We have three forms of denial in our world. We have the denial of the corporate military industrial complex that believes that its orgy of greed will go on forever just because it wants [it] to. We have the denial of the institutional religions—the belief that they've been given some mandate from God to keep their idiotic dogmas going forever and ever. And we have the denial of the New Age, which is grounded in a fundamental stupidity about the nature of the Divine. It's all about light, light, light, and love, which totally ignores the dance of opposites that is the essence of the Divine's manifestation in reality. So those three kinds of denial are incredibly powerful, because the whole of our culture is actually created out of an endless copulation between those three kinds of denial.

The corporate industrial complex gives us a completely fictitious dream of endless progress. The religions give us a completely fictitious dream of salvation through their mediation, which allows for all of this darkness to keep going on and the illusion that "all will be well." And the New Age gives us another fictitious dream that if we just sit quietly and vibrate what we imagine as love, the oil slick in the Gulf will clear away. Suddenly, miraculously, the forest will be healed—all of which is a psychotic evasion of the actual nature of this appalling crisis—and also an evasion of the incredible possibilities that come when you embrace this crisis.

So denial is overwhelmingly powerful. We're talking about something that is paralyzing the sacred energies of transformation in our culture. And you and I are absolutely with helping people to see the greatest paradox of all, which is that when you stop denying the crisis in its fullest and loudest and most intense urgency, [that] is the very moment when you start to experience inside yourself a wholly new level of hope and energy and possibility. And then you can prepare an inner container strong enough to contain that. And then you can get together with other people to share this preparation with.

CB: I love that notion of preparing an inner container. You know, so many people who are consciously preparing for collapse are doing so logistically—storing food, water, medical supplies, learning skills for living in a postindustrial world, and so on. But so very often they miss the importance of preparing the inner container. Sometimes I lead people in workshops in a visualization of what the crisis might look like at its worst. I take them into some pretty tough scenes of demise, and then when they come back from the visualization, I ask them to journal about what specific emotions they felt during the visualization. I then give them the opportunity to share in the large group what they felt and what they wrote. Without exception, people are enormously surprised by what they felt and how powerful their feelings were. I then ask them, "Do you think that the amount of food and water you've stored, the skills you've learned, the logistical preparation you've made is going to carry you through this emotional gauntlet that you have just visualized running?" Naturally, no one ever says that they believe that logistical preparation will prepare them for the emotional toll. Through this process, they realize how crucial it is to build a strong emotional container for the crisis.

I want to go back to denial for a moment and just emphasize that while we give it a lot of bad press, denial is one of our human nervous system's defense mechanisms, and in certain cases, we need denial in order to just survive, but we are now at a point in human history where we can no longer afford the luxury of denial, and we cannot keep saying, "I can't look at this." As you say, we have to create the container in people and help them create it for themselves, which will allow them to look. You can't look at this without support. Although I do know people who have. I know people who have sat in their houses by themselves for many months doing nothing but researching collapse, and were absolutely appalled and overwhelmed, then they went out and found other people to talk about this with, but I don't recommend doing that. We really need to be able to dialogue about this with other people and get support for creating that container.

AH: So how do we create the container that you call in your book, *Navigating the Coming Chaos,* "the internal bunker"? I think both of us have visions about this, but I'd love to know what your vision is. How do you advise people to start creating within themselves the kind of spiritual strength, the kind of inner bunker that can help them to look without illusion at the death and the rebirth?

CB: *Navigating the Coming Chaos* is filled with tools for inner preparation. First, we have to begin to turn our attention more from the outer to the inner. We live in a culture that says "out there, out there." Everything is "out there." The way we solve these problems is to get a new president. Or technology, which is out there, will save us. Or organic farming or going completely solar is going to do it. But we need now to be turning our attention inward to what's "in here." There are many practices that you and I both recommend that help us do that. Journaling, meditation, contact with nature—just being out in nature by oneself. And even though that's an external experience, it evokes that in us that resonates with nature, because, in fact, we *are* nature.

Another is paying attention to our feelings. In our workshop today and last night, we helped people with feeling things like grief, fear, anger, despair, regarding what's happening in the world, and they were able to do that in a safe place with the support of us and each other. And you and I have said many times how transformative it is to be able to work consciously with these emotions and allow them to take us to that "something greater" that is sacred within ourselves, which is the only thing that can help us emotionally and spiritually to get through all of this.

AH: And that's the horrible stupidity of denial—it actually prevents us from getting to our core richness. Because the things that we fear most—grief, fear, anger, and despair—turn out to be, when we truly work with them, within the sacred container, to be initiations into the deepest sacred presence of the Divine in us.

CB: And joy ...

AH: Yes, and joy! Grief takes us to compassion, which takes us to the joy of service. Fear makes us real about the situation, which galvanizes our energy, which provides the joy for action. Anger awakens our sense of justice and truth and the necessity of putting justice into action, which galvanizes our energy to start getting together to do something real about what's potentially destroying everything. And despair is the best corrosive agent for dissolving illusion, which releases us to be agents of reality. And when you really get those sacred transformations through those sacred paradoxes, denial is not only fantastically stupid, but it's also something that aborts the joy, the hope in the name of joy and hope!

The people who are promulgating denial are saying that we're the doom merchants, and what we have to say to them is, "You, by keeping us trapped in illusion, are actually preventing us from discovering the enormous, creative, sacred, joyful powers that could totally transform this situation."

CB: Yes, and some people say, "I don't want to get too involved in any particular emotion, because I'm afraid I'll get stuck there." For example, they may say, "I'm afraid that if I start crying or start feeling the grief, it will never stop." What I always say is that the word *emotion* has the word *motion* in it, which means that things will flow and move and change to something else, so you're not going to get stuck in grief forever. It's going to move into something else. And you know, emotions are an energy field. But in the West what we've done is compartmentalize them. Grief is in this box; anger is in this one; fear is in another box; despair in yet another. But the truth is that they are *all* connected. An energy field is an energy field.

AH: And in a disaster like ours, all of those energies are going to be connected. But they're essential, because the birth of a new human possibility cannot take place except by destruction of the old. And it can't take place except through a transformation of consciousness, which can only come from the human ego confronting its appalling limits. And this is what the crisis, which is designed with an almost amazingly ruthless beauty, can do for us. Because everything that we have believed in through the collective human ego—all the "isms," such as socialism, capitalism, and so on—are all going to be shown to be games of the mind and not revelations of the heart.

CB: And the answer is not another "ism."

AH: The answer is a transformation of consciousness put into sacred action by all of us together on a global level. And this is emerging— we see it emerging. Paul Hawken identified it in *Blessed Unrest,* Occupy is now manifesting it, however chaotically—it always begins chaotically. The reception that my work on Sacred Activism has had has proven to me that there are people who already know what I'm trying to say. You, Carolyn, have been bringing through this vision of collapse, and you know that although the audiences are not huge now, [you] had a day today in Denver in which almost every aspect of this culture—politicians, social workers, dancers—people from every conceivable group were there, and they are waking up. This new humanity is forming right now, and we're shaken, we're fragile, we need each other, we need each other's wisdom, but we're not despairing. We're really trying, with all our flaws and follies, to get together and invent something new in the middle of all of this. This, to me, is incredibly and radiantly hopeful.

CB: Well, one of the things you talk about in your work, and I'm right there with you, is the shadow. And I'd like to introduce our discussion of the shadow by telling a little story. As you know, I'm a storyteller, and I usually tell stories with my drum, but I don't have my drum at the moment, so I'll tell the story without the drum.

One of the stories I frequently tell is a Native American story and it goes like this.

> Once upon a time … people knew that there was a cave somewhere in this land, and that in that cave, there was an old woman who was weaving away, making the most beautiful garment that has ever been made in the world. Even now they say that cave exists, and even though there are highways going in every direction, and even though all of them seem to be full of cars and those roads are filled with people, and despite the fact that everyone seems to have an SUV and they even go off-road, tracking this way and that, for some reason, no one finds that cave. But the old ones say that cave exists, and in that cave there's an old woman weaving that beautiful garment. She's making a trim for it, elegant and beautiful, in order to finish it. And because she wants it to be the best it can be, she's making it out of porcupine quills, and in order to weave them, she has to flatten them, and in order to flatten them, she has to bite them down with her teeth, and she's been

biting down on porcupine quills for so many years—for maybe hundreds, maybe thousands of years that her teeth have been worn down to stubs that barely appear above the surface of the gums. And still she keeps biting down on the quills and weaving the trim of the garment.

She does it constantly and only once in a while stops, and when she stops, she goes to the great cauldron that is in the cave, and when she goes to that cauldron, she stirs the soup that is in it—the soup that she has been making from all of the herbs, and all of the plants and grains and everything good that grows on the earth [are] in this great cauldron. And if she doesn't stir it once in a while, it will burn, and many things will turn out badly, so she stirs it, and because she's so old and tired from all that she's been doing, she moves very slowly over to the cauldron, and stirs the thing very slowly. And while she is stirring the cauldron, the black dog that is also in the cave goes over to the garment that she has been weaving and unravels everything that she has done so that when she finishes stirring the soup that has everything in it, she has to begin the weaving of the garment all over again.

Now some people say that black dog is the cause of all the trouble in the world, and if that black dog would just stop interrupting the weaving of the old woman of the world, everything would be fine, but the elders say [that] if that black dog ever stops unraveling things, if this world ever loses the trouble that is in it, and the garment is completed, then that will be the end of the world and everything in it. That is to say, it is the unraveling that keeps everything going. It is the trouble that keeps the beauty being made. It is the taking apart that causes the old woman to begin making the world again, over and over again.

Now there is no proof that the elders are seeing this in the most meaningful way, but tell me this: if the elders don't know the answer to this, who does?

Now we notice that the old woman in the story didn't complain or curse, she just accepted that the garment had unraveled and that it needed to be woven again. Some people say that we should get rid of the black dog of trouble, but the black dog of trouble is very important in the unraveling. As a matter of fact, our friend Malidoma Somé of the Dagara tribe of West Africa says that in his tribe they don't try to get rid of trouble. What they say is, "Make sure you're in the *right* trouble." So this is a story about the shadow and how we actually need the shadow for this remaking.

AH: Without the shadow or the crucifixion, there is no resurrection. The shadow is now erupting in this immense crisis, not to destroy us potentially, but to help us accommodate the revelations that only the shadow can give. Because only the shadow can reveal to you that your ego is mad.

CB: Well, some people may not know what the shadow is. I'll give you my definition. It's anything in ourselves that we send away and say, "That's not me." So we might say, "Well, I'm not a greedy person like the person on Wall Street." Well, actually there is a part of us that is greedy, and if we dig deep enough, we'll find it. Or we might say, "I'm not a dishonest person, I always tell the truth." But paradoxically, if we really are honest, we find that there is some dishonesty somewhere in us.

AH: Well, those are relatively harmless flaws, but you really have to find your serial killer, your prostitute, your unbelievably perverted side, and we all have all of it. And it's only when you understand that and accept it and are deeply, deeply humbled by it, that you become truly open to transformative divine mercy and grace.

CB: And every person and every institution has a shadow. So as we've seen, with the Catholic Church, it has presented this beautiful appearance but behind it, as we are now discovering, which is part of the unveiling, is a long history of child sexual abuse.

The Suffering of Love

AH: Well what about fundamentalism? You were brought up in fundamentalism. Look at the homophobia, crucifixion of women, how much browbeating, lying—and look at Islam!

CB: Any kind of fundamentalism.

AH: And we're all fundamentalists until we're not. I think that's one of the most frightening realizations, because the most difficult thing for me to accept is that I'm a fundamentalist until the shadow in me is fully acknowledged and worked on with great grace and mercy. And it's a very shaming realization.

So there is no way out, especially in a crisis like this, of confronting the fundamental shadows of the collective ego and of the personal ego. We have to do it, but it's best done together, isn't it?

CB: Yes, and the way out is through—and through together.

AH: And how would you define "through together"?

CB: Well, by not staying alone with these awarenesses, [but by] coming together as we did today in this workshop, where you are with people who have the same awareness and they're on the same page, who have this passion about preparing themselves emotionally and spiritually, as well as logistically, who really get what is at stake. And through dialogue, and through really supporting each other, we can walk out the door and say, "I'm not alone, I just met thirty new friends, and I know that we're on this journey together."

AH: One thing that's very intimidating in this culture in this terminal period of the American Nightmare/Dream is that the prevailing culture is dictating one whole illusion that permeates almost every aspect of life. So the ones who are waking up feel incredibly outnumbered and incredibly alone. So what you and I are both doing are providing places for those who are awakening to come to.

The first thing we did in the room this morning was to ask people to be silent and look around at the people in the room and notice the great difference of the people in the room and then to consider that the person sitting next to you in the plane or the person you're walking past on the street, might very well be another person who is having these thoughts, who is having this awakening, and who knows that we're in the endgame of this culture and that something new is beginning.

And that by creating this kind of community, what we're doing is awakening an alternative world, a world that has nothing to do with the prevailing folly, because it is beginning to see in each other's eyes the elements of a new beginning. It's amazing.

CB: It is. Nothing I have ever done is more invigorating.

AH: Well, you know that you're doing the work you were born to do. I know I'm doing the work I was born to do. I don't know whether we'll help the human race to get through to this new stage. I don't know whether the human race is going to commit suicide or choose divine transformation. I don't think God knows. I do know that if you turn up doing your part, you will be joyful. You will be filled with passion, with energy—you will meet incredible friends. You will dance with them, and you will try your best to create a whole new way of being and doing everything. So in a sense, the birth is already taking place. In these meetings—in the pain, grief, joy, hunger, and longing—and this is very amazing, and this is the key.

CB: Well, there's one more thing I want to add that I emphasize in all my writing and workshops, and that's this: it's really, really important at this time to create beauty. To create art, music, dance, and so on. It's one reason I do the drumming and storytelling. Anything that is right-brained and anything that expresses beauty is so important now, because that allows a balance between all that we see in the external world that is disheartening and the hideous ugliness of this collapse

475

and that which expresses the sacred within us. To create beauty is a holy act, and we as elders should be doing it every moment.

AH: Well I couldn't agree with you more, because in the Koran it says, "God is beauty and loves the beautiful." And anyone who's ever had a mystical experience of any kind is overwhelmed by the unbelievable beauty of the Transcendent, and when you awaken to that, you see that beauty everywhere—in human beings and hummingbirds, rocks, leaves—you hear it in Mozart and Beethoven, and you know that that beauty is what fortifies. Beauty is the fuel of the passion that transforms the planet in the name of compassion and justice, because compassion is beautiful. Justice is beautiful. Forgiveness is so beautiful that it tears your heart out and makes you cry at its beauty. Beauty is the thread that links all these sacred enterprises. And that's why I think Rumi is coming back so strongly at this time. Because if there is a king of beauty, it is him. What, for me, Rumi does is to create in words what Shah Jahan did in the Taj Mahal, which was to bring together the most beautiful things in the whole world and just create something so staggeringly beautiful as a celebration of life. Rumi is creating a Taj Mahal of the most utmost, intense beauty, and that's why he's coming back in such force everywhere. Everybody has been reading him, and everybody is getting the perfume of the beauty of divine love and of the presence to inebriate us to make us wise, brave, and fearlessly passionate enough to set about the re-creation of the world through divine grace.

CB: Well I use all kinds of poetry in my work, as you know, but Rumi's a big one. All of these things we're talking about—drumming, storytelling, art, music, dance, poetry—these all get us into the right brain, and they get us into our bodies. Someone said today in the workshop that the body is really the corridor to go deep into the soul. It's a corridor for us to really go into the internal bunker. So I do a lot of work in my workshops with helping people get into the body.

A Conversation with Carolyn Baker

AH: Well, it's not just getting into the body being the corridor to this presence, it is that the deepest meaning of this crisis is that what this crisis is designed by the Divine to do is to shatter our dissociation from the body, because it's our dissociation from the body that is enabling us to murder the body of the planet. If we loved our own bodies and saw the body as sacred and would experience the sacred *in* the body, how could we let two billion people starve? How could we create situations that are insuring the death of all the animal species? How could we pollute the body of the seas? How could we rape nature? We would be absolutely aghast beyond belief at this desecration, this blasphemy of the sacred body of the world. So getting back into the body, honoring and loving the body, celebrating the divine presence in the body, and celebrating the divine presence in the body's appetites—such as sexuality, touching your friends, and *being* with other beings—these are the keys to the awakening that can birth a divine, embodied humanity.

And that's why I love your work so much, and one of the reasons why I *really* love it so much is because you bring together what I think are the four ingredients of this birth of the Divine, embodied humanity. The first is to get real about where we are and realize that we are in a death/rebirth process and to surrender to it and to accept it and to let it teach us. The second is to do real shadow work, because the shadow is the body for us, and without accepting how we've tortured and desecrated our bodies, dissociated from our bodies and the bodies of others, we'll never get through this crisis, and we'll only continue to perpetuate it. The third thing you bring through your work that I love so much is inspiration of the arts, music, all the things we've been talking about, because without inspiration, we will never get drunk enough on the beauty of God and the beauty of compassion and justice to be fearless enough to do this work. And the fourth thing is to really face the necessity of body work, body love, body connection, so as to enable this bringing down of the light into our illumined mind, into our open heart, and into our loving, compassionate, justice-making bodies.

477

CB: Yes, I even have a chapter in *Navigating the Coming Chaos* on "The Eros of Collapse."

AH: What do you mean by that?

CB: Well, I talk about connection, relationship—that we find eros in relationship. That there is tremendous pleasure in this connecting with each other around preparation, around simplifying our lives, around all the things we need to do to be more present and to be really prepared emotionally, spiritually, logistically, on every level.

AH: So many of my friends when I was growing up were people who had been through World War 2, and they said that terrible though the circumstances were, they never had a better time, because they were with people, facing death all the time, and you cut through the nonsense, and you got down to love. You got down to friendship, you got down to real sexual communication on a deep level, you got down to sharing, without the blah, blah, blah. What we've created in our pursuit of pleasure and money and power is a horribly lonely, isolated, atomized culture, which is killing us all and boring us all to death and preventing hardly any real communication. People sit in their mansions watching things on television and computer screens, not really relating. And what everybody I know who's been through any kind of deep shattering, especially with other people, finds is that that releases whole new energies of relationship and communication, which are the foundations of great creativity. And this is what is going to happen to us and is happening right now, and we're living proof that it's happening. And the people we meet, who come to our events, who want to really face this with us, give me such incredible hope that this is really fermenting a renaissance. But it's not a renaissance that's going to be built through denial or pretending that facing grief and other dark emotions is negative. It's only going to be built through love.

A Conversation with Carolyn Baker

CB: Well, we're running out of time, but if I may, I'd like to conclude with a poem by the great contemporary female poet Rashani who writes:

> *There is a brokenness out of which come the unbroken,*
> *A shatteredness out of which blooms the unshatterable.*
> *There is a sorrow beyond all grief which leads to joy.*
> *And a fragility out of whose depths emerges strength.*
> *There is a hollow space, too vast for words, through which*
> *We pass with each loss, out of whose darkness we are*
> *Sanctioned into being.*
> *There is a cry deeper than all sound whose serrated edges*
> *Cut the heart as we break open to the place inside that is*
> *Unbreakable and whole,*
> *While learning to sing.*

Chapter Seven

The Power of Love—Becoming a Sacred Activist in Service of Self, Other, the Planet, and the Divine

Introduction

Only a global, grassroots, sacredly inspired movement of love in action can possibly be of any use now. Such a movement will not be able to prevent the coming collapse of the industrial civilization, but it will accomplish two related, crucial tasks. First, it will mobilize, educate, and refine the special forces needed for the evolutionary leap that humanity must take in order to survive. Second, only such a group of dedicated, fearless sacred activists—human beings who fuse together the deepest stamina and wisdom with radical action—can begin to create the social and spiritual structures that can survive the storms of destruction, which are now both necessary and inevitable.

Nothing is clearer to me than this and nothing in our current orgy of denial, addiction, and dissociation is more difficult to get across to others. The illusions that the collective, hubristic false self has spun out of its dark passion for the exploitation of nature, the illusion of extreme narcissistic entitlement and worship of the false religions of science and technology are now so seeded in us that they rule our minds, institutions, corporations and media. Tunneling out of these illusions for the great majority of humanity is now all but impossible. This is why the Divine now has no other choice than to bring down, in Rumi's words, "the burning sword of justice, the sword soaked in dawn."

We have brought this ferocious cleansing upon ourselves. We have only ourselves to blame. Every possible divine grace and inspiring message about the lethal shadow of our communal addiction to power has been given us. We continue to torment the earth in sick, blind denial of our responsibility as the divinely appointed guardians and servants of life. Kali has already begun to dance. The thunder of

Her dancing echoes in the ears of those who dare to hear it. She will continue to dance, wilder and wilder, until Her dream of a transfigured human race is birthed.

No one can know what this appalling and amazing process will look like or exactly how it will unfold. As the Koran makes clear in surah 6, "With God are the keys of the unseen. No one knows them but God." What we can know, and must face squarely, without the illusion of magical thinking, is that the birth will have to take place in a humanity brought to the edge of extinction and in a nature brought to the edge by the fires of greed.

Terrible though it is to face such a scenario, it can be done in the heart and mind that has been prepared by the mystery of the dark night and the resurrection it unfolds. There are three kinds of human beings on the planet at this moment. The great majority, who are in denial and becoming more and more frantic, dissociated, soulless, heartless, and disconnected in a twittering, media-manipulated world spinning into madness. A small group starting to awaken, but in scared retreat at what they see. These people sink into false comfort with New Age metaphysics, transcendent addiction, or desperate worship of technological and social solutions, which aim to keep alive the very civilization that is destined to die. Thirdly, there is a far smaller group of people who have been seared by their own individual dark nights into an acceptance of the ruthlessness of the divine evolutionary process. They have learned to embrace an all-saving and all-grounding faith in the resurrection and divine embodiment, because the birth is happening, against great odds, in them.

My work is directed to those in the third group. The first group will continue to believe the lies of a collapsing civilization and shrink from the scalding truth, demonizing those who are compelled to tell it as doom-merchants, maniacs, or worse. The second group, in my experience, has already been driven by latent terror into such an adamant love of magical thinking that only total crisis can possibly begin to bring them to their senses. It is in the third group, the ones who have been shattered open, that the hope for the birth lives and grows. Anguish and revelation have prepared them to be willing to risk everything and to trust, bless, and accept divine ferocity as they do the grueling work to stay grounded in peace and inspired by divine passion.

This third group is the sacred activists, those who know that in a situation as finally extreme as this, nothing will work but an inner transformation, which must express itself in outer, radical action. Fortunately, through divine grace, there may be just enough of us for the birth to be accomplished. I say "may," because only time will tell. False optimism and cheerleading rhetoric is now as useless as passive, despairing pessimism. Those of us who are beginning to see the reality of where we are must now take the greatest of all adventures into divine embodiment and the transformative action that flows from it. Let the chips fall where they may. The fish who leapt out of the toxic sea into a totally unfamiliar dimension and struggled for a long time in it did not know they were going to evolve into birds. Now those of us who long to be midwives of the birth have to leap into the darkness of the mystery, have to learn to trust it unconditionally and have to gamble our whole beings and lives away for the glory of divine love.

If we do learn how to gamble in this abandoned, radiant, naked way—giving up any desire for specialness or special protection, renouncing all the fruits of our continued action to the Divine—what we will be given in return by the Beloved is the wine of radical peace and radical passion and the increasingly astounding experience of knowing the Divine is transforming our hearts, minds, and bodies.

I have found this gift of divine life not only to be enough, but to be a miracle, which constantly brings me to my knees in awed gratitude and constantly inspires me to dive into being more completely, so as to flow out in wiser, more refined and effective radical action. It is my prayer for you who are reading this and for all those on the same evolutionary journey in the world, that this book, and the ragged wisdom in it, will inspire you to evolve and journey on with great peaceful fervor, giving away everything to the transformation of humanity. "You have been weak as milk," Rumi wrote. "Now become jungle lions."

The rest is in God's hands.

Andrew Harvey

"The Ordinary Decency of the Heart"
Interview with Andrew Lawler

"This building makes me drunk," Andrew Harvey says. We're standing in the middle of Frank Lloyd Wright's Unity Temple, a century-old experiment in sacred architecture in the wealthy Chicago suburb of Oak Park. Autumn light pours through the glass ceiling onto cream walls, dark wood, and muted carpet. The temple has the solemn simplicity of a Zen shrine or a New England meetinghouse. It was this project, Wright said, that made him realize the heart of a building is its space rather than its walls. "I love this man," Harvey says. "This is unity consciousness."

Harvey is a renegade in the world of the sacred. An Englishman raised in India, he has spent much of his life attempting to unite the spiritual traditions of East and West. And like the brilliant but acerbic Wright, he has stirred his share of controversy. In his book *Sun at Midnight,* Harvey attacks the guru system as corrupt, using his own former teacher, Mother Meera, as an example. His openness about being gay has rattled many in the largely closeted religious world, and he has even taken the Dalai Lama to task for his stance on homosexuality. Harvey has little patience with what he calls the popular "vulgarization" of ancient spiritual traditions, from yoga and tantra to Buddhism and Christianity. He says, "A lot of people prefer the marzipan mysticism of the New Age," which predicts that a change in consciousness will occur by "good vibrations."

With his unruly hair, British accent, and engaging manner, Harvey seems more enthusiastic schoolboy than spiritual bête noire. Though fifty-five years old, he charges through Wright's masterpiece with youthful vitality. Afterward we walk back to his cozy third-floor apartment, which he calls "my treehouse." Adorning the walls are a Black Madonna from Venice, a Tibetan *tanka* tapestry, and a page from a Persian manuscript.

Harvey's curiosity about faiths of all sorts began when he was a boy living in India, which had then only recently shaken off the yoke of British colonialism. Though sectarian violence wracked the nation, Harvey describes his household as having been a place of tolerance, where "everyone felt free to worship in whatever way they wanted." His English parents were tolerant Protestants; his Catholic nurse imbued him with a love of Mary; the Hindu servants would take him to their temple to hear stories of Krishna; and the family's Muslim driver spoke of the greatness of Allah. One night, after his parents had left for a dinner party, six-year-old Andrew sat on the balcony and watched as their inebriated cook played a small drum until he was drenched with sweat, then began to chant in a strange tongue. Intrigued and frightened, young Andrew asked the man if he was all right. The cook explained that he was thanking God. "God is everything," he said. "God is everywhere." It dawned on Harvey then: "I could be with God directly and talk to God directly whenever I wanted to." He also concluded that each person in his multicultural house was worshiping the same God.

Harvey spent his school years in England, eventually attending Oxford University, where he studied the theme of madness in Shakespeare and Erasmus and at twenty-one became the youngest fellow ever admitted to Oxford's All Souls College, a prestigious humanities research institution. Though his intellect was well-fed, Harvey felt alone, despairing, and even suicidal. In 1977 he left Oxford to return to India, and found his way to the remote Himalayan region of Ladakh, where he met Tibetan Buddhist sage Thuksey Rinpoche. Harvey's book about the experience, *A Journey in Ladakh,* won critical acclaim for its portrayal of one of the last traditional Tibetan Buddhist societies.

Harvey then moved to Paris and began an exploration of Sufism—the mystical tradition of Islam—and the poems of thirteenth-century mystic Jalal-ud-Din Rumi. This led him to write *The Way of Passion*, in which he describes Rumi's work as "strange, fabulous, ornate, baroque, and tremendously mysterious." Other works on Rumi followed. Along the way Harvey became an ardent follower of Mother Meera, an Indian woman he heralded as an incarnation of the Divine. He broke with her in 1993, after she asked him to forsake his male lover. (This point is disputed by Mother Meera's supporters.) Since then Harvey has denounced her and other gurus as phonies more concerned with money, sex, and power than with matters of the spirit.

Shortly before his father's death in 1997, Harvey had a mystical experience of Christ that renewed his fascination with Jesus and Mary. He took a provocative look at Jesus as a radical mystic in *Son of Man* and explored the Divine Feminine in *Return of the Mother*.

Having encountered the limitations of both gurus and romantic love (he is no longer with the man he married in 1994), Harvey is devoting himself to melding spiritual disciplines with activist efforts in order to promote peace and justice. He calls the concept "Sacred Activism" and envisions "an army of practical visionaries and active mystics who work in every field and in every arena to transform the world." His vision is wildly ambitious and at times feels both messianic and apocalyptic. But sitting at a Frank Lloyd Wright–designed table in his living room and listening to him describe Sacred Activism's potential, I found his enthusiasm hard to resist.

Andrew Lawler: Why are you so critical of organized religions, including even their mystical aspects?

Andrew Harvey: Religions keep alive fantasies and dogmas, and what passes for mystical instruction most of the time is folly. There is a horrific way in which people use spirituality to sign off from the ordinary decency of the heart. I've been walking with famous Sufis who tell me I'm crazy for stopping and talking with beggars on the street. One said, "Why are you giving that beggar money? He's just going to drink with it." I said my responsibility was to help, and the beggar's responsibility was to look after himself. I couldn't force him to spend the money on food, but I also couldn't pass the man and not give him something. If you're not capable of being gracious and recognizing the pain another person is in, you're not a spiritual practitioner.

AL: How did your parents come to live in India?

AH: My father's family went to India in the 1820s, and my mother's family moved there in the 1920s. My mother still lives in south India, in a little cottage surrounded by jacaranda trees filled with monkeys, and she runs a charity for disabled children. I asked her recently what she was going to do on her eightieth birthday, and she said she was going to throw a party for the children. She has a huge heart.

My father had a deep sense of justice. He was a police officer and was in the Imperial Service Order as a young man. I went to see him when he was dying in 1997. We hadn't ever quarreled, but we'd lived such different lives. When we spoke about Jesus, however, I realized he was a mystic: he trusted absolutely, surrendered, and prayed every day. He had never told me any of this, because men don't talk about that sort of thing. I realized that I'd been roaming the world, looking for sages, and there had been a real sage right there at home, reading the *Daily Telegraph,* and I had missed him. But I didn't miss him in the end. I think my father's sense of justice and service, combined with my mother's wild heart, is what has given me my passion.

AL: How did your father's death renew your connection to Christ?

AH: On the Sunday before he died, I went to church. It was the Feast of Christ the King, and this roly-poly Indian priest gave a simple sermon in which he said that Christ is the mystical king of the world, not because of his miracles, but because he sacrificed everything and he loved and believed beyond reason. When the priest had finished speaking, I looked up at the crucifix, and it came alive.

There was this torrential flow of molten fire between Jesus and me. I can only describe what happened as: he took a knife and slashed open my heart. I felt I was going to die, because of the ferocious violence of his love. It was ecstatic and blissful, and it was terror itself. I saw Jesus in his glory, but still with the wounds, because the awakened state contains the shattered state. You're not sprung free of wound and heartbreak; rather, they are deepened but contained within a vaster consciousness.

Then I went outside, and there was this desperate young man with no legs and no arms, and I looked into his eyes and saw the same Christ that I had seen on the cross. I lifted him out of the puddle, gave him whatever money I had, and made sure he got some help. As I was staring at him, I heard this terrifying voice say, "You've been playing with your mystical experiences. You have used your grace to inflate your own ego, to write books, and to become famous. Don't you understand that this is obscene? You must do everything you can to speak up for those who have no voice and to rouse people to divine service. You have to give yourself over to that."

It was scalding. I felt seen, stripped naked, but also inspired and empowered.

AL: Was that the start of your concept of Sacred Activism?

AH: That was the beginning. I've always loved that quotation by French Jesuit Teilhard de Chardin: "Someday, after mastering the winds, the waves, the tides, and gravity, we shall harness for God the energies of love, and then, for a second time in the history of the world, man will have discovered fire." Sacred Activism is the fusion of the mystic's passion for God with the activist's passion for justice, creating a third fire, which is the burning sacred heart that longs to help, preserve, and nurture every living thing.

AL: So mysticism alone is not enough? It must merge with activism?

AH: All mystical systems are addicted to transcending this reality. This addiction is part of the reason why the world is being destroyed. The monotheistic religions honor an off-planet God and would sacrifice this world and its attachments to the adoration of that God. But the God I met was both immanent and transcendent. This world is not an illusion, and the philosophies that say it is are half-baked half-truths. In an authentic mystical experience, the world does disappear and reveal itself as the dance of the divine consciousness. But then it reappears, and you see that everything you are looking at is God, and everything you're touching is God. This vision completely shatters you.

We are so addicted, either to materialism or to transcending material reality, that we don't see God right in front of us, in the beggar, the starving child, the brokenhearted woman, in our friend, in the cat, in the flea. We miss it, and in missing it, we allow the world to be destroyed.

AL: How does a mystic become an activist? It seems an oxymoron.

AH: The mystics as we know them will be praying as the last tree is cut down. They are junkies of ecstasy and bliss, and they're hooked into their own self-created mystical experiences. There are too many bliss bunnies running around presenting the Divine as a kind of cabaret singer in hot pants, available for any kind of fantasy you may have. Then there are the activists, who are noble and righteous and give their lives to their cause, but they are divided in consciousness. They demonize others and often burn out. Neither mystic nor activist balances transcendence and immanence, heart and mind, soul and body, presence and action.

AL: But don't many traditions—from Christianity to twelve-step programs—consider service a spiritual necessity?

AH: Yes, it's essential to all the major traditions, from Buddhism to Judaism. In Hinduism it's what the self does when it recognizes itself in all reality. In shamanism, being in tune with nature leads to serving all living beings. Service is the central message of Christianity, though it's been lost for the most part.

Sacred Activism isn't anything new, but we need to bring an urgency and intensity to this message at this moment, because there is a worldwide addiction to money and power and a worldwide depression that affects even people who claim to be religious but have secretly given up on the human race.

Service, as it's usually understood, is not going to be enough. Working at soup kitchens, helping stray animals, looking after old women, sitting by the deathbeds of young men who are dying of AIDS—all these are honorable actions, but we have to go farther. What's required now is inspired, radical action on every level.

AL: Can a mayor, a congressperson, a CEO of a major corporation be a sacred activist?

AH: If that person is prepared to do some dangerous and disruptive things, yes. I don't think a CEO could be a sacred activist if his or her company was strip-mining or spreading toxic waste. A sacred activist would risk everything to transform those policies.

AL: If we want to move beyond the idea of individual service, it will require organization. But can you organize mystics?

AH: Absolutely you can. The great revolution that has to happen for the world to be saved will be organized through networks of grace. Look at South Africa's Truth and Reconciliation Commission, a court in which victims of apartheid could give testimony, and perpetrators of violence could request immunity. Look at how the people of Rwanda have come together. I am working with a child soldier from Sierra Leone who was tortured and raped. He wants to go back to his country and bring together all the people who went through the same experience, so that they can mourn together and help each other and use their tragic experiences to remake their country.

For people to come together, they must first be broken by what is happening. When people allow the horror and pain and sorrow of this time to go through their heart like a spear, the thought of hiding away in their private devotions becomes repulsive. They need to turn their love into action.

AL: So this will not be a hierarchical approach?

AH: No, the Divine Mother doesn't like top-down organization, because it is often authoritarian and patriarchal and driven by an agenda. The kind of organization I'm describing is compassionate, egalitarian, and driven by the heart. When people devoted to a cause come together and pour out their creativity, "mother power" is born. Grace comes down, creativity flourishes, and amazing things happen.

AL: Creative, passionate people don't always agree. How can sacred activists work out their differences?

AH: If Sacred Activism becomes a normal way of functioning, there will be more sensitivity, clarity, and wisdom, and less divisiveness. If people differ, they will be willing to go through a process of consensus, and once a decision is reached, their hearts will be united. We have seen glimpses of this. Martin Luther King Jr. was able to turn large numbers of civil-rights activists away from violence and toward reconciliation and peace. Many African Americans thought he was crazy at first, but he convinced them by personal example and indefatigable commitment. The same is true of Gandhi. Many Indians thought he wasn't standing up to the British. And some Tibetans believed the Dalai Lama was soft on the Chinese, but they've been convinced by his example.

The Power of Love

AL: Yet there are compassionate environmentalists at odds over whether to support nuclear power. We're human, and we get attached to our particular solutions. How do you mediate that?

AH: Painfully and slowly, as it has always been done. All divine visions are hard to embody. They require hard work. You have to keep looking at your own shadow—and sacred activists have two shadows: they have the shadow of the mystic, longing to escape into the light and leave the world behind; and they have the shadow of the activist, which is full of denunciation and divisiveness and anger. But if you examine those two shadows long enough, something amazing happens: the mystic's shadow gets purified by the activist's, and vice versa.

AL: How do these shadows manifest in you?

AH: I wouldn't be so disturbed by the mystic's addiction to transcendence if I didn't know something about it. I have felt that shadow in myself that says, "Only God is real." The rest is illusion. It comes from a psychological desire to escape the complexities of my past. On the activist side, I understand how easy it is to project my own failing onto others, to demonize the CEOs and George W. Bush and not recognize that every time I catch a plane to go and talk about saving the environment, I am polluting. Every time I think of President Bush as a psychopath who doesn't deserve to live, I'm committing a kind of murder.

AL: Author Anne Lamott writes about the necessity of loving George Bush.

AH: She puts an image of him on her altar. I've been trying to love him myself. I understand the temptation of anger. I am a passionate person, and passion's shadow is anger—ferocious and lacerating. Though I feel Sacred Activism needs the power of anger to fuel its work, we also need to purify and transmute that anger.

"Sacred Activism" Interview with Simran Singh

Q: Just as people move through dark nights of the soul for growth, it seems as if the planet is moving through a dark night of the soul. Why in either case?

Andrew Harvey: The dark night of the soul is an essential right of passage to anyone that wants to be born into Divine consciousness. There is no true, deep, profound birth without a radical death of the ego and the false self. If you choose not to go through it, avoid it, or deny it ... what you are avoiding and denying is your profoundest growth. There are two aspects of the dark night that need to be understood by everyone.

The first aspect: You need to surrender completely to the stripping, searing, and burning of the experience so that the chaos you are in can unravel and dissolve the agendas of your false self. This surrender has to be grounded in profound faith, deep prayer, and tender self-care. It is essentially a very grueling passive process.

The second aspect: The other process one needs to be able to undergo during this dark night is an active process. As the pain of what you are going through penetrates, it awakens profound heartbreak at the world and profound compassion for all beings suffering in our cosmos. What is essential is to open to that heartbreak, not to deny it. Choose to dedicate yourself to something that causes you the most heartbreak. You will discover a fountain of deathless energy hidden within heartbreak and an inexhaustible passion to do something about what you are so heartbroken about.

In order to gain the deepest wisdom and profoundest empowerment from the dark night, you need to marry the opposites of deep, trusting, passionate surrender to the disintegration process of the false self with an active, passionate commitment to do something in the real world. When you marry these opposites, you feel increasingly filled with Divine energy, love, and power.

There is no way out of the communal dark night of the species now. We have systematically ignored all of the signs. We have done very little about the horrible destructiveness of capitalism, the perversion of the planet, environmental holocaust, or the creation of billions of poor people.

The consequences for this terrifying ignorance and addiction to domination and greed are now inevitable. But even in such chaos and destruction, there is tremendous hope. As this chaos and destruction unfold, we see them not as terminal but as opportunities for us to go through a dark night, have our false identity destroyed, and be empowered directly from the Divine. What seems like the end can transform into the beginning of a new way of being and doing everything.

Q: Before we can become sacred activists, or even qualify to have hope, must we find our way back to the Divine?

AH: There is a problem of intellectualizing what sacred practice is supposed to be. In order to be able to really enter into communion with the Divine, one has to open to the heart-center. This is the crucial opening of the path.

Ramakrishna said, "Having a relatively illumined mind will only take you into the courtyard of God. Only Love will get you into the bedroom." Open the heart-center and discover in it the fundamental passion, adoration, and devotion of the soul for the Divine. With that passion and adoration, anything is possible, including going through the most terrible ordeals. Once you realize that even the most terrible ordeals are an aspect of divine Love sent to you to purify, transform, and transfigure you, then you can embrace ordeals as an aspect of Love and love the Beloved in them and through them. Rumi said, "Be grateful for the Friend's tyranny, not his tenderness, so the arrogant beauty in you can become a lover that weeps."

Our task on the divine path is to transform the arrogant beauty in us, the entitled, spoiled, narcissistic, selfish, demanding ego and false self into the humbled and transformed lover that weeps for three reasons:

Weeps for amazement.
Weeps in adoration.
Weeps in wonder.

Q: Are we overglamorizing what mysticism is, or the ability to have/ become mystical transformation or enlightened evolution as a human being?

AH: You cannot have a major mystical transformation without radical devotion and any practices undertaken without that radical devotion will have some effect, but only a very small part of what they could achieve.

I would say to everyone who really wants to find the sacred in life, you have to fall in love with life. Dare to fall in love with creation. Dare to fall in love with human beings, cats, flowers and stones ... Mozart, Rumi, and Shakespeare. Dare to let the passion for love, which is the core nature of the soul, out. Dare to experience love in all of its facets. Know that experience as radiating from the One Love as rays of the One Love. Dare to let this Great Love lead you to understand that this whole creation is a manifestation of love—radiant and saturated with this love. Everything that happens, whether good or bad, seemingly dark or light, is a manifestation of this love trying to turn you into itself. This will give a clue toward the mystical path and keep you brave, focused, calm, and grateful through everything.

Q: As humans, we get caught up in having an outcome—something measurable. How do people sacredly work toward bettering humanity without attachment?

AH: It is important to let go of the fruits of action for three reasons:

So actions you perform come from the most purified consciousness.

So the actions can respond to the given situation free of your desire to control or interpret the situation.

So the action can be directed by the Divine and not by you.

Once you have grasped the profound mystical truths and the necessity of surrendering the fruits of action to the Divine, then you need to really build, in soul, mind, and body, a profound piece of authentic detachment. This has nothing to do with not being committed to action. It has everything to do with not believing that your interpretation of action is the only possible one. Therefore, turn in peace and surrender to be guided by the Divine. It has everything to do with understanding [that] God's timing is very different than the ego's timing.

The Divine is working a transformation that depends on many mysterious factors that you cannot be aware of completely. To be brought into communion, cooperate with this mystery of transformation by surrendering to its unknowable laws in an act of profound, detached peace.

"The sage is the one that knows the inaction in action and the action in inaction." This verse from the Bhagavad Gita means [that] when you are acting from true holiness and deep identification with the Divine, then at the core of your action there is surrendered peace, surrendered devotion that has truly given up the fruits of action. There is an inaction at the heart of action that sanctifies and releases it from individual karma and allows it to be a part of the divine dance in reality.

Similarly, if you are in this state of profound peace and deep devotion when you are contemplating and meditating, your meditation and contemplation become radioactive with divine power and are form of action. Your prayer is as much a form of action as your visible action, because you have unified your whole being in the force field of divine peace and divine love.

Q: Which identifies first, the individual shadow or the collective shadow? What are we to do regarding both of these?

AH: It is essential for people to understand the collective shadow. We are a civilization doomed because of our addiction to power, lust for domination, crazy separation from nature and the belief we are special and not interdependent with the whole of the cosmos. When you put all of those beliefs together they constitute a psychosis. It is important that we own up to the psychosis and realize it is driving the whole of humanity into a lethal and suicidal insanity that could very well destroy humanity and take a great deal of nature with us.

It is important to be aware of these myths that belong to the collective shadow, as we keep them going in our personal shadows. We have to do deep enough and grueling enough shadow work within ourselves to really understand how we have accepted these myths, through cowardice, intellectual vanity, hunger for power, and/or hunger for comfort. We keep them going even when we pretend not to.

Only by opening up to our collective shadow and the way in which our personal shadow keeps it alive can we call down, into this cauldron of difficulty and darkness, the transforming powers of the Light.

Q: Does shadow work support the unfolding and work of sacred activists?

AH: When you do this grueling shadow work on the collective and personal level, three things are essential for the true sacred activist.

First, your self-righteousness and separation from those you demonize as destructive, bad, and evil crumbles. You recognize you share, in a part of your psyche, all the drives and desperate hungers that compel those beings. From that recognition of the destructive darkness that you share and separate from, a very much deeper and more profound compassion for all beings is born in you.

Second, you begin to recognize those doing the destruction are also Divine, and their divinity is camouflaged. They need—not your anger, judgment, and separation—but your deepest prayers, profoundest help, and most un-self-righteous compassion.

The third thing born from this very difficult work is the mysterious wisdom that can, in turn, birth really skillful means as to deal with the very difficult situations we find ourselves because of our addictions.

You will not be able to deal with the addict out there until you deal with the addict in here. You will not be able to deal with the power maniac out there until you have dealt with the one in here. You will not comprehend how to reach those who are engaged with a false vision of nature and a consumerist orgy of greed until you have faced those ravages within yourself, finding the secret places of emptiness and fear they are trying to cover up. Be able to reach out from a place of pure love, unconditional compassion, and fearless, grounded, embodied intelligence.

Q: There is an increase in narcissism among people. Can those on a spiritual path, or a sacred activist, encounter a narcissist within themselves?

AH: Two very powerful forms of narcissism can be found in the mystic and the activist. The mystic can have the narcissism addicted to transcendence. The mystic's narcissism is the feeling special, elect, or initiated when others are not. It is also the rapture of dropping the body, the attachments, going into the light, and the excitement of very intense experiences. The energies released by mystical experience can fuel the subtle ego's obsession with its own specialness.

The activist has a similar lethal narcissism. It is an addiction to eminence, to doing, being right and righteous. It is also reflected in a martyr complex, victim complex, an addiction to suicidal burnout to prove a level of authenticity.

These are both lethal. You have the tragic truth that the two most sensitive kinds of people, the mystics and the activist, are both trapped potentially in a narcissism that neutralizes the effect of the divine energies that are struggling to be expressed through them.

Q: If the mystics and the activists are at this degree of risk, is there hope?

AH: I am very hopeful. If you fuse the passion for God with the passion of the activist for justice, then the mystic's narcissism, which is an addiction for transcendence, is healed and transformed by the best of the activist's passion for engagement with the real world. The activist's narcissism, an addiction to doing, is healed by being nurtured and nourished from the source of love itself.

The two, the fire of the mystic and the fire of the activist, must come together to birth a third fire, sacred love and wisdom in action. This is the birth of divine love consciousness and divination of the human.

Foreword to *New Self, New World,* by Philip Shepherd

The deepest meaning of the all-embracing world crisis of our time, which threatens the future of the human race and of much of nature, is that it is an evolutionary crisis. It is, at once, a death of all our agendas; illusions and fantasies of uniqueness, domination over nature, and endless growth; and a birth—whose crucible is tragedy, heartbreak, and devastation—of an embodied divine humanity capable of and inspired to work directly with the Divine to transform all existing ways of being and doing everything. Seeing the crisis in this way—as an unprecedented and inescapable dark night of our species that could lead to the unprecedented birth, on a massive scale, of a new, embodied divine consciousness in action—not only enables us to endure its necessary horrors and ordeals with faith, perseverance, and grace; it aligns us with the design of the divine intelligence of evolution itself, a design that has been made available to us, with majestic passion and precision, in the divinely inspired works of great modern evolutionary mystics such as Sri Aurobindo, Jean Gebser, Teilhard de Chardin, Father Bede Griffiths, and Ken Wilber. It is the essence of our terrifying and amazing time—its central and potentially all-transforming paradox—that in our darkest hour, the most all-encompassing and transfiguring vision of what we essentially are and could be is also arising to give us the passion and the peace, the knowledge and hope and strength that we will need to rise to the full height of our evolutionary destiny.

Philip Shepherd, in his profound and original masterpiece, *New Self, New World,* now adds his distinctive, elegant, fierce, and tender voice to those of his distinguished evolutionary predecessors. His book—written over a decade of painstaking, grueling self-exploration, and with the highest nobility and clarity of soul—provides us all with an indispensable guide to why a radically embodied divine humanity needs to be birthed now, and birthed fast, and it also shows us how to allow this bewildering and majestic destiny to be worked out in and through us through divine grace. This is not a book to be read casually or fast; it is not a "self-help" book with easily assimilable, facile "practices," false promises of "instant healing," and risibly superficial "quick fixes." It is that rarest of works in our age—a brave, magnificent manifesto for a new kind of divine human life, a life lived in conscious, dynamic harmony of illumined mind, impassioned and tender heart, and increasingly, consciously, divinized body.

Those of us who are already experiencing the rigors, demands, and glories of the birth that is now taking place will find in *New Self, New World* both a brilliant forensic analysis of our current dead-end, flatland obsession with reason and the mind and all the tyrannical, matricidal, and suicidal structures and actions it engenders; and a luminous, inspiring, exact, and exacting description of the embodied divine human life of the birth—a life in which soul is embodied and body ensouled, and the "masculine" energies of clarity, control, and forceful action dance in abandoned, perfect, lucid rhythm with the restored and celebrated "feminine" energies of adoration; tender, erotic love of all creation; and wise, sustaining, humble, nourishing interrelationship. Both in the way it is structured and in the precise but richly poetic and full-breathed, almost mantric way in which it is written, *New Self, New World* not only describes this sacred marriage of transcendence and immanence, body and soul, masculine and feminine, but also embodies it with a magical power and force that is at once challenging and healing.

Philip Shepherd's book presents three ways of understanding ourselves that go so against the grain of habituated, sclerotic thinking that they can be considered revolutionary. These three radical contributions are: a new model of human consciousness; a new vision of our evolutionary history; and a new vision of the interrelated environmental, political, social, and economic crises that now threaten our survival and demand a collective, evolutionary leap in embodied divine consciousness.

In the new model of human consciousness that *New Self, New World* offers, Philip Shepherd proposes a conscious "sacred marriage" of what he calls "the two brains of the human being"—between, in other words, the intelligence we have ruthlessly and ruinously centered only in the cranium, with its obsessive, and dissociated, cold passion for separatist analysis, objectification, and control; and the vast, free-flowing, infinitely supple and responsive intuitive intelligence of our "second brain": that of the enteric nervous system, immune system, and genetic networks, with its locus in the pelvic bowl. In this radical new model, the psyche or spirit is shown to pervade every living part and every cell of our human organism in such a way that makes the transfiguration of the human into the divine human possible. The evolutionary significance of this very grounded and precise vision cannot be overstated: it accords, in every spiritual and material detail, with the universal law of interrelationship, intercommunion and interresponsibility that is everywhere proclaimed by both the ancient mystical systems and those of the emerging evolutionary mysticism. Our only possible release from the psychotic tyranny of a heartless and radically dissociated glorification of bodiless intelligence lies in a reclamation of the almost miraculous, sensitive awareness of all the interrelated physical and cellular systems, and in a sacred marriage of that vivid and vibrant, "feminine" body consciousness—allowed at last to speak in its own sacred language—with a purified, chastened, tenderized, "masculine" rational consciousness. It is precisely this sacred marriage and the birth of the divine human it makes possible that Sri Aurobindo, in his own inimitably grand way, celebrates in his *The Life Divine*. Philip Shepherd's particular contribution to the understanding and unfolding of the birth now taking place is that it is rooted not in grand metaphysics alone, or even exclusively in a "yogic" understanding of the mystical, tantric transformation of matter, but in the latest astounding revelations of quantum mechanics and neurobiology, which reveal to all those who dare to see the mystery of a material cosmos, everywhere pervaded by dynamic spirit-energy. Such a vision—which fuses the highest mystical wisdom, the most advanced scientific inquiry, and the greatest and most poignant historical urgency—could only be born now. It is Philip Shepherd's peculiar grace to be its midwife.

In Philip Shepherd's second great contribution to our evolutionary crisis—that of a new vision of our history—he demonstrates how the entire "progress" of our modern history has been severely maimed and distorted by a wholesale, ruthless, semi-demented denigration of the values and wisdom of the feminine. *New Self, New World* makes it fiercely clear that our now habitual neglect and ignorance of the center of our "feminine intelligence"—the second brain—is part of a much larger and now blatantly lethal denigration of the feminine in all of the values that govern our rapidly more distorted and destructive relationships to each other, to Creation, and to the political, social, and economic worlds we create and continue to keep going. Other major writers, of course, have pointed out, sometimes with as great an eloquence and elegance, this devaluation of the feminine and its increasingly catastrophic consequences in every domain of human life. What makes Philip Shepherd's work unique is that it demonstrates clearly and specifically how the orientation of our thinking about the body has determined and potentially aborted our evolution. In some of the greatest and most revealing pages of *New Self, New World,* Shepherd shows—definitively, I believe—how the center of our thinking has risen through the body over the passing millennia, starting in the belly center of consciousness in the Paleolithic and ascending to the isolated, tyrannical "cranium" center in our modern era, birthing separatist belief systems; dissociated social, political, economic, and scientific philosophies; and hierarchies of all kinds that enshrine division, injustice, horrible poverty, and inequality, and thrive on the "dominator delusion" that, if we continue to feed it blindly, can now lead only to the annihilation of humanity and the terrifying desecration of most of the natural world.

Once we truly dare to grasp how our own thinking is constricted and perverted by what amounts to the trained addiction of our body-thinking to predominantly masculine values and perspectives, then, Philip Shepherd suggests, we will begin to see clearly not only its horrific impact on the world around us but also—and this is crucial for our evolution and survival—the woeful superficiality, narrowness, and petty unwisdom of most of the proposed "solutions" to the crisis we are mired in. We seem still to want to go on believing—against mounting evidence—that the interrelated crises of the death we are passing through can all be dealt with through a hyped-up, cracked-up application of the very addicted and heart-dead consciousness that created it to begin with, through technological legerdemain and wizardry, super-smart social engineering, and political will radically dissociated from spiritual law or practice. This is a desperate, corrupt, bankrupt, and dangerous fantasy, one whose absurdity is destined now to be exploded, and in increasingly deadly and dramatic ways, as we enter into the eye of our evolutionary perfect storm. Without the revolution that *New Self, New World* proposes—a revolution of illumined mind, sacred heart, and divinized body; without entering, in fact, into the integral transformation of the birth, and acting from its healed, sacred consciousness urgently in every realm of human endeavor, we will not be able even to imagine—let alone labor to construct, enshrine, embody, and enact—the new ways of being and doing and creating that we now need if we are to rise to the challenge of our evolutionary destiny. What lies ahead for us, if we refuse the challenge of transformation, is first, unimaginable chaos and horror, and then extinction; if we accept the terrors of the challenge and submit to its rigor and demands in grateful surrender, anything is possible. The great hope that Philip Shepherd offers—and that has clearly inspired him through all the long and lonely labor of creating his masterpiece—is that the human race will wake up in time, will go on a journey into a new, vibrant, embodied wholeness of heart, mind, soul, and body, and will birth in divinely inspired, sacred action, in and through divine grace, a new and far more just and harmonious world. To that hope Philip Shepherd has devoted his life, his brilliance, his energy, and all the rich and profound wisdom and analysis of *New Self, New World*. May we all be worthy of his faith.

Interview with Philip Shepherd

Andrew Harvey: Your book discusses myth, physics, poetry, anthropology, physiology, spirituality, theater, and history—and yet its journey is really the unfolding of a single issue. How would you describe that issue at the book's core?

Philip Shepherd: Well, the easiest way to put it might be simply, "What is happening to us?" And I mean that on a societal or cultural level, of course, given our broken relationships with each other and our planet—but I am also addressing the quality of the life we settle for as individuals: our lives are chock full from dawn to dusk, and yet in many ways they also feel profoundly empty. And that intrigues me, because it feels like the frog in the bowl of water that is being heated to a boil so slowly the frog makes no effort to jump out. Life is all you've got, really, and if you harbor any reverence for it, that reverence will eventually lead you to ask some very personal questions, such as: "How alive am I on a day-to-day basis?" "How much of my life is present right now in this moment?" or "In what conditions am I most alive?" If you entertain those questions frankly, you will see that your life is most keenly felt and expressed when the energy of your entire being engages with the life around you.

So when I ask, "What is happening to us?" I am also asking how it is that our love of life is so far down the list of our priorities that people can go for decades without ever allowing their entire being to be present in the world and engaged with it. And there are very many things that can compromise our engagement, and certainly personal choices made over the years play a significant role—but the whole phenomenon is easier to understand once you appreciate that our personal choices are made in the context of a culture that is driven by a madness at its core. Our culture is deeply, deeply antilife. We violate life at every turn. What have we done to our rivers and lakes that to drink from them is to risk grave illness? We torture our livestock in the name of productivity. In our cities we reduce nature, our most intimate teacher, to the role of decoration. We take our playful, curious, outgoing young children and incarcerate them indoors at desks all day long, stunting their vitality. It goes on and on, wherever you look. But when you confront our antilife madness and chase it down to its roots, you discover that the madness we inflict on the world, all of it, is a reflection of what we do first to ourselves. It is rooted in how we relate to our own bodies. We have dissociated ourselves from them and smothered their vibrant, world-attuned intelligence—smothered their vitality—and we sit up in the head and move through the world like a driver in a car, expecting the car to behave.

AH: How can we love life, and express that love in action, when we cannot love ourselves?

PS: Exactly.

AH: But our separation from the body has been with us for so long that it's a real challenge to open our eyes to the depth of its hold on us.

PS: Yes, and that's true even for people who teach the gospel of a mind/body unity. For instance, we are coached in the importance of "listening to the body"—but when you look at the metaphor at work in that phrase, it's shocking. It's telling you in effect that you are in one room, your body is next door in another, and you should put your ear to the wall separating you and listen to what's going on over there. The advice, which espouses a healing of our body/mind divide, is actually reinforcing it.

AH: One of the strengths of your book is that it demonstrates how this fractured relationship with the body shapes our entire worldview.

PS: Well, for starters it shaped the foremost belief systems of our culture into profoundly anti-body institutions. Religion has for centuries told us the body is tainted with sin, and has urged us to transcend it. Science believes that truth is the preserve of reason and objectivity, and so seeks to cleanse itself of all feeling. As a consequence it leeches mind from the body and nature and turns them into organic machinery. And capitalism—well, the word itself comes from the Latin word for "head," and it expresses a heady, narcissistic belief in the enterprise of personal gain, urging us to seek power and control and to pursue self-gratification, as though the "bottom line" were the truth of life. Success in capitalism is biased toward those who live in their heads, unhindered by a sense of certain responsibilities. The tacit justification for capitalism is the pseudo-Darwinian phrase "survival of the fittest"—but that phrase is empty of real meaning, and the sentiment it seeks to express is simply wrong. All of nature shows us that a species is most likely to survive when it is most in harmony with its environs—which bodes ill for our own survival. You can't achieve harmony while living in your head.

AH: You call the head consciousness of our culture a tyranny.

PS: Yes. It's a tyranny of the self, first of all. To live in the head is to distance yourself from the sensations of the body and retreat into an abstract realm that cannot feel. The brain has no sensory organs. Because it is insensate, it is immune to harmony—it has no way of feeling it even. What it does understand is order, which is the opposite of harmony. If you cannot feel the harmony of the body or the world, your actions can neither enhance it nor find guidance there. So your actions will be dictated by some other source—a source that instead recognizes and promotes order. And that other source is the construct of ideas you have developed about the body and the world. So all of your actions then impose those dead ideas onto your life, seeking to order it. But what begins as tyranny of the self—trying to have the right emotions, make the right impression, show the right response, lose the right amount of weight, evolve the winning formula for your happiness—soon translates into a tyranny imposed on the world around you, dominating it with your ideas, trying to make it right, to control it, all the while oblivious to the harmony of its actual reality. While we are in that state, body and world are experienced as mere things. We mistake the avalanche of sensations within the body as "the noise of the machinery," and remain deaf to its voluble and subtle intelligence. If the body falters, we blame it, feeling betrayed, and cart it off to a body mechanic to get it fixed, heedless of its need for the dynamic, coursing energy of our love—just as we remain heedless or dismissive of the world's need for the dynamic, coursing energy of our love. And that's how we carry on: sitting up in the head, running the show, hammering the world into the shape of our ideas, deaf to its ever-present, living guidance. We take that state to be normal and even inevitable.

AH: And it seems inevitable only because we are taught that all our thinking happens in the head. But your book argues forcibly against that.

PS: There's an interesting story that shows just how stubbornly attached we are to this fantasy that the head is the sole thinker of the self. We are born not with one brain, but with two. There is a second brain in the belly, and it is not a subsection of the cranial brain or its handmaiden. It is a fully autonomous brain that perceives, acts, thinks, and remembers. We've known about this brain since 1910, when the anatomist Byron Robinson published a book about it. It was soon forgotten, was rediscovered by Johannis Langley in the 1920s, forgotten again, and rediscovered a third time in the 1960s. And still we commonly believe we have one brain. We have resisted this major piece of self-knowledge because our culture has invested ten thousand years in creating a story about what it means to be human, and that story would be radically upended by accepting the fact of this other aspect of our consciousness. But that's sort of the point, isn't it? Our story about what it means to be human isn't working. It needs upending. Interestingly, there are other cultures, such as the Japanese, Incas, Chinese, and Mayans, that refer openly to the brain in the belly, but it seems to be anathema to us.

AH: In your book you distinguish very clearly between these brains, and the role they play in our consciousness.

PS: Yes, they really are complementary opposites. The most basic difference between them is that the brain in the head is where we can consciously think, and the brain in the belly is where we can consciously "be." What that means is that when you are living in your head, you are disconnected from your being and are numb to the pulsing reality of the present. And the present is really all that exists. But there is another way to distinguish between our two brains. The brain in the head is where the male aspect of our consciousness is centered, the aspect that excels at perspective, analysis, abstract reasoning, and systemization. All of those processes require a subject/object relationship with the world, whereby you step back from the world and view it as though through a window. That is precisely the state that living in the head creates.

The brain in the belly, and more particularly in the pelvic bowl, is where the female aspect of our consciousness is centered—and I should stress that when I use the terms *male* and *female,* I am talking about the two complementary poles of consciousness that live in each of us. This is not a discussion about men and women—it is about the embodied unity of our human consciousness.

AH: And it is about recognizing how the sacred marriage of masculine and feminine can take place within us, as a union of love within the body.

PS: Exactly. And once you understand that inner union, you see that our culture's injunction to live in the head is literally a decree against the sacred marriage. As is our culture's primary orientation, which says that "up" is good and "down" is bad, tacitly instructing us to live in the penthouse of the body and to keep a safe distance from the body's underworld—an underworld that we characterize as a teeming dark hell: the belly, which we disparage unless it is a six-pack; the internal organs of digestion, with their juices and gasses; the genitalia, a cultural source of shame; and the anus, which is simply unmentionable. But suffused through those organs is the second brain, and in its neural center, resting on the pelvic floor, is the experiential core of our being. That is where the female aspect of our consciousness is centered, and it is what brings us into relationship with all things. Just as this second brain empowers us to integrate the world into our bodies through the food we eat, it empowers us to integrate the mindful present into the mind of the body. In contrast to the strengths of the male consciousness of the head, that work of integration grants insight, enables us to empathize, and attunes us to the world, that we might harmonize with it in the recognition that we are one with it.

AH: And that embodied knowledge of unity is the mystic's insight— the direct experience of our inseparability from all existence. It's an experience that reveals the utter poverty of reason alone, and yet as long as we cling to reason that experience will never be available to us—so we will go on believing reason is almighty.

PS: We are trapped in a sort of catch-22. You cannot reason your way into the present, however hard you try. And if you are unable to be present, you can live only according to your ideas about the present, which means you are living a fantasy that leaves you addicted to the abstractions of reason. And it is this fantasy that is killing us. Dissociated from the body, a virtual stranger to the female aspect of our consciousness, the self is out of balance, and so brings imbalance to all of its relationships. We cannot arrive at truly balanced relationships with our world until we deepen into the body and reclaim the sensitivities that allow us to rest in the divine present. And even then, the balance of the male and female aspects of our consciousness can occur within us, as the Tao Te Ching puts it, only when the female element of being comes first. When being comes first, doing arises naturally from it, because being calls you into relationship with the world. When doing comes first, being is kept on the sidelines, because dissociated doing puts idea in charge. The rarified upper atmosphere of abstract reasoning is rich and marvelous, but it is not home. To bring your consciousness back home—to allow it to descend through the body and come to rest on the pelvic floor—is to come home to the astonishing gift of your life, here and now, and to come into an embodied relationship with the miraculous beauty of life all around you.

"Follow Your Heartbreak into the Eye of the Storm"
A Discussion on Sacred Activism with John Malkin

John Malkin: You write about bringing together spiritual practice and social action into Sacred Activism. I'm always interested in finding that balance between being and doing, or as you put it; "The sacred marriage between serenity and urgency." Tell me about the importance of that now, especially in this country, and how best to create that balance.

Andrew Harvey: Let me back up a bit and say these three things; I believe we are heading into the eye of a perfect storm of crises that really do threaten the extinction of the human race and the desecration and degradation of a great deal of nature. I think that we have absolutely ignored all the warnings, indulged in a vast "Coca-Coma," being in denial about all the information that has been coming through about climate change. We are now in for a series of very devastating ordeals. That's the first thing, and I think that a great many people are waking up to the severity of this scenario.

The second thing I believe is that *this is not the end* for the human race. This is a massive wake-up call and a massive challenge for the human race to get real about putting love and compassion and wisdom into urgent, focused, radical action. And that if millions of us take up this challenge, then what this Great Death that is materializing all over the planet will turn out to be will be the birthing canal for a new humanity. It's what I call a *divine humanity*. This is a humanity that is being chastened by tragedy and chastened by the death of its false illusions and agendas, to start fusing together the two noblest fires in the human psyche—the fire of the mystic's passion for God and the fire of the activist's passion for justice—to bring about the birth on earth of a third fire, the fire of love and wisdom in action. It is this fire that I believe is Sacred Activism and it is this fire that I believe is destined to birth a divine humanity. A divine humanity that by fusing the mystic's passion for God and the activist's passion for justice will heal the division between heaven and earth, heart and mind and will, body and soul, prayer and action. So as to come into a fully empowered, fully active, and contemplative humanity that can turn tragedy into grace, desolation into the opportunity to build and procreate with the Divine, a new world.

You asked the question, "How can this be done? How can a deep and mystical spiritual practice that is simultaneously illuminative of the mind, expansive of the heart and invigorating of the body be combined with clear, wise radical action?" It isn't easy, but it is possible.

In the Bhagavad Gita I think we're given a great clue when Krishna says that the perfect sage knows the "action in in-action" and the "in-action in action." That sublime phrase means that when you have really developed a contemplative practice, which you are developing not for itself alone and not for the glorious experiences alone that it gives you, but to make you strong and effective in action in the world, then what happens is [that] when you are praying and meditating you are always directing the effects of that prayer and meditation toward the healing of the world. You are in a deep sense *active* in contemplation. When you are acting you are always acting from the peaceful, divinely grounded, illuminated center of being, so that you're doing is suffused by the wisdom and peace of being.

What I suggest in my book is that people combine in the core of their lives four different kinds of practice. These are the four different kinds of practice that I try to fuse into the core of my life, and these are the four different kinds of practice that I have found over years of forging this issue and trying really to become an embodied divine human being and an embodied sacred activist really work.

The first kind of practices that is essential in a world gone mad like ours, in a world of such severe and terrible turmoil, are what I call *cool practices*. These are practices like *vipassana* meditation, breathing, imageless meditation, calm saying of mantra in the heart, visualizations that imagine you in deep peace. What these cool practices do is to align you with what the Hindus call shantih; the radiant, eternal peace of divine being. So that whatever is happening in the world and whatever is happening in your life—whatever defeat and disappointment you may endure on your way to eventual victory and success in what you're trying to achieve—you remain serene and you remain surrendered and connected to the enormous, calm, loving energy that is always streaming from the silence.

The second kind of practice that is essential to anyone who is going to engage in the horror and madness and pain and violence out there is what I call *heart practices*. Heart practices enable you to keep your sacred heart open and passionate and juicy and compassionate and filled with the intense energy of love even when the world is burning. There are three kinds of heart practices that I recommended. First, there are the Christian heart practices that enable you to get into direct connection with the sacred heart. The second are the kind of Sufi practices that enable you to plunge your whole being into the fire of the beloved so that you can feel that fire penetrating every cell of your being. The third are the great Mahayana Buddhist practices. The practice of *Tonglen,* for example, which is a practice of giving and receiving, where you breathe in the pain of the world and breathe out the peace of Buddha nature into that pain, to heal it. Another is the great Hinayana practice of *metta,* "loving-kindness."

The third kind of practice that is essential is *prayer practice.* I think everybody should develop this in terms of his or her own spirituality, and it doesn't matter what religion or spirituality you are, because I think we're in the birth of a universal mysticism that understands that we are all the creatures of the eternal light, the entire cosmos is sacred, and that all of the mystical traditions have vital things to give us.

My own experience is that when you go through a severe ordeal— and I think what the world is going through is an equivalent of a dark night of the soul, it's a *dark night of a species.* And the dark night of the soul comes at a particular moment in the path when the mystic is ready to die into the Divine and have his or her false self stripped and burned from him or her so that the divine self can rise. During this period of turmoil, this period of ordeal, this period of terror and menace that I myself experienced and went through, I wasn't able to do the cool or the heart practices. My mind and my heart were too shattered. But what I was always able to do, and what was always powerful and effective, was prayer practice.

I recommend keeping prayer practice very short and intense, such as the Jesus prayer: "Lord Jesus Christ have mercy on me." Or a mantra such as the great Sufi mantra, which I love and adore and do everyday, as often as I can, "La Ilaha El Allah Hu." "*There is no other God but God.*" Or the marvelous power of a rosary, which can never be exaggerated, "Hail Mary, full of Grace, the Lord is with you."

When you pray in that passionate, intense, repetitive way, whatever is happening in your body, in your mind and heart, you remain aligned with the power and the presence and the will of the Beloved, so that the Beloved can slowly infuse you with the kind of calm and the kind of purpose, faith, and stamina that you need.

The fourth kind of practice that is essential for all those who want to become sacred activists is a *sacred body practice.* Over the last five years I have really plunged into two areas of sacred body practice. I worked for five years on a book with a great yogini, Karuna Erickson, who's a pupil of Rodney Yee, called *Heart Yoga: The Sacred Marriage of Yoga and Mysticism.*

Heart Yoga brings together yoga in its most ancient, mystical form with very intense and beautiful practices taken from all of the mystical traditions about the sacred heart and sacred body, and about the way in which the light comes into the body to transform it, so that yoga can now become what it has always, I think, been intended by the sages who formed it intended it to be; a crucible for the divinization of the body. This is very important, because the world's immune system is being destroyed. Diseases are rampant; we are eating poisoned food; the body is under threat; and you cannot do the great, powerful, pioneering work of Sacred Activism without a powerful, luminous, subtle, and deeply inspired body that has become conscious of its spiritual ground.

The body is a manifestation of the spirit; and to experience that and unite consciously the body with its spiritual ground increases the energy of the body; and this is what yoga can be and must be and will be! What has really deeply heartened me is that all of the major yoga teachers are behind this book—so they've all said that this represents the possibility of a revolution, a tender revolution of yoga, that can take it to its next stage.

I've also been working with Gabrielle Roth, the great pioneer of sacred dance, to unite her five rhythms—these five rhythms that she's noted as the fundamental rhythms of experience—with the five different stages of the path of Rumi, to divine love. So that by uniting her vision of the five stages with Rumi's passionate poetry and understanding of the unfolding of divine love in the heart and in the body, sacred dance can also become what it has been in the ancient mystical systems and of course in Rumi's own practice; a way of energizing the whole subtle field of the human being so that human beings can go into the glorious fire of sacred dance and catch fire in it and find the joy, the *ananda,* the "bliss," the power and energy to be refreshed enough to go on and on and on, working calmly for justice and compassion in a burning world.

I'm very concerned that all those who really want to fuse spirituality at the deepest level with action and the most urgent, wise, calm intensity—that all those who really want this fusion know that there is really only one way to do it. And that is through an integral, deeply thought out, continual spiritual practice. There is no other way, there is no magical formula. But there is a way through that has been enshrined in the wisest evolutionary mystical system and that is a way through that simultaneously works on opening the intellect to the divine intellect, opening the heart to the divine heart, and opening the body to the divine body, longing to be born in it through a conscious absorption of the light.

All of these amazing practices are now available because of the great mystical renaissance that's been happening in the last thirty years and because of the great outbreak of what I call *evolutionary mysticism* in the twentieth century in the work of Sri Aurobindo, Teilhard de Chardin, Wilber, and others—and my great teacher, Father Bede Griffiths. People will understand that we've come to a moment when we are being challenged to embody the Divine so as to transform a ragged and tormented humanity into a powerful, focused and passionate, compassionate and divine humanity. And that everything we need is actually here on earth to help us forward. So that in the

middle of our greatest disaster and in the middle of our greatest
challenge, in the middle of our greatest despair, we have the greatest
opportunity, the greatest help, and the greatest hope.

JM: I'd like to hear your vision about how we might strategize to
encounter specific problems in the United States. This is a country
permanently at war, where economic and retributive violence are
the status quo. There is a wider and wider gap between the very few
who own most of the wealth and the majority who have less and
less. This institutionalized violence harms people inside and outside
the United States.

AH: And also we've just been sold to the corporations by the Supreme
Court, which has given the corporations carte blanche to invest in
American politics. This is tantamount to saying that the corporations
can buy whatever politician they want. *We are in the best democracy
that money can buy.* This is an outrage and an abomination. It's
amazing to me that the American people aren't in the streets, because
this is actually the prelude, potentially, to the rule of fascism.

We saw in the horrendous Republican government of eight years
under Bush that many of the things that Hitler put in practice were
actually put in practice. The American people stood by and let torture
be used. The American people stood by and let Bush invade Iraq. The
American people stood by and let trillions of dollars be poured into
a useless war while many people here are starving and living in terrible conditions. I'm alarmed by the state of America at the moment.

I'm very alarmed, too, at the spiritual response to this. During
these years we had the rampant explosion of what I call the most
arrogant and idiotic spiritual materialism of the New Age. The most
popular book of the last seven years or so has been *The Secret.* I
consider it an almost demonic, idiotic manifestation of greed. We've
had a spirituality that's sanctified greed, sanctified consumerism,
sanctified bottom-line business thinking. It's been utterly un-awake
to the agony of what's happening and not at all concerned with either

service or political and social transformation at the very moment that they are needed most.

JM: You are pointing to the difference between authentic or mystical spirituality and Capitalist-materialist-religious spirituality.

AH: Well, Capitalist-materialist-religious spirituality has almost taken over the American marketplace of spirituality. What is almost more alarming are the Christian churches, who you'd have thought would've been trying to represent the authentic teachings of Jesus, which is one of absolute commitment to social, political, economic, and emotional transformation. Instead they are indulging in an orgy of *prosperity consciousness* at the moment when the world is groaning under the explosion of greed.

JM: In *The Hope* you write that you've spent much of the past five years reading about corporate brutality. You also describe a meeting you had with a businessman that had a big impact on you.

AH: I went to a meeting in New York to speak with the people who organized Rio. I met this very intelligent businessman who took me out to lunch and told me the skinny on the corporate mind. It was really the most frightening lunch of my life. But I'm very glad I met him because he really woke me up. Basically he said, "People like you will never be effective until you realize that there are people like me who know exactly what we are doing and know exactly how destructive we have been and who do it because we want to do it and because we like doing it. We love the power that it brings us and we're not going to be changed by all of your liberal do-gooding and we're not going to be changed by any of your spiritual precepts and your mouthing of quotations from the Dhammapada and the Sermon on the Mount. We know what we are and we love what we are and we're going to try everything to hold onto power."

When you look at the last thirty years and when you consider the horrible practices of the tobacco companies in deliberately obfuscating the research about cancer, when you really cop to what the oil and coal companies have been doing over the last twenty years in paying off corrupt scientists to do corrupt studies showing that global warming isn't happening, knowing full well that it's happening, but wanting to keep control of oil and coal, to keep us addicted to them at the very moment we need desperately to get off the heroin, selling us the heroin for ten more years so they can make more money.... Then you have to ask yourself the question—looking at all of that, knowing what we do now—what are the corporations *not* capable of?

Last night I saw the new Mel Gibson film, *The Edge of Darkness*. A defense facility is secretly making nuclear weapons with foreign components so that in an extreme situation, if the American people need to be controlled, a nuclear bomb could be launched, but could be identified as an Arab jihadist bomb, because it has components from that region of the world. This really overwhelmed me, because it's kind of a cynical twist I hadn't thought of. And I figured I'd thought of most of the dark twists, but this was one I hadn't thought of! And I asked myself, watching it, "Could this be true?" And I think it could be true. Anything could be true.

There are people who believe that many of the natural disasters that are now occurring are the result of laboratories working on trying to control nature that have actually gone out of control, or pierced a certain veil in nature, with disastrous results. This sounds like madness and paranoia, but, in fact, it very well could be true, when you remember that when the Americans exploded the nuclear bomb in 1945 in the New Mexico desert, there were many scientists who thought that it might set off a whole chain reaction that could consume the world, and still went ahead with it!

JM: Isn't that amazing!

AH: It's insane and psychotic. We have to face that there is, in the corporate minds, addiction to the bottom line. In the cold-heartedness that passes for efficiency there is a kind of frozen psychosis that is now, of course, omnipotent, because the corporations are not regulated. There is no international regulation of any significance of their activity. And now, with the Supreme Court's ruling, they've been given omnipotence over the political process. I cannot begin to describe how alarming this situation is! Eisenhower forecast the potential horror of a military-industrial complex that controlled politics, and I'm afraid that we're entering the era when his worst fears are becoming our daily reality.

JM: I often reflect on the reality that those nuclear warfare scientists were placing bets with each other, and some of them predicted that perhaps the entire universe that we knew of would be consumed by fire.

AH: Don't you remember also that when they were working on the multibillion dollar reactor that is supposedly going to discover the formation of the Big Bang—this was underground in Switzerland—there were some scientists who believed that it could, in fact, open up a black hole that could swallow up our Milky Way! And they were not fools or maniacs. It was based on mathematics. It didn't happen, but nevertheless they were prepared to go forward with it because the lunacy of pursuing the power of what they considered to be knowledge overran any kind of sane human considerations.

Look at what is happening, for example, in genetic food manipulation. You have Monsanto making it impossible for farmers in Asia and Africa to buy seeds that will last more than a year. This means that the whole agricultural cycle is broken, and they are totally under the control of the corporations selling them seeds. This is fascism!

JM: Do you have ideas about strategies to use in dealing with genetically modified foods, war, poverty, corporate control? How do we change these systems of control and violence?

AH: No. I have no specific strategies but what I am certain of is this: I'm certain that everybody needs now to face some very unpleasant facts. Everybody needs to face that the corporations are certainly not going to go through a quick change of heart. They are going to cling to their power and their manipulation and this bottom-line mentality as long as they can. This was very obvious to me when I was in Copenhagen as part of a group of world spiritual leaders there to monitor and comment on what was going on in the conference. We were all absolutely stricken and aghast by the obvious disconnect between everything the scientists were telling us about the horror of the state of the environment and everything the corporations and the politicians are doing.

The next thing that people have to face is that there is very little hope in the political system. I have a great deal of admiration for President Obama and I think he is a genuinely good man, but I think he is absolutely constricted in what he can do by the military-industrial complex and the corporations and the lunacy of the Republicans. It's almost impossible for him to get any serious changes through this time around. Maybe he'll be able to next time around, but I doubt that.

We have to face [the fact] that neither the corporations nor the politicians nor any of the so-called experts in power are going to be any help. This means that the responsibility for major change now lies in us. This means that the one hope for the world—and I think there is a tremendous hopefulness—is in a *global mass movement*. It needs to be a globalized mass movement of *love in action*. I'm devoting everything I'm doing to help mobilizing ordinary people into what I call *networks of grace*.

My vision of networks of grace is this: I didn't finish my book until I really came to understand how the vision of Sacred Activism could be radically grounded in a real mass movement. I prayed to be shown what this might be. I read deeply in terrorist literature; I read about Al Qaida and I read about different fundamentalist organizations that are very successful in organizing themselves. One of the things that absolutely struck me was that the dark forces are brilliant at organizing themselves, but those of us who are trying to be on the side of humanity—on the side of this Great Birth that is going to take place—are astonishingly disorganized, individualistic. We are pursuing private goals of liberation and not public, social, and economic transforming goals. It came to me: "Why should the devil have all of the best tunes?"

Networks of grace are cells of between six and twelve people who are gathered around a heartbreak, a profession, or a cause. They're ordinary people who come together realizing that it is up to us now. They organize themselves in a cell, and pray together, and infuse each other, and pool their resources and creativity, and start working together to try and shift all of the problems in all of the different directions.

How I see these networks of grace is this: I had a wonderful conversation once with Deepak Chopra about what happens to a caterpillar when it becomes a butterfly. The caterpillar creates a cocoon, the body of the caterpillar dissolves in the grey *gunge* of the cocoon and when the grey *gunge* is sufficiently *gungey*, what wakes up in it are what are called *imaginal cells*, which constitute together to create the body of the butterfly that will break out of the cocoon.

What I see these networks of grace being are those imaginal cells waking up in the grey gunge of our late-Capitalist disaster and coming together through the internet, through the available media that aren't yet totally controlled, to start a massive global movement of love in action. When I was meditating more deeply on this I had a vision of the Buddha of Compassion. I have spent a tremendous time studying Tibetan Buddhism and, of course, I have a very great love for the Dalai Lama. He is, in many ways, the embodiment of the Buddha of Compassion. One of the ways in which the Buddha of Compassion is represented is as a being with a thousand-thousand arms stretching out to heal in every direction. I imagine each network of grace to be one of the arms of the million-armed Buddha of Compassion, stretching out to heal different problems.

There will be networks of grace to deal with the plight of old people. There will be networks of grace dealing with the necessity for environmental protest and transformation and the creation of different forms of energy. There will be networks of grace working on poverty and famine and the transformation of our relationship to animals. The clue to the networks of grace is in the phrase *follow your heartbreak*. That is one of the core phrases of Sacred Activism.

One of the phrases that has been most misused by our fake spiritual renaissance is Joseph Campbell's phrase *follow your bliss*. In fact, on his deathbed Joseph Campbell turned to his wife, Jane, and said, "Oh, I wish I'd never said that in that way because it's just been completely taken over by the narcissism of the Western mind. What I actually meant was that when you look for your bliss you find a place where your deepest bliss intersects with the hunger of the world." The point of following your bliss is to find the place where your deepest bliss intersects with the deepest pain of the world, so that you can experience that pain with deep security and start doing something about it.

What I suggest to people who really wish to discover what their mission is in this chaos, is that they get up at three o'clock in the morning, they ground themselves in the Divine in whatever way is natural to them, and they ask themselves one question: "What of all of the causes in this world breaks my heart the most? What breaks my heart?" When you really deeply and sincerely ask yourself that question you will find that there are one or two things that really keep you up at night, that really get under your skin, that really threaten your sanity, threaten your sleep, threaten your hopes in life. That is what you should be working for. Because if you work for something that truly breaks your heart, you will always find the energy and the passion and the intense focus to be able to go on doing something you feel so deeply about. Rumi said that when you uncover your heartbreak you uncover a passion for compassion that will never run dry.

JM: I'd like to talk with you about nonviolence. In *The Hope* you write that, "As a race we have begun to believe that the only way to achieve anything is through the use of force. This is the most dangerous of illusions, as wars and genocides prove." And then you write that, "I am not a dogmatic pacifist, however. In certain extreme situations, which I pray do not arise, but could, I would be prepared to take up arms and use force." Tell me about the power of nonviolence as we've seen manifest through Gandhi, Cesar Chavez, the Dalai Lama, Dorothy Day, and others, and this paradox in nonviolence of the possibility in extreme cases of using force.

AH: On the one hand, we saw in the twentieth century astonishingly powerful people like Gandhi and Martin Luther King Jr., Nelson Mandela and Desmond Tutu and all of the wonderful beings that you mentioned, and His Holiness The Dalai Lama, who really showed us that through pursuing nonviolence with great spiritual strength, astonishing shifts in history could take place. What I believe is that everybody should, as far as possible, pursue the path of nonviolence and pursue the kinds of inner practices that can give you the strength to be compassionate, generous, peaceful, all-embracing, and focused, even in extreme circumstances. History has shown that when people pursue their goals with such a divine fervor, passion and peace then the Divine blesses those causes and over time they do have an extraordinary chance of becoming realized.

I also believe, however, that given the situation as it is—the omnipotence of the corporations, the strength of the military-industrial complex—given the horror that it manifesting all over the world, we might—and I say *might*—be brought to a situation so extreme and terrible that even those who have committed ourselves to nonviolence would then consider a disciplined and focused and economic use of force would be necessary.

When I interviewed His Holiness The Dalai Lama on the day he won the Nobel Peace Prize in 1989, he surprised me by saying that he wasn't a dogmatic pacifist. Because in the Tibetan bodhisattva tradition there are very rare and very unusual cases of bodhisattvas who did in extreme situations and on rare occasions employ force when it was absolutely the last resort. Then he said something that permanently changed my mind. If you ever have the grace to sit with the Dalai Lama and to talk with him, he *will* say something that will permanently change your mind! *[Laughter]* What he said was, "If it comes to the necessity of using force, only those people could be trusted to use force in a way that could work to change the situation who had been profoundly, and over a long time and with a deep spiritual intensity, trained in nonviolence." Only a person who is truly calm and truly centered in God could ever be trusted to use the very dangerous weapon of violence.

This is exactly the same message that Krishna gives Arjuna in the Bhagavad Gita. The Bhagavad Gita is not a pacifist document. It is about the Divine appearing to a warrior who is deeply sad about having to go into battle where, if he wins, he will probably kill not only his relations but also his own master, the most sacred of all relationships. What the Divine tells him is that he has to do it, because the cause that he represents has to win. Otherwise the destiny of humanity would be destroyed. Krishna tells Arjuna that he can only act in a divine way when he has truly surrendered his will to God and acts not from rage, not from revenge, but out of a great peace. He knows that his actions have been sanctioned by God with the view to win, but not in a merciless and ferocious way.

When you look at the practice of the prophet Muhammad, who is one of my great heroes and one of the supreme sacred activists of history, you see that he was absolutely not afraid to go into battle. He was not only a great prophet, a supreme mystic, but also a king and a general. If you look carefully at the Koran, you see that the Koran lays down in very explicit sentences and ways exactly how to proceed in war: women and children and materials and trees and the environment were never to be destroyed. And prisoners were always to be treated with mercy and generosity. He himself showed this in his practice. Muhammad represented this sacred action from a sacred consciousness even in extreme circumstances.

Another wonderful example would be Sri Aurobindo. Because of his deep passion for the evolution of a divine humanity, Aurobindo knew absolutely that the Nazis threatened the evolution of humanity and knew perfectly well that they represented the darkest imaginable forces of evil, and that there was no way that they could be stopped except by force. This is one reason that he really challenged Gandhi. He said, "Do you really believe, Mahatma Gandhi, that by linking hands and singing and praying that the Jews could somehow escape the horror of the concentration camps? Of course not! We have to get together to stop the Nazis and to eliminate Nazism. Otherwise the future of humanity is a futureless one!"

Aurobindo is a very important evolutionary philosopher, perhaps the greatest of them all. He is also what all the great mystics are, which are realists. What realism in *our* situation shows us is that we really have to be prepared for anything. If the future of humanity is at stake, we will need to get together and oppose it by whatever means necessary to prevent a monstrous abortion and the terrible death taking place.

Again the Dalai Lama's warning is a very important one. He said that only those could be trusted to use the very dangerous and ambiguous weapon of violence if they had been trained in nonviolence. So, anyone who wants to prepare themselves as a sacred activist for the potentially terrifying future needs to ground themselves in peace, compassion, and an absolute surrender to the divine world, so that if they are called to take up force, they will only do so with the divine mercy and divine compassion and effectiveness.

JM: I think it's also beneficial to remember that Gandhi was advocating some strategies that were more potent and effective than singing and holding hands. Noncooperation and constructing self-sustaining systems were integral parts of his constructive nonviolence program. Regarding the Nazis, Gandhi did advocate nonviolence and was regularly questioned about this. And actually when nonviolence was employed, it seems to have worked and saved thousands and thousands of people. Just a few examples are the Rosenstrasse incident in Berlin, when Jewish husbands were taken by the Gestapo, and the German wives of those men rallied in front of the prison and demanded their release and were successful. In Denmark, virtually all of the Jewish population was saved by noncooperation and disruption by a vast underground movement. And in Le Chambon, France, the villagers collectively created a safe haven for Jews, and about five thousand Jewish people survived with their help. I agree with the Dalai Lama and even Gandhi, that in certain cases force may be necessary, but I think the history of nonviolent success is largely overshadowed by the intensity of the history of violence, and it's important to remember the vast possibilities of nonviolence.

AH: Absolutely. I think it is one of the most important trainings that Sacred Activism needs to offer. It's a training that can really explore all of the kinds of strategies that you're describing and really solidify them so they can be used. Obviously the use of violence must be the absolutely last resort, after all of these strategies have been tried and exhausted. Thank you for pointing that out. It's very important.

JM: I would like to hear about anger, and what to do with anger in terms of being an activist and a spiritual practitioner. In *The Hope* you write, "In today's world it's not only our right to be angry, it's our responsibility. The question is do we act out of anger or love?" This is a constant question for me. A lot of activists I know go along with a sort of bumper-sticker sentiment: "If you're not angry, then you're not paying attention." But if we're acting out of that anger, then one can be simply spreading more anger. How to transform anger into compassion and peace and the kind of world we want to live in?

AH: The greatest and most holy anger arises out of deep love. When Jesus overturned the tables in the temple with such fury, it was because he loved the sanctity of the direct connection of human beings with God, and he really felt that polluting the temple in that way with merchandise and business was an abomination. So there is a holy anger and that's very important. We have to also understand that in the greatest tantric and evolutionary mystical systems, we are given a way not of suppressing and repressing anger, but of *transmuting* anger into fierce compassion and energy. This is the clue for the sacred activist. Many mystics suppress and repress anger and are secretly very depressed or stuck in a ghastly fake cheerfulness. And many activists express anger from a divided consciousness, which can only make the problem worse.

There is a very powerful way beyond both, and that is the way of the tantric systems. In those systems, what you do is to let the anger arise and offer it up to the Divine. So that the *lead* of the neurosis and the fear and anguish in the anger can be removed and the *pure gold* of the fierce energy that arises in the anger can then be employed in focused ways to affect change.

One very powerful practice that I was given by a great Hindu tantric in Benares is to allow your anger to arise and imagine that Kali, the dark goddess, appears before you and opens Her belly, and that out of your belly streams that wild rage that you're feeling in a black and gold stream. The black represents the pain, fear, and anguish, the wounded ego, the outrage. And the gold represents the fierce, beautiful energy of righteousness that is arising. They both go into the belly of the goddess, and the goddess closes Her belly and then She opens it. She absorbs the dark of that energy and She sends you back the pure, vibrant, living gold, and you imagine your whole being—your heart, mind, and body—filled with that vibrant, golden passion energy. Anger can be transmuted into a focused, passionate compassion.

All those who are really trying to be sacred activists need to learn this great tantric judo, because [if you use it,] your anger becomes your friend and not your enemy. Anger actually becomes the source of a beautiful, holy power that can help you sustain your actions through everything.

JM: I hope to put that into practice.

AH: I'm trying, too. It's something that I work with all of the time. I think that some people are too chilled out and some people are too heated up. I certainly belong to the second category and I work very, very hard to transmute my outrage and fury and my boiling passion about what is happening in the world into a calm, clear, focused, fierce, compassionate energy. Over time I've found that it has really extraordinary results to practice like that. But you have to do it constantly, because you have to combine it with shadow work. You have to try to understand the deepest levels where your shadow might be influencing your mind. By separating slowly through deep self-knowledge, your shadow from your emotions, you can purify your emotions so that they become in service to the divine will and not in service of your own agonizing ego.

JM: I tend to consider my anger as an enemy, so I always appreciate teachings that are offering ways of making friends with all aspects of myself.

AH: I think it's essential to realize that anger can be a powerful agent of love in action, but only when it's been transmuted in this way, through divine grace.

"World Crisis, Accountability, and Change"
A Discussion with Chris Wingate

A leading scholar and practitioner of the world's mystical traditions, author, teacher, and visionary, Andrew Harvey has a vision of transformation and evolution that could just save the world.

Chris Wingate: Looking at the struggles that our world is currently facing, you believe that we are in a state of crisis that will force our hands toward a new way of thinking and behaving. Is it faith in the human spirit or faith in the Divine that gives you hope for the future, or do you see this as a "do or die" situation?

Andrew Harvey: Well, very much both. I think that there is a Great Death going on and that this Great Death is obvious now to everybody with half a brain and half a heart. It involves an environmental holocaust that is devastating the environment. It involves the proliferation of nuclear and biological weapons, which threaten millions of people. It involves the escalation of a massive conflict in the Middle East, which is looking extremely dangerous. It involves the dereliction of a whole world through an obsession with technology. It involves a mass media addicted to pornography, violence, trash, and trivialization, at a moment when the whole world needs serious, deep, profound inspiration. It involves a pace of life that is so crazy it makes everybody half crazy. I think when you think of all these crises together, you see very clearly that we're in a situation that threatens the life of humanity and the life of the planet.

This would be a complete disaster if there weren't some divine meaning to it, and I believe that there very much is. I think that the divine meaning is that this Great Death is destined to compel humanity to discover its own divine nature and to work from that discovery, in unity with itself and with nature, to rebuild an almost totally ruined world.

I think that human arrogance has taken us to this absolute limit of folly in which we are so dissociated from the world that we are killing the very atmosphere that is supposed to sustain us in an act of unprecedented suicidal stupidity by any species.

So we really deeply need to embrace the truth of this death, and also to see that it is the condition of a Great Birth, that this Great Birth is going on right now. There's a Great Birth in the crisis itself, as a situation that's going to compel an evolutionary leap. It's a birth in the growth of new technologies, in the return of the Divine Feminine, and in the cultivation of the philosophy of nonviolence, which has been shown to work in extreme situations—by Gandhi, by the Dalai Lama, and by Nelson Mandela. It is also a birth in the deep, passionate growth of all kinds of people who are waking up and realizing that there is a potential extinction crisis of the human race, but also realizing that God is in us and that we do have the divine nature. We can use this death to go deeper into the birth and midwife a new humanity in harmony with nature and in a true pursuit of justice. I think this crisis is meant to be used by the Divine as a way of crucifying our illusions and being born into the world of divine humanity, which would give us direct access to unimaginable power.

This power is to be used, not for domination and exploitation, but for healing, for tremendous worldwide healing—healing of the poor, healing of the oceans, healing of the divisions, healing of all of the separations between all beings. There could be paradise on earth.

CW: It's interesting to think of the parallels between humanity as a whole and one person. Many people have to experience the dark night of the soul, or bottom out, to be able to evolve.

AH: It's essential. Otherwise you don't get to know the truth of life. You cannot go into the divine dimension standing up thinking you are something. You only enter into your own divinity by knowing that you are nothing at some very profound level. Only that knowledge and nothing else can give you access to "the everything" that you also are—it is the condition of this evolution.

Otherwise that divine knowledge would be given to the drunken and the crazy and the egocentric and the power hungry, and they would inevitably misuse it. It may only be attained by the death of the full self. Humanity is going to have to discover that too. Those who do not know the wisdom of the dark night—that there is a crucifixion process that leads to the resurrection and the new energy, the new identity, a new truth, a new power, a new strength—these people are going to be driven crazy by what's coming down.

That's why the mystical knowledge of crucifixion and resurrection are so important. That's why it's so important to understand that this Great Death is a Great Birth. That's why it's so important to become really concerned about how to become a Sacred Activist.

The only thing that will give any life, power, strength, or coherence in the years to come is the person who knows that he or she is trying to do the best he or she can to avert this madness that threatens everything.

I think it is important to be unillusioned, to be realistic, but it's also very important to understand that there is a tremendous secret in this adventure, the secret of a possible transfiguration of humanity if we go for it with all the passion, truth, humility, and deep desire to serve that we can possibly muster. Whatever happens, the only important thing will be to have lived in love, to have lived in the divine energy, to have given everything that one could possibly give to other beings to make this unendurable situation endurable.

It's really getting extremely crazy. Even the most conservative scientists are now saying that global warming is much worse than we think.

CW: It's amazing to think of how much evidence it has taken for some people to finally get over the idea of trying to conceal knowledge or spin facts so that things seem better than they are.

AH: If you could write the history of climate change as a sort of study of an advancing psychosis, you would actually get to the clue of the problem. The deepest problem is that our countries are in massive denial. Those who are not in denial are on the verge of breakdown. The only ones who are holding up are those who are doing the work of Sacred Activism, whether they know it by that name or not.

People who have a deep spiritual connection to the Divine know that they are divine, know that life is divine, the world is divine and they are actually doing things in the real world, with real resources, out of love for the world, guided by inner wisdom. Those are the people who are going to get through a time of devastating affairs. If they don't get through, those are the ones who are going to live the life that will make living here worthwhile.

CW: So sacred activists will facilitate this process of change and lay the groundwork for those who come after them doing sacred work?

AH: Exactly, there's no way out, and it's actually a tremendously joyful opportunity.

CW: Many people feel an "itch" to be active in changing our world. Some recognize that there are problems in our world but feel powerless, don't know how to facilitate change or where to begin. What do you say to people who are apathetic or feel they can't make a difference, can't kindle the "you can do it" spirit?

AH: I would tell them that I completely understand why they feel powerless. I think that first we need to understand why we all, at some very profound level, feel a tremendous depression. By trying to open up the door of desolation, we can understand that this suffering and depression at a very great level is fundamentally because we are waking up to the fact that we are really like serial killers on the loose, having destroyed ourselves, our environment, having destroyed hundreds of species in the process of burning down the rainforests. I mean, my God, what kind of people are we? I think at some profound level we all register the unbelievable shock that we are actually the people who incinerated hundreds of thousands of people with nuclear bombs, who murdered over a hundred million people in concentration camps in the twentieth century, who strip-mined the environment without giving a damn, who annihilated species after species. This is a big deal at some psychic level.

CW: A lot of people do their best to ignore these issues. Perhaps this is where apathy comes from, looking at all the various problems and feeling all the "guilts" and saying, "well, gosh, where do I start?"

AH: After having explored the foundation of depression and accepted it, we then have to realize that apathy is the last temptation. Given the depth of the problem, what possible way out of it could there be except through real, concerted action? There is no other way. So apathy is a luxury that no one can afford.

It's not realistic. It's not going to make you happy. It's not going to give you any sense of exaltation about your life. It's certainly not going to bring you into a search deep enough to uncover your divine identity. It's not going to give you any kind of clue as to why this process is happening, and it's not going to give you a role that you can feel decent about in indecent times. So you're going to be screwed from every level if you continue to indulge the virus of apathy.

I'm being very direct, because I think it's time to be direct. I think there is a coma that I call the "Coca-Coma." It is as if there's a bomb that's gone off that has killed the psyche, but not the people's bodies. So this is what is so difficult at this moment—we are facing unprecedented crises with a largely destroyed psyche. That is why the whole vision of Sacred Activism is so important. It offers a way of inner healing that leads to the desire to act and the knowledge of how to act.

My teaching is to follow your heartbreak. You can't solve all the world's problems. Decide which of them absolutely breaks your heart and dedicate your time to that, because that heartbreak will give you outrage, compassion, passion, and energy. Heartbreak is kind of a divine virtue, a divine guide into the depths of your real mission.

CW: Once you overcome apathy and recognize problems, you believe that through the process of Sacred Activism, you can form a foundation of how to go about creating change?

AH: The clue to the whole movement is the realization that the way through is to combine the true fire of the mystic (which is a very holy passion for God, a passion to unify the soul's substance with the substance of God) with the fundamental passion of the activist. The holiest impulse behind activism is the passion for justice, the fiery, compassionate passion to see justice done for all beings. If you unite these two fires within yourself, what you have is a paired fire that combines the power of those two, but goes further, because it is a new combination.

So the first thing is for people to feel this new intensity in their bodies. That is only possible through sacred practice, sacred adoration, and through a deep turning of the self toward the divine Beloved in whatever way you know. The foundation of a new form of action is a new form of feeling.

The program of Sacred Activism is a combination of mystical and intellectual work and right, practical action. We are trying to strengthen the intellectual understanding of the crisis, strengthen the heart's wisdom in the face of the crisis, strengthen the soul's awareness of its divine identity, and strengthen the body's capacity to absorb new levels of divine energy.

CW: Do you stress the importance of being grounded in preparation for dealing with struggles?

AH: I think that what is important is, in a deep sense, to be grounded in your true nature. If you have spiritual practices in your daily life that keep you calm, that keep you awake, then use them, because they will become the foundation that can produce the kind of energy, wisdom, and compassion that can guide you to act with great intelligence.

CW: One of the subjects of lectures you present is "Direct Path Yoga for Sacred Activists." How does this tie in?

AH: I believe that sacred activists are going to need sacred physical disciplines. Over the last few years I've had the great fortune to work with a true genius of yoga, Karuna Erickson. Together we have married the deep mystical roots of yoga with a whole way of looking at the divine light in a mystical way.

We believe it has created a very powerful yoga for the transformation of the human body and for the strengthening of the entire being, which is essential for Sacred Activism. What I'm doing is sharing the mystical wisdom and advice that is essential for learning how to act in Sacred Activism.

"Powered by Love: From Human to Divine, the Path of Transformation as a Sacred Activist" Interview with Louise Danielle Palmer

An Invocation

Rise and place your hands on your heart. Bow your head to your heart and in doing so, bow your mind, bow your intelligence, bow your ego, to the presence of the Living One, however you understand that within you. And as you bow your head to your heart, be real about where you and I are at this moment. You and I are in an apocalyptic situation in which the entire world is burning, in which the whole future of humanity is threatened, and in which all of the species are being decimated by our greed and our cruelty. And so, in bowing the head to the heart, we are doing more than simply enjoying a spiritual moment. We are all crying out silently and in profound pain, in an agony of compassion and in a hunger of spiritual delight, to the Beloved to dwell in us, to come and transform us, to make us wise, to make us authentic, to awaken us, and to give us the power, the grace, the intensity, and the energy to become authentic sacred activists.

Sacred Activism was born from a visionary experience, but it is much more than a vision. It is an epic narrative of birth and death. It is an invitation to undergo a radical change that ignites the divine spark deep within. It is a way through to a world so transformed that its contours cannot yet be described, only imagined. It is a plan and a promise and a prayer. If it strikes you, as it struck me, like a sword of light through the heart, if it delivers you to your highest calling and brings you to the awful grace of truth, it's because this message is delivered in a prophetic voice.

This voice is deeply rooted in mystical law, inspired by a lifetime of spiritual devotion, divined through shattering revelation. It belongs to Andrew Harvey, an Oxford-trained religious scholar and author of thirty books, and coeditor of the bestselling *The Tibetan Book of Living and Dying.* Harvey is recognized the world over as a living mystic, who has charted the journey into the great wisdom traditions of Buddhism, Sufism, Hinduism, and Christianity. He was the first major Western teacher to be openly gay and among the first to champion the rise of the feminine face of God. Spiritual and intellectual luminaries ranging from Marianne Williamson to Lance Morrow have called him a "genius" and "one of the world's irreplaceable resources." Still, Harvey has not always been popular in New Age circles. Just as he was labeled a traitor for deconstructing the Eastern guru system and advocating instead a direct path to God, some now criticize Harvey for sounding a call for Sacred Activism that is too radical.

"When the coming crisis reveals itself fully, it will threaten us at the most fundamental depths," Harvey says. "If we aren't rooted in our spiritual identity, we will be driven into meaninglessness and despair unless there are people to say, 'No, this horror can be healed through the sublime truth! We will survive and we will find purpose and joy and love through sacred practice and sacred action.' In fact, that is the whole point of the crisis—to drive us to that place where we, as a species, will have to go into our divine nature. The truth of our situation brings tremendous turmoil, a huge, sacred turbulence into the core of one's life, but this turbulence is the condition for the flowering of more and more divine grace, divine passion, and divine energy."

Larry Dossey, MD, likens Harvey to an "Old Testament prophet whose words are ignored at great peril." Indeed, in keeping with the tradition, Harvey has walked through the spiritual fire himself, emerging not with a scorched heart but with a tender one. Sacred Activism is the bright flame that burns urgently inside him, fueled by a compassion for all creatures and for all of life. His mission, as he sees it, is to exhort, compel, guide, and inspire every one of us to become fire-walkers as well. And so, into the fire we step.

We all know, on some level, that things are bad. What we may not know—and what may be Harvey's greatest contribution to shaping the story we live by—is that two realities are manifesting as a result of our actions, positive and negative, individual and collective. Harvey believes a Great Death is unfolding at the same time as a Great Birth; they are emerging simultaneously because they are interdependent. Indeed, Harvey characterizes this death as the birth canal of new life—of a new humanity that recognizes its divinity. But there's a caveat: only a powerful, loving army of sacred activists can transcend the Great Death and usher in the Great Birth.

Harvey believes that our first task is to see the crisis clearly, because it is in seeing that we will be compelled to transform ourselves—our habits of denial, addiction, and overconsumption—and from that holy place of spiritual transformation, respond with the depth of love and action that is necessary. So here are the seven aspects of the Great Death:

1. Population explosion. Demographers believe that current population is expected to triple to nine billion by 2050—three billion more people than the planet can support.

2. The growth of fundamentalism. Rather than coming together and relinquishing their claims of exclusivity, the world's religions are retreating into violent separatism.

3. Nuclear proliferation. The unprecedented spread of weapons of mass destruction is a great (and growing) threat to life on the planet.

4. Ecological devastation. One hundred and twenty species disappear into extinction every day, our seas are polluted, the Amazon is on fire, Antarctica is melting, and so on.

5. Our technological worldview. We have turned the earth into a great cement garden. Being disconnected from the natural world impoverishes our spirit and imagination.

6. Corporate media. Instead of being informed about the true dimension of the crisis and our role in it, we are subject to an avalanche of celebrity trivia, half-baked news, reality shows, pornography, and violence.

7. This "Coca-Coma," as Harvey calls it, puts us in a state of anxiety, depression, and fear, keeping us addicted to our destructive, consumerist way of life. While we chase after that day, which keeps us hectically busy but never fulfills us, we have no time and no peace, the essential ingredients of a spiritual life and the key to discovering our divine identity.

In the course of evolving as a species, we have discovered one-half of the God-power within us: the power to destroy. Now, Harvey believes, we must embody the other half: the power within us to create. This power is reflected in the golden mirror he calls the Great Birth, made up of Seven Stars that counteract the Great Death. They are:

1. The crisis itself. The forces of destruction we have unleashed will be so horrific that they have the capacity to shake awake the slumbering Divine within us and the radiant impulse to nurture and sanctify life. From that place, nothing but grace, love, and salvation flow.

2. Democratizing media. New communication technologies are a source of alternative information independent of government and corporations. They represent an unprecedented grassroots-organizing tool with global reach.

3. Creative technologies. That which brought us the cement garden can, and is, bringing us life-enhancing innovations,

including new sources of energy that are self-generating and nonpolluting. Advances, from medicine to quantum physics, will have the capacity to heal us and the planet in new ways we can't yet foresee.

4. The spiritual renaissance sweeping the globe, countering the fundamentalist impulse. In the past thirty years, most sacred texts have been translated and mystical practices that have been closely guarded secrets for millennia have been shared. It is no coincidence, Harvey says, that we are now being blessed with the divine wisdom and power that allow us to transform ourselves.

5. An evolution in the philosophy of nonviolence. In the past century, individuals such as Gandhi, Nelson Mandela, Rosa Parks, and the Dalai Lama have given us the tools, the insight, and the knowledge of how to affect fundamental change through love and compassion.

6. The return of the Sacred Feminine. The healing of the planet and humanity is unfolding as the full power of the feminine, in all Her rage, beauty, and wildness, unfolds. Sacred activism is the sacred marriage of the masculine (consciousness) and feminine (creation) forces unifying heaven and earth, body and soul, spirituality and politics, the human and the divine.

7. The will of God to allow for a humanity transformed. As well as the detached spectator envisioned by patriarchal traditions, Harvey says God is also Mother determined to save and elevate Her creation, pushing us deeper into our divine creativity and revolutionary passion.

"I know there is a way to be a conscious creator with God in this stupendous birth of the divine human taking place through the chaos of our time," Harvey says, "and that is the way of the sacred activist. But the word *sacred* carries with it the need for great inner transformation."

The Power of Love

Only when we have truly surrendered our will to God, only when our minds and hearts are shattered open by what we have created out of our ignorance, will we go deep enough to the Divine within and bring out the energies of transformation, Harvey says. "People can criticize this teaching as too morbid or too bloody, but it's neither. It's the law of transformation in all the authentic mystical traditions."

Harvey was raised in southern India, a place he credits with instilling in him a love for all religious traditions, as well as a deep sense of the sacred dimension of life. From the age of nine, he was educated in England and became the youngest person ever to be awarded a fellowship to All Souls College at Oxford. Disillusioned with academia, he returned to India in his mid-twenties, embarking on a journey across the subcontinent, during which he met a succession of saints, sages, and teachers, and began his study of Hinduism. In Ladakh he was introduced to the great Tibetan adept Thuksey Rinpoche and undertook with him the Mahayana Buddhist bodhisattva vows. After moving to Europe, he devoted himself to an Indian teacher named Mother Meera, and embarked on a decade-long exploration of the Sufi tradition. In his forties, Harvey developed a relationship with the great Christian mystic Father Bede Griffiths, who helped him synthesize his spiritual explorations and reconcile Eastern and Western mysticism.

For anyone on a serious spiritual path, Harvey learned, there are two kinds of initiations. The first is the realization that everything and everyone comes from the same divine source, or what some call "unity consciousness." It took fifteen years of rigorous practice before Harvey was graced with this experience, at the age of 37, while living in Paris.

"I saw everything vanish into light and I knew I was the light and the light was me," Harvey explained during our interviews at his home in New York City. "It was like the void exploded as the whole world blazed with light. I wasn't there in my room anymore—there was just a fiery dance of atoms, a fiery dance of bliss consciousness. The Sufis say there are two journeys, the journey to God and the journey in God. That was the end of the journey to God for me. It was the most beautiful initiation imaginable. I thought it was "it," not realizing it was just the beginning, a gift to make you strong enough to take the great shattering."

This shattering marks the second initiation, he explains. "The divine heart is really the Divine Mother's heart feeling the suffering created by our ignorance. So, as the Divine draws you nearer, it draws you through these rounds of beauty and bliss until you are ready to experience the agony of the Mother's heart, which nearly kills you."

Harvey's second initiation took place over two decades, culminating in 2000 in a pilgrimage to Arunachula, a mountain in southern India not far from where Harvey was born, a place where yogis have for thousands of years performed austerities and other acts of spiritual devotion to Shiva, the great Hindu god of creation and destruction.

"I began my walk around the mountain in the dark," he recalls. "There I was, trying to concentrate on my mantra, thinking I was going to have a transcendent experience, when out of the sacred darkness emerged all the horror and grief, the abject, unspeakable obscenity of India's suffering: deformed people, crying old women with no money, people with AIDS clawing at me—a cacophony of misery all around me. Finally, I came to this crossroads and there, strapped to a board, was an epileptic screaming and howling, his mouth foaming. That scream ended something for me. I can only describe it this way: until that moment, despite everything that had happened to me, there was a kind of invisible glass wall around me. That scream shattered that glass wall. I lost control over my whole body and started to shake and tremble.

"I walked off into this field covered with sharp stones and cut my feet open. My bowels were running all down my legs. I was a complete derelict. I had joined the people in the darkness. I was nowhere and had nothing. Someone who knew me saw me and told me: 'Shiva has struck you down, you must return and you must be peaceful.' He took me back to my hotel and I didn't leave there for three days. The first day I experienced all the suffering I've lived through in my life, and I cried and cried. And on the second, I went through vision after vision after vision of what has happened and will happen on earth, the Great Death. And on the third day, I was lifted from the dead, and I saw the Great Birth. This is where I speak from, and why I am in a state of advanced urgency. I know where we are and I know where we're going if we don't do everything we can to change."

This death and rebirth process is described in the great mystical traditions as a rending apart, a disemboweling, or a dark night of the soul. It is the crucifixion and the resurrection. It is what the shaman and the saint experience. It is represented in the life of Rumi, Jesus, and the Buddha, all of whom, it is said, differ from us only in that they know that God resides within. It is, in fact, represented in our own lives, through our own personal experience, whether we consciously recognize it or not.

"A seed has to break open for the seed to spill and a tree to grow," Harvey notes. "A woman's body is nearly torn apart when a child is born out of it. This universe was born in a vast scream of light, a stupendous and glorious Big Bang. Creation is often terrifying, bloody, ferocious, and that is how it happens in the soul."

It is also how it will now happen in the soul of the world, Harvey believes, and it is crucial to understand and to fully engage in this process ourselves so we are equipped to "midwife" this great rebirth.

"When the blood of heartbreak comes together with the light of divine joy and peace, the sacred heart of the sacred activist is born, and from that heart flows a golden, ecstatic torrent of passion to change all things out of love for all things," Harvey says. "The world is going to go through what looks like annihilation. Only those who aren't afraid of this and are able to teach about this, only those who have taken on this deep mystical practice, will be able to lead the world through this great transformation. The birth of the Divine in the human is a volcanic, cosmic event. It isn't like you wake up one day in Kansas as Jesus Christ. It's a huge, frightening, scary, amazing, incredible set of processes that unfolds over a lifetime."

Being a sacred activist means a profound engagement of this process on a personal, spiritual, and political level. Through our willingness to let our hearts break open completely, Harvey says our pain will be transformed into love—a love that is so eternal, so transcendent, so unbound that we ourselves become identified with it. This is not a rational process. It is a kind of divine alchemy.

While this process is a mystical one, it is also grounded in practical action. Harvey outlines five ways in which we can work to unleash the astounding power of divine passion and love necessary to heal and transform ourselves, and the world, step by step, one by one.

The cornerstone of Sacred Activism is serving God with our whole being. Can we have enough humility to recognize that we need the divine light to heal and change? Harvey believes we must. We must turn our whole being to God in adoration, in thanksgiving, and in longing, so that our actions are illuminated, guided, and energized by that light.

Without turning to the great source of power that transcends us all, Harvey says, we will not be able to elevate our consciousness to act wisely and precisely and powerfully enough to make a real difference. Being truly centered in our divine identity allows us to face the Great Death and respond to it with love, rather than burn out, fall into anger, or give up in frustration. Spiritual practice enables us to surrender the fruit of our actions to God, face our own shadow, and maintain faith.

Serving the Divine may include regular visits to a mosque, church, temple, or mountain; it may consist of daily meditation and prayer; it may involve chanting the names of God. Whatever it looks like for us, steeping ourselves in the depths of our divine identity must be at the core of our lives as authentic sacred activists.

We must revere ourselves as sacred instruments of God. This means trying to keep ourselves whole through proper diet and rest, regular exercise and meditation, and psychological work on our own shadow.

Of all practices, shadow work is the most challenging. It involves acknowledging that we are all colluding in this crisis in the ways we think, act, feel, eat, consume, and pollute; in the way our culture is intoxicated by money, power, and celebrity. It involves understanding that "they" are not doing it; "we" together are doing it.

"You are going to have to be the change you want to see, and you're going to have to be very strong and very powerful, and that strength and that power will not come from your ego," Harvey says. "It will come from your surrendered self. It will be God's presence residing in you, driving you on like a whirlwind into the center of the world to radiate the power of love."

Recognize that everybody and everything we meet is the face of God—the woman bagging our groceries, the dog gamboling in the garden, Democrats and Republicans. Sacred Activism is about acting from a place of "secret unity" with all beings so that we no longer hate or separate ourselves from those we consider to be our enemies. Only people who have forgiven at that depth can embody the kind of intelligent love that opens doors in locked prisons, the kind of love that will lead us out of our own folly and illusion. The Divine will not bless anything less than divine action, Harvey says, and the divine blessing is crucial.

"This doesn't mean we don't criticize and we don't fight against bad policies, it simply means we manifest respect," Harvey says. "People can feel when you patronize or condemn them. If we instead approach everyone and everything we meet as a face of God, a light will go on in our life, and the mystery of the unity of the Divine will become clear to us. We will receive the guidance we need. We will be helped—perhaps more helped—by the people in opposition to our ideas than by those who support our ideas, because they will be a face of the Divine saying to us, 'Get your ideas sharper, be more in love with Me. Do more to be real in your life so those who oppose you will be overwhelmed by the reality of your presence, because it will be My presence in you.'"

Figure out what we realistically can do in our own community with our own resources. We aren't called to save the world single-handedly (although if every person took action, it would change the world), but to do what we can in our own lives.

"One morning, wake yourself up at three in the morning and pray to the Beloved," Harvey suggests. "Open your heart to the agony of the world and listen to what comes to you. What is your heartbreak? What robs you of sleep? What makes you cry out to God in the middle of the night? What makes you yearn with your whole being to change? Find out, because if you do, you will find a source of inextinguishable flames and tears, which will open your sacred heart. When your sacred heart is open, out of it will come a torrent of focused passion, which will give you the energy to go on and on, giving of yourself. So I don't say follow your bliss; look where that has gotten us. I say follow your heartbreak."

Consider what it means to have sacred compassion on every level for all beings, including the animals, everywhere, in every community around the world. We must be determined to act responsibly and compassionately in the way we vote, the car we drive, the investments we make, the food and clothes we buy. We must educate ourselves about what is happening in the world around us.

"Learn about why two billion people are living on less than a dollar a day," Harvey suggests. "Try to understand the systems of cold evil by reading masterly analyses of the ways in which corporations are killing our world. Start waking up from what Graham Green called America's 'insanity of innocence.' Become bloodied by the real blood of the real world and start aligning your choices with all the beings of all the world as global citizens."

These five kinds of service make up a daily practice. Practice does not imply perfection, it implies slow, steady, gentle, but intense work. Then, when we are called to face situations that require of us all that we are, Harvey says, we will find that everything we need is waiting in our hearts. The blessing of the Divine will fill us with love and with joy. It will flow from our hands and our hearts, and it will transform this world, because we ourselves have been transformed: "We must live in such a way that the splendor of our lives, the passion of our lives, and the beauty of our lives is its own statement reaching out in a flame of divine passion that awakens the latent divine flame of passion in others."

"The Hope" Interview with Sharon Hall

Years ago, Andrew Harvey—mystic, poet, translator, scholar, spiritual teacher, founder of the Institute of Sacred Activism, and passionate environmental activist—helped me get through a spiritual crisis. I had not met him yet, but finding his books was like finding a friend. Andrew's passionate, poetic writing helped me realize that I was not alone.

I met Mr. Harvey this year at an expo in Los Angeles. He was there to talk about his book, *The Hope: A Guide to Sacred Activism.* After a day surrounded by psychics, mediums, and crystals, hearing him speak was like stepping from shade into brilliant sunlight. He offered hard truths: the world is crying out—do we have the guts to listen and respond? The audience that day was asked to consider an important question: "What, of all the causes in this burning world, breaks my heart the most?" Answering that with our whole being would reveal our own path of Sacred Activism.

I spoke with Mr. Harvey over the phone—about *The Hope* and Sacred Activism, about the coming global shakedown and shadow, and about his relationship to the Divine Mother, who continues to inspire and energize his life and work.

Sharon Hall: I've been thinking about Sacred Activism in light of Japan and the Middle East. You wrote and talked about the precipitating event of a global crisis before these recent events took place. Is this the beginning?

Andrew Harvey: We are going to be shaken awake. There will be a perfect storm of events designed to wake us up to the truth: all our current agendas are illusions, and we are living unsustainable lives. It is showing up in environmental disasters, financial disaster, in millions living on less than a dollar a day, in the burning down of the forests, in the pollution of our oceans. There is more to come.

SH: Is it too late for us?

AH: In a terrifying sense, it's going exactly as it has to go. We have to be shattered in order to be healed. The old ways, the old agendas, have to be deconstructed so the new that is already here has room to emerge in greater strength. The truth is, there's a Great Birth taking place in the middle of, and partly as a result of, a Great Death—this is a divine mystery. What the human race is going through on a global scale is what the mystic goes through in the dark night of the soul.

SH: You have said we won't survive this deconstruction without the grace of the Divine, our spiritual practices, and our work with our own shadow-material. You've described it as one of the key practices of a sacred activist. Many spiritual people either demonize this shadow aspect, or seem to ignore it completely.

AH: Without confronting our personal shadow, which colludes with the collective shadow, we won't get through the crisis. And, we can't do this kind of work without first being grounded in the Divine.

SH: Should we have compassion even for those who are bringing about such destruction?

AH: Of course, because they are doing the most appalling things to themselves first in order to do these dreadful things. But that should not stop us from opposing their actions with real vigor—while still holding them in our hearts.

The Power of Love

SH: That's a beautiful vision, and a hard place for many activists to hold.

AH: It's a hard place for anyone to hold. Gandhi brilliantly opposed the whole edifice of the British Empire and, at the same time, honored every English person. Martin Luther King deeply opposed the injustice and horrific cruelty that had manifested in the system against African Americans, but managed to hold the white people involved in the core of his heart. The Dalai Lama has devoted his entire life to undoing the horror of what the Chinese did to the Tibetans; he continues to treat the Chinese with respect and compassion and to pray for their spiritual liberation.

SH: Not an easy thing to do.

AH: It's an impossible thing to do in the frightened, scared, endlessly compromised, and endlessly corrupt ego. It's only possible by going into our enlightened self, where all sacred activists are being required to go, and to put in place structures that can survive.

SH: You have talked and written about such structures or cells—networks of grace—you are creating, which will hold their integrity in the midst of rapid change. Aren't people in many traditions doing this, through spiritual practices, prayer, and community?

AH: Grace and practice and prayer are essential, but they have to be backed up by actions in the real world. The new human being created by the Divine is a person rooted in the deepest spiritual practices, but who uses the fuel of love and wisdom that comes from these practices in order to be strong enough to act for justice in the world—with compassion, love, and wisdom.

SH: Jesus tossing the moneylenders from the temple.

AH: Yes. He's doing that as much for the moneylenders as for those who are being victimized by and colluding with them. He is exercising divine ferocity at that moment, as an act of compassion for those still trapped in the ego.

SH: This term—divine ferocity—reminds me of the wrathful deities in Tibetan Buddhism. Utterly fierce, full of terrifying and fearsome power, but still Buddhas!

AH: Yes! You can only obtain such divine ferocity when you can love those who oppose you as much as you love those who are with you. When you can achieve that, divinely ferocious action comes straight from the heart of Divine Love.

SH: Andrew, you have spoken and written about your struggles, your own dark night of the soul.

AH: I think we all have to go through a dark night in order to be broken down; in order to become truly empty. Then, the divine fire can awaken in us and possess us.

SH: You have said this came about, in your own case, from loss and betrayal by a beloved teacher. How did you survive, emotionally and spiritually?

AH: I think one person dies and another is born. Betrayal that deep, that cruel and ferocious, can drive a person to a place where they are the strongest—it forces one into the Divine. All the mystical traditions have talked about the necessity to die in this life before the death of the body. That is the dark night—and it's the ultimate mercy, because it saves us from being trapped in the false self. And it's very dangerous. That's why I'm trying to bring through this vision of Sacred Activism so people can be ready for what's coming.

It's a question of being able to respond—creatively, joyfully, and passionately, with one's whole being—to something that feels to the ego like total disaster. That paralysis is already here. Most Americans seem incapable of protesting against anything that is done to them, don't they?

SH: If sure seems that way. Things flash by for a moment then we're on to the next. Do you think recent events are forcing people to wake up?

AH: Look. America had 9/11 and was told to shop. You had Katrina, and that's already a distant memory. Then there was the oil spill in the Gulf. That was bad news for a while, but now it's almost forgotten. You had the 2008 financial collapse. All people can think about now are the very small signs of financial recovery. But the entire system is built on sand and it will crumble soon. It will take multiple disasters to penetrate the absolute paralysis of the human mind and heart.

We are now in the position of an addict. When you love an addict, you discover they can fall down stairs, be convicted of stealing, hurt themselves and those around them and do the most appalling things, but keep the addiction; until a devastating moment arrives. Then the addict has to face the fact he or she may die; then he's given a chance to turn it around. Many choose the addiction and die. As a species, we're dangerously close to that choice now.

SH: The Sacred Feminine is very important in your work. How does She figure in this upcoming crisis?

AH: The death aspect of this is Kali stamping Her feet, signaling the end of one kind of human being—the one that's suicidal, matricidal, and addictive. Her other side—the loving, nourishing, Mary side—is flooding us with grace and with new technologies that could wean us from our addiction to oil, and with mystical and spiritual revelations.

The vision of Sacred Activism itself is a vision of putting the Mother's love into action and finding a way out of the madness.

SH: Do you find women have more access to this vision?

AH: Both men and women have a deep wound. Women tend to be more thirsty to discover this abandoned and derelict feminine, but men are waking up to their need to come in contact with their love natures, to stop being slaves and robots. Women are becoming stronger and men are becoming gentler and wiser. This amazing alchemy of the marriage of opposites is taking place in a great many women and a great many men at this time.

SH: I have found from my own experience [that] unless people are actually doing some sort of deep spiritual work there's a tendency toward imbalance. I practice a form of Buddhist meditation and find it really helps.

AH: It's not just spiritual practices that are required; it's also shadow work, especially in groups. Spiritually aware people can disintegrate just as easily as other people. Teachers like Thich Nhat Hanh have evolved a very powerful form of engaged Buddhism. What I believe to be the essence of the Buddhist transmission is the ideal of the bodhisattva, who works ceaselessly for the salvation and good of all beings. That's the key.

I also believe the Dalai Lama is the supreme example of a sacred activist. He has offered ceaseless, loving critique again and again for thirty to forty years—about our environmental policies, our addiction to arms, our addiction to consumerism.

SH: Your book is such a call to reclaim our voices.

AH: And to reclaim the potency and power of our divine empowerment.

SH: It is not about the needs of the ego; it doesn't come from there.

AH: No! It comes from enlightened consciousness. A major misconception is that enlightenment is the end of the journey, but it's just the beginning. Once you've awakened, you have to embody that in everything you think, everything you feel, everything you do. The Divine is not static; it's evolving. Constantly.

Enlightenment is better phrased as the enlightenment field; it's an entrance into a quantum field of expansion.

SH: That idea of something we achieve—that's so Western, isn't it? We want to get the *A;* we want to win the gold.

AH: But it's an entrance into an explosion that continues to explode! I'm sure the Dalai Lama came in very awake, but I do believe that at seventy-five, his awakening is incomprehensibly greater now than it's ever been, because of the intensity of his practice and the dedication of every single moment of his life to the salvation of every being.

SH: Let's talk about love for a moment, Andrew. It's so much a part of what you have talked and written about over the years.

AH: It's a cosmic power that is manifesting everything that lives as everything that is—behind the dance of opposites. It's a gift of the Mother God; a vast, fiery, ecstatic, blissful energy.

SH: In *Return of the Mother,* you describe the Virgin Mary as tantric—ecstatic and fiery. I like that description.

AH: Well, I don't believe in the traditional idea of Mary as an actual virgin; that's a patriarchal fantasy. The woman that we revere as Mary was enormously strong and passionate—and radical. The Magnificat is the most radical thing in the New Testament. Mary calls for complete social, political, and spiritual revolution. And

Her example is of a woman who stood there, and endured, and expanded—just vibrating with the Divine Love. To this day, She inspires people who turn to Her.

SH: Is here anything else you want to add?

AH: Just that the signs of the Birth are there for everyone to see. These signs, from a mystical point of view, are that the crisis itself is both a birth and a death; that extraordinary new technologies are coming in that will show us the way through our addiction to oil; and that the mystical renaissance has made all the sacred technologies from all the mystical and spiritual sources totally available—to everybody.

SH: So, everything we need is already here?

AH: Everything we need is here for us to birth a new world—including crises to show we cannot and should not go on in the same way anymore.

SH: Sounds like a good time to buckle our seatbelts.

AH: It's going to be a bumpy ride. But everything is possible.

SH: Because we're still here.

AH: No. Because She is here, with us. She is in us, and She is guiding this huge, terrible transformation. She is blessing us with the powers and the passion and the vision and the clarity—everything we need is available from Her, because She's here. That's why we can survive. Doesn't that make sense to you, deeply?

SH: It makes complete sense; I can feel Her too.

AH: We have to come down to this place where we can feel the

One who is here already. We have to arrive in our bodies, we have to arrive on the earth, and realize it is Her body; we have to see the animals as Her glorious creations, we have to fall massively in love with the reality that is Her. Then we will know Her and feel Her and feel how much torrential grace is streaming toward us at every moment. Then we will wake up and become strong and do the work—not in the spirit of penance—but in the spirit of great, great joy.

SH: Why do we hesitate to surrender and open completely to this?

AH: Because we're afraid; it means the end of our personal agendas of power, personal satisfaction, personal manipulation—all the games of malice and cruelty, perversion and domination that we've chosen.

SH: The very thing that would save us is what we resist the most.

AH: Yes. But isn't that the drama of the human race? We come close to the fire of Love and are terrified, because we realize this is the fire that will burn our house down. That is when we have to trust the great mystics. As our personal house burns down, we receive the entire cosmos as our new dwelling place.

SH: I'm reminded of the poem about the monk whose house burned to the ground.

AH: I think it's Basho: "My house burned down. Now I own a better view of the rising moon."
Our houses will be burned down and we'll own a much better view of the rising moon. We're going to scream and think we're being destroyed, but the moon will rise on a new human race.

Bibliography

Hart, Hilary. "Blaze of Light, Blood of Creation," in *The Unknown She: Eight Faces of Emerging Consciousness*. Inverness, CA: Golden Sufi Center, 2003.

Harvey, Andrew. *The Direct Path: Creating a Journey to the Divine through the World's Mystical Traditions*. New York: Broadway Books, 2000; London: Duncan Baird, 2011.

———, ed. *The Essential Gay Mystics*. Edison, NJ: Castle Books; San Francisco: HarperSanFrancisco, 1997.

———, ed. *The Essential Mystics: Selections from the World's Great Wisdom Traditions*. New York: HarperCollins, 1997.

———. Excerpt in *Sixty Seconds: One Moment Changes Everything*, collected by Phil Bolsta. Hillsboro, OR: Beyond Words; New York: Atria Books, 2008.

———. Foreword to *Black Sun: The Collected Poems of Lewis Thompson*, edited by Richard Lannoy. Chino Valley, AZ: Hohm Press, 2001.

———. Foreword to *The Book of Mirdad*, by Mikhail Naimy. London: Watkins, 2011.

———. Foreword to *Day Breaks Over Dharamsala*, by Janet Thomas. Friday Harbor, WA: Nutshell Books, 2010.

———. Foreword to *Navigating the Coming Chaos: A Handbook for Inner Transition*, by Carolyn L. Baker. Bloomington, IN: iUniverse, 2011.

———. Foreword to *New Self, New World*, by Philip Shepherd. Berkeley, CA: North Atlantic Books, 2010.

———. Foreword to *The Other Side of Eden: Life with John Steinbeck*, by John Steinbeck IV and Nancy Steinbeck. Amherst, NY: Prometheus Books, 2001.

Bibliography

——. Foreword to *The Seasons of the Soul: The Poetic Guidance and Spiritual Wisdom of Hermann Hesse,* edited and translated by Ludwig Max Fischer. Berkeley, CA: North Atlantic Books, 2011.

——. Foreword to *Spiritual Writings on Mary,* by Mary Ford-Grabowsky. Woodstock, VT: SkyLight Paths, 2005.

——. Foreword to *Unmasking the Rose,* by Dorothy Walters. Charlottesville, VA: Hampton Roads, 2002.

——. Foreword to *The Way of a Pilgrim,* by Gleb Pokrovsky. Woodstock, VT: SkyLight Paths, 2001.

——. Foreword to *Zohar,* annotated and explained by Daniel C. Matt. Woodstock, VT: SkyLight Paths, 2002.

——. Introduction to *Songs of Kabir,* by Kabir. Newburyport, MA: Weiser Books, 2002.

——. Introduction to *Essential Teachings,* by His Holiness The Dalai Lama. Berkeley, CA: North Atlantic Books, 1995.

——. *Hidden Journey: A Spiritual Awakening.* New York: Henry Holt, 1991, 1993; London: Watkins, 2011.

——. *The Hope: A Guide to Sacred Activism.* Carlsbad, CA: Hay House, 2009.

——. *A Journey in Ladakh: Encounters with Buddhism.* New York: Houghton Mifflin, 1983. Reprinted with a new afterward, New York: Houghton Mifflin, 2000.

——. *Light upon Light: Inspirations from Rumi.* Berkeley, CA: North Atlantic Books, 1996.

——. *The Return of the Mother.* Berkeley, CA: Frog Books, 1995; New York: J.P. Tarcher/Putnam, 2001.

——. *Son of Man: The Mystical Path to Christ.* New York: J.P. Tarcher/Putnam, 1998.

——. *Sun at Midnight: A Memoir of the Dark Night.* New York: J.P. Tarcher/Putnam, 2002.

——, ed. *Teachings of Rumi.* Boston: Shambhala, 1999.

——, ed. *Teachings of the Christian Mystics.* Boston: Shambhala, 1998.

——, ed. *Teachings of the Hindu Mystics.* Boston: Shambhala, 2001.

————. *A Walk with Four Spiritual Guides: Krishna, Buddha, Jesus, and Ramakrishna.* Woodstock, VT: SkyLight Paths, 2003.

————. *The Way of Passion: A Celebration of Rumi.* Berkeley, CA: Frog, 1994.

Harvey, Andrew, and Anne Baring. *The Divine Feminine: Exploring the Feminine Face of God throughout the World.* New Alresford, UK: Godsfield Press; Berkeley, CA: Conari Press, 1996.

Harvey, Andrew, and Karuna Erickson. "Heart Yoga: A Response to Today's Stress." Huffington Post. October 4, 2010. http://www .huffingtonpost.com/andrew-harvey-and-karuna-erickson/heart-yoga-the-sacred-mar_b_741671.html.

————. *Heart Yoga: The Sacred Marriage of Yoga and Mysticism.* Berkeley, CA: North Atlantic Books, 2010.

————. "A Response to Today's Challenges: Sacred Activism and Heart Yoga." Huffington Post. September 1, 2010. http://www. huffingtonpost.com/andrew-harvey-and-karuna-erickson/a-response-to-todays-chal_b_699190.html.

————. "Yoga: The Quiet Revolution." Huffington Post. September 24, 2010. http://www.huffingtonpost.com/andrew-harvey-and-karuna-erickson/yoga-the-quiet-revolution_b_731882.html.

Harvey, Andrew, and Eryk Hanut. *Mary's Vineyard: Daily Meditations, Readings, and Revelations.* Wheaton, IL: Theosophical Publishing, 1996.

————. *Perfume of the Desert: Inspirations from Sufi Wisdom.* Wheaton, IL: Quest Books, 1999.

Harvey, Andrew, and Iain Watson. Introduction to *Peintures,* by Victor Segalen, translated by Andrew Harvey and Iain Watson. London: Quartet, 1991.

————. Preface to *Stèles,* by Victor Segalen, translated by Andrew Harvey and Iain Watson. London: Cape, 1990.

Palmer, Louise Danielle. "Powered by Love—From Human to Divine, the Path of Transformation as a Sacred Activist." *Spirituality and Health.* Sept/Oct. 2006.

Interviews and Conversations
with Andrew Harvey

Baker, Carolyn. Interview by Andrew Harvey. "Transition and Transformation: The Joy of Preparation." November 12, 2011. http://carolynbaker.net/carolyns-video-and-radio-interviews/radio-interviews/.

Fischer, Ludwig Max. Interview by Andrew Harvey, discussing *The Seasons of the Soul: The Poetic Guidance and Spiritual Wisdom of Hermann Hesse,* edited and translated by Ludwig Max Fischer. Berkeley, CA: North Atlantic Books, 2011. http://www .hermannhesseseasonsofthesoul.com/fireside-interview.html.

Fox, Matthew. Interview by Andrew Harvey. "The Unfolding of a Prophet." August 15, 2000 at the University of Creation Spirituality.

Harvey, Andrew. Interview by Chris Wingate. "Andrew Harvey and Sacred Activism. A Discussion of World Crisis. Accountability and Change." *Natural Awakenings,* March 2007.

———. Interview by Simran Singh. "Andrew Harvey: Sacred Activism." *11:11* July/Aug. 2010.

———. Interview by John Malkin. "Follow Your Heartbreak into the Eye of the Storm. Discussion on Sacred Activism." Free Radio, Santa Cruz, CA. February 3, 2011.

———. Interview by Sharon Hall. "The Hope: A Conversation with Andrew Harvey." By Sharon Hall. *The Whole Person Calendar.* http://www.wholepersoncalendar.com/library/a-conversation-with-andrew-harvey.pdf.

———. Interview by Rose Solari. "On Divine Responsibility." *Common Boundary,* September/October 1994. Also included in Andrew Harvey, *The Return of the Mother,* (Berkeley, CA: Frog Books, 1995; New York: J.P. Tarcher/Putnam, 2001).

———. Interview by Frederick Gustafson. "On the Black Madonna: An Interview with Andrew Harvey." In *The Moonlit Path: Reflections on the Dark Feminine,* edited by Frederick Gustafson. Berwick, ME: Nicolas-Hays, 2003.

———. Interview by Andrew Lawler. "The Ordinary Decency of The Heart: Andrew Harvey on Sacred Activism, the Divine Feminine, and Loving George W. Bush." By Andrew Lawler. *The Sun Magazine.* May 2008.

———. Interview by Felicia M. Tomasko. "Radical Mystic Andrew Harvey." *LAYoga.* November 2008. http://layogamagazine.com/content/index.php?option=com_content&view=article&id=143:interview-radical-mystic-andrew-harvey&catid=92:columns.

———. Interview by Michael Bertrand. "Resurrecting the Authentic Christ," www.banyen.com/infocus/Harvey.HTM.

———. Interview by Michael Bertrand. "The Sacred Activism of Heart Yoga," www.banyen.com/infocus/harvey_heartyoga_0410.htm.

———. Interview by Catherine Ingram. "Teachers and Seekers: An Interview with Andrew Harvey." By Catherine Ingram. *Yoga Journal,* July/August 1995. 56–63, 152–53. Also included in Andrew Harvey, *The Return of the Mother,* (Berkeley, CA: Frog Books, 1995; New York: J.P. Tarcher/Putnam, 2001).

Myss, Caroline. Interview by Andrew Harvey. "The Compelling Power of Teresa of Avila, An Interview with Caroline Myss." http://www.myss.com/news/archive/2007/022307.asp.

Polikoff, Daniel. Interview by Andrew Harvey discussing *In the Image of Orpheus: Rilke; A Soul History.* Mill Valley, CA: Chiron, 2011. www.andrewharvey.net/newsletter/files/Rilke_interview_edited-fnshd.pdf.

Shepherd, Philip. Interview by Andrew Harvey, discussing *New Self, New World,* by Philip Shepherd. Berkeley, CA: North Atlantic Books, 2010. http://www.andrewharvey.net/media-audio.php.

Thomas, Janet. Interview by Andrew Harvey, discussing *Day Breaks Over Dharamsala,* by Janet Thomas. Friday Harbor, WA: Nutshell Books, 2010.

Permissions

Permissions

Permissions

Permissions

"The Sacred Activism of Heart Yoga" Interview with Michael Bertrand. Printed with the permission of Michael Bertrand.

Foreword to *The Other Side of Eden: Life with John Steinbeck,* by John Steinbeck IV and Nancy Steinbeck. Copyright © 2001 by John Steinbeck IV and Nancy Steinbeck. Reprinted with the permission of Prometheus Books.

Foreword to *Hidden Journey*—2011 Edition, by Andrew Harvey. Copyright © 2011 by Andrew Harvey. Reprinted with the permission of Watkins Publishing.

From *Day Breaks Over Dharamsala: A Memoir of Life Lost and Found,* by Janet Thomas. Copyright © 2009 by Janet Thomas. Reprinted with the permission of Janet Thomas.

Interview with Janet Thomas. Printed with the permission of Janet Thomas.

Introduction to *Navigating the Coming Chaos: A Handbook for Inner Transition,* by Carolyn Baker. Copyright © 2011 by Carolyn Baker. Reprinted with the permission of Carolyn Baker.

"Transition and Transformation: They Joy of Preparation" A conversation with Carolyn Baker. Printed with the permission of Carolyn baker.

"The Ordinary Decency of The Heart" Interview by Andrew Lawler in *The Sun* magazine, May 2008. Reprinted with the permission of Andrew Lawler.

Foreword by Andrew Harvey from *New Self, New World: Recovering Our Senses in the Twenty-first Century* by Philip Shepherd, published by North Atlantic Books, copyright © 2010 by Philip Shepherd. Reprinted by permission of publisher.

"Follow Your Heartbreak into the Eye of the Storm" A discussion on Sacred Activism with John Malkin. Printed with the permission of John Malkin.

Permissions

About the Author

Andrew Harvey was born in south India in 1952 and lived there until he was nine years old. It is this early period that he credits with shaping his sense of the inner unity of all religions and providing him with a permanent and inspiring vision of a world infused with the sacred. He left India to attend private school in England and entered Oxford University in 1970 with a scholarship to study history. At the age of twenty-one he became the youngest person ever to be awarded a fellowship to All Soul's College, England's highest academic honor.

By 1977, Harvey had become disillusioned with life at Oxford and returned to his native India, where a series of mystical experiences initiated his spiritual journey. Over the next thirty years he plunged into different mystical traditions to learn their secrets and practices. In 1978 he met a succession of Indian saints and sages and began his long study and practice of Hinduism. In 1983, in Ladakh, he met the great Tibetan adept Thuksey Rinpoche and undertook with him the Mahayana Buddhist Bodhisattva vows; later, in 1990, he would collaborate with Sogyal Rinpoche and Patrick Gaffney in the writing of *The Tibetan Book of Living and Dying*. In 1984, with a group of French Sufis, he began a ten-year-long exploration and explication of Rumi and Sufi mysticism in Paris under the guidance of Eva De Vitray-Meyerovitch, the magnificent translator of Rumi into French. In 1992 he met Father Bede Griffiths in his ashram in south India near where Harvey had been born. It was this meeting that helped him synthesize the whole of his mystical explorations and reconcile Eastern and Western mysticism.

In 2005, in the historic Santuario de Guadalupe in Santa Fe, New Mexico, Harvey delivered his vision of the contemporary crisis now confronting us and its potential solution in what he has termed "Sacred Activism," which he sees as the culmination of his life's work. This extraordinary occasion was made into a documentary film by the Hartley Film Foundation and is available on DVD at www.hartleyfoundation.org.

The author of more than two dozen books, Harvey was awarded the Christmas Humphrey prize for *A Journey in Ladakh*, the Humanities Team Award for his 2010 body of work (an award previously received by Desmond Tutu), and a Nautilus Award for *The Hope*. He is the founder and director of the Institute of Sacred Activism.